Urban and Landscape Perspectives

Volume 6

Series Editor

Giovanni Maciocco

Editorial Board

Abdul Khakee, Faculty of Social Sciences, Umeå University

Norman Krumholz, Levin College of Urban Affairs,
Cleveland State University, Ohio

Ali Madanipour, School of Architecture, Planning and Landscape,
Newcastle University

Leonie Sandercock, School of Community and Regional Planning, Vancouver

Frederick Steiner, School of Architecture, University of Texas, Austin

Erik Swyngedouw, School of Environment and Development,
University of Manchester

Rui Yang, School of Architecture, Department of Landscape Architecture,
Tsinghua University, Peking

For further volumes:
http://www.springer.com/series/7906

Aims and Scope

Urban and Landscape Perspectives is a series which aims at nurturing theoretic reflection on the city and the territory and working out and applying methods and techniques for improving our physical and social landscapes.

The main issue in the series is developed around the projectual dimension, with the objective of visualising both the city and the territory from a particular viewpoint, which singles out the territorial dimension as the city's space of communication and negotiation.

The series will face emerging problems that characterise the dynamics of city development, like the new, fresh relations between urban societies and physical space, the right to the city, urban equity, the project for the physical city as a means to reveal *civitas*, signs of new social cohesiveness, the sense of contemporary public space and the sustainability of urban development.

Concerned with advancing theories on the city, the series resolves to welcome articles that feature a pluralism of disciplinary contributions studying formal and informal practices on the project for the city and seeking conceptual and operative categories capable of understanding and facing the problems inherent in the profound transformations of contemporary urban landscapes.

Enhancing the City

New Perspectives for Tourism and Leisure

Giovanni Maciocco and Silvia Serreli
Editors

 Springer

Editors
Giovanni Maciocco
Department of Architecture and Planning
Faculty of Architecture, Alghero
University of Sassari
Palazzo del Pou Salit
Piazza Duomo 6
07041 Alghero
Italy
maciocco@uniss.it

Silvia Serreli
Department of Architecture and Planning
Faculty of Architecture, Alghero
University of Sassari
Palazzo del Pou Salit
Piazza Duomo 6
07041 Alghero
Italy
serreli@uniss.it

ISBN 978-94-007-3063-2   e-ISBN 978-90-481-2419-0
DOI 10.1007/978-90-481-2419-0
Springer Dordrecht Heidelberg London New York

Cover image: "Shibuya crowd", photo by TC Lin, poagao.org

Printed on acid-free paper

Springer is part of Springer Science+Business Media (www.springer.com)

Contributors

Gregory J. Ashworth
Faculty of Spatial Sciences, University of Groningen
Postbox 800, 9700AV Groningen, The Netherlands
g.j.ashworth@rug.nl

Gregory Ashworth was educated at the Universities of Cambridge, Reading and London (PhD 1974). He has taught at the Universities of Wales, Portsmouth and since 1979, Groningen. Since 1994, he has been Professor of Heritage Management and Urban Tourism at the Department of Planning, Faculty of Spatial Sciences, University of Groningen.

Arnaldo Cecchini
Department of Architecture and Planning, Faculty of Architecture, Alghero
University of Sassari
Palazzo del Pou Salit, Piazza Duomo 6, 07041 Alghero, Italy
cecchini@uniss.it

Arnaldo Cecchini obtained his Master's degree in Physics and began his academic career at the IUAV in Venice. He is now Full Professor of Urban Planning at the Faculty of Architecture in Alghero, University of Sassari; he is an expert in urban analysis and modelling techniques including simulations, gaming simulations, cellular automata, scenario techniques and information systems for public participation.

Daniela Ciaffi
Regional Inter-Institute Department, Turin Polytechnic
Viale Mattioli 39, 10125 Turin, Italy
daniela.ciaffi@polito.it

Daniela Ciaffi is an architect working on research at Turin Polytechnic Spatial Planning Department in Italy. She has a PhD in Planning and Local Development and teaches Urban Planning and Community Capacity Building at the Turin, Alghero and Genoa Faculties of Architecture. Her main interest is the relationship between people and the urban environment.

Xavier Costa
Director, Metropolis Graduate Program in Architecture and Urban Culture
CCCB/UPC, Montalegre 5, 08001 Barcelona, Spain
metropolis@cccb.org

Xavier Costa is the Director of the Metropolis Postgraduate Program in Architecture and Urban Culture at the Universitat Politècnica de Catalunya and the Centre de Cultura Contemporània de Barcelona, as well as Curator of Architecture Programs at the Fundació Mies van der Rohe. He is an architect and has a PhD from the University of Pennsylvania.

Eric de Noronha Vaz
ISEGI, Superior Institute of Statistics and Information Management
New University of Lisbon
Campus de Campolide, 1070-312 Lisbon, Portugal
evaz@isegi.unl.pt

Eric de Noronha Vaz holds a Master's Science Degree in Geographic Information Systems and Sciences and a European Master's Degree from UNIGIS. He is at present a PhD student at the New University of Lisbon, Institute of Statistics and Information Management in Portugal. His recent research is all closely related to the use of spatial analysis methodologies, predictive modeling with a strong emphasis on artificial intelligence (cellular automata) and environmental sustainability focusing on natural and cultural heritage vulnerability.

Oliver Frey
Department of Spatial Development, Infrastructure & Environmental Planning
Vienna University of Technology,
Karlsplatz 13. A-1040 Vienna, Austria
oliver.frey@tuwien.ac.at

Oliver Frey is an Assistant Professor at the Department of Spatial Development, Infrastructure and Environmental Planning at the Vienna University of Technology. Since 2008 he is responsible for the "Urbanism" section. As an urban sociologist and urban planner he is working on the intersection of creative cities and urban renewal strategies. His recent research focuses on transformations of societies and new forms of governance.

Tony Griffin
School of Leisure, Sport and Tourism
University of Technology, Sydney
PO Box 222, Lindfield, NSW 2070, Australia
tony.griffin@uts.edu.au

Tony Griffin is a Senior Lecturer in Tourism Management at the School of Leisure, Sport and Tourism at the University of Technology, Sydney. He has published extensively on subjects ranging from hotel development to sustainable tourism. Much of his recent research has focused on understanding the nature and quality of visitor experiences in a variety of contexts, including urban tourism precincts, national parks and wine tourism.

Bruce Hayllar
School of Leisure, Sport and Tourism
University of Technology, Sydney
PO Box 222, Lindfield, NSW 2070, Australia
bruce.hayllar@uts.edu.au

Bruce Hayllar is an Associate Professor and Head of the School of Leisure, Sport and Tourism at the University of Technology, Sydney. He has an extensive portfolio of applied research projects. His most recent work has been in the area of urban tourism and in particular a series of collaborative studies examining the experience of tourists in precincts in Sydney, Melbourne and Fremantle.

Monica Johansson
Department of Political Science
Jönköping International Business School
Box 1026, Jönköping, Sweden
monica.johansson@ihh.hj.se

Monica Johansson received her PhD in Political Science from Jönköping International Business School, where she teaches Political Thought and Local and International Democratisation. She has a professional background in the field of regional development and EU structural policy. Her recent research has focused on policy analysis, citizen participation and governance.

Laura Lutzoni
Department of Architecture and Planning, Faculty of Architecture, Alghero
University of Sassari
Palazzo del Pou Salit, Piazza Duomo 6
07041 Alghero, Italy
llutzoni@uniss.it

Laura Lutzoni is a PhD researcher in Architecture and Planning at the Faculty of Architecture in Alghero, University of Sassari. She obtained a degree in Architecture and a specialism in Territorial, Urban and Environmental Planning at the University of Sassari. Her present research focuses on transformations of the urban context in relation to spatial and social processes in the city and on the territory.

Giovanni Maciocco
Department of Architecture and Planning, Faculty of Architecture, Alghero
University of Sassari
Palazzo del Pou Salit, Piazza Duomo 6
07041 Alghero, Italy
maciocco@uniss.it

Giovanni Maciocco obtained a degree in Engineering at the University of Pisa and in Architecture at the University of Florence. He is Full Professor of Town and Regional Planning. His main research themes concern territorial and urban planning, and landscape planning and architecture.

Agustina Martire
IHAAU, Institute of History of Art, Architecture and Urbanism
Faculteit Bouwkunde, TU Delft
Julianalaan 134, 2628 BL Delft, The Netherlands
agusmartire@hotmail.com

Agustina Martire is a researcher in Urban History. She obtained a PhD in Urban History at the Faculty of Architecture at TU Delft and a degree in Architecture at the University of Buenos Aires. Currently she is teaching Tourism at BA and MBA level at the European University in Barcelona and working on the research project "Great Metropolis" for the Institute of History of Art, Architecture and Urbanism at the Faculty of Architecture of TU Delft.

Brian L. McLaren
Department of Architecture, University of Washington
PO Box 355720, Seattle, WA 98195-5720, U.S.A.
bmclaren@u.washington.edu

Brian McLaren is an Associate Professor at the University of Washington Department of Architecture where he teaches design studies, as well as history and in theory seminars and lecture courses. He obtained a PhD in the History, Theory and Criticism of Architecture at the Massachusetts Institute of Technology, an M.Sc. in Architecture at Columbia University and a B.Arch. at the University of Waterloo.

Alfredo Mela
Department of Human Settlements Science and Technology
Turin Polytechnic, Viale Mattioli 39, 10125 Turin, Italy
alfredo.mela@polito.it

Alfredo Mela obtained a degree in Philosophy at the University of Turin. He is Full Professor of Urban Sociology at Turin Polytechnic and of Environmental Sociology at the Second Faculty of Architecture. His main research themes concern the contribution of sociology to urban planning, the improvement of sustainability at a local scale and the organisation of citizen participation in decisions referring to urban policies and design.

Elena Moreddu
Department of Architecture and Planning, Faculty of Architecture, Alghero
University of Sassari
Palazzo del Pou Salit, Piazza Duomo 6
07041 Alghero, Italy
elena.mor@libero.it

Elena Moreddu received her PhD in Social Anthropology/Study of Religions and Master's degree in Social Anthropology from the School of Oriental and African Studies, University of London. Her research focuses on understanding the relationship between people and places the temporary religious hamlets present in Sardinia. She is currently in charge of special projects at the Modern and Contemporary Art Museum (MAN), in Nuoro.

Peter Nijkamp
Department of Spatial Economics, Free University
De Boelelaan 1105, 1081 HV Amsterdam, The Netherlands
pnijkamp@feweb.vu.nl

Peter Nijkamp is full Professor of Regional and Urban Economics and Economic Geography at the VU University, Amsterdam. His main research interests cover quantitative plan evaluation, regional and urban modelling, multicriteria analysis, transport systems analysis, mathematical systems modelling, technological innovation, entrepreneurship, environmental and resource management and sustainable development.

Silvia Serreli
Department of Architecture and Planning, Faculty of Architecture, Alghero
University of Sassari
Palazzo del Pou Salit, Piazza Duomo 6
07041 Alghero, Italy
serreli@uniss.it

Silvia Serreli is a Researcher in Town and Regional Planning at the Faculty of Architecture, University of Sassari. She has a degree in Civil Engineering from the University of Cagliari and a PhD in "Urban Planning Methodology" after from "La Sapienza" University of Rome. Her main research trends deal with urban and territorial planning, and environmental evaluation of plans and projects.

Silvano Tagliagambe
Department of Architecture and Planning, Faculty of Architecture, Alghero
University of Sassari
Palazzo del Pou Salit, Piazza Duomo 6
07041 Alghero, Italy
tagliaga@uniss.it

Silvano Tagliagambe has been Full Professor of Philosophy of Science at the University of Cagliari, at "La Sapienza" University of Rome and at the Alghero Faculty of Architecture, University of Sassari. He has been Vice President of the CRS4. He is currently the Director of the E-learning education and training project S.O.F.I.A. He has been a member of several Commissions established by the Ministry of Education.

Contents

1. Leisure and Construction of Urban Consciousness

Places for Leisure: Places for City
Giovanni Maciocco

Places for Leisure as Interactive Space of the City
Silvia Serreli

Urban Tourist Precincts as Sites of Play
Bruce Hayllar and Tony Griffin

2. Authentic Places, Simulacrum Places

3. Creative Places and Cultural Matrices of the City

4. Leisure and Privatisation of Public Space

5. Urban Tourism and Hybrid Spaces

6. Urban Populations and Rights of Citizenship

Which Tourisms? Which Territories?
Arnaldo Cecchini

Tourist Populations
Daniela Ciaffi and Alfredo Mela

Tourism and Local Participation: What about the Citizens?
Monica Johansson

Enhancing the City: New Perspectives for Tourism and Leisure

Giovanni Maciocco and Silvia Serreli

The chapters in this book were inspired by the profusion of meanings leisure takes on in the contemporary city, where the various forms of post-modern culture occupy increasingly central positions in urban organisation and leisure and entertainment are becoming more and more active components of the wider process of regeneration of post-industrial cities.

In these times of rapid change in cultural and political paradigms, urban spaces show some of the diseases of the city which highlight a detachment from reality, false relations with place, manifest in the forms of aestheticisation, spectacularisation and thematisation that disguise a trend towards genericity. To "place themselves on this map" with leisure and tourism activities, cities put spaces on show that are out of the ordinary, themed environments in which urban landscapes are produced, marketed and consumed. The new spaces of culture, leisure and consumption become catalysts of new urban development and the new image of cities.

Leisure can also take on the shape and function of a space where reciprocal identities can assert themselves, where differences, the various ways of seeing the world and the wide-ranging styles of thought are defined, ultimately the basic elements of a collective consciousness of the city.

These tensions are measured in terms of some general issues on which the book is structured.

One of the first issues concerns the "restriction" on settlement situations through forms and modalities of private organisation of space, situations that generate an imitation-city that cuts off relationships with the outside, depriving the city of basic public spaces enabling users to experience a fictional existence. The first section of the book is connected with this theme, *Leisure and Construction of Urban Consciousness,* with the chapters by Giovanni Maciocco, Silvia Serreli, Bruce Hayllar and Tony Griffin, as is the fourth, *Leisure and Privatisation of Public Space,* with Xavier Costa and Laura Lutzoni's chapters.

G. Maciocco, S. Serreli (eds.), *Enhancing the City*, Urban and Landscape Perspectives 6,
DOI 10.1007/978-90-481-2419-0_1, © Springer Science+Business Media B.V. 2009

Themed environments entail, moreover, a "mystification" of relations with the environment that signifies exclusive attention to the visual, superficial aspects and indifference to the deeper meanings of nature and the history of regions. This theme is dealt with from different viewpoints in two sections of the book: Silvano Tagliagambe and Elena Moreddu discuss it in *Authentic Places, Simulacrum Places*, and Oliver Frey, Eric de Noronha Vaz and Peter Nijkamp in *Creative Places and Cultural Matrices of the City*.

Leisure and tourism activities involve the "production" of the holiday, with a sub-division of forms and modalities ranging from hetero-production to perspectives of aware self-production: from passive fruition as "abandonment" to holiday places, to aware fruition of the territory as an internal experience. This theme is the subject of Gregory Ashworth's reflections and the variety of experiences illustrated by Brian L. McLaren and Agustina Martire in the section *Urban Tourism and Hybrid Spaces*.

Another important question refers to the spatial experience of the different urban populations, as the quest for elements of urban vitality and new citizenships in a territory which apparently seems based only on the exclusive dimension of the holiday and play. Daniela Ciaffi and Alfredo Mela, Arnaldo Cecchini and Monica Johansson discuss this in *Urban Populations and Rights of Citizenship*.

To seek new perspectives for tourism and leisure to improve the city means to go beyond the exclusively thematic experience of the city and conceive places of leisure as places *external* to the critical dynamics of the city.

These places may be thought of as sites of reliability, resistance and potentiality, capable of opening up new possibilities for the city project. Through leisure, "spaces of hope" and "spaces of resistance" may also be revealed, in which it is possible to contribute to the formation of alternative social relations not colonised by the economic sphere of tourism. Some experiences show how leisure and tourism activities offer themselves as the opportunity to experience cultural boundaries, as spaces that keep individuals in touch. They are places where it is possible for a critical capacity on the part of inhabitants and tourists to be reasserted, both travellers who experiment, both travellers who experiment with their possible selves in them, but also where they express the need to enter into deep contact with the other and the elsewhere.

If in leisure we recognise the nature of contemporary public space, to design the city means to assert the *externity* of leisure, seek places external to the simulated public space of the thematised city and reassert the places of experience and subjectivity of individuals. It is thus necessary to think again on the role of the project and the possibility of creating contexts for tourist experience that will not solely be linked with spatial conditions and functional dynamics.

In this direction, the book enquires into the perspectives offered by the urban and regional project for reconstructing a public dimension of space through ethical action entailing an active relationship with places, a statement of difference and a capacity for understanding the dynamics of different urban populations. The project may then be an impulse for maintaining the diversity of places and their stories, and of social behaviours, for contexts are by definition pluralistic and should thus offer various possibilities of choice.

Leisure and Construction of Urban Consciousness

In his chapter, *Places for Leisure. Places for City*, Giovanni Maciocco maintains that leisure is to all effects an urban activity, in that to sustain intellectual growth and development it presupposes participation in the formulation of symbols and rites within one's own area of social and cultural life, which is indeed the city. In this sense, it can contribute to the project for the city, for it constitutes a concretely operative possibility of a necessary retrieval of individual and social spaces, times and relations.

Places of leisure are often considered places where it is possible to free ourselves from work, take our distance from reality and open ourselves up to desire, and holiday landscapes become a projection of desires. The landscape as desired product marks a distance from reality, as "repetitive, foreseeable and reassuring familiarity", an aesthetic ideal that has to do with "kitsch" in that it eliminates from our visual field all that in human existence is basically unacceptable but has an appeasing effect on the inhabitants of a world that is becoming increasingly insecure.

This completely changes the economic bases of landscape construction and favours involution of the concept of landscape towards *commodification*. But in the heart of commodification, in the advanced economies, vast alternative spaces also exist, where commodification is not present or has a slow, irregular process of penetration, spaces of hope, where leisure can play a fundamental role in the dialectic processes of construction of identity.

Commodification becomes an important part of leisure activities through tourism economics, which has become a key aspect in local economics for many urban areas and has produced tensions and conflicts between managing the city as a tourist destination on the one hand and as a space of work and residence on the other.

In the age of "urban redevelopment", art and entertainment are also used as instruments for renewal of the city, or often of its caricature, through "fantasisation" of the everyday context, as a company strategy to exploit "commodity fetishism" and extend the life of a brand geographically and symbolically. *Branding* projects may be of great importance for cities but are also accompanied by great risks that are linked with the lack of social control of the accessibility of art and culture as an instrument of collective growth.

Maciocco concludes by upholding that if leisure is understood as *intermediate space* or frontier between these tensions, it may take on the form and function of a neutral zone, where reciprocal identities may be attested, remaining separate but each beginning to have experience of the other. Where differences, the different ways of seeing the world and the various styles of thought are defined, ultimately, the basic elements of a collective consciousness of the city.

Silvia Serreli's chapter, *Places for Leisure as Interactive Space of the City,* points out how the city, through leisure, may reveal potential places for reassertion of the public sphere.

Leisure has thus taken on strong urban importance. The geographies of leisure, in its various senses, are explored by the author as important parts of contemporary spatial experience. It is emphasised how some places have become themed environments produced and transformed to be "consumed", but also how leisure has favoured new forms of social interaction around new reference spaces that seem to cause a crisis for the traditional centralities of cities. In this sense, leisure is interpreted as an expression of the power of production and subjectivisation, but also as an opportunity to construct urban perspectives and different forms of "resistance".

Particular attention is paid to the situations in which leisure and tourism activities reveal micropolitics and change tactics, promoted by the forms and modalities of interaction of the different social groups that give these spaces of entertainment and leisure a meaning.

Departing from a reflection on the effects generated by place marketing in the Øresund region of Scandinavia, territorial competition processes are dealt with which, through programmes directed at leisure activities, put on the same level strategies to hold inhabitants, to attract companies of the creative industries, as well as catalyse visitor flows. But these policies often create "imaginative space", spaces where technological skill in creating hyper-real environments is evident, to which the reality of the inhabitants does not correspond.

Some places become themed environments produced and transformed solely to attract "the eager gaze of the tourist". This is the case of ethnic tourism places in the city of Gallup, New Mexico. The outcome of tourist promotion by the business elite is the creation of "enchanted landscapes" which generate forms of conflict on the part of the inhabitants. In the dynamics of the spectacle, forms of challenge and protest are generated, which attempt to make the essence of Indian culture explicit and subtract it from myths and an idealised vision that disguises marginalisation and discrimination.

This experience, which can be traced back to other "minor" cultures, highlights the "spaces of resistance", the counter-spaces of tourism in which inhabitants and visitors are involved in a real, not simulated, experience. In this direction, spaces of leisure, too, can be configured as places of awareness, where travellers (inhabitants and tourists) exercise their freedom and participate in the construction of an urbanity that is not simply the product of imaginative geographies, places of "extraordinary experience".

Silvia Serreli ends by emphasising that the tourist experience is an entertaiment activity but at the same time a learning activity. It is experiential learning that derives from interaction between individuals and destination and takes shape in the individual's "geographical consciousness". The project for urban leisure spaces thus opposes programmes which tend to isolate men and places within a fixed temporal segment to transform them into "enchanted" landscapes, in which the action of individuals has dwindled to a form of spectacle weakening links with the past and without the strength to construct perspectives for future urbanity.

Beginning with a conceptual overview of the urban tourism precinct – an organised space for playful forms of leisure in the city – Bruce Hayllar and Tony Griffin maintain that both visitor and host engage as mutual actors in urban "playgrounds". In their chapter, *Urban Tourist Precincts as Sites of Play,* their arguments are inspired by two studies conducted in The Rocks and Darling Harbour precincts in Sydney, Australia.

While the city and its services provide the overlay for urban tourist entertainment activity, in most urban destinations tourist visitation tends to be spatially concentrated rather than dispersed. These points of concentration may include iconic sights, shopping areas, landmark cultural institutions or places of historical significance. However, where a number of attractions of similar or differing types aggregate alongside a range of tourism-related services, these areas take on a particular spatial, cultural, social and economic identity – now commonly (but not universally) recognised as a tourist precinct.

Precincts have been the subject of considerable research. This research has primarily focused on two areas, namely, describing the precinct phenomenon and some its fundamental characteristics, and developing ideas around the role of precincts in economic and urban regeneration. More recently, research has been directed towards a focus on both the experience of tourists in urban precincts and towards an understanding of the key attributes of such places that contribute to the quality of that experience.

This chapter exemplifies this new direction and examines the urban tourism precinct as an organised space for playful forms of leisure in the city. It is argued that play is the experience of control, freedom, arousal and intrinsically focused activity which brings enjoyment and satisfaction. In the context of a visit to a precinct, enjoyment and satisfaction are key outcomes for visitors. As such, the challenge for precinct planners and managers is to enhance the opportunity for playful experience through thoughtful design and management practice.

Authentic Places, Simulacrum Places

Silvano Tagliagambe takes Porto Cervo as an emblem of "tourist city", a well-known resort of the Costa Smeralda in Sardinia. In *The Tourist City, the Dream and the Reversal of Time*, he reflects on the modalities by which this resort presents itself. Altogether, the "Costa Smeralda" operation presents as a marketing operation aimed at imposing an overall "brand" or trade mark, charged with values and meanings, following the intentions of those who elaborated and promoted it.

Commenting on the slogan "Holidays-Travels-Dreams-Luxury", Tagliagambe underlines the strong tie established between the concept of "holidays" and that of "dreams".

The theme of the dream is interpreted following the reflections of the Russian philospher and theologist Pavel Florenskij, in his essay of 1922, *Ikonostas,* in which the dream is the common limit to the series of experiences of the visible world and those of the invisible world and constitutes the border between these two series, separating them, but at the same time linking them and putting them into contact with each other. The images that separate the dream from reality separate the visible world from the invisible world, and in this way join the two worlds together. In this border place of oneiric images, their relationship both with this world and the other is established.

The author emphasises how the "mystification" of the relationship between "tourist city" and environment generates the reversal of history and time. The entire Costa Smeralda "trade mark" is based on an image not aimed at communicating meanings via signs and symbols but construed and spread in order to be self-referential, not a re-presentation of anything, but a presentation, with the intention of highlighting precisely its non-naturalness and non-historicity.

In this way, the memories, distinctive traits, matrices that make up the concept itself of historical process and of place as a result of this process vanish and the *place itself becomes a simulacrum.*

Tourist destinations like the "Costa Smeralda" are constantly in a precarious position between falsehood and illusion and aimed at transforming the holiday into a "dream". They are situations that have nothing to do with actual reality, not only historic and cultural but also natural and environmental.

Tagliagambe ends by maintaining that, even if we are confused between reality and dreams, we must never lose sight of the authentic meanings, the link, if not with daily experience, in its rough effectuality, at least with that idealised vision of it that takes on consistency and finds a shape in the images it evokes, in the phantasies, in the inclination to think of it and see it otherwise. This effectuality enables projects to be created that find their route to being realised and have, consequently, the effective capacity to influence and transform it.

In *Disney-ality and Forgetfulness: the Eu-topia of a Consolatory Place,* Elena Moreddu enquires into the relationship between authentic places and simulacrum places with particular reference to some experiences in central Sardinia. In these, the consumption of images of places creates an inclination in the tourist to have simulated experiences, to seek the "game of the real" in the experience of the journey, aware of experimenting surface sensations, undertaking to explore "amazing spaces" without missing reality at all.

Moreddu carries out a reading of those mechanisms and practices of construction of the real as they are exemplified in events promoting tourism on the territory, which use the historic/identitarian value of the urban place identified as historic "centre". The so-called experiential marketing responds to those strategies directed at intercepting the desires of the visitor/consumer of places and their appeasement, by offering consumer experiences that strengthen the pre-ordained discursive strategies relating to those same places. In this way, these become contextualised and contextualising objects for consumption, to be experienced, by means of a total experience. She concentrates on showing how this reality is rather a projection, in practice, of a eutopic perspective of spatial construction, a standardising constriction, if not annihilation, of the polyvocality of place.

Creative Places and Cultural Matrices of the City

Creativity of Places as a Resource for Cultural Tourism is the title of Oliver Frey's chapter; he maintains that "creativity" is said to play a major role in the development of urban economy and the civil society in the future ("urban renaissance"). This chapter aims at two aspects: first, the identification and description of "creative places" and their resources as a prerequisite for the establishment and consolidation of urban creativity. Second, at describing the link between the model of a "creative city" and urban cultural tourism. The aim is to extract the "hard" and "soft" qualities of spaces as well as the symbols and images of creative places and to contextualise them as a resource for cultural tourism in the processes of (re)urbanisation.

Cultural tourism has become for some cities one of the most important sectors of urban development and urban economy. It may stimulate cities, governments, local authorities, enterprises and people. Today, cultural tourism does not only affect the economic development of a place/city/region, it also affects the social, cultural, political and ecological dimensions of a place. The objective of this chapter is also to describe the effects of cultural tourism on the process of gentrification of "vibrant" neighbourhoods.

Eric de Noronha Vaz and Peter Nijkamp deal with cultural matrices of the city from a different viewpoint. In *Historico-Cultural Sustainability and Urban Dynamics*, they explore themes relating to cultural heritage with a geo-information science approach to the Algarve area.

In particular, in the EU, an increasing tension can be observed between a common European economic and social ideology and the presence of a local or national cultural identity which is often heterogeneous and originates from different historical periods. Against this background, rapid urban development (for instance, related to mass tourism or leisure time behaviour) is having far-reaching and severe implications for the varied natural and historical landscapes which are part of the identity of each individual nation or locality. Challenges in understanding such different environmental changes (rise in urban land use, loss in biodiversity, environmental degradation and pollution) are currently prompting much policy and research interest in Europe. The recognition of such prominent landscape changes has specific spatial dimensions which may be assessed from the perspective of pro-active preservation in favour of sustainable development. In this context, geographic information systems (GIS) can play a key role because they offer the possibility to map out and understand the above-mentioned changing patterns more accurately.

This chapter is an attempt to understand and analyse the threats to the Algarve's cultural heritage due to the quickly changing environment as a result of mass tourism and rapid urban growth. The chapter shows how GIS and spatial analysis may provide a better understanding of pro-active policy initiatives and measures aiming at landscape protection and help to identify which strategies are currently available for the assessment of historico-cultural sustainability. By using different land use maps provided by the CORINE Land Cover study. The authors aim to interpret statistical and temporal changes in land use in the Algarve area and to understand how they relate to prior conditions. This study is undertaken using linear regression and statistical inference methods, as well as simple Markovian urban growth models aided by Cellular Automata transition rules.

As a case study, the Portuguese area of Faro-Olhão is assessed with a view to (i) a better understanding of the underlying urban growth trends and (ii) the design of analytical tools to cope with the current jeopardy of environmental and socio-cultural heritage regions in this area. The analysis attempts to shed more light on the effectiveness of local and regional policies that are being formulated in line with a common European framework in which a more sustainable cultural environment is advocated, while recognising that cities will inevitably continue to grow. In summary, the chapter outlines the foci of sustainability challenges that must be faced by the Algarve and indicates how stakeholders can actively be engaged in sustainability policies.

Leisure and Privatisation of Public Space

The theme of public space is discussed by two writers who draw attention to the fact that its privatisation is strictly tied to the variety of conceptions behind the current design of consumer spaces.

In *Spaces of Consumption*, Xavier Costa upholds that our cities are increasingly defined by the dynamics of space transformation in a world of consumption, including strategies of publicity and commodification. The traditional notion of contextualisation – which defined spatial design as a process of adjustment to "local" traits – is being replaced by thematisation processes linking architecture to de-localised meanings, thus participating in a growing, universal visual culture.

Ever since the first contemporary commercial spaces in the passages of the *fin-de-siècle* European metropolis, a typological and cultural evolution has developed. From the passage to the boulevard, from Parisian *grands magasins* to North American department stores and from *hypermarchés* to theme parks, one finds the same process in which consumption and architectural space develop jointly.

Leisure activities cannot be evaluated without taking into consideration the strong tie established between them and the spatial forms of shopping. In her chapter, *Shopping as an Urban Leisure Activity,* Laura Lutzoni highlights how places of consumption have changed from areas that tended just to sell all manner of goods to authentic areas of entertainment, their main characteristic being to simulate the urban centre, reproducing both its spaces and functions. Mass consumerism, the spreading of shopping malls, the thematisation of urban spaces and urban islands dedicated to leisure activities are phenomena that show the cultural and physical transformation of the contemporary city contributing in an important way to placing consumption at the centre of attention.

This simulation of reality does not prove to be limited and circumscribed to shopping centres alone, but the progressive standardisation undergone by urban space has led to a negation of the city in the plural in favour of continuous "recycling" of what has already been seen and tried.

The strong tie that has been established between spaces of consumption and those of leisure is implemented through projects that aim at uniting the functional form of the mall with the entertainment model typical of the theme park. Such is the case of Namba Parks in Osaka, Japan, a complex designed by Jon Jerde, which follows these principles.

Referring to the experiences of Barcelona and Reading, Lutzoni points out that leisure epicentres are in some cases located in marginal urban areas, inside abandoned industrial buildings, with the objective of setting in motion renovation and urban transformation processes.

In this perspective, edge areas, areas with great environmental worth and abandoned areas show their value as places rich in elements unexpectedly released from the inexorable process of standardisation. The chapter thus states the need to depart precisely from these edge areas to design places able to oppose the rules of consumerism and entertainment alone.

Urban Tourism and Hybrid Spaces

The relationship between cities and tourism is handled in particular by Gregory Ashworth in *Questioning the Urban in Urban Tourism.* He emphasises that most tourists come from cities and most tourists visit cities, but this says little about what is specifically urban about urban tourism or indeed about the importance of cities to tourism or conversely the importance of tourism to cities. Classification of urban is made. The topic is then approached from three directions.

Firstly, from the viewpoint of urban tourists and their motivation and behaviour. Travel in general has increased, and many facilities are located in urban areas, but this travel is not necessarily an urban tourism motivated by the distinctly urban characteristics of cities. The behaviour of the tourist in the city is characterised by consumption that is selective, rapid, non-repeated and capricious. Secondly, the approach is through the urban tourism industry, however diverse and difficult it may be to isolate. The conventional consensus of the "industry" about the nature and markets for urban tourism products is considered. The third approach departs from the city itself in search of the notion of a tourist city. Any consideration of the roles of tourism in cities confronts the difficulty of isolating the tourism function from wider urban functions and facilities. The urban policy implications of this are examined. The chapter concludes with a series of paradoxes that underline the asymmetrical nature of the relationship between tourism and cities in terms of economic, social and political significance. The consequences of such asymmetry for the tourist, tourism and the city are noted.

Urban tourism and hybrid spaces is the theme of Brian L. McLaren's chapter, *The Ambivalent Space(s) of Tourism in Italian Colonial Libya.*

In the Italian colony of Libya during the course of the 1920s and 1930s, there developed an extensive and quite elaborate tourist system that facilitated travel through the Mediterranean coastal regions as well as deep into the pre-Saharan interior. This system combined the most advanced network of transportation and accommodation of any Western colony – providing a level of comfort that was coincident with the standards of the metropole – along with a number of "authentic" settings that brought tourists in relatively direct contact with the indigenous populations – in this case offering a vicarious, though entirely safe, experience of the local culture. The ambivalence of these tourist spaces – being both continuous with and detached from Western culture – is entirely coincident with the politics of Italian colonialism in Libya, which sought to incorporate this colony into the larger Italy at the same time as it attempted to preserve the indigenous cultural heritage.

The simultaneous experience of the modern and the indigenous placed the colonial tourist in a liminal space. To be a tourist in Libya was to be continuous with the experience of modern metropolitan culture – including the methods of transportation, means of accommodation and instruments of political and social control – at the same time as being both temporally and culturally removed from it. Even though the essential experience of the Western tourist in Libya was tied to escaping their moral and cultural boundaries in favour of the experience of the indigenous culture, that culture was entirely defined by the West and that sense was already modern.

This chapter investigates the ambivalent spaces of tourism in the Italian colony of Libya through its combination of modern tourist infrastructures and carefully preserved (and even invented) environments. What will emerge from the discussion is the sense that rather than being the product of two conflicting impulses that were modernising this colony at the same time that its traditional cultural environments were being carefully preserved, the tourist space in Libya was the product of two different kinds of modernity – one tied to its aesthetic and technical demands and the other to its historical consciousness.

The same theme is approached, discussing a different experience, by Agustina Martire in her chapter *Waterfront Retrieved: Buenos Aires'Contrasting Leisure Experience.*

Tourism has transformed urban territory. Since the Grand Tour in Europe in the eighteenth and nineteenth centuries, through the later expansion of transportation, through the universal and international exhibitions, to the massification of tourism during the twentieth century, cities have been influenced by the appearance of the holiday-maker of every kind. This transformation has had different effects on the development of urban public space, especially on the waterfronts. During the last decades, the moving of harbour facilities out of urban centres has left a great amount of land close to the city's central areas free for intervention and development. Projects for the recovery and restructuring of obsolete industrial areas by the water are sprawling all over the globe. Urban ideas and interventions of various types and qualities have been applied. This action has proved to be a global phenomenon but not a new one, as explained by Stephen Ward, who describes the process of trans-national cross influences as "a significant historical phenomenon: the extensive international flows and exchanges that have been going on since the nineteenth century in the field of planning". However, leisure has many aspects other than tourism that have been present in urban waterfront transformation, and these can be seen in particular cases all over the western world.

The process of translation, transference and trans-culturation that is currently taking place on urban waterfront areas began more than a century ago with the discovery of the urban waterfront as a space for leisure. This process of transference has had different consequences on public space throughout the twentieth century, going from an appropriation of urban ideas and transformation of them according to local reality and ending up in globalised, standardised planning and use of space that lacks local identity.

A good example of this process can be found in the development of the waterfront of Buenos Aires. The lands on the southern waterfront of Buenos Aires, next to the city centre, were exploited as leisure space at the beginning of the twentieth century. They were later abandoned in mid-century until the area was rediscovered in the 1980s. Memory of place has been combined with real estate development to construct a hybrid of local and international images and uses, which depict the development of urban space in the last decades. Real estate development, offices, dwellings, parks and leisure facilities cohabit on a limited piece of land, steps away from the administrative, banking and tourist district of Buenos Aires.

Urban Populations and Rights of Citizenship

As Daniela Ciaffi and Alfredo Mela maintain in their chapter, *Tourist Populations,* one of the categories traditionally used by the ecological vein of sociology in analysing society is "populations". Tourism is one of the most suitable social phenomena for an analysis using this approach, which has many limits compared with others, but one clear advantage: the close relationship between the social sub-groups taken into consideration and respective places chosen and frequented, or, vice versa, rejected and not frequented.

This chapter proposes a possible classification of populations in relation to tourist areas. The variables taken into account refer (i) to residence, which may be stable, periodic or occasional; (ii) to work, which may be seasonal or occasional; (iii) to fruition of services, which may concern tourist services or ordinary ones. The seven populations singled out are inhabitants, tourists (loyal clients and *tout court* on the one hand, visitors on the other) and workers (commuters, seasonal and occasional).

The purpose of this description is to reflect on the relationship between tourist populations and respective attitudes to places: the relations singled out range from the classic "predator-prey" to symbiotic or competitive attitudes, then finally more unusual ties of an amensalistic or commensalistic type.

The thesis sustained is that, given such populations and conjecturing for them certain types of ecological relation, the tendency is for them to find a point of equilibrium over time, or reciprocally cancel each other out or else alternate in cycles. We might say it is a matter of a result more qualitative than quantitative, even if it may envisage the application of formally rigorous models, based on numeric data. In any case, in spite of not being immediately translatable into projectual indications, this type of result can also prove to be of great use in planning activities and the project for tourist places.

Which Tourisms? Which Territories? is Arnaldo Cecchini's chapter which draws attention to how tourists impose a new point of view on places. He maintains that a post-Fordist tourism is becoming more and more substantial and not only has growing dimensions but also a sort of cultural hegemony that is also a reference point for the prevalent consumer models of mass tourism.

Reference to the "population" approach follows a research trend that enables the different kinds of tourism to be picked out and possible policies for managing them to be defined and to describe and characterise in a dynamic manner the phenomenon of the "use" of places on the part of each population.

The writer highlights that the populations competing in the city are linked with each other, but also in conflict with each other. In his analyses, he refers in particular to the "tourist cities", namely cities where tourism has a prevalent or particularly significant economic role.

These reflections are supported by a work instrument, a model of classification of tourist populations the author devised and named with the acronym FDMP (faithfulness, duration, mobility, period). By the FDMP model, we can thus attempt to "measure" how near a certain typology of tourist comes to the figure of resident inhabitant, and it is therefore possible to define objectives governing the tourist flows brought in line with the context. With this model, an action may be chosen or sub-groups of actions selected to implement (strategy), and therefore to estimate, the consequent value of the probabilities that will be obtained following activation of the action or the strategy of single events or groups of events (scenarios) or the values of single variables or groups of variables.

In particular, Cecchini tests the model referring to a scenario he calls deseasonalisation and "fidelisation". The instrument is configured as a "dashboard" for tourist policies, to define scenarios to be publicly evaluated. But the instrument may also be useful for private decision makers, operators in the sector, resident citizens and tourists, to take into account the whole group of interests in the field and the public features of many of the "goods" put at stake by tourism.

The dashboard to govern tourism dynamics may to some extent give indications for delivering cities from the mortal embrace of tourism as a monoculture, as an elitary or pseudo-elitary good, as consumption that is doubly predatory.

In *Tourism and Local Participation: What about the Citizens?* Monica Johansson examines one case of tourism evolution which is a clear example of a setting that poses several palpable challenges to participative approaches and the development of a type of tourism that can be considered socially sustainable. The theoretical framework is built mainly on the notions of "deliberative democracy". Other alternative or complementary approaches to planning are also discussed.

Johansson refers to one specific site: the village Castelfalfi in the municipality of Montaione in Tuscany, Italy. This specific site has been selected since it can be considered a good example of a process in which participation and social sustainability appear to be two important objectives and since it throws light on challenges – difficulties as well as possibilities – facing tourism development processes. Findings and conclusions drawn from the case study may, therefore, be useful also in other (tourism) planning processes that are social sustainability oriented.

1. Leisure and Construction of Urban Consciousness

Spatial "restriction" with respect to the totality of urban life is a recurring theme in leisure, the forms and modalities of which are often linked with organisation of a private kind that deprives the city of constitutive public spaces. Being catalysers of new urban development, places of leisure may, on the other hand, be designed to contribute to the construction of a collective consciousness of the city. In this sense, to assert the externity of leisure as regards situations of restriction and privatisation means to explore unknown cultural frontiers that enable us to experience new, promising public dimensions of space.

Places for Leisure: Places for City

Giovanni Maciocco

Leisure as an Amphibian Figure

Our current society reveres aesthetic and hedonistic values centred on pleasure and lightness. A sign of this is the rapid multiplication and success of games on offer, which permeates the classic *leisure* area and risks causing and spreading superficial attitudes and styles, disillusioned to the point of being passive, in social relations and the relationship with the principal categories of civil life, such as politics and culture (Mori 2002). But there is no doubt that leisure is to some extent a constituent element of metropolitan man, in terms of the link between the culture of narcissism and the weakening of the individual resulting in flexible man, infinitely adaptable and able to be manipulated. It is a sociological phenomenon that over thirty years ago Sennett (1977) considered the result of a change that led halfway through the nineteenth century to the formation of a new capitalist, secularised, urban culture.

The hedonist, narcissist I, the I characterised by the "process of personalisation" (Lipovetski 1983), which severs any form of self-limitation previously effective, disciplinary or authoritarian, seems incapable even of those instrumental forms of binding and relationality that had marked the first phase of modernity, intent on ensuring progress, security, pacific cohabitation, entrusting their management to the State or the market (Pulcini 2001). Avid for freedom intolerant of any form of tie and bereft of the certainties granted by solid, credible institutions, it exhibits that paradoxical coexistence of omnipotence and void from which its aspirant, insatiable fabric takes origin and nourishment (Pulcini 2001). At that time, the traces needed to be sought of a process Sennett interprets in the reverse manner with respect to Riesman's well-known thesis, in which he counters an autonomous society, in which action and commitment are based on strictly personal aims and sentiments, with a hetero-directed society (Riesman 1950).

In actual fact, the direction of change should be reversed, in the sense that in the western world we are passing from a hetero-directed society to a self-directed one, even though in a situation of narrow-mindedness it is

G. Maciocco, S. Serreli (eds.), *Enhancing the City*, Urban and Landscape Perspectives 6,
DOI 10.1007/978-90-481-2419-0_2, © Springer Science+Business Media B.V. 2009

impossible to say what interiority consists of. In his quest for these roots, Sennett explores the traces of the elements that, in his opinion, concurred to lay the foundations of the affirmation of intimism and the individual personality as the dominant social principle, the reverse side of the current aridness of the public sphere and decline of current socialities (Sennett 1977). Among these, which can be linked with the current urban importance of leisure, is a new idea of secularisation, which exalts the immanence of personal emotions and the subordination of public experience to the formation of personality. Of course, many new reflections have subsequently appeared, also in the work of Sennett himself, on the transformations of the public sphere following perspectives that have tried to delve deeper into other important dimensions.

These first ideas seem nevertheless pertinent to understand the sociological roots of the phenomenon, also because according to analyses of the natural need of creative idleness (de Masi 1997), our society's near future envisages, for the specific evolution of the technological and social system, a progressive, unrelenting increase in the quantity of time to bring into play, which will be reflected in a decisive manner in our culture. And, on this subject, Huizinga (2002) asserts, re-reading cultural paradigms as interpretable and relating to the ludic form, that culture itself has indeed since antiquity revealed itself as play.

In this perspective, precisely because the availability of time for leisure has developed, the role of leisure in political life has become more important, a role that has undergone profound changes through history and culture and has always had to take account of its own times. In an interesting analysis of the recent history of the political meaning of leisure, Henry reminds us how leisure in the industrial revolution was seen by governments as the appropriate spot for popular subversion, but due to this it was also used for social control, for example to reduce the great, widespread social segregation of people (Henry 1994). Since halfway through the last century, a more paternalistic approach to welfare has emerged, seeing leisure as a resource to be enjoyed by everyone. Subsequently, welfare paternalism has let pragmatic economic calculation take over, in the sense that in recent years the return of public expense on leisure has been increasingly measured in terms of regional development (Henry 1994).

But nowadays, the role of leisure is undergoing great changes and will change more and more in the future. Professionalism of subjects is certainly growing, which reflects a shift from a relatively simple society in which the services are largely produced by the participants themselves to one where we pay for the services that are produced by a combination of providers of the public and private sectors, with the emergence of a new class of professionals. In this sense, these services have followed the social services model, highlighted by the creation of professional associations to advance the cause of the profession, associations which also have the role of the voluntary sector emerge as an instrument of leisure management policy.

Henry (1994) throws light in his book, which sketches a number of case studies in western Europe, on the absence of well-developed conceptual patterns to understand leisure policy. From this point of view, while the book does a good job of analysing the past, there are doubts as to how it is possible to develop a conceptual pattern that will help us to foresee the future. For example, on what the political implications might be of the current demographic changes whereby social groups that are increasingly larger as concerns the demand for leisure may be supported by economically active social groups which are diminishing proportional; or if it is possible to develop a universal pattern for analysing its policies.

In a period of rapid changes in cultural and political paradigms, it is quite difficult to define the role and policies of leisure most suitable for rapid changes, also because *leisure* is an amphibian figure, a term that brings to mind manifold meanings and loans itself, moreover, to interpretations of different signs, positive and negative.

Referring precisely to this large number of meanings, Marc Fumaroli has us notice that in the modern world, men are strange amphibian creatures who have taken the baton from theologians or monks: they lead two lives simultaneously; one in the world, where one needs to be accepted and listened to; the other, more internal and invisible, in the library, in the *otium studiosum et literatum,* the society of their equals, ancient and modern. Therefore the paradox of "spare time" is its bond, tight and disguised, with the surrender, the weariness of the soul, or with its inarticulate inertia. The paradox of "recreation", on the other hand, in its ancient meaning of *scholé* or *otium,* is its basic relationship with spiritual activity.

Otium and *studium* each postulate the other, therefore, placing themselves at the base of knowledge and of that internal freedom which is manifest in play and joy (Fumaroli 1996).

Departing from the idea that emotions and ludicity are the elements that distinguish the contemporary individual and ought to determine his or her modalities of learning and growth and that leisure, being the "art of knowing how to spend spare time" (Fumaroli 1996), should be interpreted as a fundamental activity and no longer as reparative and residual time; it should be made to unfold in society in its own noble forms of permanent training that man carries out in the various phases of his life, not being limited to exploring the world in a single dimension or being configured in a strictly utilitaristic sense as an instrument to produce something or being identified just as an economic factor.

Seen in this comprehensive dimension, leisure is to all effects an urban activity, in that to maintain intellectual growth and development it presupposes participation in the formulation of symbols and rites within one's own area of social and cultural life. In this sense, it can contribute to the project for the city, for it is a concretely operative possibility of a necessary recovery of individual and social spaces, times and relations. It may be the favourable environment for the capacity of analysis and continuous, creative reinvention of the world, the reconstruction of an equilibrium, of a natural need of harmony and peace (Mori 2002).

Kitsch Space and Space of Rooting

But places of leisure are often considered places where it is possible to free ourselves from work, take our distance from reality and open ourselves up to desire, and holiday landscapes become a projection of desires, in a certain sense a simulacrum, a masking of the real conditions of urban life, which is just a mere onirical invention (de Azua 2003). By "simulacrum", we mean an urban construction that imitates televised, photographic or film images, or things that are similarly, mythical or fictitious, and place in the world a city copied from a model that was never inhabited by human beings (de Azua 2003). As if the city, in its classical meaning, no longer existed, but in its place and upon it were being built a particularly convincing simulacrum of the classical city. And this simulacrum is *authentic*. And this gives origin to our disorientation.

Baudrillard (1970, 1981) links the simulacrum phenomenon with the passage from an industrial economy to a consumer and services economy. The last representation of the city divided into two ethically united categories was that of the proletariat and the middle class, but with the passage to the third world of contaminating heavy industry and advanced automatisation, the production of goods destined to cover needs has been overtaken by the production of desires as a driving force of the economy (Ritzer 1999). Thus, while man's needs have a clear, rational definition, which proves easily representable, desires, on the contrary, do not: they change constantly, do not have a fixed object, and once they have been satisfied are reborn embodied in a new fetish. Cities also follow this trend, which leads from construction to cover needs to the construction of stage-sets of desire, of the way in which the current post-cities are taking on an appearance which is indeed an onirical invention (de Azua 2003).

This invention corresponds to the landscape as desired product, being distant from reality, "repetitive, foreseeable and reassuring familiarity", a concept that has to do with *kitsch*, in the meaning this term takes on in the thought of Milan Kundera,[1] who adopts it as one of the fundamental interpretative categories of existence and, perhaps, even the central nucleus in the expression of his cognitive course. Translated up to a short time ago by the "art of showiness" or "showy art", the term was completely deprived of its philosophical and existential meaningfulness to be reduced to a category of objects (Le Grand 1996). The French translation of the German term Kitsch, *art de pacotille*, is, according to Kundera, highly reductive as regards its philosophical import. As shown by Broch, who links kitsch historically with the sentimental romanticism of the nineteenth century, it is a question of a wider, more basic category than that of artistic "bad taste", and is bound much more to human existence than the sole reference to art would suggest (Broch 1990). It is an existential category, in the sense that kitsch attitude and kitsch behaviour exist (Kundera 1988).

As it had been for Broch (1990), for Kundera, too, to reflect on kitsch was to mean above all to reflect on the human state of mind nurturing it, on the man-kitsch, on the existential need kitsch satisfied: "The kitsch-man's (Kitschmensch) need for kitsch: it is the need to gaze into the mirror of the beautifying lie and to be moved to tears of gratification at one's own reflection" (Kundera 1988, p. 135). Studying this compensatory desire and the human state of mind that nurtures it, Kundera maintains it corresponds to the clash with the daily demonstration of the unacceptability of reality. If it is beyond human possibility to eliminate imperfection from existence, the solution prepared will on the contrary be profoundly human and will consist of finding powerful mechanisms of negation of reality (Espejo 1984), eliminating from our visual field all that in human existence is basically unacceptable. This aesthetic ideal is called kitsch (Kundera 1984). It is the aesthetic ideal that seems to be at the bottom of the concept of landscape as a projection of desires, of landscape as a desired product (Vos and Meekes 1999).

Kundera makes particularly interesting observations on the relationship between kitsch and repetition, in the sense that happiness, understood as an engine of kitsch mystification, is "desire of repetition" (Kundera 1984): the finiteness and linearity of the course of time in which human experience takes place, if allowed, reveal all the tragicness of the human condition or rather its lack of weight and necessity.

The desire for happiness, namely, the desire for repetition, is therefore nostalgia for the Eden we were sent away from, the lost idyll, an image that has stayed within us as a memory of Paradise, the monotony of which was not boredom but happiness (Le Grand 1995). Losing the possibility of the idyll and repetition, man can only preserve nostalgia for it, and it is for this nostalgia that kitsch seems to suggest a convincing consolation.

From a social-psychological perspective, the fortune of kitsch has been due to its capacity to satisfy the human desire for happiness, thanks to the "averageness" of its values. According to Abraham Moles, kitsch is people-oriented, for it is created by and for the average man, and is more relaxing and easier to live with than great art with its elevated values; it opposes transcendent, cumbersome beauty with the more measured values of tranquillity that the average man seeks (Moles 1971). The pleasure that the kitsch object offers is due to its capacity to produce, more easily than a functional object does, a lifestyle able to satisfy the average man.

For this reason, perhaps, planners often support "kitsch" aesthetic values to characterise the cultural patrimony in an attempt to commercialise and promote it. This is the case, for example, of a redevelopment project for a port area in Hull, England, analysed by Atkinson (2007), who studies the way in which the values of the patrimony are understood by the inhabitants of the area. Kitsch aesthetics are criticised and judged as common, mundane and typical of a "low" culture, but according to Atkinson, the "repetitive, foreseeable and reassuring familiarity" and nostalgic sentimentality have a appeasing effect on the inhabitants of a world that is becoming increasingly insecure and "disembedded".[2]

In this sense, he tries to show how residents interface with kitsch landscapes and how they interpret them and he tries to understand whether kitsch contributes to giving them a sense of rooting. One hypothesis is that the analyses based on "everyday spaces" enables us to understand how the identities of sites are constructed and continually remodelled by everyday practices and by social memory interpretation (Atkinson 2007).

This concept binds the landscape with social memories in the sense that the landscape patrimony is not a story but a reconstruction of the space of social memories. It is an interpretation that has been progressively developed by researchers and highlights the close relationship between memories, the memory and space, sites and landscape. The link becomes particularly clear in sites dedicated to memory and to the historic patrimony, where it remains concentrated and frozen such as in museums. This interpretation of social memories risks, however, ignoring the fact that they are interpreted through society. Though the memory is also generated in non-planned sites pertaining to everyday life (and not by the usual "high profile projects") and it is a nomadic, dynamic phenomenon, as sustained by various researchers such as Bruno, Terdiman and Thrift

(Bruno 2003; Terdiman 2003; Thrift 1999), who Atkinson quotes as support for his theses.

Basing himself on the stories of people who have a relationship with the research site, Atkinson reaches certain conclusions. The reconsideration of social memories as the product of a dynamic process of production and mobilisation of a context, rather than a phenomenon that is the fruit of a relationship made between space and memories, enables the study and analysis of how architects, promoters and managers of the site produce routine spaces, where the spaces are transformed by the continuous interpretation of inhabitants and visitors. An example of such a negotiated transformation taken from the "Victoria Dock village" research in Hull is the fact that one of the pubs that had initially adopted the maritime kitsch envisaged in the planners' work, subsequently abandoned it. Another example is that a part of the port, Quay 2005, which had been greatly discussed and contested in the past, has now been realised. Thus, even though the initial planning of these sites departs from history for the sites to be interpreted and understood, we must also take into consideration their gradual transformation and how they are understood, contested or reinterpreted by the subjects who form their sense of place, social memory and appropriate aesthetics through these sites (Atkinson 2007, p. 537).

As demonstrated in the description of the kitsch concept above, new theories suggest that kitsch may be appreciated by the residents of Victoria Dock, not because they are common or ironically sophisticated but because in this form of aesthetics they find simple, ready convenience. The people interviewed in the research recognised the planners' intent to use kitsch aesthetics in maritime style as a sales instrument for the "target", the middle class. The planners' commercial objectives caused ambivalent reactions among the inhabitants. Those interviewed described Victoria Dock as a pleasant, safe, attractive place, even though none of them admitted that the introduction of kitsch aesthetics led them to feel more "embedded". Some of the people interviewed stated they approved of the introduction of the kitsch style in the area.

These results demonstrated, according to Atkinson, that kitsch aesthetics should be taken more seriously in the interpretation of space. The shift of research towards "everyday spaces" may enable deeper interpretations to be developed of the complex, spatial social memories in the contemporary world (Atkinson 2007, p. 537).

Commodity Space and Citizen Space

We have seen how planners often support kitsch aesthetic values to distinguish cultural patrimony in an attempt to commercialise and promote it for leisure. Kitsch aesthetics in places of leisure therefore also have to do with commodification of the landscape, which – as we have seen – from place experienced becomes a "projection of desires", a shopping object. Man is at a distance from the landscape and this distance, which indeed marks the involution of the landscape concept in contemporary post-cities, is also a distance from the project in that the glance of contemporary man is a passive, contemplative one that is reflected on our perceptive worlds and behaviours (Vos and Meekes 1999). One feature of our times is the rapid change in production and information technology. This completely changes the economic base of landscape types and favours involution of the concept of landscape towards commodification.

The process of development and penetration of commodified economics into several spheres of life within society has been touched on by a number of analysts of the large transformation processes (Polanyi 1994; Castells 1996; Mckay 1998), but according to Williams and Windebank, little attention has been paid to the dimensions and modalities of the penetration of commodification into our organised life. Through a critical analysis of the statements of various researchers, who generically maintain that our modern economic lives have been almost completely penetrated by economic relations, they highlight the need for a more critical, precise and scrupulous evaluation of the nature and extension of commodification penetration (Williams and Windebank 2003).

The study conducted by these two researchers suggests a series of queries, which for us take on particular importance in that they are to do with the possibility of revealing spaces of freedom, not governed by commodification, in the city project: how deep has the penetration of the logic of commodification been in the advanced economies? Does the trend show a route towards economies that are even more commodified? Do non-commodified spheres still exist? In which case, what form do they take? Where are they? And why do they persist?

Vast non-commodified spaces do exist. Even in the heart of commodification – the advanced economies – vast alternative spaces exist, where commodification is not present and its penetration process is in any case irregular and slow. Williams and Windebank refer to a series of case studies to manage to explain the irregular, slow process of commodification (Williams and Windebank 2003). But to understand the phenomena of the commodification process neither strictly "economic" explanations nor investigations of the "cultural" aspects alone are sufficient; it is a combination of both that is needed.

For leisure, too, there may be alternative approaches and new possibilities, "spaces of hope" – "spaces of resistance" as Silvia Serreli (2009) reinterprets them – that do not necessarily entail the inevitability of commodification, spaces that we may define as edge spaces, in that they are external to some critical dynamics of the city. At the *edge*, it is possible to gather everything that is considered rejected by the "normality" of the urban machine, a condition that emerges just when different ways of thinking of the settlement space open up. Edge spaces may favour the development of public awareness (Décamps 2000) to re-establish the role of public space in the contemporary society, a modality of public space in which we can move without feeling manipulated, the space par excellence of the *polis* (Abalos 2004). This possibility of "moving without feeling manipulated" where it is possible to mediate and transform the messages coming from this immense visual flow of competitiveness and commercialisation.

In the context of our contemporary metropolises, *edge areas*, obsolete, forgotten by development, seem to offer possibilities for new urban situations to emerge. These marginal situations, which escape clarity of description and institutionalisation, are particularly fit to reveal that void which common sense understands as the exclusive space of action, which is the meaning of the project for space. As Paola Pittaluga (2006) indeed notes, the resulting physical spaces, the non-planned edge spaces, appear as places where creativity, subjectivity, the construction of new moments of communication assert themselves.

These situations cause us to have doubts about the affirmations often made by sociologists on the hypotheses that the penetration of economic aspects into other spheres of our everyday life is inevitable as well as deep and rapid.

There are therefore new opportunities to challenge the inevitability of the commodification process and hope for the construction and development of alternative social relations, which may avoid being colonised by the economic sphere. In this perspective, spaces of leisure may also contribute to the formation of alternative social relations to those linked with commodification and, in this sense, the construction of *civitas* and, ultimately, of the city.

Tourism Economics and Dialectic of Identity

Commodification becomes an important part of leisure activities through tourism economics. Tourism has become a key aspect in local economics in many urban areas, a phenomenon due to the transition process of cities from place of industrial economy to area of recreation and the consequent reassessment of urban space as leisure commodity. This process has also entailed changes in city planning, affected by tensions and conflicts which exist between managing the city as a tourist destination on the one hand and as a space of work and residence on the other (Meethan 1997). They are tensions that affect the link between tourism and policy, between policy and the subordination of a series of values to other values. In this sense, each shift or change in the representation of space involves power, given that tourism, in any form, is the domination of a series of values rather than others (Hall 1994).

This type of domination and control over space is taken into consideration by Meethan, with particular reference to the ways in which economic restructuring has been conditioned by local contingent circumstances (Meethan 1997). These circumstances have accepted conceptual reassessment of space. The relations existing between the modalities of space production and the specificity of a place have to do with both the history of material production of spaces and social and economic practices, but also with ideas and representations (Harvey 1989, Lefebvre 1991). Values, ideas and symbols thus carry out an important role in the reassessment and promotion of cities and are attributed to urban areas. Cities are promoted and planned as places of consumption and recreation, placing the accent on qualities and aesthetic values of the landscape and expressing architectural and cultural specificities.

The reassessment of cities is a response to changes in economic conditions, but should rather be interpreted as a local process of negotiation, which involves both institutional elements and everyday empirical micropolitics (Meethan 1997).

These changes in economic conditions in the evolution from post-industrial to tourist city are analysed in a study on the city of York, where, before the eighties, local authorities did not lay their stakes on tourism as an important resource as they considered it a secondary, seasonal sector, not very well remunerated. As in many other tourist destinations, there were conflicts between the economic interests of organisations and of the local elites – who wanted to earn from investments in a short-term perspective – on the one hand, and the management of the image of the place in a more long-term perspective, on the other hand. Conservative politicians had developed a "hands off" type of approach; the city was not promoted at a tourist level, and this strategy contributed to limiting the number of tourists. This passive or "indirect" stance towards tourism in territorial and urban policies paradoxically contributed to preserving the city and improving its chances of becoming a tourist city (Meethan 1997).

City planning and administration aimed at providing technical and rational solutions to urban problems has the dimensions of an administrative space, which is not the same space as that experienced by the people (Lefebvre 1991). This different perception or view may lead to a conflict between the needs perceived by residents and those of visitors, considering that the space of the tourist city is continuously being transformed. Space control therefore involves both economic elements and institutional ones, but also acts as an instrument by which cultural identities are created and maintained.

The promotion of a city should be aimed at influencing not only potential visitors but also the inhabitants, and policies must create an inclusive image of the city in which the control of space has a strategic role, in that it serves to understand how to promote tourist development in the city within the local community, trying to explore the cultural and perceptive worlds of the inhabitants in the centre, in the suburbs and in the various social classes (Meethan 1997) and to understand what are defined as the inhabitants' spatial images. As Paola Pittaluga notes, this concept, of a psychological, sociological and geographical matrix, refers, on the one hand, to understanding the modalities by which individuals acquire, store, recall and decode environmental and spatial information and, on the other, to pinpointing cared-for places belonging to spaces lived in by a society – highlighting the value and significance, the relations linking them, the symbolic projections of which they are the subject – and the hopes, aspirations and anxiety of the populations inhabiting a territory (Pittaluga 2008). To render explicit the spatial images of the inhabitants, it is important to emphasise that an individual's portrayal of space derives from psychological and cultural processes, life and everyday experience, and reveals a distance from an image yielded by traditional territorial and urban analysis.[3] Descriptions change as their perception varies, influenced by the expectations and hopes of local societies: a change that may be considered partly *external*, related to objects, for the object of the perception changes, and partly *internal* in the sense that it is the result of a substantial shift in the perceptive viewpoint (Maciocco and Tagliagambe 1998).

Places of Leisure and Intermediate Spaces

To understand current leisure policies, we must, however, analyse the relations between the policies and the mechanisms of planning at various levels of government, which are significant in two ways. On the one hand, the role played by local authorities has changed. Local authorities have become "entrepreneurial authorities" instead of authorities supplying services. Thus, coalitions of interests have been formed and policies have been worked out that are pro-active for economic development. On the other hand, the statutory planning frame and regulatory mechanisms entail reconciling conflicts between new development and the need to protect the environmental resources that attract both investments and visitors. Local authorities play two roles at the same time: that of authority-entrepreneur, working out strategies for economic development, and that of defender of the environment, attempting to limit the impacts of economic activities. There is therefore a link between policies and the dominant role of space over the values of the city (Meethan 1997).

But the authorities are not the only actors to have economic interests in the city, and the use of aesthetic, historic and architectural values does not belong solely to them. There are also the private actors and the city inhabitants.

The power of space is to be obtained through the capacity of groups of interest to establish or impose a vision of the city. Therefore, the development of partnerships and alliances in planning and implementing tourism policies is crucial. Collaboration between the authorities must involve both the interest groups and the entire population of the city and the hinterland. These alliances are important for regulating the influx of tourism and creating a link between the authorities and the inhabitants, but also to establish and implement a new view of the city, which is not confined to the use, development and influence of the centre but which prevents the formation of a social, economic periphery. This process of reassessment of the city is not only a strategic planning practice but also the retrieval of a process of non-planned spatial organisation, which materialises in the experience of living in the city every day and in the creation of identity through continuous projectual activity (Meethan 1997). In this sense, leisure may be considered an opportunity for the city project, an "intermediate space" between everyday reality and the possible, to make up for a lack of projectuality which makes itself felt more and more in our times and culture, which often digresses into the justification a posteriori and at any cost of the "strength of reality" and the reasons for it. This is why leisure can play the role of a space that is not trapped by the need to follow and reproduce a pre-established route but is always open to new solutions, determined by the "friction", by what Florenskij calls *sdvig* (displacement), between the results which our thought and culture are accustomed to and an inexhaustible wealth of events and processes which make up its body of study and research (Tagliagambe 2008).

The holiday, being an essential part of leisure, causes the inhabitant to not withdraw within himself but also to not project himself completely outside himself and alienate himself, taking his mind off himself. He must learn to inhabit the intermediate space between himself and the "other", between his internal and external worlds and between natural and artificial so that the border between these dimensions never becomes a clear, insurmountable line of demarcation, such as would prevent reciprocal communication and fruitful interaction, but neither does it thin down to the point of becoming no longer recognisable. But to obtain these results, rather than "go beyond" the real world, plunging directly into virtual reality, we need to work at the border between inside and outside the latter, namely at the interface between it and ordinary reality (Tagliagambe 2008).

Understood as intermediate space or frontier, leisure takes on the form and function of a neutral zone, where reciprocal identities may be attested, remaining separate but each beginning to have experience of the other. Where differences, the different ways of seeing the world and the various styles of thought are defined. In leisure, apart from habits, the misunderstanding also performs a social function, as a stimulus and opportunity for translating languages, a sort of compromise aimed at achieving an understanding (La Cecla 1997). This is because the misunderstanding is strongly correlated with the idea of encounter, namely with the possibility that two dissimilar people, through messages initially not completely understood either by one or the other, manage gradually to become familiar and understand each other, establish reciprocal harmony, a sort of "third entity", within which the better features of the two original subjects can emerge and progressively be asserted (Maciocco and Tagliagambe 2009). In this "third entity" are found the matrices of the construction of *civitas* and, ultimately, the city. Thus, leisure as a frontier, as the place where conflicts may be generated but also fruitful experiences of translation.

Taking up again the important distinction between frontier and border made by Piero Zanini (2000), La Cecla asserts that the border indicates more an internal or external limit not to be crossed, whereas the frontier recalls the idea that there is a place where two diversities face each other. If this is true, if frontiers are the face-to-face between two cultures, then it is fundamental that they take place so that they may really be the filter and stage of "difference" (La Cecla 1997).

If leisure is configured as the opportunity for a holiday from normal practice and a chance to experience a cultural frontier, this space between men may legitimately be considered an essential prerequisite and precondition of freedom and consequently becomes an increasingly important, fascinating theme for the idea and vision of the city, since it is indeed this gap that ensures plurality, the existence of individuals not crushed one against the other. It is a space that maintains relations between individuals: they are together but are also separate from each other. In leisure there is in a certain sense the nature of contemporary public space, which allows us both social contact and the idea of the "individual isolated in the midst of a crowded environment" (Abalos 2004), a concept of public space which combines a collective ideal with an individual ideal.

Public Identity and Brandscapes

We have seen how one meaning of leisure has to do with overcoming the hindering force of reality as a habit and how this overcoming is necessary to make up for a lack of projectuality which – as we have said – often digresses into the justification *a posteriori* and at any cost of the "strength of reality" and the reasons for it. But this taking distance from the strength of reality may project us, indeed through leisure, into an exclusively thematic experience of the city.[4] In this way, leisure, in the carefree experience of the city as a theme park, is configured as a form of detachment from reality.

The link between the place of leisure and thematisation of the city lets us glimpse the acritical, reassuring side of this experience, more and more controlled by the new urban economy of entertainment. Hollands and Chatterton (2003) report that entertainment and spare time have been incorporated in the new urban economy, characterised by the phenomenon of "theming of entertainment and leisure" (Sorkin 1992; Gottdiener 2001) and promoted by the large multinational brands. If we do not stop at the triumphalistic descriptions on the rebirth of urban culture (Worpole and Greenhalgh 1999; Landry 2000), we cannot but emphasise how multinational control deprives people of alternatives, commercialising public space, splitting up and gentrifying the supply and marginalising alternative local, creative development (Zukin 1995).

We are therefore living in an era in which the great corporations are tending to expand their power in the entertainment and spare time sector, dominating the market with their brands, market segmentation and the concentration of ownership of the businesses of the sector (Hollands and

Chatterton 2003). It is a phenomenon linked with a tendential picture that features the increase of globalisation and the concentration of economic activities (Sassen 1996, 1997; Klein 2000; Monbiot 2000). These effects are also reflected in the process of *branding* and the dominance of nightlife by large businesses. As Hollands and Chatterton emphasise, quoting an expression of Monbiot's (2000, p. 4), we have reached a situation in which "corporations, the contraptions we invented to serve us, are overthrowing us". Concentration on the market, new global actors, a new more entrepreneurial State, gentrification and segmentation of the supply aimed at the professionals of the services sector have, all together, contributed to replacing the old, the historic, with ways of interpreting entertainment and spare time in nightlife that have different consequences. A fundamental consequence is indeed branding in entertainment and spare time, which we are used to accepting as a normal aspect, a part of contemporary life in the public sphere. This constitutes great change with respect to a recent past when places of entertainment were more detached from the contemporary public sphere, such as the large entertainment centres like Disneyland. In cities, various processes of gentrification have occurred: old industrial zones have become centres of the new nightlife, infrastructures for a new, well-to-do urban class in search of pleasure and entertainment (Zukin 1992, 1995). The multinational corporations of the media world and entertainment are the planners of these new "urban landscapes" (Hollands and Chatterton 2003), characterised to such an extent by branding that they have generated the neologism "brandscapes" instead of "landscapes" (Hart 1998).

In spite of the fact that the demand tends to be flexible and consumers' preferences may change, the supply takes on a more and more standardised, universal form, and it is precisely because it is impossible to take one's distance from this standardisation that the spatial forms linked with this supply do not express contemporary spatiality, which has diversity and specificity as its constituent features. For this reason – as Hollands and Chatterton emphasise – it is important to remain critical towards those rumours that maintain that "post-modern consumerism" or post-Fordism represent flexibility and the possibility of choice for the consumer. Actually, the choices will almost certainly be limited and will tend to resemble each other rather than express unicity. In effect, in the epoch of "urban redevelopment", art and entertainment are used as instruments for renewal of the city, or better of its caricature, through "fantasisation" of the everyday context (Hannigan 1998), as a company strategy to exploit "commodity fetishism" and extend the life of a brand geographically and symbolically (Evans 2003, p. 417).

A condition of this kind does not imply or require active participation on the part of the consumers. Urban life becomes something that happens rather than an environment created and participated in by people (Hollands and Chatterton 2003, p. 380). What is *branded* in these cities is not the immediate event or something like a collection in a museum but the city itself. The museum becomes an icon and a magnet for post-industrial urbanity (Ryan 2000 quoted by Evans 2003).

Branding is not, however, a new phenomenon. Simmel maintains that a sort of branding of cities already existed in the eighteenth century and that it contributed to the creation of a culture, a collective identity and a sense of belonging. Names like Hollywood, Guinness World and Silicon Valley are all examples of the branding phenomenon and have been known and linked with certain cities for decades.

Branding, can, in actual fact, be described as the use of symbols or logos. Logos were already used in ancient Greek times as carriers of specific information, using a minimum of visual support to refine and condense a range of complex, even disparate, meanings in a single symbolic image (Lip 1995 quoted by Evans 2003).

Some tendencies in the *hard-branded* cities are that the products – which in the past were predominantly consumed by private subjects – have been transformed into a space of collective consumption. An example of a space of this kind is Nike Town in London. The impact these spaces have on the urban landscape clearly constitutes the commodification of spaces of consumption. In these contexts, two twin systems of symbolic and political economy exist and interact; the physical representation of promotion of the product and the opportunity to strengthen both client loyalty and synergy between the physical and symbolic values of the brands (Evans 2003).

In the last few decades, the great artistic and cultural projects have been implemented by planners and architects using such attributes of art and culture to express a sense of civic or national pride. These phenomena, too, are a sort of urban "branding". Different monuments, entire museum districts, etc. have been created. As Evans notes, such a transformation occurred for the last time in the nineteenth century and now we are experiencing a new one (Evans 2003). An interesting phenomenon is that the form rather than the function of the facilities seems to be of great importance in attracting visitors. In a survey carried out a year after the Guggenheim Museum was opened in Bilbao, 40% of visitors maintained that they had come above all to see the facility, and only 5% had come to see the art collection (Stern et al. 1995). Moreover, buildings become a sort of icon, symbols of cities, even though the architecture of new (cultural) facilities has been designed not to idealise but to mirror the context, including its contradictions. A position in a certain sense similar to the phenomenon of "reflective sliding", being a reflection of the contradictions of the world, without addressing the problem of facing them, almost an escape from the need to solve the social conflicts of an "already become" city. This causes architectonic and urban space production to be reduced to a spatial replica of daily behaviours, as happens among the supporters of "reflective sliding", in which the said behaviours, the apparent manifestations of the social, become the primary content of architecture, often "at a level of clarity that transforms them into advertisements for themselves" (Gregotti 1993).

In any case, the large cultural projects, contemporary art museums and other cultural complexes seem to be irresistible for politicians and other cultural producers, who often maintain that the purpose is to reconnect the city with its own context. But very often the self-referential approach used by the planners and architects is contested, which actually excludes the context since the residents and the local dimension are not taken into consideration and involved in projects of this type (Evans 2001).

Branding projects may be of great importance for cities but are also accompanied by great risks that are linked with the lack of social control – in the case in point the accessibility of art and culture – as an instrument of collective growth. A problem aggravated by the decline of the public dimension in man of the post-modern society, characterised indeed by a subjectivist trend responsible for the crisis of the social bond and disaffection for public life (Sennett 1977). There are therefore advantages and disadvantages produced by branding in the development of the city through the use of art and culture. There is, for example, the opinion that brands bring a sense of order and coherence to a multiform reality and enable us to interpret more easily the context of spaces and products in which we find ourselves, as is the case of some symbol-architectures that project cities into the limelight of the international map via sophisticated campaigns and carefully selected images (Mommaas 2002). A role of branding is similarly acknowledged in the creation of public identity and culture (Zukin 1995 quoted by Hollands and Chatterton 2003).

But one disadvantage or rather a challenge that many cities or sites that have experienced a branding process have to face is the risk of losing the charm linked with their being a city if the same attributes, symbols or brands are always referred to, to achieve notoriety, promote the city and attract visitors. Competition between the various cities is strong, and it is not enough to copy the methods or processes used by other cities to be successful. Another challenge linked with the branding phenomenon is that symbols and values are less tied to cities or specific sites. They are universal and for this reason also placeless. Evans suggests, however, that the values and symbolism connected with universal phenomena or brands have a limited existence (Evans 2002). In recent years, examples have arisen of new practices in consumer tendencies which indicate the return to a link between space and city as a way of life (including systems of consumption, architecture and spare time) on the one hand and a departure from mass production on the other.

The managers, researchers and curators of museums and monuments of past times have been replaced by the new *elite* of promotion organisers, experts in redevelopment and merchants. Culture, which once represented aesthetic quality, now becomes standardised to be able to offer "an *elite* experience for everybody" (Zolberg 1994 quoted by Evans 2003). This tendency also creates a replica of architectural style, which produces a link between culture and commerce. Suffice to think of the economic benefits that can be considerable if *branding* and the transformation of the city are successful. An example mentioned by Evans is the MoMa Museum in New York, where the turnover per square metre of the boutiques inside the museum exceeds that recorded in the large American chain of supermarkets, Wal-Mart (Evans 2003). This is branding with a strong commercial connotation, which often arouses negative reactions, and various researchers have characterised it as an example of commodification and privatisation of a non-democratic nature, a process which, according to Mari Paz Balibrea (2001), represents the erosion of the public sphere and privatistic redefinition of accessibility to spaces of culture.

Examples exist, however, of places and movements where the inhabitants have resisted the branding process, expressing their opposition to the domination of the public sphere and public spaces by corporations. Hollands and Chatterton report on them as a reaction that places a counterweight against the tendencies of domination and control by the large chains. Places with a strong local entrepreneurial culture have managed to resist branding tendencies at length. Unfortunately, it is difficult (sometimes impractical too) to resort to the law to defend consumers against producers, also because WTO anti-protectionist regulations exist. On the other hand, the defence of human rights addresses States and not the large corporations, so this is not of use either to defend people from the interests of the big businesses (Hollands and Chatterton 2003).

The consumers, the citizens, should achieve more frequent interaction with and better knowledge of the big businesses, their marketing and branding strategies, their domination and segmentation. This would be the first important step on the way that might lead to the creation and realisation of a more democratic, creative and diverse nightlife (Hollands and Chatterton 2003).

Symbolic Construction and Urban Consciousness

In the previous sections we have emphasised that among the urban phenomena linked with leisure there is the transformation of citizens into passive consumers as an effect of the *fantasisation* of the everyday context, a misunderstood form of urban upgrading that transforms the city into a pervasively branded environment, where urban life "happens" without citizens actively living it (Jacobson 1998). The branded city is a city that is reduced to a theme park strewn with pavilions for consumers, which enables and propitiates losing oneself within it (Costa 1996). Pleasure consists of yielding, letting oneself mingle, be influenced and even intoxicated by the spatial experience. It is a phenomenon in which urban strategy and company strategy merge and support each other reciprocally. At the same time, fantasisation needs to recreate the city in stage-sets that are often a caricature of the city and reduce its complexity,[5] portraying it as a simulacrum, a virtual image that is a copy of a copy of a city that never existed and was never inhabited by any man (De Azua 2003). A city that, as the film *The Truman Show* recounts, is only a set, in which Truman, a metaphor for the post-citizen, risks being shipwrecked in the simulated storm as the sailor cannot help him: he does not know how to *do*, he only knows how to *act*. Almost as if to point out that it is indeed this difference between doing and acting that marks the distance between the true city and the simulacrum city. Where *doing* is closely connected with *inhabiting*.[6]

The detachment of the images of reality represents a loss because by entrusting its image to the virtual the real becomes residual. But if we do not go to meet the real, lived-in space, worrying pairs will assert themselves opposing the city to its simulacrum – represented by its image linked with a *brand* – and the non-citizen to the citizen (De Azua 2003), where the figure of "non-citizen" will correspond to the loss of the collective urban conscience and with it the loss of the city as a conceptual unit.

What interests us is precisely the space of the conscience which develops gradually as the subject understands, while acting and often after he has acted, the sense of his actions and those of others, and which, in this sense, opens up to the world of relations that nurture the collective consciousness. For which the expressive force of the symbol is essential for taking on a collective conscience of the elements that preside over our spatial life. In the current epoch, too, permeated by rationalism, the language of figures and images keeps its expressive force intact (Tibaldi 1986). We have been able to note how leisure may also be considered an intermediate space, a *frontier* between reality and possibility, where it is possible to open up to the project of possible worlds. There is therefore a constituent relation with the symbol in the sense that, in its deepest etymological origins, the symbol is a "bridge thrown" between reality and possible worlds. But this bridge cannot but be built via a project, which makes relations between the project and symbolic language indissoluble. Here, the importance of leisure takes shape as the space of one's own cultural growth and the construction of one's own symbolic patrimony and its collective dimensions.

But, as Maurizio Ferraris (1993) notes, we can argue that the whole of reality is a symbol. If this is true, the process of symbolic construction that activates the collective consciousness cannot but depart from a regained relationship with reality, through which to encounter a new concept of public space. This process may not, however, develop in the thematised space of the contemporary post-city, which is a figure of detachment from reality. How, then, is it possible to recuperate a relationship with reality in places of leisure? And how is a concept of public space conceivable through the retrieval of this relationship at a moment when we are experiencing a sort of crisis of public space deriving from its commercialisation, privatisation and *theme parking*, from the form of the "city without a city" (Sieverts 2002)? In this picture, places of leisure external to the public space simulated by the thematised city are to be explored, places of individuals' experiences and subjectivity, who with their practices end up creating various types of "public dimension" (Williamson et al. 2002). To design the city in the thematised "urban" means to assert this *externity* (Maciocco 2008) of leisure which, as a frontier space, external to habitual spaces, has within it the possibility of covering various dimensions of *contemporary public space.*

These marginal areas, the portrayal of the bad conscience of a city, rejected, residual spaces seem to offer the possibility for new participatory situations to emerge, where the city of places re-emerges as a set of traces of the city of communication flows and competitiveness. In these spaces, it will be the project's task to reveal the *traces* (Derrida 1998) of the city of places.

In these spaces, far from the flows, there are favourable conditions for social practices, including new ones, that make a new concept of public space constructed by people's habits conceivable, what we call "contemporary public space", beyond the monumentalised public spaces of the institutions or the spaces of commercial representation.

Through their individual subjectivity and their social practices, citizens can create a new public sphere suitable for the contemporary condition. Thus, every gesture, even the smallest, has the task of revealing the meanings of this common world.

Notes

[1] See entry "kitsch" in Kundera (1988). Kitsch in Kundera's work was brilliantly researched by Anna Davini in her degree thesis, which has constituted a rich store of critical references for this paragraph, enabling the implications of kitsch for the city project to be explored. Cf. Davini (2003-2004).

[2] Giddens (1991). In actual fact, the term *disembedding* was coined by Giddens not to mean the absence of reference points but to register the detachment of the community from an organisation at a local level. It does not, however, just mean the separation of a single organisation but also a process of "disembedding" of sentiments, values and traditions attached to or identified with the place. The term "disembedding" should be interpreted with care. It does not mean alienation from the local level but rather a participation in various "new" communities and informative, communicative environments, which have common experiences as their reference point rather than the territory *itself.*

[3] On this theme Lardon et al. (2001), Lardon and Debarbieux (2003).

[4] Cf. for example Sorkin (1992), Jacobson and Warren (1998), Augé (2001), Glaeser et al. (2001).

[5] *Ibidem.*

[6] This is a concept Heidegger (1971) faces in his analysis of Holderlin's line *Worthfully, but poetically Man inhabits the Earth* referring back to the Greek root of poetry, ποιέω, the Greek expression for the word *do.*

References

Abalos I (2004) *Metamorfosi pittoresca.* Focus, 9° Mostra Internazionale di Architettura, Fondazione La Biennale di Venezia, Venezia.

Atkinson D (2007) *Kitsch geographies and the everyday spaces of social memory.* Environment and Planning A n. 39, pp. 521–540.

Augé M (2001) *Finzioni di fine secolo seguito da Che cosa succede?*, Bollati Boringhieri, Torino.

Balibrea MP (2001) *Urbanism, culture and the post-industrial city: challenging the "Barcelona model".* Journal of Spanish Cultural Studies n. 2(2), pp. 187–210.

Baudrillard J (1970) *La Société de Consommation*, Denoël, Paris.

Baudrillard J (1981) *Simulacres et Simulation*, Galilée, Paris.

Broch H (1990) *Il Kitsch*, Einaudi, Torino.

Bruno G (2003) *Havana: memoirs of material culture.* Journal of Visual Culture n. 2, pp. 303–324.

Castells M (1996) *The Rise of the Network Society*, Blackwell, Oxford.

Costa X (1996) *Ciudad Distraída, Ciudad Informe*. In: Collegi Official d'Arquitectes de Catalunya/Centre de Cultura Contemporània, *Presente y futuros. Arquitectura en la ciudades,* Actar, Barcelona, pp. 184–189.

Davini A (2003–2004) K*itsch e romanzo come figure dell'esistenza,* Degree Thesis in Philosophy, Facoltà di Letteratura e Filosofia, Università di Padova.

De Azua F (2003) *La necessidad y el deseo.* Sileno ns. 14–15, pp. 13–21.

Décamps H (2000) *Demanding more of Landscape Research (and Researchers).* Landscape and Urban Planning n. 47, pp. 3–4.

De Masi D (1997) *Ozio Creativo,* Ediesse, Roma.

Derrida J (1998) *Addio a Emmanuel Lévinas,* Jaca Book, Milano.

Espejo M (1984) *La ilusión lírica: Ensayo sobre Milan Kundera,* Hachette, Buenos Aires.

Evans GL (2001) *Cultural Planning: An Urban Renaissance?,* Routledge, London, New York.

Evans GL (2002) *Living in a world heritage city: stakeholders in the dialectic of the universal and particular.* International Journal of Heritage Studies n. 7(5), pp. 117–135.

Evans GL (2003) *Hard-branding the cultural city – from prado to prada.* International Journal of Urban and Regional Research n. 27(2), pp. 417–440.

Ferraris M (1993) *Il ritorno del simbolo.* Il Sole 24 Ore, 28/02.

Fumaroli M (1996) *"L'arte di sapersi ricreare". Loisirs et loisir. Considerazioni e riflessioni in margine a un convegno dedicato al tempo libero e all'ozio degli antichi,* Il Sole 24 Ore 01/12/1996.

Giddens A (1991) *Modernity and Self-Identity: Self and Society in the Late Modern Age,* Polity Press, Cambridge UK.

Glaeser EL, Kolko J, Saiz A (2001) *Consumer city.* Journal of Economic Geography n. 1, pp. 27–50.

Gottdiener M (2001) *The Theming of America. American Dreams, Media Fantasies and Themed Environments,* Westview Press, Boulder CO, 2nd Edition.

Gregotti V (1993) *Teatranti della cultura,* Casabella, n. 606, November.

Hall CM (1994) *Tourism and Politics: Policy, Power and Place,* John Wiley and Sons, Chichester.

Hannigan J (1998) *Fantasy City. Pleasure and Profit in the Postmodern Metropolis,* Routledge, London, New York.

Hart S (1998) *The Future for Brands.* In Hart S, Murphy J (eds) *Brands: The New Wealth Creators,* Macmillan, London.

Harvey D (1989) *The Condition of Postmodernity,* Blackwell, Oxford.

Heidegger M. (1971) *Building, Dwelling, Thinking. Poetry, Language, Thought,* Harper Colophon Books, New York.

Henry IP (1994) *The Politics of Leisure Policy,* Macmillan, Basingstoke.

Hollands R, Chatterton P (2003) *Producing nightlife in the new urban entertainment economy: corporatization, branding and market segmentation.* International Journal of Urban and Regional Research n. 27(2), June, pp. 361–385.

Huizinga J (2002) *Homo Ludens,* Einaudi, Torino.

Jacobson JM (1998), *Staging difference. Aestheticization and the politics of difference in contemporary cities.* In: Fincher R, Jacobs JM (eds), *Cities of Difference,* Guilford, New York, pp. 252–279.

Jacobson JM, Warren S (1998) *Disneyfication of the metropolis: popular resistance in Seattle.* Journal of Urban Affairs n. 16, pp. 89–107.

Klein N (2000) *No Logo,* Flamingo, London.

Kundera M (1984) *The Unbearable Lightness of Being,* translated by Heim HH, Faber and Faber, London-Boston.

Kundera M (1988) *The Art of the Novel,* translated from the French by Linda Asher, Grove Press, New York.

La Cecla F (1997) *Il malinteso. Antropologia dell'incontro,* Laterza, Roma-Bari.

Landry C (2000) *The Creative City. A Toolkit for Urban Innovators,* Earthscan Publications, London.

Lardon S, Debarbieux B (eds) (2003), *Les Figures du Projet Territorial,* Éditions de l'Aube, Paris.

Lardon S, Maurel P, Piveteau V (eds) (2001) *Représentations Spatiales et Développement Territorial,* Editions Hermès, Paris.

Le Grand E (1995) *Kundera ou la mémoire du désir,* XYZ, Montréal.

Le Grand E (1996) Introductions: *Séductions du kitsch: roman, art et culture.* In: Le Grand E (ed), *Séductions du Kitsch: Roman, Art et Culture,* XYZ, Montréal, pp. 13–25.

Lefebvre H (1991) *The Production of Space,* Blackwell, Oxford.

Lip E (1995), *The Design and Feng Shui of Logos, Trademarks and Signboards.* Prentice Hall, New York.

Lipovetski G (1983) *L'ère du vide. Essais sur l'individualisme contemporain,* Gallimard, Paris.

Maciocco G (2008) *Fundamental Trends in City Developement,* Springer-Verlag, Berlin, Heidelberg, New York.

Maciocco G, Tagliagambe S (1998) *La città possibile,* Dedalo, Bari.

Maciocco G, Tagliagambe S (2009) *People and Space. New Forms of Interaction in the City,* Springer-Verlag, Berlin, Heidelberg, New York.

Mckay G (ed) (1998) *DiY Culture. Party & Protest in Nineties Britain,* Verso, London-New York.

Meethan K (1997) *York: Managing the tourist city.* Cities n. 14 (6), pp. 333–342.

Moles A (1971) *Psyhologie du kitsch: l'art du bonheur,* Mame, Paris.

Mommaas H (2002) *City Branding: The Necessity of Socio-Cultural Goals.* In: Patteeuw V (ed) *City Branding: Image Building and Building Images,* Nai Publishers, Rotterdam, pp. 32–48.

Monbiot G (2000) *Captive State,* Macmillan, London.

Mori A (2002) *L'importanza di giocare sul serio.* Il Sole 24 Ore, 22/12/2002.

Pittaluga P (2006) *Aree di bordo: possibilità di integrazione e coevoluzione.* In: Maciocco G, Pittaluga P (eds) *Il progetto ambientale in aree di bordo,* FrancoAngeli, Milano, pp. 35–54.

Pittaluga P (2008) *Images of local societies and projects for space.* In Maciocco G (ed), *The Territorial Future of the City,* Springer-Verlag, Berlin, Heidelberg, New York, pp. 87–104.

Polanyi K (1994) *The Great Transformation: The Political and Economic Origins of Our Time,* Beacon Press, Boston.

Pulcini E (2001) *L'Io globale: crisi del legame sociale e nuove forme di solidarietà.* In: D'Andrea D, Pulcini E (eds), *Filosofie della globalizzazione,* Ets, Pisa, pp. 57–82.

Riesman D (1950) *The Lonely Crowd,* Yale University Press, New Haven.

Ritzer G (1999) *Enchanting a Disenchanted World: Revolutionizing* the *Means of Consumption.* Pine Forge Press, Thousand Oaks CA.

Ryan R (2000) *New Frontiers.* Tate (Tate Modern Special Issue) n. 21, pp. 90–96.

Sassen S (1996) *La città nell'economia globale,* Il Mulino, Bologna.

Sassen S (1997) *Città globali,* Utet, Torino.

Serreli S (2009) *Places for Leisure as Interactive Space of the City.* In: Maciocco G, Serreli S (eds), *Enhancing the City. New Perspectives for Tourism and Leisure,* Springer-Verlag, Berlin, Heidelberg, New York, pp. 45–65.

Sennett R (1977) *The Fall of Public Man,* Knopf, New York.

Sieverts T (2002) *Cities Without Cities: An Interpretation of the Zwischenstadt,* Spon/Routledge, London, New York.

Sorkin M (ed) (1992) *Variations on a Theme Park: The New American City and the End of Public Space,* Hill and Wang, New York.

Stern RAM, Mellins T, Fishman D (1995) *New York 1960: Architecture and Urbanism Between the Second World War and the Bicentennial,* Monacelli Press, New York.

Tagliagambe S (2008) *Lo spazio intermedio. Rete, individuo e comunità,* Università Bocconi Editore, Milano.

Terdiman R (2003) *Given Memory: On Mnemonic Coercion, Reproduction and Invention.* In: Radstone S, Hodgkin K (eds) *Regimes of Memory,* Routledge, London, New York, pp. 186–201.

Thrift N (1999) *Steps to an ecology of place.* In Massey D, Allen J, Sarre P (eds), *Human Geography Today,* Polity Press, Cambridge, pp. 295–322.

Tibaldi G (1986) *Cantaci o simbolo.* Il Sole 24 Ore, 02/02/1986.

Vos W, Meekes H (1999) *Trends in European Cultural Landscape Development: Perspectives for a Sustainable Future.* Landscape and Urban Planning n. 46 (1), pp. 3–14.

Williamson T, Alperovitz G, Imbroscio CM (2002), *Making a Place for Community: Local Democracy in a Global Era,* Routledge, New York.

Williams CC, Windebank J (2003) *The slow advance and uneven penetration of commodification.* International Journal of Urban and Regional Research n. 27(2), pp. 250–264.

Worpole K, Greenhalgh L (1999) *The Richness of Cities – Urban Policy in a New Landscape,* Comedia & Demos, London.

Zanini P (2000) *Significati del confine. I limiti naturali, storici, mentali,* Bruno Mondadori, Milano.

Zolberg, VL (1994) *"An élite experience for everyone?" Art museums, the public, and cultural literacy.* In: Sherman D, Rogoff I (eds), *Museum Culture: Histories, Discourses, Spectacles*, Routledge, London, New York, pp. 49–65.

Zukin S (1992) *Post modern urban landscapes: Mapping culture and power.* In: Lash S, Friedman J (eds), *Modernity and Identity*, Blackwell, Oxford, pp. 221–247.

Zukin S (1995), *The Cultures of Cities*, Blackwell, Oxford.

Places for Leisure as Interactive Space of the City

Silvia Serreli

Places of the City as Places of Movement

The spatialities of contemporary social life derive from the systematic movement of people for their work and everyday life, leisure and pleasure (Sheller and Urry 2006). Urban behaviours are affected by continuous dematerialisation practices and by a large number of link-ups that are constantly being redefined. In universal mobility and interchange, subjects operate in networks interacting on different scales within multiple geographies (Oakes 1993).

In this trend, leisure activities are more and more structured and inter-related with other everyday activities (Short 1999), and the concept of spare time as regeneration and rest, or as dynamism and a break with everyday patterns, has been surpassed. If the limiting of leisure to the active search for gratification had "alienating" work as its opposite in the past, currently the opposition between spare time and work time has become only apparent. The loss of this dichotomy presupposes real and virtual movement from place to place, person to person, event to event, physical movement, but also the transfer of images and data, favoured by the immaterial infrastructures that organise intermittent flows of people, cultures and images, as well as regulating and anticipating such traffic.

Contemporary mobility entails urban spaces which link up new forms of social interaction around new reference points that seem to cause a crisis for the traditional centralities of cities and their public sphere. These centralities are tied to the infrastructures (airports and stations), places of high culture (museums, theatres, concert halls and convention centres) and places of leisure (large leisure complexes, roadside parks and resorts). Urban spaces show some of the diseases of the city, which highlight a detachment from reality, a "loss of the centre", false relations with the place that are reflected in forms of aestheticisation, spectacularisation, thematisation, discomposition and genericity (Maciocco 2008). They are spaces that show a lack of hierarchies; in them the boundaries between different cultural forms are removed (art, education, architecture, but also tourism, television, music, sport and shopping) – between the artistic and

G. Maciocco, S. Serreli (eds.), *Enhancing the City*, Urban and Landscape Perspectives 6,
DOI 10.1007/978-90-481-2419-0_3, © Springer Science+Business Media B.V. 2009

the commercial. Thus, consumption and culture become two indissolubly interrelated aspects (Urry 1990; Miller 1998; Jackson 1999).

The leisure spaces where the different forms of culture, shopping and leisure are confusedly activated are urban spaces of movement that are often consumed in a state of absent-mindedness and "alienation". In the seventies, Jean Baudrillard was already describing situations of alienation as intrinsic in society. He maintained that in contemporary societies, the consumer sphere prevails over that of production: in a society where everything is a commodity that can be bought and sold, alienation is total, and reality is transformed into a *pastiche* of images and pseudo-events bereft of meaning. Further, according to the French theorist, the *need* of a commodity is not considered a relation between an individual and an object but is called up by signs that are part of a cultural system in which a contingent mode of needs and pleasures prevails (Baudrillard 1970). Symbols and signs create those same needs that lead to consumption; product and production permeate social life and dominate the individual's thought and behaviour, constituting a universe of illusions and fantasy which manipulates his subjectiveness. The "production system" creates the "system of needs". The origin of needs, as Baudrillard further stresses, is to be traced back to publicity and marketing activities, to the capacity of creating general willingness to consume, a desire to desire.

Following this introduction, some remarks seem relevant as to how urban leisure activities respond to the needs and desires of society and how the forms of power of multinational organisation for the management and development of the spare time industry find expression in branding processes (Selby 2004; Arvidsson 2006). The brand may be considered "as a node in a memory-based chain of associations" (Cai 2002, p. 723). The construction of a strong brand image is linked with the capacity to make evident the more pertinent associations that strengthen ties between brand and place.

Spaces of consumption and leisure (Fig. 1), the *funscapes* described by Tracy Metz (2002), offer the city new branding opportunities, as they are situations that give shape to the "urban imagination", and they structure norms and visions to project visitors towards fun destinations. In these places, the relationship between individual imagination (dream), collective imagination (myths, rites and symbols) and narrative fiction changes, breaking down the frontiers set up by each culture between dream, reality and invention (Augé 1997; Tagliagambe 2009).

The planned mega-events that produce consistent shifting of persons are brand spaces and places of movement, those which Maurice Roche (2000) describes as social spatial-temporal *hubs,* shifts that channel, mix and redirect global flows.

Fig. 1 Places for leisure as places for shopping

The development and popularity of these world fairs represent a growing intrusion of leisure, tourism, the aesthetic into urban landscapes that become enriched with a great number of thematic environments (McNeill 2004). The events are often based on national stereotypes[1] and themes designed to enhance the specific cultural attractions of a destination: nations are basically represented as places of spectacle, as signs in the branding processes that the events construct and celebrate. The event transforms the places into specialised leisure spaces and moves them into new, distinct niches of the global market.

In this chapter, contemporary landscapes are explored, where leisure has taken on strong urban importance. Departing from a reflection on the current ways of designing leisure spaces, some experiences are illustrated, where places for leisure are conveyed as enchanted landscapes, imaginative geographies and places of "extraordinary experience". Forms of leisure as active components of the city may be interpreted within "new mundane geographies" (Binnie et al. 2007, p. 518), a reflection which makes clear how city spaces can be conceived as and designed to become interactive spaces, in order to favour social construction that enhances subjectiveness, making individuals free and aware.

Leisure Landscapes as Mundane Geographies

The various forms of urban tourism make the increased mobility of contemporary society apparent. Various authors recognise that leisure and tourism are central elements of social life and above all are decisive for space. Leisure and culture attractions are increasingly configured as active components of the wider process of regeneration of post-industrial cities. Changes in the heart of society during recent decades have generated structural transformations, some of which derive from the fact that the various forms of post-modern culture occupy increasingly central positions in urban organisation (Zukin 1995; Hall 2000). Nevertheless, leisure landscapes are often denied the possibility of being configured under an urban dimension. They take the shape rather of monofunctional epicentres (malls, amusement parks, leisure islands, tourist villages, etc.), characterised by a lack of multifunctionality and plurality of activities belonging to urban life. They are spaces of consumption, new urban geographies distinguished by "inauthentic diversity" (Jacobs 1998, p. 252), which substitute the hierarchical orders of the traditional city.

Some authors associate the connotation "mundane" with these landscapes, including "the notion of it as something lacking in force, capturing the sense of it as dull, bland and boring" (Highmore 2002; Seigworth and Gardiner 2004; Benni et al. 2007). Reference is often made, in the interpretation of "mundane" urban places, to the concepts of subjectivisation, sameness, homogeneity or a sense of placelessness. The banal and the mundane are associated with alienation, de-identification and constant repetition in and through time and space; they support levelling of experience, repetition.

Compared with these positions, research exploring mundane geographies as spaces that can become "extraordinary" for "a variety of practices, materialities and forms of habituation" seems more fruitful. It is necessary, therefore, to explore whether there are alternative opinions that refer to places of leisure as sites of reliability, resistance and potentiality (Aitchison et al. 2002; Binnie et al. 2007). Following Michel Foucault's point of view on the modalities by which power mechanisms affect daily life, a reflection on the forms of resistance to power seems relevant on this subject. If, as Foucault maintains, power takes life as the object of its exercise, research into what in life resists it and, by resisting, creates forms of vitality that escape power itself seems more pertinent. In spite of the fact that everyday spaces can be seen as spaces of subjectivisation and consequently some practices subjugate individuals and bring them into submission, for Foucault (1980) forms of power surpass the dichotomy "dominators and dominated", and in these same forms, spaces of comparison and strength may be revealed.

Departing from these ideas, mundane geographies are explored – including urban leisure spaces among them – as places where micropolitics and change tactics are revealed, promoted by the forms and modalities of interaction of the different social groups that have an impact on these spaces of significance. In these geographies, the dialectics of everyday life are expressed to which the following opposing pairs correspond: habit-event, repetitiveness-uniqueness, predictability-unpredictability, routine-impulse, alienation-liberation, repetition-creation and safety-threat (Lalive d'Epinay 1983). In the field of the psychology and sociology of communication, these reflections tie up with the fact that the infrastructures of the moral universe in which individuals conduct their daily existence have, as fundamental elements, routine, habits and safety that are often highly ritualised. As Roger Silverstone (2006) maintains, the media belong to the ordinariness of everyday life and contribute to sustaining its "normality" by continuously recreating common sense with their arguments and generating "ontological safety". Anthony Giddens points out on this matter how individuals tend to emotively take on an attitude of trust in the continuity of their identity, the constancy of the social and material environment in which they act, and the sense of predictability of the daily routines to which their sense of security is bound (Giddens 1990). The proliferation of risk situations in contemporary society implies that "the assurance derived from habitualised and routinised forms of practice allows us to see the value of mundane" (Beck, 1992, quoted by Bennie et al., 2007, p. 516).

On the dialectics of the everyday, the "big businesses" of leisure pursue their profit logic, promoting new lifestyles based on the needs of daily life, trying to grasp the habits and behaviours involved to give answers with products and services for the needs and desires of individuals/clients. The meaning of leisure geographies as an expression of the power of production and subjectivisation, but also as an opportunity to construct urban perspectives and different forms of resistance, is studied through certain experiences that permit clarification of leisure landscapes on the basis of certain recurring situations.

Situations emerge from some experiences in which different forms of leisure and cultural regeneration are implemented, in particular in the inner city and the cities of industrial decline; these situations characterise cities that have promoted through branding processes urban strategies linked with leisure and culture-based economies. They are places that may be configured as places of high culture and arts (museums, galleries, theatres and concerts)[2] but also as places of entertainment and "popular culture"

(Zukin 1991, 1995; Tallon et al. 2006). The majority of regeneration processes of the leisure-related and culture-related city are accompanied by the creation of "enchanted" landscapes in the shape of a *cultural cluster* or *themed quarter* (Zukin 1995; Scott 2000; Hall 2000; Gospodini 2006). Cultural quarters are distinguished by a wide variety of forms and features including (a) a mixture of activity (e.g. diversity of uses, an evening economy and a small-firm economy); (b) an appropriate built environment (e.g. fine-grained morphology, a variety of building types and good quality public space) and (c) cultural meaning (e.g. a sense of history and progress, identity and design appreciation and style) (Montgomery 2003, quoted by Tallon et al., 2006).

In other experiences, situations are faced that are found in the contexts of tourism development among ethnic minority groups (Oakes 1993), permitting reflection on the concept of locality, local resistance and local knowledge (e.g. ethnic tourism in China, Greece and native American reserves of southwest America). In these contexts, the places of tradition are reproduced, reconstructed within the new contexts characterised by staged authenticity (MacCannel 1973) and "reality effects" to attract flows of nostalgic visitors. Such "geographies" mediate between the predefined structures of tradition (which are given) and the needs and possibilities of global economy structures with their tendencies towards homogenisation.

These situations show forms of attrition of the transformation processes induced by capital arriving from the outside, a resistance that asserts the present and its unease, which opposes the need to copy landscapes no longer existing, considered "more traditional" just to increase the capacity to attract.

Enchanted Landscape as a Place of Extraordinary Experience

We have seen how the new developing urban economies are nurtured by the industries of culture and leisure and how new forms of renewal and regeneration emerge, encouraged by the creation and expansion of new spaces of culture, leisure and consumption, which become catalysts of new urban development and the new image of the city. More and more often, they include agglomerations of services which contain a concentration of propulsive companies of the knowledge-based economy that are directly based on the production, distribution and use of knowledge and information.

Cultural consumption economics in the post-industrial city has been widely discussed and systematically highlighted by various authors. Peter Hall (2000) points out the fact that cities have passed with extraordinary speed from a manufacturing to an informal economy and from an informal to cultural economy. He considers that culture has become a magic substitute for factories and their plant, a stratagem which will create a new urban image, making the city more attractive for mobile capital and new profiles of mobile professionals.

The city that adapts to a culture and consumerism economy has been described by John Hanningan (1998) in the book *Fantasy City* in which the following attributes have been used for the city: theme centred, aggressively branded, in constant operation, modular in design, separate from existing neighbourhoods, post-modern and clustered.

Culture industries have developed as an interface between global and local (e.g. based on the way global distribution networks rely on the distinctive features of the local), and it is from this that their most important potential derives, exceeding in importance the economic activities based on data and knowledge. Sharon Zukin has widely illustrated different types of urban landscape based on consumerism, maintaining that in many cities, with the disappearance of the local manufacturing industries, culture represents business, the basis of tourist attraction. The growth of cultural consumption (of art, food, fashion, music and tourism) and the industry providing for this fuel the economy of the city and its visible ability to produce both spaces and symbols (Fig. 2).

Dominant urban policies are focused on the supply of attractive lifestyles both in terms of visitors and with regard to possible new residents. The public sector and city administrations have promoted a shift towards leisure activities in their programmes, from a policy aimed at organising opportunities for entertainment to a policy more oriented towards the creation of spaces, quarters and *milieus* for cultural production creativity.

Fig. 2 Places for leisure as places of cultural consumption

Various regions and cities have for this reason invested in a strategy of positive image-forming, better known as "place marketing" or "branding", public policies to communicate the attractiveness of their territory as an ideal space in which to live, work and carry out leisure activities. Thus, places intensify their promotion activities to put themselves on the map. Territorial competition processes put on the same level strategies to hold inhabitants, to attract companies in the creative industries, as well as to catalyse visitor flows.

A clear example is represented by the effects generated by place marketing in the process of economic and spatial transformation in recent decades in the region of Øresund in Scandinavia.

The region – which was transformed from peripheral area into a west European metropolis – is often quoted as a European model of international cooperation as it is a cross-border area connecting Denmark with Sweden. However, as the economist Gert-Jan Hospers (2006) maintains, the region represents an "imaginative space" to which the everyday reality of the region does not correspond. To create greater interest for external investors, the region was presented at Expo 2000 with the slogan "Øresund: The Human Capital". Branding was founded on three principal clusters: media technologies, leisure and the quality of life. The region was meant, according to the aims of a plan agreed between the regions, to be a dynamic localisation in which new inhabitants would be able to find a high quality of life.

Leisure, one of the principal strategies, does not include activites based on tourism only in its programmes but also the development of cultural activities and of the communication and entertainment sector. As Hospers explains, the region is still a space endowed with an identity created artificially by political strategies which does not reflect the expectations of the majority of the inhabitants: "the conurbation is branded as an exciting Euregional hub, whereas the region's inhabitants still cope with many day-to-day problems of cross-border integration" (Hospers 2006, p. 1015). "Urban entrepreneurialism" policies have conveyed throughout the world a strongly attractive image of the region, favoured by innovative branding strategies, and have brought new institutional forms into the field, such as the creation of the Øresund Committee. The unreal branding of real places has, however, favoured the creation of the Øresund region as "imagined spaces". The criticalities of the region suggest that external marketing policies have been activated to the detriment of the bottom-up processes of "internal marketing".

The leisure areas are spread through the city in the form of clusters, a division that is not a recent phenomenon. Two temporal phases can be pinpointed.

In the first phase, policies for the agglomeration of places of culture were the instruments for urban regeneration and were conceived as catalysts for revitalising inner-city decline and discarded areas (previous industrial areas). Examples of this are the cities that have promoted intra-urban competitions and cultural mega-events (e.g. Olympic Games, international expositions, culture capitals and world expos). Subsequently, an increase was seen in the size of clusters and a tendency towards functional specialisation, the generation of sub-clusters of homogeneous activities and the involvement of various types of product and cultural activity (from the theatre and visual arts to music, the new media, spaces of entertainment), grouped together in a variety of spatial forms. This tendency to expand and cover vast areas corresponds simultaneously to an inclination towards monofunctional specialisation.

In the second phase, some cultural clusters develop as spatial concentrations of cultural activities, to then become functionally specialised cultural quarters (e.g. islands of museums, fashion quarters and multimedia quarters). As Aspa Gospodini (2006) illustrates, examples are the fashion quarter of Nottingham; the multimedia cluster of Hoxton, London; film-making in Bristol; the popular music cluster of Westergasfabriek, Amsterdam, and the leisure cluster in Witte de Withstraat, Rotterdam; London's "ethnoscapes", i.e. clusters of ethnic culture and leisure – such as "Banglatown" in Brick Lane and the Asian-fashion cluster in Green Street.[3]

To "put themselves on the map", cities draw attention with leisure clusters to spaces that are out of the *ordinary*. And indeed because the traveller's out of the ordinary experience is constructed with respect to its opposite, Dean MacCannel, in his essay of 1973, *Staged Authenticity*, maintains that it is an active response to the difficulties of modern life; tourists seek authentic experiences so as to overcome the difficulties of daily life.

There are various modalities by which the difference between ordinary and extraordinary is established and maintained. If sometimes the *extraordinary* is a unique object to see and visit at least once in a lifetime, at other times the extraordinary is an ordinary aspect of one's own social life experienced in an unusual context.

But it is precisely to satisfy the traveller's search for extraordinary experiences that the city should devise its own uniqueness and recognisability. To design the city through leisure, the fact that there is no universal experience that is true for all tourists at all times needs to be taken into account. As emphasised by the authors of this book,[4] the "traditional" tourist no longer exists, but there are a variety of tourist profiles and ways of tourist experience. This experience, in Cohen's definition, is a relation between the individual and a variety of "centres" whose meaning derives from the "person's worldview, depending on whether the person adheres to a centre". The definition does not necessarily imply a concept of geographic centrality on which the vital space of individuals is based: "It is the individual's spiritual centre, which for the individual symbolizes ultimate meaning" (Cohen 1979, p. 181).

And in this sense, places are not given as relatively fixed elements, separate from the subject – "places are seen as pushing or pulling people to visit". In extraordinary experience, the journey towards places is also an image of the self apart from an authentic encounter with the "elsewhere". The individual attends to his deepest personal identity. The traveller travels in search of authentic experiences without perceiving daily life distorted by the rhythms and values of productivity. The tourist experience therefore becomes the quest for new experiences to bring into play a comparison with different norms, values, habits and cultures.

As Yiping Li remarks, the diversity inherent in tourist experiences is the outcome of worlds that tourists "privately" build for themselves and represents the modalities by which the widest personal needs can be satisfied, from pleasure to the search for new meanings.

Imaginative Geographies and Spaces of Dissonance

Modernity has created a unified set of practices, completely changing the spaces of authentic places to replace them with "homogenized landscapes in which place-based identities were artificially and inauthentically constructed" (Oakes 1993, p. 51). Technological skill in creating hyper-real environments (Eco 1986), new themes that seem more real than the original, has gone beyond the tourist attraction.

The concept of themed environments, often highlighted by the authors of this book, emphasises how urban landscapes are produced, marketed and consumed. As Elena Moreddu (2009) states in theme parks, the object observed should seem real and absolutely authentic. Settings should in a certain sense be more real than the original, a world of signs and entertainment, in which each thing is a copy, a text on a text, where something false may seem more real than the real: a "flimsiness of reality", as Lash (1990, p. 15) defines it. In the behaviour of the tourist or the consumer, a reciprocal game of cross-referencing between motivations and images occurs. This behaviour is often conveyed by the language of advertisements, with their predominantly conative function, in an effort to persuade the consumer-spectator, usually disguised and mystified under other functions. Persuasion appeals, rather than to rational means, to the addressee's affective or subconscious sphere, because it is there that motivation originates to purchase or be persuaded to make a journey to a place not directly known. To support these ideas, the experience discussed by the geographer Bruce D'Arcus seems interesting, regarding how certain places become themed environments produced and transformed to attract "the eager gaze of the tourist" (D'Arcus 2000, p. 696). As is known, John Urry maintains that the gaze is socially organised and systematised: there are different professionalities that contribute to constructing and developing the tourist gaze. This poses an important question for city transformation processes: what are the consequences for the places that are the object of this gaze and how do they link up with the variety of other urban practices?

D'Arcus highlights how, in the city of Gallup, New Mexico, some of the transformation processes of places of ethnic tourism by the elite business have generated "imaginative geographies", responded to by forms of conflict and resistance on the part of the inhabitants.

The city of Gallup is located in one of the main travel corridors of the United States, Route 66; in spite of its strategic position, it is a border town with a number of Indian reserves situated nearby. The city grew up in connection with the presence of coal mines and has tried to counter the economic decline linked with the mines but also the creation of the new highway, which as far back as the twenties began to transform its image into one of the emerging tourist landscapes of the Southwest. One of the specificities of the tourist destination found expression in the Inter-Tribal Indian Ceremonial which, in exhibiting the traditional rites of the Indians, had the objective to "keep vigorously alive a timeless heritage from the challenges of a swiftly changing world".[5]

From the sixties onwards, American Indian activist forms of opposition resisted the US Department of Commerce Planning Rules, aimed at transforming a local event celebrating authentic Indian culture (Inter-Tribal Ceremonial) into a year-round event. The event, which endeavoured to create the National Indian Memorial Park,[6] was designed by some private consultant companies – active in theme-park design such as Disney World – to tempt and attract "the white tourists… driving down 66", who, pursuing the myth of the American Dream, would find "a taste of the authentic Southwest" in the city of Gallup. In crystallising the image of the Ceremonial and an entire region of the Southwest, the tourist's enchanted gaze would be attracted by the great open-air museum by staging the different Indian cultures of North America. The tourist would have the chance to plunge into an authentic experience (namely, primitive) depicting "the ways they lived when the country was theirs",[7] with the possibility, of course, of visiting unusual shops where they could purchase "moments of experience".[8]

The project focused particularly, in order to respond to the rules of the tourist industry market, on the relationship between "visitor interest quotient" and "landscape production". According to the designers, competition between "themed" tourist destinations in attracting flows of visitors relies on the capacity they have to create unusual out of the ordinary environments: "Tourists are first of all sightseers, and the beauty and appropriateness of scenery and 'staging', both nature's and man's, are a key factor in determining whether they will be prompted to make a return visit".[9] In actual fact, the perspectives of the arguments on tourism were not a reflection of the authentic "essence" of the region but aimed at creating a particular view of this "essence", "one which caters to tourists' desires for an experience of enchanted otherness" (D'Arcus 2000, p. 694). From this viewpoint, the dominant symbolic construction of the Southwest attempted to convert the problematic aspects of this place and the local society into something fantastic, a "fascinating land", and to link up the construction of a subject (the tourist) with the object of his gaze (the "authentic" Indian). In the final parade of the ceremonial, the Indian audience would become part of the landscape to give shape to the show, transforming what was a mundane landscape into an exoticised space. To give life to the entertainment, tourists move around freely, as they are consumers of goods, and the Indian stays frozen as the object of the gaze, being a commodity to be visually consumed (Dilworth 1996, quoted by D'Arcus 2000). The representative policies of this project construct symbolic geographies that do not have ties with the spatial policies of everyday life (Fig. 3). D'Arcus thus investigates the role that urban space has in these dynamics of entertainment. The forms of challenge proposed by Indian activism try to make clear the contemporary conditions in which Indian culture is expressed, subtract it from myths and an idealised vision that disguises intrinsic problems of marginalisation, discrimination and inequality.[10]

The "spaces of resistance" of the protest, the counterspaces of the ceremonial, were manifested in different ways, all having the purpose of raising awareness not only of the ceremonial sponsors but, above all, of those very tourists awaiting the show. Signals of this were conveyed by the local press by which tourists were incited to boycott the shows and not buy Indian arts and crafts from Anglo traders. This was followed by certain actions: "In particular, in 1970 IAE sponsored two Indian markets which sold arts and crafts, and also 'planned an Indian pow-wow ... on the mesa north of the Ceremonial grounds to hear speeches from an open platform and to take part in Indian social dances'".[11]

Fig. 3 Places for leisure as places of memory. Picture by Niala Branson

Thus a "social" dance rather than a "ceremonial" in which visitors could be involved in the real experience of their world; this gives visibility to the contradictions of a culture with no "official" spaces to express the unease of segregation.

Places of Leisure as Spatiality of Learning

As has been stressed, places of leisure can be interpreted through the theme of mobility that counters the ontology of the distinction "places" and "people". It has also been pointed out that the mundane landscapes of work, production, consumerism and residence may not be considered bland and banal or associated exclusively with concepts of monotony and alienation. These spaces may be spectacular or extraordinary due to different urban behaviours and practices which concern different types of resident and different types of visitor, both "traveller" figures in leisure urban spaces (Maitland 2007).

Thus, some queries arise: how is it possible to design contemporary spaces through leisure activities which stimulate interaction and social aggregation; but more generally speaking, on what spatial conditions can the project for places of movement be founded?

Leisure places depend partly on what is practised in them, they are produced and reproduced, they are hybrid systems of materialities and mobilities, in which objects, technologies, socialities intertwine; dynamic places, places of movement (Hetherington 1997). For this reason, they cannot be considered fixed and stable.

The project for leisure spaces is called upon to act against some of the criticalities of social reality, characterised by the trend of subjectivism in which mainly desire and personal need are pursued, seconded more and more often by operative routines of the tourism and leisure industry. In these routines, the vision of reality – to take up Foucault once more – is that of a "panoptic gaze", a typical vision of closed systems and devices in which the idea of space management is based on the normalisation of situations, the elimination of every form of diversity and the possibility of exerting constant, continuous control.

These possibilities of control are enacted through processes of standardisation of places, not only from a spatial point of view but above all from the viewpoint of the behaviours that unfold in them.

In contemporary cities, the loss of "sacrality" of many places and the associated behavioural rigour required within them has generated, on the contrary, attention for thematised environments, spaces of leisure and entertainment. They are spaces that do not have particular situational requirements and offer themselves as pleasure places where the spectator abandons himself without aiming to understand. In them, individuals follow abstract, impersonal instructions; they merge with the place, and their losing themselves in it gives shape to a personal experience split into many fragments, isolated from each other; each experience takes on a relative meaning and burns itself out.

But we cannot think that the operative routines of the tourist industry are the only components contributing to nurturing the break in the link between place and social behaviours. This break concerns inhabitants and tourists, both figures of a social universe evading enactment of behaviours determined by the specificity of the physical place.

The social reality of the destination of a journey and tourist cognition and awareness also affect place transformation and urban behaviours. Both behaviours are the outcome of the loss of an active glance over the landscape which is, moreover, at the base of the project for the city (Maciocco and Tagliagambe 2009). This lack of projectuality in the construction of experience is a lack of rooting on the part of the inhabitants but also the loss of sense of experience of the journey as a possible form of interaction with places. The crisis of the glance over the city weakens individual's trust – a raising of their awareness, according to Giddens (1990), of the possible alternatives that may be adopted to act and change their own space of action.

The reassertion of a critical capacity on the part of travellers enables leisure places to be reinterpreted as spaces where possible selves may be tested but also where the need to enter into deep contact with the other and the elsewhere may be expressed. In leisure places, the traveller expresses behaviours coming from different cultural experiences; he acts following the dictates and rules of the culture he belongs to or through behaviours linked with the new culture he is entering into relations with. In combining elements of one's own culture and organisational models external to it, the traveller reinterprets himself on the grounds of the new experiences, making room for new ways of growth and enrichment. The traveller enters into relations with persons, objects and cultures that cannot leave him unchanged and produces new meanings, interiorised, so alive and active as to produce expansion and reassertion of his own cultural self. In this sense, the project for the city may conceive leisure urban spaces to accommodate the variety of possibilities for interaction that can be generated in them.

In the experience more closely linked with tourism, this comparison between (ordinary) daily life and otherness (holiday destination) surpasses the conception of tourism as a totalising expression, suspends roles, enables familiarisation with the host culture previously completely unknown and generates new patterns of thought and action. From this point of view, the interpretation of leisure places as *chora* is interesting, which presupposes the fact that the space offered to tourists is interactive. "The tourist then becomes a creative, interacting 'choraster' who takes home an experience which impacts on the self in some way" (Wearing B and Wearing S 1996, p. 234). The passage proposed by various authors on the figure of the traveller as a *flâneur* seems relevant, confirming himself and his own image by placing himself in concrete urban contexts, a choraster expressing the need to test himself in new situations and to grow according to contingent needs, contributing to shaping reality by interacting deeply with the place visited (Wearing B and Wearing S 1996; Nuvolati 2006).

The figure of the choraster suggests different spatialities of interaction. As Chris Ryan emphasises (1997), the tourist experience is a multifunctional leisure activity that involves individuals both in entertainment activities and in learning activities. Leisure as a learning activity does not respond to any programme; it is a process that develops in unexpected ways and projects places towards different meanings which may be assigned to them. It is experiential learning that derives from interaction between individuals and destination and takes shape in the individual's "geographical consciousness" (Li 2000, p. 863). It is the experience in space, places and the landscape with which individuals are enriched, be it pleasurable or troublesome and problematic. This awareness is the "essence" that involves individuals in other different worlds from their own and affects the emotions, the mind and the individual's whole personality sphere. The interpretation derives from the spatial-temporal relations that connect individuals with places. Yiping Li's research conducted at the University of Hong Kong describes, through the experiences of Canadian tourists travelling through China, the way geographical consciousness conditions tourist experience. He demonstrates how the experience of the journey is closely tied to other dimensions of the life of these individuals: the socio-economic sphere, and impersonal and spiritual worlds, both factors that build up geographical consciousness. The study demonstrates that tourist experience is not an exclusively commercial fact but a learning activity that establishes relations between the self (tourist) and the other (host), relations that contribute to the development of individual's personalities in a relationship of coevolution with the environment. This presupposes abandoning an inert position and taking on an active gaze that will enable the traveller to express a constructive, projectual position.

In the interactive modalities between travellers and places, micro-openings arise, which counter the forms of closure proposed by the large leisure complexes. These forms of interaction, invisible and perhaps also useless for the dynamics of the tourism and leisure industry, nurture the city and its places of movement. They stimulate forms of resistance and dissonance, as highlighted in the practices of the Indian natives of New Mexico, in which interaction with tourists is constructed through primary relationality with people, with whom – in a climate of affective solidarity and learning – a vital everyday world is shared, expressed through a plurality of values, ideas and conceptions of the world.

The project for urban leisure spaces thus opposes programmes which tend to isolate them within a fixed temporal segment to transform them into "enchanted" landscapes, in which the action of individuals has dwindled to a form of spectacle, weakening links with the past and without the strength to construct perspectives for future urbanity. Through the leisure dimension – being an important part of contemporary spatial experience – the city may reveal potential places where the public sphere may be reasserted. It is therefore necessary to reconsider the role of the project and the possibility of creating contexts for tourist experience that will not only be tied to spatial conditions and functional dynamics.

The project may be an impulse to maintain the diversity of places, their stories and social behaviours, because contexts are by definition pluralistic and should therefore offer plurality of choice.

Leisure spaces may then be configured as geography-aware contexts in which travellers, exerting their freedom, will feel the responsibility to participate in the construction of urbanity that is not only the product of imaginative geographies.

Notes

[1] Examples are British pubs, German beer-gardens, South Sea islands' exotic dancing, etc.

[2] The Department for Culture, Media and Sport (DCMS) defines "culture" as encapsulating visual and performing arts, audio-visual industries, architecture and design, heritage and the historic environment, libraries and literature, museums, galleries and archives, and tourism relating to these sectors (Tallon et al. 2006).

[3] The geographer Aspa Gospodini (2006) quotes the different case studies enriched with an interesting interpretation of them. For further study, cf. Crewe (1996), Attfield A (1997), Bassett et al. (2002), Hitters and Richards (2002), Shaw et al. (2004).

[4] See in particular articles by Cecchini (2009), Ciaffi and Mela (2009).

[5] D'Arcus quotes this phrase from the document of the Inter-Tribal Ceremonial Association of 1922.

[6] As D'Arcus explains, "The project was to be an expansion of the annual four-day event into a year-round attraction, and was to include an amphitheater to stage the Ceremonial performances and other such events, an 'Arts and Crafts Center', a large entrance plaza, an 'Indian Villages Complex', a trading post, various 'amusements', a visitor center, campgrounds, and a covered wagon train to serve as transportation to and from the parking lot" (D'Arcus 2000, p. 699).

[7] ERA, 1967, "Expansion Program for the Inter-Tribal Indian Ceremonial at Gallup, New Mexico: A National Indian Memorial Park", Economic Research Associates; available at Gallup Public Library. Quoted by D'Arcus, 2000, p. 700.

[8] *Ibidem.*

[9] *Ibidem.*

[10] One of the protest leaflets says, "Do not let the Ceremonial let you forget that Indians have the highest unemployment rate in the country, the highest infant mortality rate in the country, the lowest average income of any group in the United States, the highest suicide rate in the U.S., and don't forget that many of the Indians you see are suffering from malnutrition. You will see many drunk Indians. Ask yourself why you see so many. Is it because they are happy and proud?" (D'Arcus, 2000, p. 703)

[11] IAE, 1970, "The Ceremonial, an Indian point of view" press release; available at Gallup Public Library. (Quoted by D'Arcus 2000, p. 705).

References

Aitchison C, MacLeod N, Shaw S (2002) *Leisure and Tourism Landscapes: Social and Cultural Geographies*, Routledge, London, New York.

Arvidsson A (2006) *Brands: Meaning and Value in Media Culture*, Routledge, London, New York.

Attfield A (1997) *Bread and circuses? The making of Hoxton's cultural quarter and its impact on urban regeneration in Hackney*. Rising East n. 1(3), pp. 133–135.

Augé M (1997) *La Guerre des rêves. Exercises d'ethno-fiction*, Éditions du Seuil, Paris.

Bassett K, Griffiths R and Smith I (2002) *Cultural industries, cultural clusters and the city: the example of natural history film-making in Bristol*. Geoforum n. 33, pp. 165–177.

Baudrillard J (1970) *La societé de consommation. Ses mythes, ses structures*, Denoël, Paris.

Beck U (1992) *Risk Society: Towards a New Modernity*, Sage, London.

Binnie J et al. (2007) *Mundane geographies: alienation, potentialities, and Practice*. Environment and Planning A n. 39, pp. 555–569.

Cai LA (2002) *Cooperative branding for rural destinations*. Annals of Tourism Research n. 29(3), pp. 720–742.

Cecchini A (2009) *Which Tourisms? Which Territories?* In: Maciocco G, Serreli S (eds) *Enhancing the City. New Perspectives for Tourism and Leisure*, Springer-Verlag, Berlin, Heidelberg, New York, pp. 277–312.

Ciaffi D, Mela A (2009) *Tourist Populations*. In: Maciocco G, Serreli S (eds) *Enhancing the City. New Perspectives for Tourism and Leisure*, Springer-Verlag, Berlin, Heidelberg, New York, pp. 313–332.

Cohen E (1979) *A Phenomenology of Tourist Experiences*. The Journal of the British Sociological Association n. 13(2), pp. 179–201.

Crewe L (1996) *Material culture: embedded firms, organizational networks and the local economic development of a fashion quarter*. Regional studies n. 30(3), pp. 257–272.

D'Arcus B (2000) *The "eager gaze of the tourist" meets "our grandfathers' guns": producing and contesting the land of enchantment in Gallup, New Mexico*. Environment and Planning D: Society and Space n. 18, pp. 693–714.

Dilworth L (1996) *Discovering Indians in Fred Harvey's Southwest*. In: Weigle M, Babcock BA (eds) *The Great Southwest of the Fred Harvey Company and the Santa Fe Railway*, The Heard Museum, Phoenix AZ, pp. 159–167.

Eco U (1986) *Travels in Hyper-Reality*, Picador, London.

Foucault M (1980) *Power/Knowledge: Selected Interviews and Other Writings 1972–1977*, Pantheon Books, New York.

Giddens A (1990) *The Consequences of Modernity*, Polity Press, Cambridge.

Gospodini A (2006) *Portraying, classifying and understanding the emerging landscapes in the post-industrial city*. Cities n. 23(5), pp. 311–330.

Hall P (2000) *Creative cities and economic development*. Urban Studies 37(4), pp. 639–649.

Hannigan J (1998) *Fantasy City: Pleasure and Profit in the Postmodern Metropolis*, Routledge, London, New York.

Hetherington K (1997) *In place of geometry: the materiality of place*. In: Hetherington K, Munro R (eds) *Ideas of Difference*, Blackwell, Oxford UK, pp. 183–199.

Highmore B (2002) *Everyday Life and Cultural Theory: An Introduction*, Routledge, London, New York.

Hitters E and Richards G (2002) *The creation and management of cultural clusters*. Creation and Innovation Management n. 11(4), pp. 234–247.

Hospers GJ (2006) *Borders, bridges and branding: The transformation of the Øresund region into an imagined space*. European Planning Studies n. 14(8), pp. 1015–1033.

Jackson P (1999) *Consumption and identity: The cultural politics of shopping*, European Planning Studies n. 7(1), February, pp. 25–39.

Jacobs, JM (1998) *Aestheticization and the Politics of Difference in Contemporary Cities*. In: Fincher R Jacobs JM (eds), *Cities of Difference*, Guilford, New York, pp. 252–279.

Lash S (1990) *Sociology of Postmodernism*, Routledge, London, New York.

Lash S and Urry J (1994) *Economies of Signs and Space*, Sage, London.

Lalive d'Epinay C (1983) *La vie quotidienne*. Cahiers Internationaux de Sociologie n. LXXIV pp. 13–38.

Li Y (2000) *Geographical Consciousness and Tourism Experience*. Annals of Tourism Research n. 27(4), pp. 863–883.

MacCannel D (1973) *Staged authenticity: arrangements of social space in tourist settings*. American Journal of Sociology n. 79(3), pp. 589–603.

Maciocco G (2008) *Fundamental Trends in City Development*, Springer-Verlag, Berlin Heidelberg New York.

Maciocco G, Tagliagambe S (2009), *People and Space. New Forms of Interaction in the City Project*, Springer-Verlag, Berlin, Heidelberg, New York.

Maitland R (2007) *Conviviality and everyday life: the appeal of new areas of London for visitors*. International Journal of Tourism Research n. 10(1), pp. 15–25.

McNeill D (2004) *New Europe: Imagined Spaces,* Arnold, London.

Metz T (2002) *Fun! Leisure and Landscape*, NAI Publishers, Rotterdam, The Netherlands.

Miller D (1998) *A Theory of Shopping*, Polity Press, Cambridge.

Montgomery J (2003) *Cultural quarters as mechanisms for urban regeneration part 1: conceptualising cultural quarters*. Planning Practice and Research n. 18, pp. 293–306.

Moreddu E (2009) *Disney-ality and Forgetfulness: the Eu-topia of a Consolatory Place*. In: Maciocco G, Serreli S (eds) *Enhancing the City. New Perspectives for Tourism and Leisure*, Springer-Verlag, Berlin, Heidelberg, New York, pp. 107–132.

Nuvolati G (2006) *Lo sguardo vagabondo. Il flâneur e la città da Baudelaire ai postmoderni,* Il Mulino, Bologna.

Oakes TS (1993) *The cultural space of modernity: ethnic tourism and place identity in China.* Environment and Planning D: Society and Space n. 11(1), pp. 47–66.

Roche M (2000) *Mega-events and Modernity*, Routledge, London, New York.

Ryan C (1997) *The Chase of a Dream, the End of a Play.* In: Ryan C (ed) *The Tourist Experience: A New Introduction*, London, Cassell, pp. 1–24.

Scott A (2000) *The Cultural Economy of Cities*, Sage, London.

Seigworth GJ, Gardiner ME (2004) *Rethinking everyday life: and then nothing turns itself inside out.* Cultural Studies n. 18, pp. 139–159.

Selby M (2004) *Understanding Urban Tourism. Image, Culture & Experience*, I. B. Tauris, London.

Shaw S, Bagwell S and Karmowska J (2004) *Ethnoscapes as spectacle: reimaging multicultural districts as new destinations for leisure and tourism consumption.* Urban Studies n. 41(10), pp. 1983–2000.

Sheller M, Urry J (2006) *The new mobilities paradigm.* Environment and Planning A n. 38, pp. 207–226.

Short JR (1999) *Urban Imaginers: Boosterism and the Representation of Cities.* In: Jonas AEG, Wilson D (eds) *The Urban Growth Machine. Critical Perspectives, Two Decades Later*, State University of New York Press, New York, pp. 37–54.

Silverstone R (2006) *Media and Morality on the Rise of the Mediapolis*, Polity Press, Cambridge.

Tagliagambe S (2009) *The Tourist City, the Dream and the Reversal of Time.* In: Maciocco G, Serreli S (eds) *Enhancing the City. New Perspectives for tourism and Leisure*, Springer-Verlag, Berlin, Heidelberg, New York, pp. 85–106.

Tallon AR et al. (2006) *Developing leisure and cultural attractions in the regional city centre: a policy perspective.* Environment and Planning C: Government and Policy n. 24(3), pp. 351–370.

Urry J (1990) *The Tourist Gaze. Leisure and Travel in Contemporary Societies*, Sage, London.

Wearing B, Wearing S (1996) *Refocussing the tourist experience: the flâneur and the chorister.* Leisure Studies n.15, vol. 4(1) September, pp. 229–243.

Zukin S (1991) *Landscape of Power: from Detroit to Disney World*, University of California Press, Berkeley.

Zukin S (1995) *The Cultures of Cities*, Blackwell, Cambridge MA.

Urban Tourist Precincts as Sites of Play

Bruce Hayllar and Tony Griffin

This chapter examines the urban tourism precinct as an organised space for playful forms of leisure in the city. We argue that these spaces create an environment for leisured interaction where both visitor and host engage as mutual actors in urban "playgrounds". The chapter commences with a conceptual overview of the urban tourism precinct. It then considers the notion of play through an analysis of selected seminal discourses. These discourses are linked to the precinct in the context of a play "space" within the city using data gathered from two studies conducted in The Rocks and Darling Harbour precincts in Sydney, Australia (Hayllar and Griffin 2005, 2006). The chapter concludes with a discussion on the implications for the design and management of urban tourism precincts.

Tourists and the City

Urban environments have for many years been among the most significant of all tourist destinations. Considering this phenomenon in the historical context Karski notes:

People with the means and inclination to do so have been drawn to towns and cities just to visit and experience a multiplicity of things to see and do. Pilgrims in the fourteenth century were urban tourists visiting cities like Canterbury. The historic Grand Tour of Europe, in the eighteenth and nineteenth centuries was essentially an urban experience for the rich, taking in more spectacular towns and cities, usually regional and national capitals. These were the melting pots of national culture, art, music, literature and of course magnificent architecture and urban design. It was the concentration, variety, and quality of these activities and attributes ... that created their attraction and put certain towns and cities on the tourism map of the day (Karski 1990, p. 15).

The attraction of cities as tourist destinations has continued into contemporary times. The centrality of cities to tourism is primarily due to their inherent scale, locational attributes and opportunities for diverse experiences (Law 1996). Indeed the intrinsic attributes of modern cities – large populations, important cultural infrastructure, significant accommodation

G. Maciocco, S. Serreli (eds.), *Enhancing the City*, Urban and Landscape Perspectives 6,
DOI 10.1007/978-90-481-2419-0_4, © Springer Science+Business Media B.V. 2009

stocks and highly developed transport services such as airports and rail connections – make urban destinations a focal point for both tourist and commercial activity. The scale of cities also provides opportunities for different types of visitors who may be seeking quite diverse experiences; from the younger groups who are drawn to sites of intense consumption such as entertainment quarters or major sporting venues through to older and perhaps better educated groups who might wish to engage with the cultural life and heritage of a city (Hayllar et al. 2008).

Sites of Experience

While the city and its services provide the overlay for urban tourist activity, in most urban destinations tourist visitation tends to be spatially concentrated rather than dispersed. These points of concentration may include iconic sights, shopping areas, landmark cultural institutions or places of historical significance. However, where a number of attractions of similar or differing types aggregate alongside a range of tourism-related services, these areas take on a particular spatial, cultural, social and economic identity – now commonly (but not universally) recognised as a tourist precinct. As Stevenson (2003, p. 73) observed, "Cities divide into geographically discrete precincts which rarely conform to imposed administrative or political boundaries. Rather, they form around the activities of commerce, sociability, domesticity, and/or collective identity. The resulting precincts have a vitality and a 'look' that marks each as unique".

However, these spaces are not just for visitors. Rather, they are typically spaces shared with others who are the majority – it is the residents and the aesthetic and culture of the city that greet the visitor. Given the diversity of urban forms and culture, precincts represent a pastiche of conflicting and complementary forms. They are modern and ageing. They are both part of, and apart from, the city. They are confined and open, colourful and plain, commonplace and unique. They are organic and highly structured. They serve different purposes and perform a range of functional roles. However, underpinning these diverse expressions of a distinctly organised city space is their fundamental human dimension. They are human spaces, where visitors and locals create places for civil interaction – to meet, eat, amble, spectate, shop, observe or simply pass time.

Debates around terminology, and discussions as to what encapsulates a tourist precinct, have been ongoing. For our purposes we have defined an urban tourism precinct as

A distinctive geographic area within a larger urban area, characterised by a concentration of tourist-related land uses, activities and visitation, with fairly definable boundaries. Such precincts generally possess a distinctive character by virtue of their mixture of activities and land uses, such as restaurants, attractions and nightlife, their physical or architectural fabric, especially the dominance of historic buildings, or their connection to a particular cultural or ethnic group within the city. Such characteristics also exist in combination (Hayllar and Griffin 2005, p. 517).

This definition has spatial, functional and embedded psycho-social dimensions. The latter dimension is suggestive of the view that one psychologically engages with a precinct. This movement is also a recognition of how space, people, activity and architecture dialectically interact and shape the experience of the precinct visitor – an experience that may be qualitatively different for each of them.

Much research on urban tourism precincts has focused on describing the phenomenon and some of its fundamental characteristics. There has been a particular preponderance of studies that have examined precincts from a geographic or planning perspective (Stansfield and Rickert 1970; Ashworth and de Haan 1985; Law 1985; Jansen-Verbeke 1986; Meyer-Arendt 1990; Burtenshaw et al. 1991; Getz et al. 1994; Fagence 1995; Pearce 1998). In a similarly descriptive vein, others have developed ideas around the economic development or urban regeneration role of precincts (Judd 1995; Stabler 1998; Montgomery 2003, 2004; McCarthy 2005) while a few studies have examined precincts from a sociological perspective (Mullins1991; Conforti 1996; Chang et al. 1996). There has been some focus on particular types of urban tourism precincts, such as the festival marketplace (Rowe and Stevenson 1994) or revitalised waterfront (Craig-Smith 1995), but these studies have tended to deal with precincts in a development process-focused fashion. Some studies have emphasised the politics of precinct development (Hall and Selwood 1995; Searle 2008) and others offered cultural critiques (Huxley 1991).

More recently, a new research direction has emerged that focuses on both the experience of tourists in urban precincts and attempts to develop an understanding of the key attributes of such places that contribute to the quality of experience. Maitland and Newman (2004), Maitland (2006) and Hayllar and Griffin (2005, 2006) exemplify this new experience-focused direction.

In the context of this chapter, Fainstein and Stokes (1998) and Fainstein and Judd (1999) were among the first authors to characterise and consider precincts as a specific leisure landscape for "play". In developing their ideas, Fainstein and Judd (1999) describe various precinct forms such as resort cities, tourist-historic cities and what they label as "converted cities". The latter form is particularly apposite and is characterised as a type of tourist city in which specialized tourist bubbles are carved out of areas that would otherwise be hostile to or inconvenient for tourists. …The aim is to create an illusory world within an otherwise ordinary setting…giant billboards, movie multiplexes, superstores, and themed restaurants combine to create a kinetic environment that overwhelms the visitor. Its spectacular quality virtually insists that to be there is to participate in excitement, to stand at the crossroads of an exotic urban culture (Fainstein and Judd 1999, p. 266).

In these spaces, the city landscape is theoretically transformed into a "playground" of colour, movement, complexity and engagement. The position of Fainstein and Judd (1999) is implicitly compelling. It recognises that notions of play are not uniquely linked to the experience of children. It introduces the idea that these archetypal symbols of post-modern urban culture are also sites for playful experience. Finally, their position intimates a relationship between consumption and adult "play". In the following, we take Fainstein and Judd's proposition on precincts and play and develop it both empirically and theoretically (Fig. 1).

Fig. 1 Waterplay

Experiencing the Precinct: Empirical Studies

The authors' work in The Rocks and Darling Harbour precincts (Hayllar and Griffin 2005, 2006) set out to understand the precinct experience from the tourist's perspective using an approach grounded in phenomenology. As we argued, "understanding how the tourist experiences a precinct, and in particular the attributes, both tangible and intangible, which engender a certain quality to that experience, can produce implications for the effective and appropriate planning, development, management and marketing of the precinct" (Hayllar and Griffin 2005, p. 518).

The two precincts are areas of substantial contrast. The Rocks is located on the western side of Sydney Cove, directly opposite the Sydney Opera House and adjacent to the Sydney Harbour Bridge. It is one of Sydney's most visited precincts, receiving over 13 million visits annually (Sydney Harbour Foreshore Authority 2008a). Half of all international tourists to Sydney visit The Rocks at some time during their stay. This historic area contains some of Australia's earliest residential and commercial buildings. Tourism activities and land uses now predominate, with few residents remaining, although the adjacent area of Millers Point to the immediate west retains both its historic built fabric and a significant resident population. The Rocks retains an historic "feel" by virtue of its narrow laneways, broken cobbled streets and its remnant colonial architecture.

The second precinct, Darling Harbour, is acknowledged as Sydney's most successful tourism precinct, hosting over 27 million visits annually (Sydney Harbour Foreshore Authority 2008a). As a former wharf and railway goods marshalling area, the area was transformed into a modern precinct to coincide with the bicentennial of European settlement in Australia. Formally opened in 1988, it has continued to grow and develop. It now contains a range of museums, including the National Maritime Museum, and commercial attractions such as the Sydney Aquarium and IMAX Theatre. Darling Harbour also features extensive tourist shopping areas, restaurants and cafés, public open space, children's playgrounds, hotels, open air performance areas, the Sydney Convention and Exhibition Centre and is adjacent to the Sydney Casino. Data for both sites were collected by way of in-depth interview. In The Rocks, 20 interview sessions, involving 31 participants, were held. At Darling Harbour, 36 interviews were conducted involving 59 participants. Data analysis was undertaken in accord with the phenomenological methods recommended by Van Manen (1990) and Moustakas (1994) – see Hayllar and Griffin (2005, 2006) for a detailed explanation of the methodology. In the following, direct quotes taken from participants in the studies have been noted in *italics*.

Playing in the City

In the psychological sense, play implies a letting go of everyday reality, a psychological shift in consciousness from the confinement of the everyday to a sense of personal choice and freedom. In his seminal work, Seppo Iso-Ahola (1980, p. 85) notes that play is arousal-seeking behaviour and that "exploration, investigation and manipulation are at the heart of play".

Freedom and control are particularly important to the play context. Freedom implies the ability to make choices – to be with others or alone, to engage in one type of experience in preference to another, in essence to play or not to play. Control is related but subtly different to freedom. Control is concerned with personally managing the play experience to ensure arousal is maintained at its optimal level. Optimal arousal is a key motivator of play. According to Iso-Ahola (1980, p. 82), maintaining the "optimal level of arousal (stimulation or interest) ranges from person to person..." but due to this drive "an individual is in a continuous process of seeking and avoiding interactions with the environment, striving to maintain his (sic) optimal level of arousal....play is motivated by the optimal level of arousal both in childhood and adulthood".

Iso-Ahola (1980, p. 86) goes on to define play as "behaviours which are intrinsically motivated and engaged in for their own sake" and which bring enjoyment and satisfaction. He concludes, after Ellis (1973), that play spaces substantially influence the quality of these playful experiences. Iso-Ahola (1980) also notes the importance of the social context and social interaction as key influencers of play behaviour.

The ideas of choice, freedom, control, arousal, exploration, investigation, manipulation (in the sense of personally shaping experience), social interaction and all within a specified "play space" noted by Iso-Ahola (1980) resonate with the type of experiences and spaces one might expect of tourists in an urban precinct. Indeed, data from both The Rocks and Darling Harbour support such a proposition.

The importance of others (social interaction) emerged as a significant theme in both precincts. Visitors to The Rocks acknowledge the social aspects of their experience in general terms but in particular note the social context of their experience. Visitors recognise that The Rocks is an urban fusion of international tourists, domestic tourists, local residents, office workers and Sydney residents "in town" for the day. One visitor noted that The Rocks is *like a community, not just like packed up when people leave at night; it doesn't just shut down.* The social aspects of Darling Harbour were particularly noted. It is seen as a place for meeting, a place for families, a place to "do" things together. *It's a people place* commented one couple.

The opportunity for "play" provided in each precinct is a point of significant contrast.

The Rocks is a more "urbanised" experience and is a place to meet, eat, drink and shop. In contrast, *Play it your way* is the SHFA-developed theme for Darling Harbour. There are numerous tourist attractions, ongoing public events and open-air concerts (such as the annual Jazz and Blues Festival or Spanish Fiesta), children's play areas and open space to promenade along the waterfront – all in addition to the ubiquitous restaurants and cafés. As one respondent observed, *It is a big entertainment centre.* Differences between and within these sites give visitors the opportunity to manage and shape their experience.

Further support for the idea of managing and determining both the type and form of activity and levels of arousal to produce a playful experience can be found in the work of Mihalyi Csikszentmihalyi (1975, 1990). Csikszentmihalyi's research set out to understand the nature of enjoyable experience. He argues that enjoyable experience, expressed through his notion of "flow", is achieved when there is an optimal relationship between the level of challenge required for an activity and the level of skill of the participant. These challenges are not necessarily of a physical nature but rather are experience-based opportunities presented to the individual. Accordingly, when there is a sense of "match" (arousal is at its optimal), the "flow" or enjoyable experience is manifested. Conversely, if an experience is not sufficiently challenging (or interesting) for the level of experience (or skill) of the visitor, boredom results. By way of contrast, if there is too much arousal, anxiety may be the outcome. Thus to be in the flow of enjoyable experience requires the visitor to constantly play an active role in managing the type of experience(s) they are seeking.

Support for the above reasoning is evident in the three visitor types – explorers, browsers and samplers – that were identified from the current data sets and in two subsequent studies (see Griffin and Hayllar 2007). The explorers are those visitors who want to move beyond the façade of a precinct, to find their own way and discover its inner complexities and qualities. An explorer in The Rocks described his way of moving through the precinct: *You're walking along one street and then all of a sudden without realising it there's a kind of ... this little alleyway off to the left that might take you to something a bit more interesting around the corner.*

The second group, the browsers, are more content to stay within the confines of the main precinct area and to follow the tourist routes – such as a walk along the main street in The Rocks or to follow the water's edge in Darling Harbour.

The third group, the samplers, are those who visit precincts as just another stop on their schedule of moving through the attractions of a city and are often focused on visiting a specific attraction rather than experiencing the precinct for its own sake. The sampler may also use the precinct as a place of respite or refuge but will not move beyond the fringe or specified refuge point, a café for example. Indeed the theme of "refuge" is consistent with earlier reasoning on managing arousal. For many visitors in these studies, precincts are experienced as places of refuge, typically from the cacophony of the city or the dissonance of the tourist experience itself. On average, approximately one-third of visitors to both precincts use them as a place to "kill time" or "relax" (Sydney Harbour Foreshore Authority 2008b). A visitor to Darling Harbour noted that when *you come down here and you've got the water there and it's a bit more laid back and a bit more, kind of "ahh", a bit more relaxing, you can sit down and take a breath.*

The visitor typology also reflects the reality that different people can simultaneously experience a precinct in quite different ways. The extent to which people wish to explore, be aroused, seek points of contrast, or to seek the company of others can be dealt with at both the individual and collective level. Indeed the extent to which this can be managed is also a consequence of the precinct's morphology. Precinct design may limit the individual's opportunity for optimal experience, through less complex or simplistic presentation, or enhance it by the provision of interesting, engaging and multi-layered experiences. The experiential space is therefore critical in shaping the preconditions for play.

The importance of space as a facilitator of playful experience is integral to the work of Johan Huizinga (1955). In his influential work *Homo Ludens* (literally, *man the player*), Huizinga (1955) argues that play was, and is, central to the formation of culture. However, Huizinga was not interested in all forms of play. In language echoing the post-modern sensibilities of Fainstein and Stokes (1998), his concern was with "contests and races, of performances and exhibitions, of dancing and music, pageants, masquerades and tournaments" all of which can be located within a cultural context (Huizinga 1955, p. 7).

According to Huizinga, play has six defining characteristics. The first concerns its voluntary nature that clearly delineates it from other forms of social activity. "Play is superfluous. The need for it is only urgent to the extent that the enjoyment of it makes it a need. Play can be deferred or suspended at any time. It is never imposed by physical necessity or moral duty. It is never a task" (Huizinga 1955, p. 8). The second characteristic of play concerns its "unreal" quality. Play is not real life, rather it is a stepping out of "real" life into a temporary sphere of activity with a disposition all of its own. However, the fact that there is a consciousness associated with this lack of reality does not prevent play proceeding with seriousness. While play is "unreal", it has an important role as an interlude in our daily lives by complementing our ongoing seeking of real world "satisfactions and appetites" (Huizinga 1955).

The separateness of play from the ordinary is Huizinga's third characteristic. According to him it is "played out" within given limits of time and place. "Play begins, and then at a certain moment it is 'over'. It plays itself to an end. While it is in progress all is movement, change, alternation, succession, association, separation" (Huizinga 1955, p. 9). In a specific reference to play spaces, Huizinga argues that all play takes place within a predetermined "play-ground" either beforehand or as the play experience develops. "The arena, the card table, the magic circle, the temple, the stage, the screen, the tennis court, the court of justice, etc., are all in form and function play grounds, i.e. forbidden spots, isolated, hedged round, hallowed, within which special rules obtain. All are temporary worlds within the ordinary world, dedicated to the performance of an act apart" (Huizinga 1955, p. 10).

The formation of a type of play community is Huizinga's fifth characteristic. He notes that following a game, there is recognition that something mutually agreeable has been shared by those within the circle. "...the feeling of being 'apart together' in an exceptional situation, of sharing something important, of mutually withdrawing from the rest of the world and rejecting the usual norms, retains its magic beyond the duration of the individual game" (Huizinga 1955, p. 12).

The idea of being apart from "others" is further enhanced within Huizinga's final characteristic, that of "secrecy". Some of these may be "open" secrets such as particular types of dress, which distinguish the playing group, yet others are more secretive. Dress is particularly interesting in the tourist context. For example, clothing purchased as a type of souvenir, or particular sartorial affectations of the visitor, both define the players and the play space. What may be appropriate and "normal" within the "play-ground" may be quite disconnected, inappropriate or pretentious when one leaves the play space or returns home.

Huizinga's spatio-temporal dimension of play, where experience is played out within a given time and within a given space, is consistent with the visitors' experiences of a precinct. Inside the world of play, a community that is "apart together" shapes and shares meanings that are captured within the spirit of the playful experience. However, they are meanings that are bounded and only have relevance to a given play space and given play time.

The temporal dimension of the play space also emerges within the work of the phenomenologist Alfred Schutz (1899–1959). Schutz's primary interest was in the ordinary, the day-to-day interactions between people and their social environments and how these interactions took place. According to Schutz, the *world of daily life* is the intersubjective world to which we are born and upon which we now have to act. He argues that "all interpretation of this world is based upon a stock of previous experiences of it, our own experiences and those handed down to us by our parents and teachers, which in the form of knowledge at hand function as a scheme of reference" (Schutz 1970, p. 72).

Schutz (1970, p. 61) argues that our experiences are not "a being that is discrete and well-defined but a constant transition from a now-thus to a new-thus" Schutz's notion of "finite provinces of meaning" or "multiple realities" (after James 1890/1950) that conceptually links this argument. Reality for Schutz (and James) is situationally contextualised. Schutz identified the specific finite provinces of meaning as "the paramount world of real objects and events into which we can gear by our actions; the world of imaginings and fantasms, such as the play world of the child; the world of the insane; the world of art; the world of dreams; and the world of scientific contemplation" (Schutz 1970, p. 253). Each of these, he argued, has their own cognitive "style", and it is this style which constitutes them as a finite province of meaning.

In the paramount world, the world of work and our everyday lives, we move in what Schutz calls the "natural attitude". Accordingly, we remain in the natural attitude until we receive a specific "shock" which compels us to shift the accent of reality. The shocks discussed by Schutz are transition points between the paramount reality and other finite provinces of meaning. For example, when the curtain is raised at the beginning of a theatrical performance or film, we suspend the reality of the natural attitude and reorient ourselves to this "new" reality. Equally when the curtain comes down, there is another point of transition back to the paramount reality.

It is Schutz's world of "imaginings and fantasms" that embraces among other things daydreams, play, fairy tales, myths and jokes that is of particular interest to this discussion (Schutz 1970). In this world, our mind undergoes decreasing "tensions of consciousness" and withdraws from "certain of its layers the accent of reality…" (Schutz 1970, p. 257). As a corollary, the playful world of Schutz is a world of freedom, "We are free from the pragmatic motive which governs our natural attitude toward the world of daily life, free also from the bondage of "interobjective" space and intersubjective standard time. No longer are we confined within the limits of our actual, restorable, or attainable reach. What occurs in the outer world no longer imposes upon us issues between which we have to choose nor does it put a limit on our possible accomplishments" (Schutz 1975, p. 257).

While the free time or tourist experience itself is a point of contrast to the paramount reality of work and everyday life, precincts have the potential to provide clear points of transition to move visitors into the playful reality. As visitors move from the paramount world of the adjacent city into The Rocks, there are "signs" which convey transition points: older buildings, a reorientation of scale, decreased traffic and a slowing of pace. Once entered, visitors are suspended in this new reality by The Rocks experience – a place of pointed contrast to adjacent modernity. Here the *architecture is quite colonial and you notice the kind of old-fashioned buildings.* This old world site with its partially hidden walkways and colourful history is a place of imagination, arousal and exploration.

A similar transition awaits the visitor to Darling Harbour. Here, the contrast to the adjacent city is also important. *It's out of the city but it's in the city. It's got it's own little atmosphere.* However, Darling Harbour overtly invites the playful. Its character is *all leisure. People sort of passing through, sort of strolling through....It is a big entertainment centre.* As one international visitor commented it is also a site to distinguish the city itself. *I mean it is comparatively similar to an equal city in the US and so, but when I go, when I come here* (Darling Harbour) *I feel like I'm in Sydney, I feel like I am somewhere else.*

The maintenance of the experience in this non-paramount world rests on the extent to which the precinct itself sustains its non-paramount character during the visit. An inappropriate architectural form or a cacophony of external noise in The Rocks, or an out of character social intrusion in Darling Harbour, may challenge the flow of the experience and "shock" participants back to the paramount reality.

Arguably, this type of visitor might also affect the extent to which an experience is more playful. Perhaps the depthlessness of the browser's visit in contrast to the "depth" of the explorer may manifest itself in a type of liminal experience where one is engaged by the experience but "on the edge" of the paramount reality.

The shifts in space and consciousness found in the theorising of Huizinga (1955) and Schutz (1970, 1975) are also evident in the work of Gregory Bateson (1973). Bateson's (1973) ideas on play arose primarily from his work in the area of communication and his hypotheses concerning the various levels of abstraction in which communication operates. For example, the phrase *this is serious* could communicate at one level the genuine "seriousness" of a situation. Yet at another level (of abstraction), *this is serious* could imply quite the opposite – this is not to be taken seriously. For Bateson, both content and context were important.

Bateson uses the analogy of the picture frame to place boundaries around the context of play. He proposes that the notions of "frame" and "context" are psychological constructs. The frame bounds the play (somewhat similar to the ideas of Huizinga's imagined or real "play ground"); the players move into the frame, a type of psychological shift and actions taking play within the context of the frame are subject to the real, unreal, paradoxes of metacommunication.

There is also a dialectic in the play frame of Bateson. At the level of player, the frame is both inclusive and exclusive. By including particular messages within a frame, others are excluded. By excluding some, others are included. Thus, there is a form of metacommunicated negotiation about what is, and what is not, "play". While the frame may be an unconscious arena for the players, it also has a type of functionality for observers. In the city context, the precinct is understood to be an "unreal" place, or equally, the players are "unreal". To this end, normatively inappropriate forms of public behaviour may be tolerated in the precinct yet unacceptable beyond the play space.

While Bateson does not speculate as to how these movements from the play frame to the serious world move, there is perhaps some mutual recognition, some shift in consciousness on behalf of the players, as to what these "unframed" actions now represent. It may be there are subtle transitions or "micro" shocks of the Schutzian type that signify movement in and out of the play frame (Fig. 2).

Fig. 2 Establishing the "play frame" in Darling Harbour

Discussion and Implications for Management

The notion of play in the city has been explored through engagement with seminal discourses in phenomenological sociology (Schutz 1970, 1973, 1975), sociology (Huizinga 1955), communication/philosophy (Bateson 1973), phenomenological psychology (Csikszentmihalyi 1975) and social psychology (Iso-Ahola 1980). Each of these writers provides conceptual insights into the phenomenon of playful or ludic behaviour in the city.

The arguments of Huizinga (1955), Schutz (1970) and Bateson (1973) collectively embrace the idea of a shift in consciousness provided by the "playground". For Schutz (1970), this shift in consciousness is towards a different playful reality shaped by movement into different finite provinces of meaning. Huizinga (1955) too links a change in consciousness with theoretical and actual play spaces. Bateson (1973) encapsulates both ideas in his notion of a play "frame", which is linked to the metacommunicated message – this is play – that passes between players and observers.

Feelings of flow (Csikszentmihalyi 1975), which are a response to the engagement of individuals in play-like experiences, are motivators for enjoyable and intrinsically driven behaviour. However, there is also the potential for dissonant experiences in the playful domain of Csikszentmihalyi. Csikszentmihalyi (1975) believes that flow is experienced when there is a perceived psychological match between the demands of given tasks and an individual's skills to meet such demands. If the playspace does not provide the opportunity for such a "match", visitors may find themselves dissatisfied with their city experience.

This theorising is also supported by the empirical data gathered in both study precincts (Hayllar and Griffin 2005, 2006). The reports of study participants highlight the roles played by precincts in both shaping and facilitating playful experience. This role is also acknowledged in the data of the managing authority (see Sydney Harbour Foreshore Authority 2008a,b).

As argued, precincts are sites for adult play. The challenge for precinct managers is to understand the foundations of this form of individual consciousness and collective action and to act upon it. To maximise the potential for playful engagement, managers need to understand the nature of the experiences they help create and shape. Precincts are not a disjointed collection of attractions, buildings, walkways, pedestrian plazas, restaurants, cafés, cinemas or retail outlets. These characteristic forms are "experiential architecture" which only takes on experiential resonance when they are acted upon and in turn act upon individuals and groups of players. This interaction between people and space creates experience in its phenomenological sense – the metaexperience of play.

Play is the experience of control, freedom, arousal and intrinsically focused activity which brings enjoyment and satisfaction (Iso-Ahola 1980). In the context of a visit to a precinct, enjoyment and satisfaction are key outcomes for both visitors and managers. Satisfied visitors are implicit advocates for word of mouth recommendations and are likely repeat visitors.

The challenge for precinct planners and managers is to enhance the opportunity for playful experience through thoughtful design and management practice. In terms of design, some important considerations include the need for precincts to have identifiable boundaries or signifiers of place indicating the shift from one area to the other (Schutz 1970); a degree of complexity to design which facilitates the creation of multi-layered and explorative-type experiences (Iso-Ahola 1980; Ellis 1973; Hayllar and Griffin 2005, 2006); quiet, respite or refuge spaces (Csikszentmihalyi 1975) and recognition of the specific needs and requirements of different user types (Hayllar and Griffin 2005, 2006).

While effective design provides the infrastructure for play, specific management practices also impact upon the potential play experience. These practices might include the ongoing renewal of experience through the staging of events (Iso-Ahola 1980; Csikszentmihalyi 1975), "soft" regulation to ensure that the experience is not being undermined by surveillance or over zealous intervention (Bateson 1973; Iso-Ahola 1980; Huizinga 1955), adequate security to minimise feelings of uncontrollability and anxiety (Csikszentmihalyi 1975), maintenance of consistent thematic or experiential atmosphere (Schutz 1970), provision of an environment where the tourist has freedom to wander and explore (Ellis 1973), provision of opportunities for convivial encounters with other visitors (Iso-Ahola 1980), and enabling the tourist to experience a more distinctive sense of place (Huizinga 1955, Schutz 1970).

Through an engagement with some of the foundational writers in play theory and reference to two empirical studies, we have argued in this chapter that urban tourism precincts present visitors with a landscape of opportunities for engagement in adult play. Further, it has been argued that design and management practices conspire to facilitate or bound the extent and quality of these experiences. However, playfulness in the city is not unproblematic. Invoking Batesonian sentiments and the need for the subtle yet deliberate management of experience, Kleiber pointedly remarks:

> Play has a Dionysian character, entertaining the unbridled and the uncivilized in the interest of manipulating the world to its own design. While this tendency can be a source of creativity, it can also lead to deviance of one kind or another.

Indeed, the tendency to idealize and romanticize play must be tempered with the realization that playful impulses may be "dirty", antisocial, degenerate and even destructive. Torturing the cat may be great sport for a couple of five year olds (Kleiber 1999, pp. 68–69).

Hence questions of balance emerge in the management of such places. Engendering a sense of play is an important attribute of urban tourism precincts, but one that is not without limits.

References

Ashworth GJ, de Haan TZ (1985) *The Tourist-Historic City: A Model and Initial Application in Norwich. U.K.* Field Studies Series n. 8, Geographical Institute, University of Groningen.

Bateson G (1973) *Steps to an Ecology of Mind*, Granada, St. Albans.

Burtenshaw D, Bateman M, Ashworth G (1991) *The European City*, David Fulton Publishers, London.

Chang C, Milne TS, Fallon D, Pohlmann C (1996) Urban *heritage tourism: The global-local nexus.* Annals of Tourism Research n. 23 (2), pp. 284–305.

Conforti JM (1996) *Ghettos as tourism attractions.* Annals of Tourism Research n. 23 (4), pp. 830–842.

Craig-Smith SJ (1995) *The role of tourism in inner-harbor redevelopment: A multinational perspective.* In: Craig-Smith SJ, Fagence M (eds) *Recreation and Tourism as a Catalyst for Urban Waterfront Redevelopment: An International Survey*, Praeger, Westport CT, pp. 15–35.

Csikszentmihalyi M (1975) *Beyond Boredom and Anxiety*, Jossey-Bass, San Francisco.

Csikszentmihalyi M (1990) *Flow: The Psychology of Optimal Experience*, Harper Collins, New York.

Ellis MJ (1973) *Why People Play*, Prentice-Hall, Englewood Cliffs.

Fagence M (1995) *Episodic progress toward a grand design: waterside redevelopment of Brisbane's South Bank.* In: Craig-Smith SJ, Fagence M (eds.), *Recreation and Tourism as a Catalyst for Urban Waterfront Redevelopment : An International Survey*, Praeger, Westport CT, pp. 71–90.

Fainstein SS, Stokes RJ (1998) *Spaces for play: The impacts of entertainment development on New York City.* Economic Development Quarterly n. 12 (2), pp. 150–166.

Getz D, Joncas D, Kelly M (1994) *Tourist shopping villages in the Calgary region.* Journal of Tourism Studies n. 5 (1), pp. 2–15.

Griffin T, Hayllar B (2007) *Historic waterfronts as tourism precincts: an experiential perspective.* Tourism and Hospitality Research n. 7 (1), pp. 3–16.

Hall CM, Selwood JH (1995) *Event tourism and the creation of a postindustrial portscape: The case of Fremantle and the 1987 America's Cup.* In: Craig-Smith SJ, Fagence M (eds.) *Recreation and Tourism as a Catalyst for Urban Waterfront Redevelopment*, Praeger, Westport CT, pp. 105–114.

Hayllar B, Griffin T (2005) *The precinct experience: A phenomenological approach*. Tourism Management n. 26 (4), pp. 517–528.

Hayllar B, Griffin T (2006) A tale of two precincts: a phenomenological analysis. Presented at *Cutting Edge Research in Tourism – New Directions, Challenges and Applications*, CD-ROM University of Surrey UK, 6–8 June.

Hayllar B, Griffin T, Edwards D (eds) (2008) *City Spaces: Tourist Places*, Elsevier, Oxford.

Huizinga J (1955) *Homo Ludens: A Study of the Play Element in Culture*, Temple Smith, London.

Huxley M (1991) *Darling Harbour and the immobilisation of the spectacle*. In: Carroll P, Donohue K, McGovern M, McMillen J (eds) *Tourism in Australia*, Harcourt Brace Jovanovich, Sydney, pp. 141–152.

Iso-Ahola S (1980) *The Social Psychology of Leisure and Recreation*, Wm. C. Brown Publishers, Iowa Dubuque.

James W (1890/1950) *The Principles of Psychology:* Vol I–II, Dover New York.

Jansen-Verbeke M (1986) *Inner city tourism: Resources, tourists, promoters*. Annals of Tourism Research n. 13 (1), pp. 79–100.

Judd DR (1995) *Promoting tourism in US cities*. Tourism Management n. 16 (3), pp. 175–187.

Judd DR, Fainstein SS (eds.) (1999) *The Tourist City*, Yale University Press, New Haven, London.

Karski A (1990) *Urban tourism: A key to urban regeneration?* The Planner n. 76 (13), pp. 15–17.

Kleiber D (1999) *Leisure Experience and Human Development: A Dialectical Interpretation*, Basic Books, New York.

Law CM (1985) *Urban Tourism: Selected British Case Studies Salford, UK*. Urban Tourism Project Working Paper n. 1, Dept. of Geography, University of Salford.

Law CM (1997) *Tourism in Major Cities*, International Thomson Business Press, London.

Maitland R (2008) *Tourists, conviviality and distinctive tourism areas in London*. Paper given at *Cutting Edge Research in Tourism – new directions, challenges and applications*, Conference University of Surrey 6–9 June 2006.

Maitland R, Newman P (2004) *Developing tourism on the fringe of central London*. International Journal of Tourism Research n. 6 (5), pp. 339–348.

McCarthy J (2005) *Cultural quarters and regeneration; the case of Wolverhampton*. Planning, Practice & Research n. 20 (3), pp. 297–311.

Meyer-Arendt K (1990) *Recreational business districts in the Gulf of Mexico seaside resorts*. Journal of Cultural Geography n. 11, pp. 39–55.

Montgomery J (2003) *Cultural quarters as mechanisms for urban regeneration. Part 1: conceptualising cultural quarters*. Planning, Practice & Research n. 18 (4), pp. 93–306.

Montgomery J (2004) *Cultural quarters as mechanisms for urban regeneration. Part 2: A review of four cultural quarters in the UK, Ireland and Australia*. Planning, Practice & Research n. 19 (1), pp. 3–31.

Moustakas C (1994) *Phenomenological Research Methods*, Sage, Thousand Oaks CA.

Mullins P (1991) *Tourism urbanization.* International Journal of Urban and Regional Research n. 15 (3), pp. 326–342.

Pearce D (1998) *Tourist districts in Paris: Structure and functions.* Tourism Management n. 19 (1), pp. 49–66.

Rowe D, Stevenson D (1994) *"Provincial Paradise": Urban tourism and city imaging outside the metropolis.* Australian and New Zealand Journal of Sociology n. 30 (2), pp. 178–193.

Searle G (2008) *Conflicts and politics in precinct development.* In: Hayllar B, Griffin T, Edwards D (eds.) *City Spaces: Tourist Places,* Elsevier, Oxford, pp. 203–222.

Schutz A (1970) *On Phenomenology and Social Relations,* University of Chicago Press, Chicago.

Schutz A (1975) *Collected Papers 111: Studies in Phenomenological Philosophy,* Martinus Nijhoff, The Hague.

Stabler M (1998) *The economic evaluation of the role of conservation and tourism in the regeneration of historic urban destinations.* In: Laws E, Faulkner B, Moscardo G (eds.) *Embracing and Managing Change in Tourism,* Routledge, London, New York, pp. 235–263.

Stansfield C, Rickert J (1970) *The recreational business district.* Journal of Leisure Research n. 2 (2), pp. 209–225.

Stevenson D (2003) *Cities and Urban Cultures,* Open University Press, Maidenhead.

Sydney Harbour Foreshore Authority (2008a) *Visitor Snapshot: Darling Harbour-January/December 2007,* www.shfa.nsw.gov.au

Sydney Harbour Foreshore Authority (2008b) *Visitor Snapshot: The Rocks-January/December 2007,* www.shfa.nsw.gov.au

Van Manen M (1990) *Researching Lived Experience,* State University of New York Press, New York.

2. Authentic Places, Simulacrum Places

"Mystification" of the relationship with the environment is the prerequisite for creating themed environments, which brings with it indifference for the deep meanings of the nature and history of territories. Insensitivity to the distinctive traits of places and the creation of simulacrum places marks the loss of the constitutive matrices of the city, the loss of the meaning of history and time. Only by being rooted in effectuality and in the quest for the polyvocality of places, can the project aim for authentic situations, taking its distance from exclusive attention to branding processes and forms of spectacularisation.

The Tourist City, the Dream and the Reversal of Time

Silvano Tagliagambe

What We Say about ourselves...

Let us take, not very imaginatively perhaps, Porto Cervo as an emblem of the "tourist city" and remark to begin with on the way this place presents and depicts itself on the Portocervo.net site. With the full title "Porto Cervo and Costa Smeralda. All the information on the most famous holiday resort in the world ... Holidays-Travels-Dreams-Luxury-Charter of Sardinia-Vip Services", on this site the birth and history of the place are reconstructed as follows:

In 1962 a group of international financiers led by Karim Aga Khan set up the Costa Smeralda Consortium to create a tourism venture of vast proportions on the territory of Arzachena. The zone involved was the place the locals called *Monti di Mola* (millstones). We may state that since then for Arzachena, and to a certain extent for Sardinia, things have never been the same. The tourism phenomenon hit the territory and began to transform it, modelling it on the grounds of its own requirements. At that time the most important tourist resort in Italy, in terms of quality, was being born. The first luxury hotels and exclusive villas began to spring up, which would become the summer meeting point for high society and world economic power.

Magazines took hold of the news and gossip about the golden world and publicised it worldwide with plenty of details. Transparent seas, beaches covered with granite sand, jagged rocks, age-old trees, Mediterranean macchia crowning bays with their wild beauty became the other powerful publicity vehicle. Everything that was done in this first phase bore the stamp of exclusivity. Hotels, villas, night-spots and harbour were destined for a select clientele that would act as an attraction. Even the architecture adopted, defined as fascinating or influential, depending on the point of view, was placed at the service of this objective. It was not a building venture aimed at destroying nature but at safeguarding it, above all encompassing and therefore privatising it: nature itself became an integral part of the constructions.

The cornerstones on which this self-presentation was based consisted, as can be seen, of the idea of the *privatisation of nature* and of the emphasis placed on the process by which the latter becomes an integral part of buildings. It is an interesting and instructive example of "reverse

G. Maciocco, S. Serreli (eds.), *Enhancing the City*, Urban and Landscape Perspectives 6, DOI 10.1007/978-90-481-2419-0_5, © Springer Science+Business Media B.V. 2009

perspective" (it is nature that must become an integral part of the constructions and not vice versa) and a reversal of the "figure-background" relationship, to which we will have reason to return.

What They Say about us...

In Wikipedia, the most widespread on-line encyclopaedia, we read under the entry "Porto Cervo":

A district of Arzachena in the province of Olbia-Tempio in north-east Sardinia, a historic-geographic region known as Gallura. It is the main resort of the Costa Smeralda and has a resident population of less than 200 inhabitants.

Geography

A renowned holiday resort, it was built up around the deep natural harbour, with its shape similar to that of a deer, dominating the promontories out to sea, the curve of the harbour and the dotted villas immersed in the green. The town is built on a raised level with respect to the harbour, and has a very famous square, shops and boutiques, while all around the restaurants, hotels, night-spots and villas ascend the slopes of the surrounding hills.

History

The old harbour goes back to the sixties when Prince Karim Aga Khan, fascinated by the beauty of this stretch of coastline, decided to buy the very poor land of this corner of Gallura and to give birth, together with the greatest architects of the time, Luigi Vietti standing out among them, to the paradise of international elite tourism that we know today. In the eighties work began on construction of the new harbour, much more capacious and better equipped.

Architecture

At the project stage, the Prince and his architects decided to create an architecture that would maintain as much as possible continuity with that typical of Gallura, with its simple, rudimental look though perfectly at one with the surrounding environment, and this was the key to success. This type of architecture spread throughout the north-east coast and is still up-to-date and imitated today.

Worldy life

The new harbour at Porto Cervo is one of the best equipped in the Mediterranean, with a capacity of 700 places, and as you walk along the quays you can admire the most beautiful boats, cruisers and yachts owned by rich, famous people. At the centre of Porto Cervo there are the mythical waterfront, the *Chiacchiere* square and the *Sottopiazza*, a series of narrow lanes, multi-coloured balconies and windows, built in typical Costa Smeralda style. Whereas the suburbs host the most fashionable night-clubs and the most prestigious restaurants, the real centre of nightlife of the coast.

A Dream Holiday, or Better: the Holiday as a Dream

Let us concentrate on the link "Holidays-Travels-Dreams-Luxury" which, as we have said, is found in the heading of the site and characterises it and, in particular, on the strong tie established between the concept of "holidays" and that of "dreams".

The atmosphere in which it is aimed to immediately immerse the potential addressee by this method of presentation is magnificently expressed by what Pedro Calderón de la Barca, in his work of art written in 1635, the philosophical/theological play entitled *La vida es sueño* (Life is a dream), has Segismund say, when confused between reality and dream:

What's life? An illusion,
a shadow, a fiction,
and our greatest good is but small;
for, all of life is a dream,
and even dreams are dreams
(Calderón de la Barca 2002, p. 123).

Among the many things written about the dream, the fascinating reading proposed by the Russian philospher and theologist, Pavel Florenskij, in his splendid essay *Ikonostas* (1993), dating back to 1922, deserves particular attention for the purpose of our argument.

The dream, according to Florenskij, is the first and most common step in life which joins heaven and earth, visible and invisible, and which leads us to understand that these two worlds are separated by a boundary that separates but also unites them. What distinguishes it is the new time gauge acquired by the sleeper, who, isolated from the external world, passes in his consciousness into the oneiric world and experiences a spectacular increase in the rhythm of time which reaches infinite speed and actually ends up turning head over heels. This collapse is made possible due to the fact that a single equal current event is conceived in two minds: in daytime consciousness – as Ω – and in night consciousness as x (Florenskij 1977, p. 21). Let us take the example of a dream in which the sleeper is transported into the chaotic atmosphere of the French Revolution and condemned to death: let us imagine that he awakens, appalled, as the cold blade of the guillotine is about to descend on his neck and that, once awake, he realises that the whole experience has originated from the fact that the iron bedhead was pressing against his bare neck. If no doubt arises in us on the internal coherence and completeness of the dream from the beginning of the revolution (a) to the contact with the blade (x), even less may we doubt that the oneiric sensation of the cold blade (x) and the pressure of the cold iron of the bed when his head was resting on the pillow (Ω) form a single phenomenon, but perceived in two different consciousnesses. There would be nothing special about the fact that the pressure of the iron (Ω) has shaken the sleeper and simultaneously, in the same time lapse by no means long in sleep, has taken on the symbolic image, though still remaining iron, of a guillotine blade and that the image, expanded by associations, though still on the same theme of the French revolution, has developed into a more or less extended dream. Except that this dream, like many others of the same kind, takes place, Florenskij (1977, p. 29) writes, *as reversed.*

In the visible world, in effect, the external cause (Ω) of the dream precedes in time the event a, psychically deriving from the event x. But in the time of the invisible world, the reverse occurs, and the cause x does not show itself before the consequence a, and usually not before all its consequences b, c, d ... r, s, t, but after them, crowning the whole series and determining it not as efficient cause but indeed as final cause – $\tau\acute{\epsilon}\lambda o\varsigma$. So that in the dream time flows, and it flows rapidly, *towards the present, backwards* with respect to the movement of vigil consciousness. The first *capsizes upon itself* and with it all the concrete images capsize. But this means we are taken onto the plane of an *imaginary space*, so that the same event triggered from the outside, from the plane of real space, is also seen in an imaginary way, that is, first of all, as if it were taking place in teleological time, as the purpose, the object of a tension (Florenskij 1977, p. 30).

And it is exactly in this sense and due to this aspect that the dream is the common limit to the series of experiences of the visible world and those of the invisible world and constitutes the border between these two series, separating them, but at the same time linking them and putting them into contact with each other, in that the images that separate the dream from reality separate the visible world from the invisible world, and in this way join the two worlds together. In this border place of oneiric images, their relationship with both this world and the other is established. The dream is therefore a sign of stepping over from one to the other dimension and indeed the world we are faced with cannot therefore be considered flat, a horizontal space into which to extend itself, with time measured out by a unilinear succession of facts. Instead, it always suggests to us a vertical space, to be negotiated from the top downwards and vice versa, presenting a symbolic nature: seen from above, it is a symbol of down here and seen from down here, a symbol of up there (Florenskij 1977, p. 33).

In Lotman's (1993, p. 53) opinion, here we have a brilliant hypothesis, according to which when the dream is narrated and transformed into a narrative plot, it undergoes transformation in four principal directions:

– A clear increase in the degree of organisation, due to the fact that the narrative structure is superimposed on what has been seen.

- The removal from the memory, following the process of narration, of the real traces of the dream, to such a degree that the person is sure he has really seen exactly what he has narrated. Afterwards, the verbally narrated text remains impressed on his memory.
- The reversal of the verbally organised text with the visual images stored in the memory and the memorisation of it in a visual form. Thus, the structure of the visual narration is created, which unites the sense of reality, belonging to all that is visible, with all the grammatical possibilities of unreality.
- The exchange between the beginning and the end and the change in direction of the dream.

The dream is an unreal reality. It is distinguished by its plurilingualism: it immerses us not in, for example, visual, verbal, musical spaces but in their merging, the same as true reality. Translation of the dream into the languages of human communication is accompanied by a decrease in indefiniteness and an increase in communicability (Florenskij 1977, p. 30). Following this process, it is observed and read "backwards": the dream that was originally indescribable and unpredictable, characterised by a state of incompleteness, the result of a process of random explosion of visual fragments scattered in all directions, is "rectified", set and confined within a linear temporal composition that gives it a complete form, and subjects all the events it is composed of to a reassessment in the second instance that transforms the casual into the inevitable. What was originally one of the many possibilities of development of the multilingual process of which the dream consists is placed in a perspective of meaning originally unpredictable. Then, rethinking of the whole previous story occurs, so that the unpredictable is retrospectively reconsidered as the only possibility (Florenskij 1977, p. 192).

What was just *one* possibility among many is, therefore, transformed into the *only* possibility, in that it is considered an intermediate stage of the process that has to necessarily lead to the final outcome, namely the end of the dream, its narrative epilogue. The tree-like structure, rich in ramifications and different courses of the "dream-event", weakens at the level of the "dream-tale", following the choice the narrator has made, until it disappears completely and irreversibility enters the scene. Although in effect no choice has been made, the dream is reconsidered and relived as a choice and direct movement towards a purpose: after that, the explosion loses its unpredictability and presents itself in people's minds in the form of predictability of the dynamics it has generated.

In Lotman's opinion, the interesting thing in this "rereading" and transformation process to which, according to Florenskij, the dream is subjected, is that it shrewdly grasps the destiny of all artistic creation. All the forms of the latter can be represented as varieties of an intellectual experiment. The essence of the phenomenon subjected to analysis is placed in some system of relations not right for it. Thanks to this, the event passes as an explosion and, consequently, has an unpredictable nature. The unpredictability (the unexpected) of the development of the events constitutes the central element of the work (Florenskij 1977, pp. 190–191). But it is the destiny of the work itself to be observed and read backwards, just like the dream.

The transformation to which the real moment of the explosion is subjected is filtered through the selection carried out by the mind, which provides us with an artificial, simplified version of that original explosion, and thus a *model,* in which sphere what is casual is seen as the result of the sequence of events preceding it, and thus transformed into something normal. On this process is then grafted the memory, which enables a return again to the moment preceding the explosion, and the entire process to be represented in the reverse order compared with what was effectively observed, therefore retrospectively. Consequently, in the mind there will now be three different layers: the moment of the original explosion, the moment of its version in the mechanisms of the mind and the moment of new duplication of these in the structure of the memory. The last layer constitutes the basis of the mechanism of art (Florenskij 1977, p. 187).

Within this complex picture, articulated in three layers, the work of art, which is different from reality because it always has an end, is looked at retrospectively precisely from its "significant finale", namely from the conclusive place to which the threads of its plot seem to converge in their aims. And the reader may assume different points of view of it, moving from one episode of the plot to another, or carrying out a second reading by which from the end he returns to the beginning. In this case that which was organised on the temporal axis occupying the reading is transferred to the synchronic space of the memory. Consequentiality is substituted by simultaneity, and this grants a new sense to the events. The artistic memory in this situation behaves in a manner equivalent to that attributed by Florenskij to the dream: it moves, that is, in an opposite direction from the temporal axis (Florenskij 1977, p. 191).

Attributing a meaning to reality, in particular in the process of artistic understanding, inevitably includes segmentation: in actual fact what has no end has no sense either, so understanding is tied to the segmentation of non-discrete space. The human tendency to attribute a sense and purpose to actions and events underlies the disassembling of continuous reality into certain conventional segments. Art is the inexhaustible space of freedom, of the exploration of ever-new possibilities, continuously straining against the limits placed by the norms: the extreme liberty it enjoys compared with reality makes art an unparalleled pole of experimentation. Art creates its world, which is thus constructed as a transformation of extra-artistic reality, according to the law of implication: "if ..., then ...". The artist concentrates the strength of art in those spheres of life in which he investigates the results of the increased freedom he can enjoy. The object of his attention can therefore become the possibility of violating not only the laws of the family, society, those of common sense, customs and tradition but even the basic ones of nature, the laws of time or space (Florenskij 1977, p. 188). When this "field of creative experimentation", the result of an exercise of freedom and of an investigation not restrained or bound by too many ties, is enjoyed by any kind of addressee it inevitably undergoes a metamorphosis. What is created in the reading process is a *time lag* between the present and the past that is transformed into synchrony. The account of the work of art, its plot, is for the reader something that has already taken place and been accomplished, which precedes, obviously, the narration given of it. This development of the plot, collocated therefore in the past, is, however, experienced at the moment of reading, especially if this is participated in and reaches the necessary level of emotional involvement, like something immediate which arouses sentiments and reactions, such as crying or laughing, that belong to the present time. The text fixes the paradoxical property art has of transforming the conventional into real and the past into present. In this lies, moreover, the difference between the time of flowing of the plot and the time of its accomplishment. The first exists in time, the second is converted into a past, which simultaneously represents an exit from time in general. This difference of principle in the spaces of the plot and its accomplishment makes reasoning on what has happened to the characters after the end of the work futile. If similar reasoning appears, it bears witness to a non-artistic perception of the artistic text and is the result of the reader's inexperience (Florenskij 1977, p. 189).

The most significant steps of this process, reconstructed by Florenskij with reference to the dream and also applied by him personally to artistic experience, may be applied, too, to the golden world of holidays, as it presents itself in the case of Porto Cervo (which is certainly not an isolated case but may be considered emblematic of a certain way of meaning tourism and holidays).

The Reversal of the Relationship between Nature and Artefact

The first common aspect is the reversal of history and time due to the "mystification" of the relationship between "tourist city" and environment, with exclusive attention to the visual, superficial, spectacular aspects and a marked, flaunted indifference to the deep meanings of nature and the history of the territory.

The entire Costa Smeralda "trademark" is based on an image not aimed at communicating, via signs and symbols, meanings of a certain type, cultural, intellectual, political, religious, mysterious, etc. but has been construed and spread in order to be self-sufficient, set apart, self-referential, not a *re-presentation* of anything but a *presentation*, with the intention of highlighting precisely its *non-naturalness* and *non-historicity*. This image, after losing any link with any kind of reality, intends to promote itself and operate as a reality in itself, with a claim to comprehensiveness and fullness aimed at not letting the lack of any referential mechanism be felt. It is the result of the same internal dynamics of the sign and its tendency to put itself forward as *signum sui* (Sini 2001), to show itself and impose itself not as a sign but as a domain capable of granting and fulfilling every demand, appeasing every desire.

In this way, the memories, distinctive traits and matrices that make up the concept itself of historical process and of place as a result of this process vanish and the *place itself becomes a simulacrum,* a visual illusion, a figment of the imagination. It is interesting and important to recall in this connection that the word "simulacrum" derives from an ancient root "sim-" which originally indicated one, the unity, and not reproduction, duality. Precisely because it does not presuppose reference to other than itself, to a *gap to be filled by a process of more or less abstract representation*, the simulacrum is an image freed from reference to any origin, any tradition. Indeed for this reason, it is *immediate, visual, transparent,* capable of *visually communicating by its simple presence.* It is not a *symbol,* which is the expression and manifestation of something lacking, being a window towards another essence not directly given, the product of two parts of a unit which, being separate, yearn to be reunited. But neither is it a *sign,* which, however, contains within it the idea of *duality,* of *reference,* of a process by which a replacement mechanism is implemented, thanks to which any reality is represented by something else that is different. The simulacrum does not repeat, nor reproduce, nor represent the real, it substitutes it, it *sets itself up and is configured as a reality apart,* completely new and different, without referring to anything, no enigmas, no effort for understanding. A container without content, no depth, no reality to which it refers and thus deprived of that friction that is the heart and fundamental nucleus of each authentically aesthetic experience.

The function of this nucleus has been well grasped and explained by Cora Diamond in her shrewd criticism of the relationship "container/contained", by which it is usually presented and experienced. "What interests me", she writes, "there is the experience of the mind's *not being able to encompass something which it encounters.* It is capable of making one go mad to try, to bring together in thought what cannot be thought" (Diamond 2003, p. 2, my italics). The example to which the authoress refers to illustrate this attempt is particularly significant for the purposes of our argument. It is a poem by Ted Hughes, composed halfway through the fifties, entitled Six Young Men.

The speaker in the poem looks at a photo of six smiling young men, seated in a familiar spot. He knows the bank covered with bilberries, the tree and the old wall in the photo; the six men in the picture would have heard the valley below them sounding with rushing water, just as it still does. Four decades have faded the photo; it comes from 1914. The men are profoundly, fully alive, one bashfully lowering his eyes, one chewing a piece of grass, one "is ridiculous with cocky pride" (1.6). Within six months of the picture's having been taken, all six were dead. In the photograph, then, there is thinkable, there is seeable, the death of the men. See it, and see the worst "flash and rending" (l. 35) of war falling onto these smiles now forty years rotted and gone (Diamond 2003, p. 1).

The experience that Hughes' poem evokes is, for Diamond, an example of what she calls *difficulty of reality*, its friction with respect to thought, that residue of opacity that prevents the latter from dominating it, rendering it completely transparent to itself and containing it, representing it in its fullness. "…experience in which we take something in reality to be resistant to our thinking it, or possibly to be painful in its inexplicability, difficult in that way, or perhaps awesome and astonishing in its inexplicability. *We take things so.* And the things we take so may simply not, to others, present the kind of difficulty – of being hard or impossible or agonizing to get one's mind round" (Diamond 2003, pp. 2–3).

It is indeed in this difficulty and in this agony, *in feeling things in this way,* which prevents the mind from containing them, that the deep sense of ethical and aesthetic experience resides: and indeed for this reason, these experiences express and grasp.

The sense of a difficulty that pushes us beyond what we can think. To attempt to think it is to feel one's thinking come unhinged. Our concepts, our ordinary life with our concepts, pass by this difficulty as if it were not there; the difficulty, if we try to see it, shoulders us out of life, is deadly chilling.[…] In the latter case, the difficulty lies in the apparent resistance by reality to one's ordinary mode of life, including one's ordinary modes of thinking: to appreciate the difficulty is to feel oneself being shouldered out of how one thinks, how one is apparently supposed to think, or to have a sense of the inability of thought to encompass what one is attempting to reach (Diamond 2003, p. 12).

To feel this difficulty, this separation between thought and reality, means that it is an emotion that is, precisely, felt and cannot simply be described, represented or pondered, exactly because it "belongs to flesh and blood" (Diamond 2003, p. 25) and thus to the body in all its physicality: we all know these moments and feel that the perception we have of them is profoundly rooted and innervated within our limbs, so that the type of knowledge emerging is not conceptual and abstract but *embodied*. To feel the fact that in Hughes' poem young people are profoundly alive and, *simultaneously, absolutely dead* means to refuse the linguistic game in which there is no contradiction between these two aspects, in that they are placed, as successive moments, in the time sequence of before and after, which tones down and eliminates all dialectic tension between them. The aesthetic and ethical sense of Hughes' poem is lost completely if it is introduced into this game, which deprives it of its capacity to refer to "presences that may unseat our reason" (Diamond 2003, p. 22) and to "experience nothingness" (Weil 1950).

This nothing is the result of the capacity to keep the two contradictory dimensions of life and death together, the visible and the invisible, maintaining their co-presence, and to project them onto a space (the intermediate world between them) in which the boundary crossing them is not the line of demarcation that separates them but the interface that takes shape, takes on consistency and has us feel we are in some *other place* that thought does not manage to contain. Language, on the other hand, has this capacity, in that it has the possibility of letting itself be questioned. From Cora Diamond's works on Wittgenstein this is exactly the interpretation that emerges of his mature reflection as the capacity to explore the idea that language involves a variety of possibilities so open and complex – not pre-established from the beginning but largely to be determined – as to include even the option of its own conceptual horizon being questioned and being as if flung out of it. According to this reading, the *Tractatus* itself already establishes, as a work, this type of overthrowing and emptying out, when it asks the reader to abandon the sentences composing it and to manage to acknowledge them as senseless, once he has followed them and has gone back up them like climbing a stairway. The coincidence of ethics and aesthetics, which we have dwelt on previously, suggests and requires, from this point of view, a type of experience based on the awareness that words are not enough to express an intermediate world like that at the centre of Hughes' poem, which therefore contains "what is mystical" (6.522) and that we "will see the world aright" (6.54) only once the sentences we used like a stairway in order to go back up the various steps of conceptual understanding are surpassed and we manage to get out of the horizon and the context arising from it and be flung outside them. Through this experience, instead of proceeding with images that replace the life we have with the words, thoughts and perceptive and cognitive style construction that we force on reality, we come to dissolve this tranquillising *adherence* of reality itself to our linguistic expressions and conceptual schemes, to rediscover its resistance and friction in respect of the latter, without, however, falling prey to panic or yielding to the flattery and traps of recurrent forms of skepticism. These are satisfied to take note of the acknowledgement, in itself quite banal, of the fact that reality and our thought may not meet each other, not adhere one to the other. The difficult and the beautiful lie in the challenge of *placing oneself in the impossible and living it,* of feeling the co-presence and coincidence of life and death, which is the centre of Hughes' poem, "not to be thought of as outside life with the words we use for thinking of life and death" (Diamond 2003, p. 25), but as something that is fully part of that linguistic game.

This type of game, in order to succeed, obviously has to be made of *opacity* and *transparency and* of the *expressible* and the *inexpressible*, kept in constant reciprocal dialectic tension: it is in this capacity to assure the presence of both these dimensions that the strength of the symbol indeed lies in comparison with the sign and its irreplaceability when it is a question of living and rendering these experiences by language. The symbol is *translucent*, it enables us to feel the presence and perceive the image of something that is beyond it, without distinguishing its outline or form and without being able to represent it. The symbol is the instrument which thought and language use while the mind undergoes the experience, as Cora Diamond writes, of not being "able to encompass something which it encounters" (Diamond 2003, p. 2). Its efficacy lies in the fact of not aspiring to presenting itself as a container that encloses a content within it in such a comprehensive, complete way as to be able to substitute it and represent it totally, but of offering itself as the expression of a relationship between container and content that may never be put aside and extinguished, in which the container, precisely for this reason, may never be put in the place of the content. This relationship in the symbol is not, however, just the *potentiality of an encounter not yet realised,* which thus gives the prospect of a situation of perennial waiting, like that of the shipwrecked person in the sea who sees a ship pass on the horizon and wonders whether he will be seen and therefore saved. In this case, the wait may be transformed into anguish and become an authentic situation of panic. To place oneself in the impossible and to experience it means to realise an encounter, thanks to which not only the content is transformed but also the container: this transformation is the result of the capacity to shift the frontier between opacity and transparency more and more forward, to the advantage of the latter, though in full awareness that we will never be able to completely demolish it. The symbol is thus the expression of consciousness of the fact that nothing can be contained without there being a relationship and that the latter can and must offer us the possibility of transforming both our emotions and sensations, and the words and thoughts we express them with. Aestheticisation suffocates and dissolves all this. Precisely because it leaves out, intentionally, reference to any type of specific life experience, external reality, it loses its transcendental connotations of perennial appeal to ulteriority and changes into a perfectly visible, transparent trace that does not expect to be questioned, interpreted and understood but is content to be *seen* and appreciated by the eye, by anyone, in an undifferentiated way, with no breadth or depth. In this way, the friction between the way in which reality *presents* itself and the way it is *represented and narrated* through signs is eliminated, with the consequent sterilisation of all emotion.

What is more, in this case the mechanism of the falling back of time on itself and its being overthrown is repeated, taking on a teleological course which, according to Florenskij, characterises the event of the dream and its transformation into a tale. The previous history of the place (that corner of Gallura, in the case of Porto Cervo) counts for nothing, has no meaning or value: it seems that the entire cycle of its duration takes on a sense dictated and imposed by the final phase alone, since, that is, its transformation into the "Costa Smeralda".

An explicit symptom of this attitude and conviction is the reversal of the relationship between nature and the built-up area, between natural and artificial, to which we have already had reason to draw attention. It is not the buildings and constructions that should try via the project to become a part, without force or violence, of the landscape, adopted as a tie in the sense of respecting its fundamental characteristics and configuration but, on the contrary, it is nature that has to become an integral part of the constructions "becoming privatised", namely, conforming with the specific requirements of the tourists and adapting (or rather becoming forcibly adapted and moulded) to them. The same is to be said (all the more) for history, which is looked at retrospectively indeed from the position of its "significant finale", that is, from the conclusive place towards which the threads of its plot appear to converge in their aims. In this way, time is overthrown, transformed and reversed upon itself: just like the end of the oneiric vision coincides with the beginning of the awakening and the logical breaking-up of the dream (the blade of the guillotine) with the impulse that at the time of awakening caused the events that had been dreamt (the iron bedstead pressing against the bare neck), thus the history of places in the Costa Smeralda, instead of following the actual process of the succession and importance of events, organised according to their reciprocal relations of cause and effect, or rather through the introduction of a causal factor, is completely reconsidered and rewritten around what we may call a *semantic dominant*.

The Dream and Awakening and the "Semantic Dominant"

To illustrate the concept behind the expression "semantic dominant", we will take the explanation Boris Uspenskij provides of it, also linked (and not by chance, at this stage) to the question of the relationship between the dream and awakening.

Let us imagine that in a dream more or less casual, dark (amorphous) images flow before our eyes, which nevertheless become fixed in our memory. It is a case, we could say, of polyvalent images, in the sense that they are easy to transform (re-interpretable) and are mostly able to combine (unite, intertwine) with each other in a great variety of ways. These images may not have any importance in the dream, but are stored in the memory, in passive consciousness. And then a door slams, and in the dream we perceive (interpret) this sound as a shot; in other words, we perceive the event as a sign and relevant; we link it to a precise meaning. This perception becomes, so to speak, the semantic dominant, which suddenly illuminates the previous events left in our memory, determines our reading of them, that is, connects them through cause/effect links, and in a flash weaves them into a string of narrative. This final interpretation (perception, attribution of sense) we could say establishes the point of view, the perspective in which the events are seen. It is like a sieve, a filter, through which the images that are not bound up with the final (relevant) event are discarded, and are therefore forgotten and disappear from our memory; all of a sudden it lets us see other images, as if tied to each other by a similar content, and lets us set them out in a succession of narrative. The events thus organise themselves instantaneously, and are set out in a linear series; in a flash we see them as if illuminated by the sudden lamp of a projector. Thus the semantic orientation (semantic code) is established which determines the reading of what has been seen: the events are perceived to the degree that, in the mind, they are linked with the final result (Uspenskij 1988, pp. 14–15).

Before embarking on applying the concept of "semantic dominant" to our problem, clarification of a historical nature should be made. This concept has been taken, though Uspenskij omits stating it, from a fundamental work by the physiologist Aleksej Alekseevic Uchtomskij (1875-1943). A student and heir of Nikolaj Evgen'evic Vvedenskij (1852-1922) and a follower of the ideas of Ivan Michajlovic Secenov (1829-1905) on biological determinism and the systemic character of central nervous system activity, Uchtomskij continued the research of these two very great scientists and, in the work quoted, put forward the hypothesis that the time-space relations of the environment are acknowledged by the body through the processing of the signals transmitted by sense organs (sight, hearing and smell), which is carried out in what he calls, indeed, "the dominant", conceived and presented by him as a centre of excitation of the nervous system, which determines the body's reactions to external and internal stimuli. The dominant nerve centre (or group of nerve centres) possesses high excitability, accompanied by a notable degree of inertia, that is, by the capacity to maintain this state even if the initial stimulus ceases its activating effect. Adding to itself the relatively weak excitation of the other nerve centres, the dominant uses these to strengthen itself and at the same time inhibit the other centres: in this way, it guarantees the coordination of the body's efforts in a single direction and quashes any elements of disturbance. At lower levels of the nervous system, the dominant is manifest as the availability of a given organ to always be ready to go into action and as a capacity for maintaining this state of alertness for a long period. Whereas, going back to higher stages, we find ourselves faced with the cortical dominant, which constitutes the physiological base of a whole series of psychic phenomena, including, for example, attention, memory, logical activity and susceptibility. The possibility of concentrating attention on particular objects and the selectivity of learning are therefore physiologically determined by the characteristics of the dominant, which is a constellation that works at a particular rhythm, optimal for certain conditions, and is able to strengthen its capacity for excitation with constant impulses. At the same time, it is able, in relation to this increment in excitability, to inhibit the other reflexes present in common nerve-life termination. In this way, by inhibiting the other centres, selectivity of learning is determined; on the other hand, there is concentration of attention, favoured by stimuli of medium intensity.

The dominant therefore begins to take shape as the fundamental structure of human behaviour: but it is also something more, in that "each of us can notice, through introspection, that when it is present, the capacity to glean and observe particular aspects of reality is greatly accentuated and, at the same time, insensitivity to other features of the environment grows. In this sense, the dominant may be considered not only the physiological prerequisite of behaviour but also the physiological prerequisite of observation" (Uchtomskij 1966, p. 126).

The inertia which characterises the activity of the dominant is, in one way and up to a certain point, useful for developing and strengthening systematic, rational behaviour, since it is precisely to it that both the constant prevalence of one mechanism over all other possible ones, and the origin, strictly connected with this prolonged predominance, of an organising principle of intellectual life, are due. But it can also in another way, and beyond a particular threshold, lead to behaviour and the personality closing up and fossilising altogether in a rigid structure, to the point of preventing the individual who falls into this "vicious circle" from opening up to the outside:

Because of the very fact that I am inclined to act in a particular direction and that the work of my reflex apparatus is polarised in a particular sense, my reflexes prove to be depressed and transformed with respect to many phenomena underway, to which I would have reacted in a very different way in other, more well-balanced circumstances […]. At every moment of our activity enormous sectors of vivid, unrepeatable reality pass us by unobserved, without leaving any trace, just because our dominants were concentrated elsewhere. In this sense they stand between us and reality. The general colouring the world and people take on for us is determined to a very great extent by how our dominants are and how we ourselves are. A scientist who works quietly in his laboratory and enjoys great stability and calm, who is fully satisfied with his state of isolation, will tend to describe the world as a quiet, harmonic flow and, even better, like a crystal in its infinite stability, and he will presumably consider men an element of disturbance, whose presence jeopardises this so ardently desired quietness. A businessman, on the other hand, will see in the world and in history just an environment purposely pre-arranged for his commercial and financial operations […]. The dominant is often unilateral, and to a much greater extent the more it is expressed. This is why in the history of science the so typical phenomenon occurs of different abstract theories regularly following each other, then followed by a return to itineraries which seemed abandoned forever […]. Two opposing abstractions are correlative and each recalls the other (Uchtomskij 1966, p. 90).

The remedy for this unilateral nature of the dominant cannot consist of the attempt to extract it from our physiological and psychic reality, in that "in a normal nervous system it is difficult to imagine a state characterised by the complete absence of any dominant" (Uchtomskij 1966, p. 102). But the route to pursue is a different one: "To not be a victim of a dominant, we must manage to exert our dominion over it. What is needed is for us to be able to subordinate our own dominants as much as possible and guide them according to a clear-cut strategic plan" (Uchtomskij 1966, p. 127).

Strategic design can, however, also be piloted from the outside. And this is just what happens in the case of the tourist city, by stages which, in my opinion, trace quite accurately what Uchtomskij speaks of in the passage previously quoted on the dream.

To be able to subject the images and representations proposed for the recodification process guided by the semantic dominant, these need, as we have seen, to be easy to transform and reinterpret, i.e. not strongly characterised, thanks to a notable trademark. They need, that is, to present themselves as amorphous and casual as possible, or at least polyvalent, and if, therefore, at their origin they do not present in this way, need to be subjected to a progressive process of *sterilisation* of all those traits that make them easily recognisable and linkable with a precise environment. Subsequently, into the historic and cultural context thus weakened, as regards its native meanings and values, at least in the eyes of those coming from outside, a strongly marked perceptive and cognitive style is introduced, able to impress itself easily on the memory and fulfil the double function of filter – which selects within the context in which it works the elements, factors, aspects and processes in harmony with the image of the latter which it wants to accredit, discarding and putting in a marginal position all the others – and of *catalyst*, able to easily and rapidly aggregate the traits selected and organise them according to a guiding idea capable of weaving among them a coherent and convincing string of narrative. To this same strategy responds the introduction of spurious elements that have nothing to do with the cultural styles of the territory on which intervention has taken place but which, perhaps through a process of assonance and analogy, may be linked, either on the linguistic plane or on the perceptive one, with aspects that in some way refer to it.

To understand how this can happen and what the "key" to the success of a similar operation is, we need to refer to the analysis of the metaphor proposed by Max Black, an author to whom we owe the most in-depth study of the mechanism of functioning of this rhetorical figure, on the basis of the conception he himself calls *interactive* (Black 1962).

It is a way of "reading" the rhetorical figure in question that begins with acknowledging that, when a metaphor is used, *two thoughts* are simultaneously activated of different things sustained by *a single word* or phrase, whose meaning is the result, indeed, of their interaction. In this way, a new meaning is produced, different from the literal one, i.e. there is an extension or variation of the meaning determined by the fact that the word is activated in a new context. We therefore have a first element to take account of: the metaphor is always the result of interaction between a word (or entire sentence) and the context it belongs to; it is therefore always a piece, though small, of text. Any word may be used on its own, but if used in this way, it will never be able to give rise to metaphorical effects. The word and the context constitute together, in an indissoluble unit, the metaphor. But what type of association between text and context produces the metaphorical effects?

To answer this question, we need first of all to bear in mind that the meaning of a word consists, basically, of a certain expectation of description. This expectation is guided, so to speak, and conditioned by the semantic and syntactic laws that govern the literal use of the word and the violation of which produces absurdities and contradiction. In addition to this, it should be emphasised that the literal uses of a word normally require the speaker to accept a package of standard beliefs that are the common possession of a given community of speakers. The metaphor acts precisely on this system of ideas normally associated with a word: this, in particular, entails the transfer of the commonplace expressions usually implied by the literal use of a term and its use to construct a corresponding system of implications to refer to a second term, for which, in literal use, these implications are not valid. "Let us try, for example, to think of the metaphor as a *filter*", which thus acts exactly like the semantic dominant Uspenskij speaks of.

Consider the statement, "Man is a wolf". Here, we may say, are two subjects – the principal subject, Man (or: men) and the subsidiary subject, Wolf (or: wolves). Now the metaphorical sentence in question will not convey its *intended* meaning to a reader sufficiently ignorant about wolves. What is needed is not so much that the reader shall know the standard dictionary meaning of "wolf" – or be able to use that word in literal sense – as that he shall know what I will call the *system of associated commonplaces* [...] The effect, then, of (metaphorically) calling a man a "wolf" is to evoke the wolf-system of related commonplaces. If the man is a wolf, he preys upon other animals, is fierce, hungry, engaged in a constant struggle, a scavenger, and so on. Each of these implied assertions has now to be made to fit the principal subjects (the man) either in normal or in abnormal senses. [...] Any human traits that can without undue strain be talked about in "wolf–language" will be rendered prominent, and any that cannot will be pushed into the background. The wolf-metaphor *suppresses some details, emphasizes others* – in short, *organizes* our view of man (Black 1962, pp. 39–41, my italics).

This authorises us to assert that "the metaphor creates the similarity, than to say that it formulates some similarity antecedently existing" (Black 1962, p. 37). The main subject, in effect, is "seen through" the metaphorical expression or, in other words, projected on the field of the secondary subjects. A system of implications (or "commonplace expressions") used within a certain field is used as an instrument to select, highlight and construct relations, briefly, to structure and organise, also in terms of perception, a different field. This operation, which thus has an authentic *perceptive* as well as *cognitive* nature, in that through the secondary subject it leads to features and properties of the main subject, till then totally unheard of, being highlighted and seen, can only be successful on two conditions: (1) that both terms or subjects are simultaneously present in the operation itself and interact with each other and (2) that the implications that are transferred from one subject to the other remain, at least to a certain extent, *implicit*. For, if the metaphor "man is a wolf" were substituted by a literal paraphrase, making *explicit* the relevant relations between the two subjects, it would lose a large part of its efficacy, that is, its "illumination" value. The set of literal sentences thus obtained would inevitably end up saying too much and emphasising things different from the metaphor, with the result of nullifying the metaphor's cognitive content. Finally, it should be borne in mind that through the superimposed elements, the production of the metaphorical tie also modifies the system of implications associated with the secondary subject, and not just that connected with the main subject. If to call a man "wolf" is to put him in a particular light, then it should not be forgotten that the metaphor also makes the wolf seem more human than it otherwise would be.

We can therefore say, at this point, that the metaphor acts by violating the expectation of description predisposed by the meaning of a word and consequently generates an effect of surprise and a tension between the original meaning of the word itself and the idea now deliberately provoked by the context in which it is placed. If we call this process "counter-determination", to emphasise that the description provided by the context proceeds in the opposite direction from the expected one, namely violates the system of standard beliefs associated with the term involved, we may say, with Weinrich (1976, p. 89), that the metaphor is a word in a "counter-determining" context. This same aspect may be highlighted by speaking of the tension between significance (*Bedeutung*) and meaning (*Meinung*), where the first term indicates the habitual content of a word, considered on its own, and the second its conforming to the global sense of the discourse, to the context which, in its turn, expresses the meaning of the person speaking.

This conception of the metaphor is distinct from the traditional one, which has its origins in the classical analysis provided by Aristotle in his *Rhetoric*, which, though celebrating the faculty belonging to the rhetorical figure in question for linking terms unrelated to each other, nevertheless still associates with it a paraphrasable meaning in code language. On the contrary, the metaphor Black speaks of is neither true nor false, i.e. does not constitute a good candidate for calculating truth functions, since by definition it is a break with ordinary code language. It proves translatable into the latter when it has lost its features of originality and novelty, or when it becomes literalised, giving rise to ordinary, institutional language.

Precisely because it has nothing to do with true or false, with the authentic or inauthentic, this conception of the metaphor permits the grafting of that mechanism Dieter Lohmar calls the "as if" (Lohmar 2005, pp. 155–167) way, which is triggered when at the base of the explanation of the way we produce in ourselves the experiences of other people, there is the "phantasmata thesis". According to this thesis, perceiving the sensations of someone else, feeling the other's sentiments, experiencing their will is based on the phantasmas of perceiving, feeling sentiments, wanting and acting that we have produced in ourselves. A phantasma is "something like" a sensation, which means it is given by a sensation. But it is not a real sensation, in that phantasmas occur where what the respective sensation normally leaves behind it as its consequence is missing. We experience the same sensation as the other "almost in the same way" (as if) the other person is experiencing it. We do not need language to represent for ourselves the reasons and sensations of others. The phantasmas with which we perceive (or feel) other people's feelings, sentiments and coinesthesia, inasmuch as they are sensations, already convey a definite sense. The "voices" of others are really present in us: we feel them as though they were authentic sensations of our own, but they are weaker.

With our Feet on the Ground: the Return from the Dream to Reality

Altogether, the "Costa Smeralda" operation presents as a marketing operation aimed at imposing an overall "brand" or trademark, charged with values and meanings which, following the intentions of those who elaborated and promoted it, prove the most effective in attracting a certain type of clientele to this place on the basis of psychological dynamics revolving around the message developed and its semantic dominants, mostly unnoticed by the addressees, who undergo their effects unawares.

By itself this operation, constantly in a precarious position between falsehood and illusion and aimed at transforming the holiday into a "dream", with all the implications and consequences that have been highlighted, is in no way reprehensible. It cannot, however, be said that it has anything to do with the actual reality, not only historic and cultural, but also natural and environmental, of Sardinia. And if it is true, as Calderón de la Barca's Segismund said, that "dreams are dreams", it is also true that this character ends his reflection by saying, not by chance: "but, whether it's reality or a dream, to do good is what matters" (Calderón de la Barca 2002, p. 137), thus emphasising that in the end the only really important thing is the precious sense of the value of an ideal, running through and permeating life, whether experienced, imagined or dreamt, and innervating it with authentic meanings.

Calderón de la Barca was thus already inviting us almost four hundred years ago to meditate on the fact that, even if we are confused between reality and dreams and perhaps are satisfied with this situation, we must never lose sight of the link – if not with daily experience, in its rough effectuality – at least with that idealised vision of it that takes on consistency and finds a shape in the images it evokes, in the phantasies, in the inclination to think of this effectuality and see it otherwise, to the point of arriving at projects that find their way to being realised and have, consequently, the effective capacity to influence and transform it.

There is a great difference, in other words, between the dream and ecstasy, on the one hand, and the capacity to allude, on the other, to a *virtual*, not effectual, presence, i.e. not able to be found *here* and *now*, in the reality that currently shows itself before our eyes, but nevertheless always possible, which constitutes, precisely for this reason, potential value-seeking opportunities to express itself and be recognised.

It is, moreover, in this sense, in connection with virtue and its meanings of capacity and power, that medieval Latin used the word *virtualis,* which derives from *virtus,* virtue, value meant originally with reference to Roman virtue, namely *vir romanus* – strength in the military sense. Subsequently, following the trials faced with courage by the first Christian martyrs, the term *virtus* took on a moral meaning.

This reference to *virtualis* in its original meaning enhances the function of creative activity which, *departing from the real,* explores the possible and enables achievement of the capacity to carry out a series of references back to other possibilities of experiencing and acting – alternatives compared with those in force and operative. Its keystone is, therefore, as we have said, the possible set against the actual (that which currently exists, spatially and temporally determined). In this sense, a *strategy considered as continuous creation of possibilities* is implemented and practised, in which each choice, each act, each behaviour, actualises a part of the possible and simultaneously creates a new possible. What it is intended to highlight through creative activity meant in this sense is not, therefore, possible in its pure state, as a generic, indefinite notion, the result of the exclusion both of what is necessary and of what is impossible, but the inclusion of what is given (experienced, expected, thought, planned and dreamt) on the horizon of possible modifications. This means that we depart from the general situation we are experiencing, which is taken as a prerequisite, trying to see it from the point of view of possible diversity, i.e. alternatives not only conceivable but also concretely realisable. It does not, therefore, designate the possible as such, but possible alternatives, seen departing from reality. This is an important clarification for, by itself, the fact of multiplying what is possible ad infinitum adds nothing to what is becoming current. By multiplying opportunities and the need for choice, we can simply increase the volume of what will never be realised. And, as Calvino shrewdly notes, "futures not realised are only branches of the past: dry branches" (Calvino 1979, p. 34).

This is certainly not what is needed. For as Umberto Eco observes, a correct meaning and interpretation of what we usually designate with the expression "possible worlds" entails adopting the following conditions:

We establish that:
a) possible worlds are linguistic (or semiotic in general) constructs;
b) they reflect propositional attitudes (believing, wanting, desiring, dreaming);
c) as *constructs* they are produced by negotiating the conditions according to which individuals are described in them (only some properties are relevant);
d) they are compared with a real world which also has to be reduced to a construct, which obeys the same restrictions of the possible world with a small

number of individuals and properties. [...] Why does this epistemic and non-ontological vision of counterfactual worlds interest us [...]? Because the counterfactual may be imagined provided there are restrictions of a narrative, or literary, type in the sense (used metaphorically) of desire. And in this sense the counterfactual has to do with the unrealistic in literature and in philosophy with the utopian (Eco 1981, pp. 258–259).

There is a substantial difference between the desire and the possible world meant in this way and the dream as it was previously presented also in the wake of Florenskij and Uspenskij's ideas. The latter, as has been seen, perhaps takes inspiration and cues from reality (the iron bedstead pressing against the bare neck) but then proceeds by himself, with a logic and a temporal succession all his own, which completely leaves aside those distinguishing the said reality. Whereas the possible world, and the creativity and projectuality expressed in it, cannot do without the link with effectuality, though possessing the capacity to raise themselves above it and filter perception of it through the ideal. It looks elsewhere, upwards, but keeps its feet solidly on the ground and for this reason always knows *where* it is and *why*.

The diversity of perspectives and orientation, as regards the conception of the holiday and the idea of the tourist city project, is not negligible. It is the same as that existing between a context like that of the Costa Smeralda, which departs from "being constructed", namely from a project thought up and elaborated *a priori*, following its own logic, like that of the dream, which takes only inspiration and opportunity from the environment to which it belongs and then proceeds expecting to forcibly encompass nature as it effectively is in this scheme, which acts as an authentic Procustes bed; it is the effort of proposing an environment that is ideal but is respectful of the history, culture and traditions of the host system and community and committed to assimilating their distinctive traits and seeking at the same time to raise their quality and general level without unsettling them. Basically, it is a question of deciding what to offer tourists: a dream which has no link with reality, or an ideal which pursues what is fair and authentic and has them taste at least a little of the actual flavour of the land hosting them and its history.

References

Black M (1962) *Models and Metaphors*, Cornell University Press, Ithaca NY.
Calderón de la Barca P (2002) *Life Is a Dream* (Original title: *La Vida es sueño*, 1635) edited and translated by Stanley Appelbaum, Dover Publications, Mineola NY.

Calvino I (1979) *Le città invisibili*, Einaudi, Torino.

Diamond C (2003) *The Difficulty of Reality and the Difficulty of Philosophy.* Partial Answers n. I, pp. 1–26.

Eco U (1981) *La combinatoria dei possibili e l'incombenza della morte.* In: Romano R (ed) *Le frontiere del tempo*, Il Saggiatore, Milano, pp. 258–259.

Florenskij PA (1977) *Le porte regali. Saggio sull'icona*, edited by Zolla E, Adelphi, Milano.

Florenskij PA (1993) *Ikonostas*, Mifril, Sankt-Peterburg.

Lohmar D (2005) *On the function of weak phantasmata in perception: phenomenological, psychological and neurological clues for the transcendental function of imagination in perception.* Phenomenology and the Cognitive Sciences n. 4(2), January 2005, pp. 155–167.

Lotman JM (1993) *La cultura e l'esplosione, Prevedibilità e imprevedibilità*, Feltrinelli, Milano.

Sini C (2001) *La libertà, la finanza, la comunicazione*, Spirali, Milano.

Uchtomskij AA (1966) *Princip dominanty* (The principle of dominant). In: Uchtomskij AA *Dominanta*, (The Dominant), Nauka, Moscow-Leningrad.

Uspenskij BA (1988) *Storia e semiotica*, Bompiani, Milano.

Weil S (1950) *La personnalité humaine, le juste et l'injuste, in "La Table Ronde"*, n. 36, 1950, poi in Ead, Écrits de Londres, Gallimard, Paris, 1957.

Weinrich H (1976) *Metafora e menzogna: la serenità dell'arte*, Il Mulino, Bologna.

Disney-ality and Forgetfulness: the *Eu-topia* of a Consolatory Place

Elena Moreddu

Introducing Reality-Proof Images

The mystique of any place (sacred, magical or simply romantic) is managed by practices intended to exert control over its "reality claims". [...] Under what circumstances do we think things are real? The important thing about reality, ... is our sense of its realness in contrast to our feeling that some things lack this quality. One can then ask under what conditions such a feeling is generated, and this question speaks to a small, manageable problem having to do with the camera and not what it is the camera takes pictures of (Caron 1993, p. 126).

Erving Goffman's words lead us to reflect on what he metaphorically defines as the *camera,* that is the mechanisms and practices of "construction" of reality and their legitimisation at a social level, rather than on reality itself. Dwelling on these mechanisms leads us at the same time to think about the desire for experiencing these "constructions" as though they were "real". Places, declined in their infinite phenomenology as tourist places, comprise unusual modalities of construction of their reality which can take on "completely different connotations and worth depending on the desires aroused and the appeasement brought to those who consume them". The mental and physical experiences produced are all "equally real in the minds of those who experience them", so as to offer the subject's perception "a plurality of levels of the real" (Giannone 1996, pp. 302–303).

The ambiguous, and more than ever imaginative, dimension pertaining to these places of tourist consumption, increasingly focused on the production and commercialisation of images of the self, asserts a somewhat pre-emptive right as concerns experiential modalities and orientation of the communities of users compared with a dimension of daily life: this, far from any logics of simulation, is in effect lacking in appeal within a market of artificial images of reality which makes its own a dimension of place that is spectacular and thus propulsive on a market of simulacra. The image is *proof* of reality, but at the same time a form of testimony that this can be constructed and manipulated (Harvey 1993, p. 380). In the post-modern society, as Featherstone (1994, p. 91)

G. Maciocco, S. Serreli (eds.), *Enhancing the City*, Urban and Landscape Perspectives 6, DOI 10.1007/978-90-481-2419-0_6, © Springer Science+Business Media B.V. 2009

maintains, the consumption of images of places creates an inclination in the tourist to have simulated experiences, to seek the "game of the real" in the experience of the journey, aware of experimenting surface sensations, undertaking to explore "amazing spaces" without missing reality at all.

It is our intention to attempt a reading of these mechanisms and practices of construction of the real as they are exemplified in events promoting tourism on the territory, which use the historic/identitarian value of the urban place identified as historic "centre".[1] Through a careful examination of the peculiar modalities of construction of the reality of a place, responding to an ideal of "centre", we will concentrate on showing how this reality is rather a projection, in practice, of a *eu*topic perspective of spatial construction, a standardising constriction, if not annihilation, of the polyvocality of the Place reduced to listening to the incessant echo of one's *own* voice.

The utopia[2] of the thematic project is easily capable of conveying (in an unconscious manner on both sides) the structural and structuring pair city-inhabitants within a pre-ordained discursive structure: the said "centre", pre-ordained space,[3] frozen in its pre-ordained state, determines the modalities of access that suit it and even transmits the perceptive modalities of the visitor (Granelli 2005, p. 7).

The Centre actually takes on a "spectacular" guise, it becomes the stage for promoting visions that it, itself, suggests in a desire to deny the insecurity arising from dialogue, the seed of discord, criticism, the unacceptable. Becoming the theme of a place thus produces a *mono*-tonous withdrawal into itself, into its own performance, into a time that "expels all interference, a permanent synchronic time" suspended and immobile (Basso 2005, p. 8). It is a happy place, so it seems, as it is always the same. But "what should we think if this island no longer appeared as a space kept up with the rules of gardening, but as a case of [urban] *sauvagerie* and became colonised by makeshift dwellings and drifters' camps?" (Granelli 2005, p. 9).

It is perhaps useful to take up again that "becoming a whole" of city and citizens which Basso indicates as "elements realised and syntagmatically related in view of precise strategies of signification", a "structural coupling between inhabitant and urban space" which "presents as circulation and continuous transformation of the sense it informs and constitutes both the identity of the city and that of its citizens" (Basso 2005, p. 1).

Recuperate the significance of Place, which needs to be able to be freed from its own utopian charge and reintroduced into an ecosystemic perspective that sees it open to spatialising, signifying practices, advocates of the social change that can still take place in those city spaces. Dismantling the stage and turning off the lights implies an opening of the unresolved and somewhat vague sides of the relationship between Centre, urban "fullness" and citizens/visitors, which remains, however, a relationship (and therefore intrinsically fertile) even if it opens itself up to "processes of distanciation (rejection) or adhesion (symbolisation)" (Basso 2005, p. 11).

The Consumption of Places

The reality of the tourist place/space occurs following a dynamic alternation between creative processes due to numerous *f*-actors, often concomitant, so as to make it a place to be experienced, as already emphasised, as a differentiated series of levels of the real, all accessible to the visitor. The visitor is thus not only urged but also literally drawn towards particular, specific interactive dynamics with such a place which, in a pre-ordained manner, leads him along a certain interpretative route complying with the image of self chosen to be conveyed. It thus proves clear to what extent factors belonging to the single subject/user, which involve his cognitive and emotional spheres and cultural traits, are used as connotative elements through which to guide the strategy of construction of reality of the tourist space. A kind of condition appears to exist, therefore, in that not only are products subject to particular rules of commercialisation that will pinpoint particular desires and needs of potential consumers, upon which to create communicative promotional projects that will encounter and respond punctually to them, but this condition will also be detectable in a parallel manner for the tourist spaces and their images/realities (Mondardini Morelli 2000). It thus seems possible to us to discover in so-called experiential marketing those strategies directed at intercepting the desires of the visitor/consumer of places, and their appeasement, by offering consumer experiences that strengthen the pre-ordained discursive strategies relating to those same places. In this way these become contextualised and contextualising objects for consumption, to be experienced, by means of a total experience.

Experiential marketing is "based on the experience of consumption [...] rather than on the product itself. From this perspective, the sales strategy aims at picking out which type of experience can promote the product best, to then propose it to the public, reconstructing it *ad hoc*".[3] The experiential marketing model distinguishes various "strategic experiential modules" which can also be combined with each other to form total experiences: "*sense* experiences, namely experiences that involve sensorial perception, *feeling* (*sensory and affective*) experiences, which involve the sentiments and emotions, *thought* (*creative-cognitive*) experiences, *act* (*physical*) experiences and *relate* (*social-identity*) experiences, resulting from relations within a group [...]" (Aiello and Donvito 2005, p. 3). Another form of marketing exists, closely connected with experiential marketing, known as "polysensorial", in that it proposes techniques of communication and selling founded on the "strategic solicitation of the consumer's five senses".[4]

We wish to clarify better this process of construction of the reality of tourist space by describing a case study below.[5]

The event called *Mastros in Santu Predu* which takes place in the "historic" quarter (Pinna 1997, pp. 28–29) of Nuoro[6] is part of a more general strategy of support and promotion of the territory and economy of the municipalities of the internal areas of the island, derelict places[7] as Silvia Serreli defines them, fitting indeed into a strategy of commercialisation of local products according to the dictates of the above-mentioned experiential marketing, the object of which is to "establish a sort of empathy between the agency and the client that will increase both the consumer's involvement and his differentiation perceived during the process of consumption, which translates into a new source of competitive advantage" (Baglini 2006).

Over the years the event, which is part of a wider circuit of tourism promotion called *Cortes Apertas*,[8] has been used as a vehicle of rediscovery of the quarter, of the existing handicraft work and some specifically imported for the occasion that use this context to show their products. The urban place, and in particular some points considered of greater significance like larger spaces and squares, ruins of the walls of old abandoned houses and courtyards are used as the simple, though effective, scenic structure to exhibit handmade goods and stage the processes of workmanship that have led to their creation. The handicraft workshops permanently present in San Pietro quarter are few: they include mostly artists and sculptors, potters, goldsmiths, carpenters or woodwork artists, blacksmiths, those making typical cakes, shoemenders and saddlers. The event is spread over three days: for those who come from different parts of the town posters erected on rigid supports accompany the effect of entry into the place, emphasising its character of urban island distinct from the rest of the town.

Opening the "*cortes*" (Pinna 1997, pp. 69–70) responds punctually to a communicative strategy aimed at selling the typical, authentic nature of the product and producer even to the local consumer. The "traditional" architectural context of the courtyards and their situation inside an urban context that is also of "historic" value, justify, granting at the same time validity, not only the type of event but what is shown at the event, men and goods.[9] The use of the word "courtyards", with the aim of including and characterising the whole group of events promoting the typical quality of local handicraft work, thus refers back metonymically to the idea of traditional constructions, which, too, are indicative, quite spontaneously, of an identitarian feature it is intended to preserve to assure that authenticity is still present.

The urban place exhibits to itself its own authentic character, for the places, handicraft products and production modalities it refers to should, and mean, to be authentic. It seems to us that this self-representation fits, though in a partially unaware manner, within the logics of identitarian creation and "authentication of identity" which otherwise show a certain incapacity to substantiate their own self in the present:

Friedman and Sagalyn (1989) provide a particularly incisive analysis of the coalitions of private capital and municipal government necessary to the successful development of the new urban retail built environment. In creating these spaces, developers and public officials articulate an ideology of nostalgia, a reactionary modernism that expresses the "dis-ease" of the present ..., a lament on the perceived loss of the moral conviction, authenticity, spontaneity, and community of the past [...]. More specifically, we collectively miss a public space organized on a pedestrian scale, that is, a setting for free personal expression and association, for collective cultural expression and transgression, and for unencumbered human interaction and material transaction (Goss 1993, pp. 24–25).

The community has to meet up in "those" streets of the town to be able to be capable of portraying itself as such: this modality of "social construction" (Shenhav-Keller 1995, p. 144; Urry 1994) of the identity of urban centres similar to the case study in point is also implemented through the display of products in which a constant reference can be traced back applicable to a "traditional" aesthetic that recurs in the symbolism used as decorative elements for the objects produced mostly following modern stylistic features.[10] "Recycling forms and languages of the past thus gives life to thousands of landscapes original in their genre, all recognisable by a tourist public, as they consist basically of surfaces, signs, references to the narration of the place rather than the place itself" (Minca 1996, p. 126).

Disney-ality and Forgetfulness

Thematisation of place, as made clear in the case study previously quoted, unfolds from a set of practices of construction of reality (Augé 2002). The urban place thus becomes an image of itself, an image to whose construction a set of *f*-actors contribute, namely experiential marketing strategies, strategies of communication of the event and modalities of use of some features of the said place: "These mental stimuli ... merge naturally with the core of the cultural, psychological, physiological and biological elements that are the patrimony of each of us. The result of this mixture is made up of many mental constructions to which just as many realities correspond" (Giannone 1996, p. 302). These elements not only transmit a certain prepacked image of the place but subtly operate on the imagination of the local visitor that was already close to it and has memories of it, leading him to experiental, interpretative modalities of the event that are strongly anchored in a pre-existing emotional experience he has had. This makes constructed reality a desired dimension into which he wishes to return.

The visitor is required to go through the experience of an event, tied to local traditions, within an urban context asserting its historic/identitarian value and providing, meanwhile, a spatial and, in turn, temporal,[11] frame in keeping with the event. The centre actually sets itself up, moreover, as a closed urban context, we might say isolatable if not isolated (isolated like Utopia, a happy island) and strengthens all the more the feeling of entry into the town's place "of the past" for all citizens (Fig. 1). A sort of subtle sensorial stimulation exists to which the individual *ken* (Caron 1993, p. 127) of visitors is constantly induced to respond, a condition that is indeed produced within a physically and historically closed context which does not permit, in the "lived" experience produced by the event, acquisition of a clearer glance, more inclined towards "doubt" on what has actually remained a place "without":

Is this the historic centre [...]? Or is it, rather, minced and digested by presumption and indifference? Is it not perhaps the reflection of the choreographic and folkloristic taste of the last to arrive, the mirror of the fashions of the moment, the sitting-room furnished with vulgar bad taste? Is it or not the perverse result of an activity of stratification and substitution in which the true foreigner is the residual historic building patrimony, strangled by irreversible demolition work, conducted in a systematic, mystifying way? How many of us, as we walk along the streets of an old town, perceive an exciting place, a wealth of values conserving memories, showing the passing of its forefathers, a place that has lived through other stories that deserve to be narrated and conserved, and how many, on the other hand, have the feeling of being just anywhere, the result of a mere repetition of brutally current interventions, equal to each other and incongruous and detached from any historic reference, logically irrational (Carcassi 2007).

The denunciation of an objective condition of *lack* of value of what nowadays may be defined as the historic architectural "patrimony" of the quarter, and of a gap we might almost call *emotional* linked with it, lies in the irrationality and iniquity of interventions carried out on it.

Fig. 1 Between the two buildings the entrance can be seen to the old town where the Cortes Apertas are held

We therefore seem to glimpse, without fear of opening ourselves to simple generalisations, direct correspondence between what in the collective imagination is considered historic and *memorable* and what is perceived as worth being experienced, being *felt*. All the more, therefore, the image of the quarter transmitted in that of the theme park requires the use of practices and mechanisms of construction of a reality (also linked to perceptive systems) that no longer belongs to it and that deliberately leads it towards the re-creation of that above-mentioned correspondence. The logics underlying the construction of a *Disney-ality*[12] operate, in effect, not to create a "completely different" reality, foreign also to the social dimension of the urban place; imaginary worlds are not represented there, rather, there is an attempt to reformulate that same reality in the closed space that the theme park always constitutes, offering it for a reading that has a strong emotional impact because it draws from those aspects most representative of the local culture, accentuating, caricaturing ways, colours, dimensions (Codeluppi 2005; Moore 1980). A "different" dimension of reality is thus produced, one of spectacularisation of the self, of closure of the being-place of the place, whose reality remains subjugated to itself. It seems to us that the logic inherent in the thematisation of these places is to be sought indeed in the absence, perceived and real, of significance: significance of the current place, significance of the social relations. Its own past, the history of what it has been, weighs on it, so much so that it is unable to avoid continuous withdrawal into a self-referential dimension that guarantees nourishment (Fig. 2). Thus, where an emptiness exists (or something which compared with what was perceived as a place once "full" of significance now becomes perceived as an emptiness), the idea arises of formulating an icon of the place and using it as an element for filling. Becoming an icon of itself lays down the prerequisite for the place of having to avoid the risk of finding itself in a dimension permitting dialogue, wanting it open to critical relations with its past, leading it, rather, to barricade itself behind its own reassuring image (Nelson 2005).[13]

A place that withholds sacred "knowledge" is this. Its sacrality belongs to it, is entirely intellectual, for the birthplace of the greatest local thinkers of the twentieth century, as the text just quoted states, was there; they, the most important exponents of "making culture", to whom sooner or later each inhabitant will refer (Gupta and Ferguson 1992). The said policies of cultural promotion localise events and highest institutions representing the culture of the town and its "still" being a town of culture indeed within the limits of the quarter or close to it, the place of its history. This dimension it possesses, which transcends though at the same time does not disregard the merely architectural/urbanistic one, refers back to the "invisibilities" that cannot be revealed. These are re-proposed, still hidden, in its dimension of theme park.

Fig. 2 A poem by Sebastiano Satta[14] accompanies visitors walking through the quarter

The place is not shown, therefore, *as it no longer is:* there is rather an attempt to shift the attention of the visitor to what can still arouse in him the image of what it *was* rather than the reality of the here and now.

As Caron observes: "Forgetting one's doubt is simply a cover-charge one pays to experience the place-as-place. The desire to forget (which is different than the desire to believe) underlies all of the practices that provide such an experience of place. A Disney park's seamless semiological and physical place saturates the consumer's ken for the duration of the visit, prompting the forgetting, [...] precisely what the consumer pays for" (Caron 1993, pp. 126, 128; Bell 1998). The efficacy of what is constructed of reality therefore revolves around the visitor's need to believe what his senses are suggesting to him, to abandon himself to it, in a sort of implicit request leading him to "forget", put aside his doubts about the craftsmanship of what is being shown to him and, above all, those mechanisms that create it, letting himself be involved somewhat in the agreeableness of the experience which always refers back, in our specific case, to itself, to the personal identity of inhabitant: the happiness of Utopia is shown in this case in its being closed in a time which we have already said was synchronic and permanent, which projects in a loop the same happy images: "the complicity of the consumer is generally required for this forgetting. The consumer agrees to accept the circumstances as they are presented. [...] Doubts are not actually abandoned in this process, but rather they are temporarily ignored, forgotten but not gone" (Caron 1993, p. 130).

It is perhaps possible to define and understand the experience of promotion of the territory in smaller towns as a series of elements that structure themselves to make "syncretic texts" of them (Fabbri and Marrone 2000).

Nowadays the syncretic text, one that uses several expressive codes such as an advertisement or an internet site, is becoming more and more open to the synesthesic. Ceriani says it well [...]: "by emphasising contaminations and equivalents on the plane of the sensitive, advertising manages to create closer relations with the receiver and activate his consent, both by lowering the cognitive threshold responsible for judgement in favour of the affective/sensorial, and by multiplying the cognitive routes in respect of the senses called into action"

(Baglini 2006).

A complex series of references and representations conveyed within the experiential marketing strategy, elements used as notification of the event,[15] just as other references pertaining specifically to the place, in the place, concur to structure these events as syncretic texts. The analysis of these factors is useful for the purpose of understanding how it is intended to transmit an identitarian message to the visitor/addressee.[16]

The identitarian message contained in the texts used in the communicative project of such events is not immediately intelligible; it is conveyed rather by continuous reference to a dimension of the *sensitive* into which the visitor is introduced: thus "suggestive atmospheres" appear, "shapes and colours", "immersion" in a route that is "out of time", "genuine flavours", images of "houses of stone and cobbled streets", "embracing the guest", the "thousand-year-old culture", "noble materials" and "expert hands". What is conveyed by the texts then finds greater expressive strength through the use of images that refer explicitly to elements of an "authentic past" (Bendix 1999).[17] Recurrent use is made of images whose subjects are a portrayal of a *time* conveying to the hypothetical visitor the emotion of his own memories linked with it (Fig. 3). They seem to promise, for those who would like to go to the place during the event, the possibility of finding themselves once more in that world, that time, in the company of those people. They seem to promise the possibility of forgetting the present and descending spiritually and emotionally into those atmospheres that lead back to ourselves and to our past: "Spectacularisation of the retail trade ... aspires to creating a new urban sociality that closely recalls that of holiday packages. The nostalgic retrieval of traditional urban places betrays this aspiration [...]. Goss (1993) calls this phenomenon *agoraphilia,* namely an almost obsessive architectural recalling of the idea of the street, the walk, the square of Mediterranean memory as a place of social interaction" (Minca 1996, pp. 129–130).

Fig. 3 Visitors enter into a captivating atmosphere that takes them back to familiar images

The visitor's involvement on the emotional/"passionate" plane is then strongly supported by the use of place as an active tool in the experiential marketing strategy: the choice of particular glimpses to present handicraft products and the respective work carried out in real time following traditional techniques has offered men, products and actions a certain plausibility as concerns authenticity and, as a reflection, traditional identity of what is presented (Cohen 1989a). A precise conceptual reference is that constructed between places, objects, persons where the place does not take on a simple cloak of sterile container but justifies and strongly connotes, being connoted in turn, the identitarian character of men and handicrafts. Traditional objects in a "traditional" place.

To give greater strength and concreteness to the evocative character triggered by clever use of the peculiar elements of the architectural context (Aiello and Donvito 2005, p. 4), other sensorial stimulation intervenes: the embers burning in the open, used by the blacksmith to shoe the horse, benches laden with cheeses and salami, others where cakes are being made, yet others where bread is being baked in a wood-fired oven. Later on local choirs will harmonise traditional songs, a smith concentrates on striking the red-hot iron, etc. (Zanini 2004, p. 137). Sounds and smells "are registered in the form of emotions, closely linked with the situations in which they were perceived for the first time".[18]

The need to trigger different "cognitive-evocative processes" (Ruffini and Turchini 2006) in the visitor is also found in the use of cultured quotations by distinguished personages continually referring to the place and its history.[19]

The process of what we have defined *forgetfulness* is thus conveyed not only by awareness of the symbolic value of the place where the event is carried out (past and identitarian) but even more by the whole series of sensorial stimuli. The synesthesic character of the manifold pressures[20] to which the visitor to the place/theme park is exposed as it takes shape in some urban spheres of smaller towns, especially on the occasion of events to promote the territory, thus leads to a lowering of that "cognitive threshold" within which it would be natural to wonder about the truthfulness of what is experienced to nurture, on the contrary, the *affective* and emotional part of the experience (Simpson 1999). It is also true, though, that in spite of the fact that the most recent marketing theories maintain that the consumer is not a totally rational person, the dimension of *forgetfulness* into which the visitor will fall is mediated by a certain dose of control on his part (Pericoli 2003): however much he obeys the logics and institutional dictates that want him "lost" in a past world but without time (such as that proposed by the theme park), because of what Featherstone defines as his "urge to merge", this obedience is part of a practice of management of his own emotional life. A "de-controlled control of the emotions" is what permits the visitor/consumer to "dive into" a place, emotionally immerse himself in it and "re-emerge later unaltered (emotionally dry), ready for the next dive (Ferraresi and Schmitt 2006). This ability to control the de-control of emotions is a fundamental consumer skill in cities where each doorway on the market street offers up a highly aestheticized ambiance in competition with its neighbor [...]" (Featherstone 1991, p. 126).

The thematised nature that we mean to assign to the urban place in question raises, however, the need to throw light on one aspect that, if not clarified, would appear misleading with respect to what we have maintained up to now; we know a certain projectual specificity belongs to the theme park in the construction of reality and respective hiding of the practices and mechanisms used for this construction. What is relative to our case study on place/theme park is, however, a modality of construction of the real similar to that which Cohen has described as "substantive staging", which is distinguished by the will to not show excessive commitment in the creation of simulated environments:

> while mass tourism appears to be caught in an artificial tourist space, alternative tourism seems to hold forth the promise of enabling the individual to visit authentic places and meet real people. Such experiences can in fact be achieved by individual travelers on unconventional trips off the beaten track. However, as alternative tourism becomes popular, it offers commercial opportunities for enterprising locals, who seek to cash in on the alleged authenticity of the attractions which they offer. The fact that mass tourist attractions are seen by many as overtly staged and inauthentic, opens to these local entrepreneurs a chance for a more subtle, covert and insidious form of staging. This is precisely because the customers believe that the alternative tourist establishment will provide them with the very authenticity which they miss in the contrived attractions of routine mass tourism (Cohen 1989b, p. 58).

This is why the visitor finds he is following routes and entering places that do not show themselves as clear reconstructions of authentic realities. The fact is not concealed from him that the craftsman may wear clothes that he does not use in everyday life for his work, in the same way as craftswomen do not wear traditional costumes but simple working clothes. Behind the scenes appears to remain an open world, accessible to the visitor. What remains hidden, in actual fact, is indeed the fact that there is nevertheless strong cognitive and emotional conditioning conveying a message of authenticity precisely where elaboration of the real is actually less. The parallelism "greater elaboration/greater fiction, less elaboration/less fiction" does not seem to be applicable in our case. The said opportunities for experiential acquisition that distinguish promotional events for the territory, in offering the visitor the chance to have direct access to handicraft work and visit the places where it is carried out, lead him to not doubt that what is being shown to him corresponds to the truth, precisely because baring the mechanisms of the work sends a message of authenticity and negation of manipulation: "[...] a tourist experience is always mystified, and the lie contained ... presents itself as a truthful revelation, as a vehicle that carries the onlooker behind false fronts into reality. The idea here is that a false back is more insidious and dangerous than a false front, or an inauthentic demystification of social life is not merely a lie but a super-lie, the kind that drips with sincerity" (MacCannel 1973, p. 599; Waitt 1997; Wang 1999). Even those places that are "caskets" of art, and the events, as convincing elements, merge to give life to a sort of "trademark" of authenticity within which the entire scenic apparatus and its products fit (Shenhav-Keller 1995; Lanfant et al. 1995).[21]

A Consolatory Place

Places thematised in this way ask the visitor to halt, they open up to him offering a fruitless delay, inviting him to find himself again in time immobile, like that symbolically marked by the history of the place, the architecture of the *open* courtyards, the trades that take him back to a time of infantile naivety and carefree youth. The historic dimension formulated and portrayed by the theme park is that of an inert synchronism that easily leads him into an out-of-time "becoming" dimension:

in effect a precious peculiarity of the historic centre is that sensation of sudden suspension of movement we feel within it. Rhythms slow down, sounds are lower, activity elsewhere and the atmosphere is meditative as was the custom. Some distinct sound of steps, a door slamming, a subdued conversation in the background, then a bell (Zanini 2004, p. 136).

Promotional events for the territory frequently use in the same communicative project[22] a clear reference to a "different" time which, though easily placed in a given past epoch, often going back to the first half of the last century, still remains "different", or foreign to what is there nowadays in that place. It is "different" because it is a time of the mind, of memories, that will remain such, unchanged, in the future.

It is this place "the temple of reconstruction, iconism, that mania for reproduction that seems to characterise contemporary tourist space more and more pervasively. [...] Nature, the remote, history are portrayed in episodic frames and (con)fused in a magma of fragments... unconnectable" (Minca 1996, p. 128). In these icon-places the simulacrum dimension is realised thanks to getting beyond dialectics like authentic/inauthentic, true/false, real/imaginary: the life dimension into which the visitor is welcomed does not actually hide the truth but rather makes of that hiding its own reality, as the root of the word simulation suggests, simul- "in the same place as" and "at the same moment in which".[23]

The techniques of management and practices of construction of reality of the place, clearly conveyed by promotional events, have shown to what extent appeal is made – we do not yet know if in a completely unaware way – precisely to the dimension of the desirable, held in the memory of emotional experience of users. The "desire to believe" that runs together with the "desire to forget" is, as Caron has already observed, what steers the experience of place and underlies all those practices that supply such an experience to the visitor almost according to "dynamics of a hegemonic type" (Vidili 2000, p. 79; Urbinati 1998) underlying the dialectic between local institutions and resident population.

A certain co-responsibility of visitors is therefore implicit in this making and representing, traceable in the "nostalgia we experience for authenticity", "for real places and historic roots" (Goss 1993, pp. 83, 86).[24]

What then concurs with a process of "malling"[25] already begun (Goss 1993, p. 24) in our place/theme park is an instrumental use of the built-up environment and its architectural peculiarities espoused with knowledgeable management of multiple demands all referable to the sphere of the senses: sounds, smells, colours, images, lights of the place, together with sounds, smells, colours, images, lights of the demonstrative "set" of the craftsman, stimulate towards "total experiences" (Ruffini and Turchini 2006, p. 59) based on the need to evoke memories that substantiate the same experience [26] (Fig. 4).

Beyond the *Eu-topia* of the Centre

The appeal of thematisation examined up to now induces us to reconsider what the being-place of the place means, the hope of signification of a city and citizens that appear to have lost their capacities to understand, to understand *each other* reciprocally. The city has taken on its own *centre* as a trademark, practising in it a "[e]utopic model of spatial construction" that the thematisation of that centre represents[27] (Dall'Ara 2004, p. 145; Musarò 2005, 2006). The exchange dimension in view between the historic centre/theme park therefore proves socially sterile: what has been shown to the visitor/observer cannot prove productive of anything at all in that it is connoted within a dimension we would call "spectacular", and makes of the stage and self-exhibition (how one *would like* to be, that is one's realisation of the utopian ideal) its own existential horizon. In processes, too, it is a show: there cannot be a dialogue between place and inhabitants/observers (spectators). Relations are denied, dialogue is denied, barricaded behind the will to be and refusing the *possibility* to be. Possibility, it is easy to understand, includes the alternation of unpredictable happenings which would threaten the alienation of the glance whose fixity, ever directed at its own realised immanence, would be deviated towards the dangerousness of the unforeseen, discord, criticism. Possibility is excluded from Utopia (Resta 2004). Island isolated from the rest of the world, beyond an ocean of water, Experimental laboratory in which to develop a perfect, "happy" society. Utopia lays claim to the quest for a uniformity it has taken from the sea, from its surface always and everywhere the same as itself: this is how this place is, which is not a place, lacking any reference to ripples that would create friction: the land dimension is rich in these ripples, uneven surfaces that might stop or cause one to stumble along the way.

Fig. 4 A stall in one of the town streets with traditional men's clothes on sale

But Utopia has chosen not to be any part of the land place, dissimilar throughout, freeing itself from any *ethos*, forcing itself thus on itself, making itself One, smooth, uniform, synchronic, releasing itself from that past which would prevent its continuous, eternal looking at its own reflection. Man's will for emancipation from what ties him to this world and the Other lies in this, in its realisation: time and space are denied, halted, crystallised in a finite universe sufficient for themselves (Sorkin 2001, p. 9; Viceconte 2004). This is how social harmony ought to be realised, by achieving uniformity in perspectives, behaviours, points of view. It does not matter if we have to give up what idiosyncrasy there is in these perspectives, behaviours and views: what remains is an order, an orthodoxy of thought, transmitted through a dimension clear and remote from human discord, "the orthodoxy on which every utopian totalitarianism is founded" (Resta 2004, p. 3). Thus having emancipated itself, free from the liberty of the singular, this order revolves incessantly around itself, imposing itself as a unique, ever repeatable, order, to the point of *boredom:* "If perfection is achieved and the ideal realised, how can time continue to pass, what *novitas* should further be announced?" (Resta 2004). The happiness of a utopian society, therefore, is sadly reduced to the incessant return of what is already known, nothing is made to filter from what is outside, nothing *new* that could settle and undermine that absolute order.

The utopian ideal of the community, a happy community, harmony that is public, that belongs to everyone, is lost in this place that does not want to be Place and does not let itself be. The Town Centre is closed, like the isolated island of Utopia. Its aim is for self-realisation within and not beyond its confines, incorruptible bulwark of a utopian ideal of civil society, realised, perfect, happy even. The Centre becomes a theme, always the same as itself, an urban "fullness" closed and isolated with respect to empty urbanity, dissimilar and chaotic, out there: in here iron rules, homologating, were established, that have been lost in the achievement of the mirage of meaningful perfection. This Centre-Utopia is self-legitimising, it conveys as much as it can the unaware observer's glance towards certain modalities of reading and not others, leads him through certain pre-ordained interpretative and perceptive routes and not others, forcing him within a temporal and spatial circularity that is always the same: "*Concrete Island* (1974) by James Ballard, is [a novel] dedicated to the theme of an unfortunate motorist who crosses the guardrail (Maitland). After overstepping the central reservation in a rough area between three converging motorways, following an accident, he cannot get out" (Granelli 2005, p. 9). The centripetal logic of the thematised Centre draws to it but does not *accommodate* the "victim", making him a hostage instead, an involuntary spectator of its continuous, eternal make-up. It denies him speech, or better frames words in its own totalitarian logic within a certain type of argument that will not allow him to move away from what it is envisaged he will say (Dall'Ara 2004, p. 148); like Maitland, our spectator does not manage to leave the traffic island: "... it is not possible to know whether the centre is really the way out of the city or just another trap [?]" (Garofalo 2005, p. 8); which alternative route should be suggested to change this state of affairs? A possibility is given to us by the being-place of the place: "In the term utopia, prevalently used in the meaning *eu-topia*, a place not real but imaginary, in which to be able to project the aspiration of a happy city, the dream of a perfect society, Schmitt invites us, on the contrary, to perceive, in that negation of place (non-place), not so much the negation of reality in favour of imagination, as the drastic negation of *what is* place" (Resta 2004, p. 2). It is thus (a peculiarity of) place to abandon the utopian totalitarian project of reduction to Uniformity of what, on the contrary, resists and is dissimilar, surrendering to what exists that is unalterable outside one's own limits, in the willingness to welcome Other's values, and breaking with the fixedness of one's own glance at oneself, blinded by the richness of the complexity and dissonance of the innumerable voices that compose it. It is place to recompose oneself continually through practices, to recuperate an "ecosystemic" perspective that does not insert solidarity in values given within a fixedness once again utopian, but realises how much that ecosystem "rather than develop, balances, supports tensive relations between two paired subjects (city and inhabitant), which incorporate and manage circulating values", "enacted values and crystallised values" (Basso 2005, p. 1). The thematised historic centre, once island of Utopia, becoming place again, thus departs from these presuppositions.

It is perhaps useful to request a glance at this urban "fullness" where, on the contrary, it is vagueness that sets the pace: the vagueness of those *terrains* that are rich in ripples and cause us to stumble, of which the smooth, uniform sea of Utopia is free. Of course, for this step a certain humility is imposed, this also belonging to the being-place, humility "from *humus*, land, to indicate a type of 'moral and spiritual inclination towards modesty and smallness'" [...] "an honest recognition of what they are, what they could become; being near to the land, of the land..." (Burton-Christie 2003, p. 499). Strenuous defence of the identitarian values of the city, to the point of thematic persistence and sterile withdrawal into them, could be replaced by a mature recognition of shared historic values with which to accompany one's journey towards the realisation of a new order, simultaneously social and urban:

[...] the historicity of identity is given within a narrative perspective that brings values onto the scene, selecting those that need to be preserved and those that may be sacrificed. The axis of the connection between town and citizens is constituted by the practices, which are optimised in view of the possibilities/constructions offered by urban organisation and the cognitive and affective possibilities/skills of subjects. Social changes act and unfold in the relations between these variables [...] given that experiential meanings are constituted and regenerate in *being* and *acting in the city* (Basso 2005, p. 1).

To be and act in the city: it is perhaps possible that the Centre recuperates the inclination and above-mentioned willingness to (transitively) be of significance, and yet again, within a perspective "strongly encouraging dialogue" (Pozzato and Demaria 2005, p. 4). Far from the frills that produce nothing in this part of the town, the Centre, thus deprived of make-up, may let its imperfections, potholes, ugly parts, contradictions be evident, and thus possibilities, too: beneath a powder that covers and makes everything uniform this Centre shows those "traces, vision-arousers *par excellence*" (Ciuffi 2005, pp. 6–7), signs of past presences, emptiness, just as traces are empty and invite whoever wants to fill them with sense to try to translate their origin, and make of this lack a source of richness for future meaningful encounters. Our intent is risky of course to project the vagueness of sense within an urban universe that up to now has shown itself inflexible to any vivifying appeal coming from the outside: we also consider that it is precisely this vagueness, this emptiness that needs to be recuperated, not in abandoning care but in reformulating it, so as to leave ample spaces of thought, vision and filling, that will grasp in the capacity of losing oneself a new, fruitful possibility of finding oneself again, passing through different routes not pre-ordained and thus incomplete: this, moreover, is what the *terrains vagues* are, places that impose "putting into brackets what is defined, regulated, productive and civil, to contemplate as a cursive, emerging possibility what is vague, anomic, unproductive and rough. These spaces and these places are [...] opaque objects, the result of ambiguous perceptions [...] without being able to achieve the reassuring grip of a widespread, codified meaning..." (Granelli 2005, p. 2). This should be the starting point then; to move away from "conservative ethics" (Basso 2005, p. 13), and become, rather, defenders of the lack, as a "grip" for future continuous re-thinking, re-signifying. Make of the possibility and the happening, the interval, the interruption, the pause of an uninterrupted (urban) fullness, the possibility of one's *r*-existence (*r*-esistance). It will then be easier to enable a constant, fruitful dialogue to be established with a *com*munity "always open from what interrupts it, preventing its closure within itself", a community that is nothing more than "co-existence happening", "an event" (Resta 2004, p. 5).

Notes

[1]   This essay originated from a short piece of anthropological research in the field conducted by the author in the town of Nuoro in Sardinia between October and December 2007. The study aimed at identifying the strategies of construction of the real and thematisation of the urban place articulated at an institutional level. Although it was our desire to try to understand what the reaction to a similar strategy was by so-called users, via focused interviews and the distribution of questionnaires, we are compelled for editorial reasons not to give specific space to this type of response, which will be dealt with elsewhere. More than one hint will, however, be given for reading the pages that follow, at the type of interaction that has come about between institutional strategies of construction of the reality of the place and visitors/users/consumers of it.

[2]   The term *utopia* derives from the Greek *ou+tópos*, "non-place", and at the same time from *eu+tópos*, "happy place". A non-place is thus simultaneously a happy place. The outcome of such reciprocal meaning bears interesting consequences, as we intend to show also in connection with the case study referred to.

[3]   The author intends to give reasons for the complex phenomenology of the *terrains vagues* in relation to the position and relationship these places have with the city: Hall's classification (1966) adopted by him and to which we briefly refer here (a pre-ordained, semi-determined and informal space), aims at reflecting on spaces as active frames, culturally connoted, suggesting particular modalities of access, behaviour and expectations for those who have relations with them.

[4]   Pericoli G (2004) *Appunti sulla comunicazione polisensoriale*,
http://www.comunotazione.it/leggi.asp?id_art=744&id_area=143[12/07].

[5]   *Ibidem.*

[6]   Capital town of a province stretching across the central-eastern part of Sardinia, Italy, enclosing mountainous territory.

[7]   The term "derelict places" is used by the author to indicate "vast territories distinguished by the decline of small centres, whose slight demographic dimensions determine the closure of basic public services. They are often the result of excessive dependence on mono-productive activities, as arises in places historically involved in agro-pastoral activities", such as the territories in question (Serreli 2008, p. 145).

[8]   The latter has become an umbrella trademark under which a series of initiatives are also of a promotional kind have been directed and to which numerous municipalities of the interior have adhered with different events aimed at promoting their cultural and productive specificities. Many of the local realities involved are situated in mountainous territories and their production is concentrated mostly in the autumn period, so that it was decided to have the already existing religious and feast days organised by single organisations for themselves join in a coordinated communicative project called "Autumn in Barbagia", giving an image to the autumn season that would be a reference point

for all these events. An ill-concealed will to keep their distance and differentiate exists on the part of the organisers with regard to the events planned for the other municipalities on the territory. This need is visible even in the graphic project designed for the event. Although images we might call "indicative" of the productive and cultural specificities of each village were acquired with the aim of giving life to a communicative project conveying a common message for the entire event, the event organisers chose to go ahead with their own, completely separate, project, parallel to the institutional one. The logo they chose was that of the bronze sculpture entitled *Il pane (Bread)* by the sculptor from Nuoro, Francesco Ciusa. Mastros in Santu Predu "is not an extemporary initiative addressing the tourist but a route dedicated first of all to the people of Nuoro, and then the Sards. It is an element from which to depart on a process of stable construction, an opportunity for growth and visibility [...] so that everyone can rediscover the trades able to offer quality and uniqueness of goods, a concentrate of craftwork apace with the times. Mastros in Santu Predu will be an opportunity for cultural exchange where visitors may ... observe the manuality that enhances arts and crafts, combining cultural visits to churches, museums of popular traditions, modern art, archaeology and manor houses of distinguished fellow citizens" (Mastros in Santu Predu Catalogue, Studio Stampa, Nuoro, 2004, p. 8).

[9]   "The original idea was to use particular frames, the cortes, namely the courtyards of old houses in historic centres, a place already well defined, therefore, to present both products and craftsmanship, a classic case of experiential acquisition: I see when they make *carasau* bread within a frame ... I see, I am a participant in the productive process of something typical in its natural environment. *Carasau* bread is certainly not made in factories or in what are these days artisans' workshops equipped with electric ovens; *carasau* bread was born in that context there and it is beautiful and fascinating to see it in that context there; carasau bread, just like the knives, the salami, all those typical products of our territories" (Chamber of Commerce operator).

[10]   As well as ceramic goods there are numerous examples of handicraft work exhibited during this event in which we were able to find the same references to symbolism that is, let us say, traditional. Editorial reasons, however, oblige us to give a list of these in another context.

[11]   It is important to emphasise that what we are referring to and what is, moreover, a function of the event, is the temporal dimension in which the quarter is placed in its form of portrayal. To simplify, whereas the urban place San Pietro persists in a contemporary temporal dimension, the portrayal given of it is almost a-temporal, as it is crystallised in a past epoch in which features, at this point lost – and the subject of research – can now be found, as is shown by events like this one.

[12]   Caron (1993, p. 127). With this neologism we mean to draw attention to the mechanisms of construction of reality practised in theme parks.

[13]   Another example referring to our case study, in which the place is constructed as an imagined image of itself, withdrawing itself into a self-referential dimension and becoming consecrated in terms of what grants it sense: 'In this

sense the unusual position of the building [Mulino Gallisai, centre of the future "Museo e Laboratori dell'Identità"] in the Santu Pedru quarter where, a few metres from Deledda's house, the homes stand of the sculptor, Francesco Ciusa, and the poet, Sebastiano Satta; the library and the square, designed by Costantino Nivola, bearing the poet's name; the Cathedral of Santa Maria della Neve, the church of the Rosario and that of San Carlo, where Francesco Ciusa is buried. The pages of Salvatore Satta's novel *Il giorno del giudizio* (Day of Justice), an international literary case, have contributed to the consecration of the cultural relevance of the entire quarter, as has the opening of the MAN Contemporary Art Museum (Regione Sardegna 2007). This example clarifies better the intent to thematise the urban place that becomes an icon of itself and reiterates with strength its intention to call itself the place of the lost identity of the town.

14 A poet and writer of Nuoro, this artist presents a cross-section of life in Nuoro and, in general, describes the minds of men who are born and live in inland Sardinia. As occurred with Grazia Deledda, his personality and work constitute a reliable cultural approach which lends itself well to events exploiting recent experiential marketing strategies.

15 It is useful to remember that the communication strategies for events have implicit time and space references. What we are keen to point out in this chapter is how much the place/quarter has also been used as an object in this strategy. An example is the choice on the part of the organisers, of particular views inside the quarter such as places with an immediate historic reference (the house where Nobel prize winner Deledda was born, Ciusa's house, buildings not yet subjected to such formal and structural handling as to modify their "traditional" character, etc.).

16 "To walk among the stone houses of the historic centres, watch the craftsmen at work, taste the genuine flavour of typical products, discover the secrets of a thousand-year-old culture with the splendid backdrop of uncontaminated nature [...]. Week after week the inhabitants of each village will gather round their guests with an embrace from the whole community, and will leave unforgettable emotions in the heart of the visitor [...]. Above everything the belonging to an authentic land stands out, with a precise soul of its own, with a profile that is both austere and gentle at the same time" (Information leaflet for Autumn in Barbagia and Cortes Apertas 2006). "[...] it will be possible to become immersed in a pathway out of time, in search of flavours and more authentic flavours" (Information leaflet for Autumn in Barbagia and Cortes Apertas 2007). At "Mastros in Santu Predu" [...] visitors can savour suggestive atmospheres, observe the manuality that enhances arts and crafts..." "Cobbled streets and squares are an enchanting frame for their path, and lead them by the hand to welcoming workshops, offering a concentrate of art, history, culture and the fruit of creative minds. Expert hands will be seen, moulding noble, natural, precious materials ..." (Mastros in Santu Predu Catalogue 2004, p. 8). "For the Mastros in Santu Predu daily life is transformed into shapes and colours. Here we see pottery and jewelry, sculptures and paintings, skins and woodwork, typical cakes. Thanks to these workers the old heart of Nuoro is

revived. A path through memory to rediscover local traditions and craftsmanship. What a feeling then, to see the Mastros in Santu Predu intent on their work in an unforgettable Autumn in Barbagia" (Mastros in Santu Predu Catalogue 2004, p. 6).

[17] The 2006 leaflet for the event includes a drawing in naïf style showing a square in front of a church that appears to have a central role in a small urban dimension. In the square a group of children are intent on traditional street games; in the background a cart has been left in front of a house, two women wait to draw water from the spring, while courtyard animals scratch freely in the wide open space.

[18] *Le nuove frontiere del marketing della comunicazione: la forza delle emozioni,* http://www.ideateca.it/focus/com_nuovefrontiere.asp

[19] "[…] nowadays, to wander round the district of s'Ispina Santa means to know close-up the troubles and dark thoughts of Pietro Benu and Maria Noina, the tragic heroes of *La via del male,* while grandmother Agostina Marini continues to reign in Via Chironi […] you can almost hear, from *L'incendio nell'oliveto* and in Piazza del Rosario, the songs of the *novenanti* (women participating in ancient rites) round the bonfire at the feast of St. Francis of Lula, admirably narrated in Elias Portolu by the great authoress of Nuoro. These writings help us to recuperate the noble identity of the town, for the thoughts, atmospheres, dreams of our artists have contributed to including this small provincial capital in the vast patrimony of the geography of world literature". The visitor to San Pietro makes "a journey among characters, images, atmospheres, flavours, perfumes and colours of the Deledda universe", *Nuoro città da leggere. Una strada, un romanzo,* project of the *I segni delle radici* (Cultural Association). This project ideated by "I segni delle radici" resulted in the realisation of a series of writings on the walls of the buildings along various paths of the San Pietro quarter, written by the author of the project himself, in connection with the themes treated in some of Deledda's novels. These writings each quote an extract from one of the authoress' novels.

[20] Among the visual stimuli are the writings on the walls evoking images and stories of other times, writings involving direct reference to the Nobel prize winner; sound, traditional choirs; smell, tasting of typical products like cheese, salami, wine, (etc.).

[21] "A theme also shown as central is the investment the community of Nuoro has made in the old centre as a treasure chest of art, with the written inscriptions and routes through the Deledda park, the evocative sculptures of modern artists but also contemporary ones, the MAN... Basically, places of official identitarian recognition may be the subject of a cultural marketing project" (Zanini 2004, p. 136).

[22] We refer to both the reference to the Mastros and the choice of the logo (the sculpture "Il pane" by F. Ciusa, the famous sculptor of Nuoro), which portrays a woman intent on kneading bread dough, sitting on the floor – now no longer the custom.

[23] *See the entry Simulacrum,* http://design.iuav.it/~comunicarti/simulacro.htm

[24] The event "Mastros in Santu Predu was born from the need to revitalise and recuperate the historic centre where values of solidarity and unity have remained alive through time. A mirror of the social and cultural identities that characterise it, the historic centre gives life to new creative experiences that lead to it being an element of identification of the town". (Mastros in Santu Predu Catalogue 2004, p. 8).

[25] The use of the term *malling* may be referred in this instance to the progressive appropriation of features and themes peculiar to the urban place and their use for commercial purposes. The image itself of the place is sold, for what it represents for the whole town and the surrounding territory.

[26] "[…] sometimes they are values that seem very basic, but let us discover them ..! to see the hearth inside Chironi's house has a very important meaning, it is an ancestral instrument in a town, in such an important dwelling as Chironi's house would have been, compared with the other homes of the epoch; the hearth was there, like in the sheep-pen with the four stones … and then there was the oven next to it, the washtub, etc…, namely it could be seen that communities were there, from there we came and have to rediscover ourselves in the city – even though everything is taken for granted, actually it is not. Here, we have stopped" (TF, Associazione Tracas).

[27] 'Urban confectioner's', is how Wim Wenders defines the gestures of cleaning up and restoration which instead of establishing a link with the past are transforming it into a cliché, "dressed up past", says the film producer, "made to shine" (Ciuffi 2005).

References

Aiello G, Donvito R (2005) *Comunicazione integrata nell'abbigliamento: strategie di marca e ruolo del punto vendita nella distribuzione specializzata statunitense.* In: Andreani JC, Collesei U, *Le tendenze del marketing in Europa*, Paris, 21–22 gennaio, Congress organised by the École Supérieure de Commerce, Paris (ESCP-EAP) and the Ca' Foscari University of Venice http://www.escp-eap.net/conferences/marketing/2005_cp/Materiali/Paper/It/Materiali/Paper/It/Aiello_Donvito.pdf

Augé M (2002) *Disneyland e altri nonluoghi*, Bollati Boringhieri, Torino.

Baglini (2006), *Il turismo e il marketing esperienziale* http://www.psicologiaturistica.it/topic.asp?TOPIC_ID=44&FORUM_ID=4&CAT_ID=1&Forum_Title=Turisti+per+caso%2E%2E%2E&Topic_Title=Turismo+e+Marketing+Esperienziale[12/07].

Basso P (2005) *Identità della città storica, identità dei cittadini* http://www.ec-aiss.it/archivio/tematico/spazialita/citta.php

Bell J (1998) *Disney's Times Square: The New American Community Theatre.* TDR n. 42(1), pp. 26–33.

Bendix R (1989) *Tourism and cultural displays: Inventing traditions for whom?* The Journal of American Folklore n. 102(404), pp. 131–146.

Burton-Christie D (2003) *The wild and the sacred.* Anglican Theological Review n. 85(3), pp. 493–510.

Carcassi M (2007) *Nuoro e il piano urbanistico da discutere. Un'occasione per la "città senza" che non ha mai saputo costruirsi un futuro.* L'Altra Voce.net http://www.altravoce.net/2007/12/07/senza.html[12/07].

Caron BR (1993) *Magic kingdoms. Towards a post-modern ethnography of sacred places.* Kyoto Journal n. 25, pp. 125–130.

Ciuffi V (2005) *Terrains vagues: il rovescio dei vuoti urbani.* In: *Per una semiotica della città. Spazi sociali e culture metropolitane,* 33rd Conference of the AISS, San Marino, 28–30 October
http://www.associazionesemiotica.it/index.php?option=com_content&task=view&id=59&Itemid=67

Codeluppi V (2005) *La città come vetrina* In: *Per una semiotica della città. Spazi sociali e culture metropolitane,* 33rd Conference of the AISS, San Marino, 28–30 October
http://www.associazionesemiotica.it/index.php?option=com_content&task=view&id=59&Itemid=67

Cohen E (1989a) *The commercialization of ethnic crafts.* Journal of Design History n. 2(2/3), pp. 161–168.

Cohen E (1989b) *Primitive and remote. Hill tribe trekking in Thailand.* Annals of Tourism Research n. 16, pp. 30–61.

Dall'Ara E (2004) *Costruire per temi i paesaggi? Esiti spaziali della semantica nei parchi tematici europei.* Quaderni della Ri-Vista Ricerche per la progettazione del paesaggio n. 1(3), pp. 144–161.

Fabbri P, Marrone G (2000) *Semiotica in Nuce. I fondamenti e l'epistemologia strutturale,* Meltemi, Roma.

Featherstone M (1991) *Consumer culture and postmodernism,* Sage, London.

Ferraresi M, Schmitt BH (2006) *Marketing esperienziale. Come sviluppare l'esperienza di consumo,* FrancoAngeli, Milano.

Garofalo F (2005) *Città e cultura. Analisi di La città di Ricardo Barreiro e Juan Gimenez.*
http://www.associazionesemiotica.it/index.php?option=com_content&task=view&id=59&Itemid=67

Giannone M (1996) *Le immagini e le realtà dello spazio turistico: l'esperienza virtuale del viaggio.* In: *Il Viaggio. Dal Grand Tour Al Turismo Post-Industriale,* Papers of International Conference, Rome 5–6 December 1996, Edizioni Magma, Napoli.

Goss J (1993) *The magic of the mall: an analysis of form, function, and meaning in the contemporary built environment.* Annals of the Association of American Geographers n. 83(1), pp. 18–47.

Granelli T (2005) *Per una semiotica del terrain vague: da luogo anomico a dérive passionale* In: *Per una semiotica della città. Spazi sociali e culture metropolitane,* 33rd Conference of the AISS, San Marino, 28–30 October
http://www.associazionesemiotica.it/index.php?option=com_content&task=view&id=59&Itemid=67.

Gupta A, Ferguson J (1992) *Beyond culture: space, identity, and the politics of difference*. Cultural Anthropology n. 7(1), pp. 6–23.

Hall ET (1966) *The hidden dimension*, Doubleday, Garden city NY.

Harvey D (1993) *La crisi della modernità*, Il Saggiatore, Milano.

Hughes G (1995) *Authenticity in tourism*. Annals of Tourism Research n. 22(4), pp. 781–803.

Lanfant MF, Allcock JB, Bruner EM (eds) (1995) *International tourism. Identity and change*, Sage, London.

MacCannell D (1973) *Staged authenticity: Arrangements of social space in tourist settings*. The American Journal of Sociology n. 79(3), pp. 589–603.

Minca C (1996) *Lo spazio turistico postmoderno*. In: *Il Viaggio. Dal Grand Tour Al Turismo Post-Industriale*, Papers of International Conference, Roma 5–6 December 1996, Edizioni Magma, Napoli.

Mondardini Morelli G (ed) (2000) *Miti della natura. Mondi della cultura. Turismo, parchi e saperi locali in Sardegna*, Edes, Sassari.

Moore A (1980) *Walt Disney World: Bounded ritual space and the playful pilgrimage center*. Anthropological Quarterly n. 53(4), pp. 207–218.

Musarò P (2005) *Ci vediamo in centro. Pratiche di consumo e nuovi significati dei luoghi* http://www.associazionesemiotica.it/index.php?option=com_content&task=view&id=59&Itemid=67

Musarò P (2006) *Ci Vediamo in centro, Pratiche di consumo e nuovi significati dei luoghi*, Rivista dell' Associazione Italiana di Studi Semiotici Online.

Nelson V (2005) *Representation and images of people, place and nature in Grenada's tourism*. Geografiska Annaler n. 87 B(2), pp. 131–143.

Pericoli G (2003) *Il Marketing Esperienziale* http://www.mercatoglobale.com/index.php?option=com_content&task=view&id=558&Itemid=8>[12/07].

Pericoli G (2004) *Appunti sulla comunicazione polisensoriale* http://www.comunotazione.it/leggi.asp?id_art=744&id_area=143[12/07].

Pinna L (1997) *Le culture costruttive nel quartiere di San Pietro a Nuoro*, Degree Thesis, Facoltà di Lettere e Filosofia, Università di Sassari, Sassari.

Pozzato MP, Demaria C (2005) *Etnografia urbana: Modi d'uso e pratiche dello spazio* In: *Per una semiotica della città. Spazi sociali e culture metropolitane*, 33rd Conference of the AISS, San Marino, 28–30 October http://www.associazionesemiotica.it/index.php?option=com_content&task=view&id=59&Itemid=67

Regione Sardegna (2007) *Nuoro. L'ex Mulino Gallisai ospiterà il Museo dell'Identità*, http://www.regione.sardegna.it/j/v/13?s=56229&v=2&c=57&t=1[12/07]

Resta C (2004) *L'utopia della felicità pubblica*. Comunità, Round Table at the Festival of Philosophy of Cosenza on the theme: Utopia/Eresia, Cosenza, 21–23 May, http://www.geofilosofia.it/pelagos/Resta_utopia2.html [02/08].

Ruffini A, Turchini F (2006) *Marketing esperienziale: sentimenti ed emozioni... vendesi*. Federmobili n. 5, pp. 58–60.

Serreli S (2008), *Derelict Places as Alternative Territories of the City*. In: Maciocco G (ed), *The Territorial Future of the City*, Springer-Verlag, Berlin, Heidelberg, New York, pp. 145–159.

Shenhav-Keller S (1995) *The Jewish pilgrim and the purchase of a souvenir in Israel*. In: Lanfant MF, JB Allcock, EM Bruner (eds) *International tourism. identity and change*, Sage, London.

Simpson F (1999) *Tourist impact in the historic centre of Prague: Resident and visitor perceptions of the historic built environment*. The Geographical Journal n. 165(2), pp. 173–183.

Sorkin M (2001) *La tematizzazione della città*. Lotus n. 109, pp. 7–17.

Urbinati N (1998) *From the periphery of modernity: Antonio Gramsci's theory of subordination and hegemony*. Political Theory n. 26(3), pp. 370–391.

Urry J (1994) *Time, leisure and social identity*. Time & Society n. 3(2), pp. 131–149.

Viceconte E (2004) *L'esperienza del luogo e del tempo*. Working Paper, Stoa' http://eprints.stoa.it/180/

Vidili M (2000) *Paradisi Incontaminati. Metafore del puro e dell'esotico nella rappresentazione dei parchi marini*. In: Mondardini Morelli G (ed) *Miti della natura. Mondi della cultura. Turismo, parchi e saperi locali in Sardegna*, Edes, Sassari.

Waitt G (1997) *Selling paradise and adventure: representations of landscape in the tourist advertising of Australia*. Australian Geographical Studies n. 35(1), pp. 47–60.

Wang N (1999) *Rethinking authenticity in tourism experience*. Annals of Tourism Research n. 26(2), pp. 349–370.

Zanini L (2004) *Il centro storico di Nuoro: percorsi tematici e luoghi*. In: Falzetti A (ed) *Riscoprire la città. Nuovi paesaggi per lo spazio urbano*, Argos, Roma.

3. Creative Places and Cultural Matrices of the City

The city is the privileged place for the production and fruition of cultural patrimony; regeneration processes are activated within it that link up with the culture and leisure economies. The attractiveness of cities is based on the local spatial landmarks that incorporate their cultural history patrimony but also on ties with the dimensions of innovation and creativity, with more universal and global reference points. Creativity does not just involve physical places but the processes of interaction and communication that favour the generation of cultural and social innovation. Creativity may then become the precondition for organising change and building future perspectives for the city.

Creativity of Places as a Resource for Cultural Tourism

Oliver Frey

Creativity and Knowledge as a Factor for Local Identity

Over recent years there has been much talk about creativity – as an individual property, as capital, as a "connecting device" in the context of new networks, as a model of governance based more on the civil society with regard to the relationship between state, community and market and, most notably, as a starting point for cities and regions to survive economically or to provide position features that can be sold even more effectively in the competition of metropolises and regions.

This new embedding of social and economic processes in local or regional spaces becomes particularly clear with bigger cities. Cities have always been the place where radical social change becomes visible first of all. They underlie permanent change at the macro-level of economy and culture, driven by the motor of changing social structures (Zukin 1995). Also, cities are themselves the cause and location of processes of social change. In particular, big cities create stimulation of structural change for society as a whole by the momentum of how they are socially, politically, culturally and economically constituted.

The social, economic and cultural change which results in new developments of urban culture influences the meaning and perception of cultural tourism. The basic thesis of this paper is that by way of these transformation processes towards a knowledge-based "services city" a new way of embedding social and economic processes into local places is happening. Creativity and different types of knowledge play a major role in the development of cultural tourism. The interaction of built environment, social structures and processes at creative places in some neighbourhoods is seen as a resource for cultural tourism. The basic thesis acts on the assumption that places express their complex urban identities by way of different "languages" (physical morphology, social and economic structuredness and communicative interaction). These "languages of creative places", the spatial complexity of structural, social, economic and cognitive factors are seen as a specific local identity which can be read and understood by a certain milieu of cultural tourists.

G. Maciocco, S. Serreli (eds.), *Enhancing the City*, Urban and Landscape Perspectives 6,
DOI 10.1007/978-90-481-2419-0_7, © Springer Science+Business Media B.V. 2009

Creativity and the "Renaissance of the City"

Within the discourse on the "renaissance of the cities" theoreticians and practitioners argue in favour of economies which are highly dependent on being embedded in an urban context and which may thus contribute to restructuring the urban landscape (Judd et al. 1999; Läpple 2003; Dangschat 2006). The paper will take up theories on the knowledge society and will consider the meaning of images and symbols to be highly significant for the production and consumption of urban places (Featherstone and Lash 1999). Terms such as "cultural economy", "cultural industries" or "creative economy" (O' Connor 1999) raise hopes of an economic upswing and urban-spatial re-evaluation among urban politicians, urban developers or economic developers.[1] The social-scientific diagnosis of a knowledge-based services society indicates that concrete places in the city are of increasing significance for the production and consumption of specific, individual services (Castells 1996). In this context, cities are considered privileged places for both the production and the consumption of cultural goods and services but also places of social innovation. In this sense an urban cultural tourism contributes by its economic and social effects to a "renaissance of the city".

For this paper, creativity will be defined as the ability to produce new original ideas with the help of knowledge. Based on creativity, innovation is considered a general term for the ability to develop new and original solutions. The precondition for this is the ability to give up old ways of thinking or points of view and to make new, surprising connections, to find new connections between given data and structures (Kunzmann 2004).

In the context of the theoretical debates on the "renaissance of the city", the "creative milieus" (Hall 1998; Landry 2000; Florida 2002) play a particular role as bearers of civil society innovations and stimulators of urban development and renewal. They are said to represent an economic added value in the field of cultural industry as well as to stimulate civil society innovation for the related concepts of "innovative milieus" (Aydalot 1986; Camagni 1995), "knowledge milieus" (Matthiessen 2004) and the "creative milieu" (Frey 2008). The thesis of this paper is that the "creative milieu" as a specific social group within cultural tourism is highly mobile and internationally connected by the spheres of work and leisure.

The Role of Cultural Tourism as a Sector of Urban Development

Cultural tourism started to be recognised as a distinct product category in the late 1970s when tourism marketers and tourism researchers realized that some people travelled specifically to gain a deeper understanding of the culture or heritage of a destination. In the 1990s cultural tourism was recognised as a high-profile, mass market activity (Richards 1996). Cultural tourism was seen as a double-edged sword by the cultural heritage management community. On the one hand, increased demand by tourists provided a powerful political and economic justification to expand conservation activities. On the other hand, increased visitation, overuse, inappropriate use and the commodification of the same assets without regard for their cultural values posed a real threat to the integrity and – in extreme cases – to the very survival of the assets (Law 1993).

Ritchie and Zins (1978) defined cultural tourism as one of the key elements that attract tourists to particular destinations. Furthermore, they identified the 12 cultural elements which attract tourists to these destinations. These are briefly the handicrafts, traditions, gastronomy, leisure activities and dress. Some other elements that they identified are the educational system and the religions. Cultural tourism is recognised as a form of special interest tourism, where culture forms the basis of either attracting tourists or motivating people to travel.

Cultural tourism is concerned with a local culture, especially its arts and involves the interrelationships between people, places and cultural heritage (Zeppel et al. 1992). For this paper cultural tourism is focused on urban areas and their cultural facilities such as museums and theatres in "creative districts". The World Tourism Organization (WTO) defines cultural tourism as "movements of persons essentially for cultural motivations such as study tours, performing arts and cultural tours, travel to festivals and other events, visits to sites and monuments, travel to study nature, folklore or art and pilgrimages" (WTO 1985, p. 6). Cultural tourism activities include the use not only of cultural heritage assets like archaeological sites, museums, castles, palaces, historical buildings, famous buildings and ruins but also vibrant cultural urban areas with their festivals, events, music and dance or subculture communities.

The aim of this paper is to determine the effects of cultural tourism on cities and their neighbourhoods in the context of gentrification. Culture according to Brislin (1993) consists of ideals, values and assumptions about life that are widely shared among people who guide a specific type of behaviour – in the sense of this paper: the "creative milieu". Culture or civilization is that complex whole which includes knowledge, beliefs, art, moral law, customs and other capabilities and habits acquired by man as a member of society. Culture is an essential part of human and urban life, a dynamic and evolving component of community, a continuous link from the past to the present and through to the future. Cultural tourism does not have much effect on buildings but on social structures of neighbourhoods. In this sense cultural tourism influences the images, experiences, actions and cultures of neighbourhoods. The social, cultural and environmental impact of tourism will be presented in the following section.

Impacts of Cultural Tourism

Cultural tourists usually get involved in special events and festivals and they participate in the normal daily life of their destination. They buy some goods or services from the residents, spend some time with the people in the neighbourhood and meet and share ideas and information with the residents. Cultural tourism has an intercultural dimension with many different cultures being related and integrated in a communication process (de Kadt 1979). Nonetheless, it may also bring forth a clash of cultures. There may be a face-to-face encounter between the new, arriving culture and the local culture. Tourists' attitudes may be construed as inappropriate and excessive and these attitudes can be annoying for the local people. The cultural tourist may erode the local culture and this may result in the loss and even disappearance of the unique identity of the local cultural heritage. This encounter may also decrease the demand on the tourism of this area and the area may lose ground day by day.

The main negative impact induced by the tourist-host relationship is the economic effect, when the consumption of cultural goods by residents changes the identity of the place. The tourist-host relationship is characterised by four major features. These are the transitory, the unequal and unbalanced, lack of spontaneity and limitation by spatial and temporal constraints. These impacts arise when tourism brings about a change in value systems and behaviour and thereby threatens indigenous identity (Boniface 1998).

The most negative impacts on the place visited are the commercialisation of local cultures, the revitalisation or commoditisation, the loss of cultural authenticity and damaging of the heritage and historical sites by cultural tourists. Furthermore, there is the issue of changing the language usage of the host. Tourism may turn local cultures into commodities when religious rituals, traditional ethnic rites and festivals are reduced and sanitised to conform to tourist expectations.

A negative impact on local culture is, for example, habits concerning food and alcohol, and dress which can bring about a change in the traditional attitudes of the residents. These impacts can be observed with a specific social group of tourists, especially in underdeveloped countries. As an impact on the environment: more obsolescence, waste pollution, garbage, noise and air pollution. A rise in prices, such as rents and the cost of land, may constitute an impact on economy, also the clothes, finery and catering costs in the process of the gentrification of neigbourhoods (Smith 1979).

In regions or deprived areas which are undergoing rapid urban change, the benefits of cultural tourism lie in a potential increase in economic development As a result, some beneficial effects on communities and their cultures can occur (Besculides et al. 2002). The appropriate presentation of assets may assist the tourists' understanding of the need for the revitalisation and retention of important cultural heritage assets in general. Opportunities may arise to develop local economies to be more entrepreneurial and self-reliant. Revenue from tourism can be directed towards local infrastructure improvement. Reinvigoration of traditional culture can occur. Cultural exchange with tourists may lead to greater tolerance of cultural differences in multicultural societies. Revenue from tourism can be reinvested in the documentation, planning and management of heritage assets. This is important for the sustainability of assets that attract heavy visitation.

Tourism may provide cultural exchange, revitalisation and enhanced quality of life. Community life, sharing ideas and social interaction may be the positive impacts of tourism (Law 1992; Jafari 1997).

Places as Socio-Spatial Entities and their Cultural Capital

This paper is based on preliminary theoretical works on the complexity of places as rational socio-spatial entities consisting of (a) physical structures like housing and infrastructures, as well as people as physical bodies, (b) regulation regimes (like urban planning and design) and processes like markets, (c) symbolisation of places by architecture, social groups and images and (d) the behaviour of social groups as a result of the construction of the socio-spatial realities of socially constructed, relational spaces (Lefebvre 1991; Thrift 1996; Crang 2000; Löw 2001; Soja 2001).

Places tell the stories of their structural environment; they have identities which go beyond physical structures. Places and their cultural capital differ in their social and emotional structuredness, their creative potential, the "language spoken" (in a metaphorical sense) and in the built environment through its appearance and form. Research on the cultural capital of places focuses on methodological debates and approaches in order to make the practical, emotional, social and structural identities of places visible, in the sense of a kind of "language matters" by way of architecture, utilisation and consumption (Lash et al. 1994; Bryan 2001; Markus et al. 2001).

The cultural capital and creative resources of places are a resource for attracting cultural tourists. In this context, "creative milieus" – as specific social groups of cultural tourists – are considered cultural pioneers who by their ways of producing and consuming space in the "niches" of neighbourhoods re-evaluate "doubtful" places and have a decisive influence on them (revitalisation). This process of producing and perceiving public spaces affects a neighbourhood by changing its economic and social structures.

The public space is used and consumed by cultural tourists, and they construct their own social-spatial reality and their ways of perception and cognition. The cultural capital of creative places might contribute to supporting a kind of "creative" city marketing or kinds of "place-making" strategies (Healey 2004). Furthermore, different aspects must be considered, such as legal regulations for adjusting to new demands for space by cultural tourists or possible spatial effects on creative industries. The mode of restrained planning is necessary or reasonable for letting creative milieus become established and develop in certain quarters. On the other hand – in the sense of "empowerment" – it must be determined which kinds of support for creative processes are suitable for making the self-management of those open structures possible which "creative people" need for their work and leisure. Thus, apart from focusing on the place as a creativity-developing resource, there must be consideration of "producers of creativity". In this context the functions of trust, solidarity and context-bound, implicit knowledge in "creative milieus" are of particular importance. They are supposed to impart information on the organisational, networking, work and life patterns of creative milieus, so that requirements for the support of culture and economy or incentive-based creativity development can be derived from them.

The connection and interaction between tourism, place, space and creativity raises the following questions: Which are the social-spatial conditions for which kind of creativity? Which structural-spatial and social constellations make a place a creative place and attractive for cultural tourists? How may the social-spatial resources of a place be "understood" (by reading and listening) by the creative milieu of cultural tourists? The field of cultural tourism, urban planning, urban design and creativity raises the following questions: How could the informal, creative potential of places be employed for urban development with the help of direct or innovative, indirect ways of steering? What tools and methods of urban development and tourist marketing are to be used to exploit the potential of creative places?

Creative Places and their Neighbourhoods as a Resource

The urban research scientific community increasingly supports the idea that globalisation has enhanced the importance of (urban) places such as districts and public spaces for the self-organisation of both knowledge-based services society and the civil society ("glocalisation"). Even if virtual communication is opening up completely new worlds of information exchange and communication, the local/regional level based on face-to-face contact becomes more and more important for anchoring economic, cultural and social processes. This paper will suggest some of the ways in which places and districts at inner-city sites are contributing to a renaissance of the European city by way of their role as "vibrant places", both through processes of gentrification and by being a leisure location for cultural tourism.

"Place matters!" This is true – despite increased mobility and cultural globalisation – also for cultural city tourists. They search for local identity and the atmosphere of a city. In this context a particular creativity for developing local, locality-related identities, specific for the place and its people, plays an important role for the city visitors. Cultural city tourists do not only want to watch, they want to experience or live and "feel" a city. For this, place-related knowledge and an understanding of the "languages of places" are necessary.

Those artists' milieus as they developed in certain quarters in Berlin, Vienna, Zurich, New York, Paris or London in the nineteenth and early twentieth centuries were often fertile ground for place-related creativity of a neighbourhood. As characteristics of neighbourhoods and cities which are fertile ground for creativity and culture we may give the following conditions: the city as a social space which, due to its density, size and heterogeneity, offers places of encounter and exchange. In the city creativity finds its place for socially heterogeneous, different life profiles, values and ways of life. There the "creative milieu" develops places and neighbourhoods which – through the process of social interaction and communication – find it easier to create cultural innovations and are attractive for cultural tourism in cities.

Creative places, visited as such by a certain kind of city tourist are found in neighbourhoods where the (intermediate) use of former sites of industrial trade, empty ground floor places, deserted former industrial sites or other "niches" offer potential for attracting urban cultural tourism. Due to their physical-material predispostion and their urban-developmental and social-structural neighbourhood, these places offer a resource. Also, the social-spatial structures of these places make communication between, and the encounter of, different social worlds possible. By means of place, city tourists, being a certain milieu, may mobilise a kind of knowledge which, thanks to cultural codes, images and symbols, makes commonly shared social interpretation possible. Thus, the capital of the place is twofold: as a structural-spatial structure where it is possible to experiment and which allows for creative actions and ways of behaviour and, on the other hand, as a store of signs and symbols which makes identification possible for the milieu. Through place, knowledge and information are handed over via networks as social capital.

The "resource of place" is structured in three dimensions: (a) the physical-material constitution of the place and the consequent possible forms of utilisation, (b) a cultural symbolism of the place which uses symbols and systems of symbols to secure the milieu's preferences in taste and thus contributes to creating an identity. This atmosphere of local identity marks the "*habitus* of the place" (Dangschat 1996), (c) the neighbourhood environment of the place, which by its utilisation and activation structures the socio-spatial habitat of the place and (d) infrastructural features and the connection of the quarter to city structures.

The symbolism of the old industrial place with its historic narratives and images was not disposed of in this context but re-contextualised. The product of this re-interpretation of place-memory is an amalgamated superstructuring of many different narratives which constitutes the "genus loci". The atmosphere of the place thus created takes up a habitus which relates the current form of creative work and development of immaterial ideas to the historic-material production of goods at the former industrial location. These derelict industrial sites in the inner city give evidence of past industrial production and – as "the old shell of labour" (Dangschat 1999) – are newly attractive for cultural tourists.

Creativity and Cultural City Tourism

Tourists identify first with these neighbourhoods (Scheunenviertel or Prenzlauer Berg in Berlin, Ottensen, Schanzen- or Karo-Viertel in Hamburg,

Gallus and Ostend in Frankfurt, the East End of London, Belleville in Paris, Bronx in New York), and, second, they arrange their tourism time in flexible patterns of use of time and space. The latter requires that the local infrastructure be similarly flexible: breakfast until 4 p.m., hot meals until 5 a.m., shopping, pizza delivery and mobility round the clock. Beyond that, Sundays are no different from Wednesdays, the annual holiday is not taken by everyone at the same time – work is determined by the date of completion of a contract, according to the rhythms of the availability of creativity.

These city districts have long been a component of (inter)-national urban tourism, recommended by countless "secret tips", they are the destination and meeting point of weekend party-goers from the entire region; the mainstream continues to dance on the remnants of the "hip" scene, which has long since fled, thus making the "vibrant city" a self-fulfilling prophecy. These districts have long been entrusted to the gentrification process, although perhaps today the contrast of the various gentrifying stages appear much more reassuring than at the time of the housing battles.

Although no longer the site of open violence, these neighbourhoods are nonetheless contested. They reflect a succession of appropriation of those sites that are marked by a high "value gap" – an income deficit between what the property actually brings in and its potential yield. This marks out the "urban borders" between those who gain profit from growth and competition processes and those who fall victim to them (Smith 1996); a border which is drawn just as much by means of architecture and urban planning as with surveillance technology, which provides a service to safeguard against, and to criminalise, groups that are refused the right to occupy a certain space because of the way they look.

The sites of opaque forms of non-commercial creativity look quite different. They, too, can be found in industrial districts which, however, appear raw and not at all aesthetic – harbours and warehouse sheds, designed by "trash-aesthetics" (Pratt 2002, p. 41). From the outside, their function is barely legible, there are no illuminated signs or company names; there are graffiti, but they do not have anything to do with the actual users. Squatting activities are, in any case, temporary, project-oriented and built upon common experience. Forms of appropriation are informally organised and not always legal in a strict sense, but they are fun-loving. Artistic or documentary products are created; one participates, takes the stage or simply shares the moment.

Gentrification by Way of Cultural City Tourism?

Since the 1970s, in the field of urban-sociological research, the term "gentrification" has been used for the description of the change in neighbourhoods in cities (Blasius et al. 1990). Due to the change in the economic, social, cultural and urban development-architectural structure, these changes in city neighbourhoods are depicted as a process. This restructuring process can be seen by a change in the population structure, rising rents, re-evaluation of the environment, improved infrastructures and the redevelopment of building structures.

One thesis of this paper is that the cultural process of appropriation and consumption by city tourists must be seen as another driving force for the gentrification process. Although some cultural city tourists are not provided with much capital, they are able to increasingly reach back to cultural resources and local knowledge from their own lifeworlds to be able to touristically open up places. The function of cultural tourism in these "vibrant" quarters is an essential driving force for changing a neighbourhood. Here, gentrification is seen as a process in the course of which the production and consumption of space takes place by a social group, the "cultural city tourists" described here. In these neighbourhoods the internationalisation of tourism has resulted in the development of new spaces for a variety of services. After all, the fact that the original cultural pioneers have been driven out may also be given as a negative result of the gentrification of neighbourhoods due to increased tourist activities.

The Concept of the "Creative City" and Cultural City Tourism

Cities have always been creative places where philosophers, painters, musicians and authors found sources of inspiration for their creative work. In his book *Cities in Civilization*, Peter Hall gives evidence of the historic function of cities for innovation and creativity; from Pericles' Athens via Florence during the Renaissance up to Vienna, the City of Music in the nineteenth century. Cities have always been the place for visitors to consume cultural goods and services. The following features may be given as conditions for the development of creativity and innovation in cities: a certain size and fragmentariness, a certain degree of communication between the inhabitants, heterogeneity of life profiles, foreigners and outsiders meeting each other, as well as existing insecurities (Hall 1998, 2000). Hall distinguishes artistically-culturally creative cities which have offered creative stimulations in the fields of literature, music, painting, theatre, cinema and fine arts from natural scientifically-technologically creative cities where new technologies developed, new ways of economic organisation, new enterprises and new industrial branches (Hall 2000, p. 640).

Often the debates on the "creative city" combine creativity and economy and then explain the concept of a "creative city" as an economic hope: creative branches, be they designers, artists, architects, authors, scientists or engineers, are said to increasingly contribute to economic prosperity – even by way of tourism. Thus, quite obviously these concepts are essentially involved in the economic question, whether overall economic developments, urban economies or indirect effects such as the image of a "creative city" in the competition of cities over the location of enterprises and being an attraction for cultural city tourists.

The challenge of this debate is in connecting the vision of a "creative city" not only with the prospect of economic success. The potential beyond the economic aspect which is inherent in the creative performance of individuals culminates in a self-determined way of outlining one's own life, in the context of which the development of creativity may result in a positive way of organizing change. The challenges of a creative city are in providing individuals and social groups with spaces for experimenting and trying out, even if they do not posses much economic capital. Places which might preserve and create cultural variety, where different people and those previously unknown to each other may meet. The danger of this debate, however, lies in a narrow-minded way of understanding "creativity". If this is only understood in the sense of the work and economic success of creative managers, advertisers or event organizers, the concept of a "creative city" falls short. Most of all, the not purely economic ways of creativity consisting of social and societal innovations, which result in civil society inventions and combine self-responsibility with public welfare, should be the focus of interest (Frey 2008a).

From the year 2002 with his book *The Rise of the Creative Class*, Richard Florida made the concept of the creative city one of the essential models of urban development. His main thesis is that a city being attractive for a creative bohème and its economic success are the same. By way of the so-called "three Ts" – talent, tolerances and technology – he established a graded scale of the creativity of US American cities. Most of all, apart from hard factors such as research and education, a successful economic policy must encourage a tolerant and cosmopolitan atmosphere to improve its ranking. The great response to his ideas is due to the fact that he provided the urban political class with a simple marketing concept which may basically be understood to be a festivalisation of urban politics and a competition for the urban middle classes.

The two research concepts by Richard Florida in the "Creative Class" (2002) and Dieter Läpple in "Renaissance of the European City" (2003) will be compared to each other and referred to cultural city tourism. Both approaches start out from the increasing significance of inner-city residential and work places for a knowledge-based cultural economy and its actors. Richard Florida finds an open and pluralist value structure of the population as one essential feature of these creative centres of cities: in these places immigrants, artists and homosexuals create a culture of variety and openness which is attractive for cultural tourists. Dieter Läpple describes an economic, cultural and social functional mixture as a condition and prerequisite for these urban quarters. Essential for both approaches is the significance of a lively urbanity which makes it possible for tourists to become part of the local atmosphere. Public and semi-public spaces also play an essential role for tourists as network junctions and communicative exchange points.

As Läpple (2003) has clearly shown, at "successful" creative places there is a close relationship between new "weak ties" of civil society supporting new forms of social cohesion. The variety of creative industries ranging from successful market presence networks to fluid cultures/scenes of events and recreation has developed creative clusters in inner city districts. Moreover, economically successful creative industries need the "amalgamation" of these "sticky places" to build these creative clusters and networks.

Cities have always had places where the production and consumption of cultural goods takes place. In this context, creativity and knowledge have played an outstanding role in the development of new ideas and goods. During recent years, scientific literature has again addressed these creative characteristics: terms such as "Creative City" (Landry 2000), "Cultural Industries" (Wynne 1992), "Milieux Innovateurs" (Aydalot 1986) or "Creative Class" (Florida 2002) are examples of combining creativity and urban life. The common diagnosis is that cities and particularly urban inner-city districts provide specific conditions for creative innovation in the context of knowledge and culture production and that there are new kinds of social community in the sense of newly regulating ways of work and life. This potential of cities in the context of a knowledge society might contribute to a "renaissance of the city" (Läpple 2003).

The reorganisation of work is accompanied by the development of new lifestyles, new spatial arrangements and requirements of urban spaces. The borders between work and leisure time become more permeable and flexible; there is a tendency towards dissolving the division of labour and a blurring of borders between work and private life (e.g. working from home) as entrepreneurs develop new flexible forms of work to exploit chances for action and organisational streamlining, all of which can be used to promote individualised professional activity and lifestyle. The "creative milieu" within the field of cultural tourism is one factor of this economic and social change. With the term of "informational capitalism" Castells (1996) diagnosed the increasing significance of knowledge in the current capitalist society. Social and also urban development is increasingly dependent on knowledge-based and culturally communicated economies. In the context of this development, combinations of cultural and knowledge-based action structures both of individuals and of economic logics begin to occur. Those economic branches seen as increasingly integrating varieties of cultural knowledge have become the hope of urban economies.

Urbanity and Public Spaces as a Resource of Tourism

Public spaces have a binding power for both tourists and the residential population to identify. For city tourists it is most of all central public spaces which offer a possibility to read "the city's identity". At central places – most of all inner-city places – they believe they recognise something of the city's nature (e.g. Heldenplatz in Vienna, Alexanderplatz in Berlin, Place de la Concorde in Paris, Trafalgar Square in London). For the local residential population other public spaces are of particular significance as places of appropriation, communication and socialisation.

The creative aspect of urbanity is due to the fact that in the urban space foreign people meet, there are unexpected situations, spontaneous actions, as well as heterogeneous and varied lifeworlds and that in this way points of view besides usual paths and routines may develop. Nowadays urbanity and the consequent connected public space are alive where the unequal, the unparallel, the unexpected and the different become combined in spatial density (Häußermann 1996). In current metropolises a diversity of cultures and ways of life develop which, by their chronological and spatial eclipsing, their parallelity and their mutual permeability, create new ways of urban living in the respective public spaces and characterise them.

For many urban developers the model of the European city and thus the model of urbanity with its characteristics of compactness, density, heterogeneity and variety serve as a model for urban development (Siebel 2004). They consider public spaces a quality typical of European cities. These days the European city is identified in particular by its public spaces. For the inhabitants and also for city tourists these places within the city structure are potential points of identification, just as cities, too, represent themselves by the quality of their public spaces (Kazig et al. 2003).

In many European cities the public space, in the form of urban developmentally structured squares surrounded by buildings, is an historic heritage of building culture. By way of squares, streets and other outside spaces the building structure of this relationship between private and public spaces creates that public space where the urban way of living and the urban kind of society may develop.

Not only the political socialisation of an urban population finds its place in the public space but public space also takes on an essential significance for the most varied events, parties or leisure events. The event society (Schulze 1992) creates new ways of consumption-event-oriented life resulting in the new wave of cultural tourism. The people's search for entertainment, consumption, events or sports activities increasingly also discovers public space as a scene of (self-) staging.

In this context public space serves as a stage where there is play, which attracts the masses and creates a sense of community. Love Parades, public viewing, Rainbow Parades, music parades or city marathons give evidence of entertainment and sports industries which, against the trend of "retreating to the private", propagate "going to the public" (Selle 2002, p. 61).

Staging in the public space is not only something for entertainment-oriented city dwellers but public space is also used as a place of urban politics. The increasing competition between cities (on attracting the attention of investors or tourists) results in advertising the quality of public spaces. They display the state of the city. Marketing strategies of cities sketch pleasant images of public space for the cities' self-representation by means of labels and symbols. In this context urban development draws attention to its contribution to securing the quality of representative public spaces.

Creativity and City Marketing in the Context of Increasing Competition between Cities

For city marketing the essential question is which kind of creativity should be supported and made visible at urban places to make them look attractive for cultural tourism. In the last couple of years the support of culture and creativity has become an essential model for urban development and city marketing (Kunzmann 2004; Peck 2005; Scott 2006). City marketing has discovered the cultural field as a driving force and has integrated it into its tools, such as strategic models, urban development planning or framework plans. The increased acceptance of this "soft" cultural field of politics in the context of urban development and city marketing is due to a fundamental change in society towards a knowledge society, which has been going on since the 1970s (Evans 2001). In the course of this social, economic and cultural change, traditional tools of location development – such as extending the infrastructure or connecting to traffic networks – have become less significant for urban development. Social change has resulted in a gain in significance of immaterial values such as knowledge, culture and creativity in a number of areas of life. The field of urban renovation strategies was the first to take cultural aspects into consideration. In this field the support of cultural events or festivals was tried out in terms of stimulating urban renewal processes (Frey et al. 2006). These strategies of cultural renewal encountered a particular response in the context of steps for the support of disadvantaged urban quarters. By way of cultural initiatives and measures these target areas of urban renovation are hopefully prevented from further decline. These processes are also aimed at economically re-evaluating these areas by making them attractive to city tourists. Cultural tourism is connected to local economy and urban developmental goals. The classical, sector-immanent focus is on the support and funding of classical culture such as museums, opera houses and theatres. In the course of the past few years understanding of the classical policy of culture support has been extended and based on a wider concept of culture. Cultural ways of life and practices, everyday cultures, local cultural initiatives, symbolic cultural productions of places by certain social groups and the like have been taken into consideration as a precondition for the variety of urban life. City marketing is able to employ the resources of local identities as a feature of uniqueness in the competition between cities. In the following, three strategic goals of cultural city marketing shall be distinguished:

Strategies for increasing the inhabitants' identification with their city and their urban quarter. The everyday cultures of city dwellers are the precondition for the variety and heterogeneity of urban life. During the course of immigration of ethnically diverse social groups a multicultural urban society has developed. In this context, culture is considered a key for the integration and identification of different groups of the population. In this sense, urban development strategies illustrate that the population's lifeworlds, value attitudes and everyday cultures are of essential significance for identifying with the city or the urban quarter.

Strategies for positioning the city in the competition between cities. In strategies for city marketing, and thus positioning in the competition between cities, culture is considered to have a significant function. Models such as the "creative city" or "cultural capital" are used to attract international attention – also that of city tourists. This strategy aims, too, at getting visitors to the respective city. In this field, the strategy of planning refers mostly to the development of flagship projects which are supposed to create an image. Being image projects of cultural urban development with unique languages of architectural symbolism, the Guggenheim Museum in Bilbao or the Museum Quarter in Vienna have developed a cultural uniqueness of the respective city which results in increased attractivity.

Strategies for re-evaluating urban sub-areas. Culture is used as a driving force for the process of re-evaluating disadvantaged urban sub-areas. In the context of this strategy, city tourism is also supposed to provide disadvantaged urban quarters with additional economic capital. Many alternative city guides and marketing concepts praise "vibrant" urban quarters with their infrastructures, bars and restaurants. In the context of this strategy, culture and city tourism are connected to urban economy. Urban development and city marketing consider cultural tourism a hope for inner-city economy. Some cities employ integrated concepts of economic development, cultural support, tourism and urban development to utilise the economic resources of cultural activities.

Cultural City Tourism and the Model of the "Amalgamated City"

Cultural city tourism looks for local identities of living urbanity. In the knowledge society this urbanity has changed. New social and territorial borders and connections have developed. Due to the mobile, internationally networked group of "creative milieus", which are a part of cultural city tourism, a demand has developed for places and neighbourhoods which by the (a) eclipsing of their uses and functions and (b) their mixture of social groups, create a varied urban, creative structure.

The "creative milieus" of city tourists look for those kinds of places and neighbourhoods in a city that they are familiar with in their "home" local living environment, but which nevertheless have a specifically local touch. They are attracted by places where rent is cheap, where deserted backyards and commercial buildings or empty ground floor places stimulate new ways of use.

In these places and neighbourhoods the "amalgamated city" (Frey 2008) names (a) the melting into one of places (physically-materially) and the social (at least temporarily for the moment) and (b) the interdependence of places by way of actors moving between them. The same is also true for information, images and the flow of money and goods as a result of city tourism. The concept of an "amalgamated city" aims at a mixture of different places making the urban-spatial environment of utilisation, perception and life. These places are in some way spatially linked with each other. Their connections and melting into each other happen by way of social practices of individuals and by cultural as well as symbolic codes, which can be "read" by the specific group of city tourists.

These "amalgamated places" are created by mixing the functions of work, leisure and tourism, where work and life are organised in new temporary, flexible modes. This means places where a mixture of gainful work, leisure and tourism occurs.

This model of a city aims at a mixture of different places (respectively understood as expressing the mutual relationship between social world and physical objects) to form the urban-spatial environment of utilisation, perception and life. These interconnected places and neighbourhoods in the cities visited are linked with each other. Quarters and neighbourhoods in the different cities are connected to each other by international exchange and a mutual relationship of social practices, cultural codes and images. These interconnections and melting into one happen by way of social practices of city tourists and by way of cultural as well as symbolic codes. The networked places of the social space structure of the "amalgamated city" are characterised by two contradicting features. On the one hand, there is a diversity and difference of places and their social-spatial rooting, while on the other, a number of common ground features and homogeneities exist which are respectively kept up by way of the scenes and milieus of cultural tourists in the course of an exchange process.

Notes

[1] Florida (2002, 2005), Landry (2000), for a critical debate on the role of creative industries, see Peck (2005), Dreher (2002), Liebmann (2003).

References

Aydalot P (1986) *Milieux Innovateurs en Europe*, GREMI, Paris.
Besculides A, Lee M, McCormick P (2002) *Residents' perceptions of the cultural benefits of tourism*. Annals of Tourism Research n. 29, pp. 303–319.
Blasius J, Dangschat, Jens S (eds) (1990) *Gentrification – Die Aufwertung Innenstadtnaher Wohnviertel*, Frankfurt am Main, New York.
Boniface B (1998) *Tourism culture*. Annals of Tourism Research n. 25, pp. 961–976.

Brislin RW (1993) *Understanding Culture's Influence on Behaviour*, Harcourt Brace College Publishers, Fort Worth, TX.

Bryan L (2001) *The Language of Space*, Architectural Press, Oxford.

Camagni R (1995) *The concept of innovative milieu and its relevance for public policies in European lagging regions*. Regional Science n. 4, pp. 317–340.

Castells M (1996) *The Rise of the Network Society*, Blackwell Publishers, Malden Massachusetts.

Crang M (2000) (ed) *Thinking Space*, Routledge, London, New York.

Dangschat JS (1996) *Raum als dimension sozialer ungleichheit und ort als Bühne der Lebensstilisierung? – Zum Raumbezug sozialer Ungleichheit und von Lebensstilen*. In: Schwenk OG (ed) *Lebensstil zwischen Sozialstrukturanalyse und Kulturwissenschaft*, Leske & Budrich, Oplade.

Dangschat JS (1999) *Der Schweiß der Maloche und der Lebensstil der kreativen Flexiblen*. Baumeister n. 10, pp. 50–53.

Dangschat JS (2006) *Creative Capital – Selbstorganisation zwischen zivilgesellschaftlichen Erfindungen und der Instrumentalisierung als Standortfaktor*. In: *Veröffentlichungen des 32. Kongresses der Deutschen Gesellschaft für Soziologie*, Campus Verlag, Frankfurt am Main, pp. 615–632.

De Kadt, E (1979) *Tourism: Passport to Development*, Oxford University Press, Oxford.

Dreher C (2002) *Be creative – or die*. Salon June 6, http://www.salon.com

Evans G (2001) *Cultural Planning – An Urban Renaissance?*, Routledge, London, New York.

Featherstone M, Lash S (1999) *Spaces of Culture*, Sage, London, Thousand Oaks, New Delhi.

Florida R (2002) *The Rise of the Creative Class*, Basic Books, New York.

Florida R (2005) *Cities and the Creative Class*, Routledge, London, New York.

Frey O, Smetana K (2006) *Vienna's "Gentle Renewal" while Being Confronted with "Robust" Challenges by the Present: A Discourse between Management, Diversity, and Prevention of Disintegration at the Level of Neighbourhoods*. ISOCARP-Review 2006.

Frey O (2008) *Die amalgame Stadt: Orte. Netze. Milieus*, VS-Verlag, Wiesbaden.

Frey O (2008a) *Creative Clusters and Loft-Working in Vienna*. In: Illmonen M, Kunzmann K (eds) *Culture, Creative Industries and Urban Development*, Ashgate, London.

Hall P (1998) *Cities in Civilization, Technology and Urban Order*, Pantheon Books, London.

Hall P (2000) *Creative cities and economic development*. Urban Studies n. 4/37, pp. 639–649.

Häußermann H (1996) *Stadtentwicklung im labor Berlin-Mitte*. In: Wentz M (ed) *Stadtentwicklung*, Campus Wentz, Frankfurt am Main, pp. 76–89.

Healey P (2004) *Creativity and Urban Governance*. DISP 3/158. 2004 http://disp.ethz.ch, 15.10.2006.

Jafari HB (1997) *Culture, tourism, development: Crucial issues for the twenty-first century*. Annals of Tourism Research n. 24, pp. 474–476.

Judd DR, Fainstein SS (1999) *The Tourist City*. Yale University Press, New Haven/London.

Kazig R, Müller A, Wiegandt CC (2003) *Öffentlicher Raum in Europa und den USA*. Informationen zur Raumentwicklung, Heft 3/4, pp. 91–102.

Kunzmann KR (2004) *Culture, Creativity and spatial Planning*. Town Planning Review n. 75/4, pp. 383–404.

Landry C (2000) *The Creative City – A Toolkit for Urban Innovators*, Charles Landry, London.

Läpple D (2003) *Thesen zu einer Renaissance der Stadt in der Wissensgesellschaft*. In: Gestring N et al. (eds), *Jahrbuch Stadtregionleske*, Leske & Budrich, Opladen, pp. 61–77.

Lash S, Urry J (1994) *Economies of Signs & Spaces*, Sage, London, Thousand Oaks, New Delhi.

Law CM (1992) *Urban tourism and its contribution to economic regeneration*. Urban Studies n. 29, pp. 599–618.

Law CM (1993) *Urban Tourism: Attracting Visitors to Large Cities*, Mansell Publishing Ltd, London.

Lefebvre, H (1991), *The Production of Space* (Originally Published in 1974), Blackwell Publishing, Oxford.

Liebmann H; Robischon T (eds) (2003) *Städtische Kreativität – Potential für den Stadtumbau*, Erkner, Darmstadt.

Löw M (2001) *Raumsoziologie*, Suhrkamp, Frankfurt am Main.

Markus TA, Cameron D (2001) *The words between the spaces: Buildings and language*, Routledge, London, New York.

Matthiesen U (ed) (2004) *Stadtregion und Wissen. Analysen und Plädoyers für eine wissensbasierte*, Stadtpolitik VS Verlag, Wiesbaden.

O'Connor J (1999) *The Definition of "Cultural Industries"* http://www.mipc.mmu.ac.uk, 15.07.2007

Peck J (2005) *Struggling with the creative class*. International Journal of Urban and Regional Research n. 29, pp. 740–770.

Pratt AC (2002) *Hot jobs in cool places. The material cultures of new media product spaces: The case of south of the market. San Francisco*. Information, Communication & Society n. 5(1), pp. 27–50.

Richards G (ed) (1996) Cultural Tourism in Europe CABI Wallingford http://www.tram-research.com/cultural%20tourism%20in%20europe.PDF, 10.06.2008

Ritchie JRB, Zins M (1978) *Culture as determinant of the attractiveness of a tourism region*. Annals of Tourism Research n. 15(2), pp. 252–267.

Schulze G (1992) *Die Erlebnisgesellschaft – Kultursoziologie der Gegenwart*, Campus, Frankfurt am Main, New York.

Scott AJ (2006) *The Cultural Economy of Cities. Essays on the Geography of Image-Producing Industries*, Sage, London, Thousand Oaks, New Delhi.

Selle K (ed) (2002) *Was ist los mit den öffentlichen Räumen? Analysen, Positionen Konzepte*, Dortmunder Vertrieb für Bau- und Planungsliteratur, Dortmund.

Siebel W (eds) (2004) *Die europäische Stadt*, Edition Suhrkamp, Frankfurt am Main.

Smith N (1979) *Towards a theory of gentrification: A back to the city movement by capital, not people*. Journal of the American Planning Association n. 45, 1979, pp. 24–35.

Smith N (1996) *The New Urban Frontier: Gentrification and the Revanchist City*, London, New York.

Soja EW (2001) *Postmodern Geographies: The Reassertion of Space in Critical Social Theory*, Verso, London.

Thrift N (1996) *Spatial Formations*, The Cromwell Press Ltd, London.

World Tourism Organization (1985) *The State's Role in Protecting and Promoting Culture as a Factor of Tourism Development and the Proper Use and Exploitation of the National Cultural Heritage of Sites and Monuments for Tourism, WTO*, Madrid.

Wynne D (1992) *The Cultural Industry: The Arts in Urban Regeneration*, Avebury, Aldershot.

Zeppel H, Hall CM (1992) *Arts and heritage tourism*. In: Weiler B, Hall CM (ed) *Special Interest Tourism*, Belhaven Press, London, pp. 45–60.

Zukin S (1995) *The Cultures of Cities*, Blackwell, Oxford.

Historico-Cultural Sustainability and Urban Dynamics

Eric de Noronha Vaz and Peter Nijkamp

Dynamic Urban Spaces and their Historico-Cultural Heritage

Over the past decades, the history of human geography in many countries has shown a tendency towards more urban patterns of living accompanied by an extension of people's action radius. Urbanization has become a worldwide phenomenon. This is exemplified in Europe, with an average urbanization rate of 70–80%. We observe not only a rise in "urbanity", seen from the perspective of urban or metropolitan population densities, but also new tendencies towards more distant suburbanization or de-urbanization patterns. Even rural areas are increasingly being turned into accessible areas that are well connected to urban centres and also display urban lifestyles. "Accessibility" and "mobility" are key words in a modern dynamic space-economy, not only at intraregional scales but also at interregional and even international scales.

The dynamics in settlement and mobility patterns is prompting a wide array of research and policy questions on socio-economic equity, spatial disparities, growth differentials and sustainable development. Nowadays, many cities and regions exhibit a tension between competitive growth strategies and sustainable community strategies (e.g. environmentally benign initiatives, preservation of socio-cultural heritage). Consequently, in various countries, cities and regions have currently become battlefields between growth advocates and conservationists. As well as being global command and control centres (Sassen 1998), urban spaces appear to be concentrations of ecologically and historically valuable assets which reflect a memorable past.

The socio-economic, political-geographic and cultural-scientific history of the dynamics of places and localities on our earth is reflected in their historico-cultural heritage. This patrimony comprises cultural assets such as old churches, palaces, museums, urban parks, historical architecture of cities or landscapes of historical interest. Historico-cultural heritage also includes archaeological sites, which sometimes not only have a local value but may have a worldwide significance (e.g. Pompei). All these assets mirror the rich history of a city or region and are a permanent source of scientific and cultural inspiration for researchers, planners, and the public

G. Maciocco, S. Serreli (eds.), *Enhancing the City*, Urban and Landscape Perspectives 6, DOI 10.1007/978-90-481-2419-0_8, © Springer Science+Business Media B.V. 2009

at large. This ongoing interest in socio-cultural heritage originates from two sources: (i) a society in motion is prompted to ask new questions about its past in order to better understand the choices to be made concerning its future pathways and (ii) the progress in scientific research and in research techniques (e.g. infrared technology) allows researchers to investigate cultural assets in a different way that often leads to novel findings.

These developments have also generated new departures for research in the cultural and archaeological sciences, as is witnessed by the following quotation: *Archaeology has traditionally possessed strong conceptual divides between data collection and data analysis, manifested most obviously between excavation and post-excavation activities* (Conolly and Lake 2006, p. 36). Actually, the emphasis in modern archaeology is not so much on excavation and material reconstruction of a historico-cultural asset, but increasingly on data analysis using geographical information system (GIS) and spatial modelling techniques (Renfrew and Bahn 2004). Exploratory research is increasingly giving way to contextual and explanatory modes of research based on advanced data analysis. For example, the geographic identification of the position of observation towers on the walls of ancient cities or the search for vestiges of carbonized animal bones ("blue collar research") is nowadays followed by massive data analysis linking these findings to research outcomes elsewhere ("white collar research"). These changes in research style call for creative modes of new analytical investigation. In this context, Schiffer argues:

Human behaviour consists of activities, which can be aggregated by the investigator to create analytic unities at many scales. Virtually every activity consists of interactions among people and one or more technologies. Along with technologies for procuring raw materials and preparing food, there are, for example, religious, social, recreational and political technologies, which enable people to interact with plants and animals, other people, and, as Walker (2001) has pointed out, even supernatural entities (Schiffer 2004, p. 579).

Thus, research on historico-cultural assets in an urbanized society is increasingly characterized by modern digital data analysis.

This paper will address research and policy issues on sustainable development in the Algarve region, Portugal. This area used to be a peripheral natural area with rich flora and fauna, but in recent decades its pleasant climate has attracted massive flows of foreign tourists, to the extent that the entire coastal zone of the Algarve shows clear signs of being an urbanized environment. This new development may endanger the historical and natural character of the areas whose cultural assets date back to the period of the Phoenicians, Romans and Moors. Its unique physical geography has led to a specific environmental, agricultural, architectural and social constellation whose roots can be found in the Neolithic period.

The socio-historical complexity of this area calls for sophisticated research methods in order to unravel the location and functions of different civilizations, their cultural complexity and their local identity.

The research for our Algarve case study has three characteristics:

- Strategic: identification of geographic patterns and historic remains to trace the historic patrimony of this area.
- Scientific: use of modern GIS and satellite information complemented with cellular automata (CA) approaches to better map out and examine historical and modern artifacts.
- Human-historical: tracing the behavioural and social interaction patterns of ancient civilizations in connection with modern development in the area.

The tools used in our research are as follows: database design and conversion into shapefiles using DB4, spatial analysis in combination with GIS technology (ArcMap®), topographical reference using ortho-photomaps from satellite information including archaeological data (see Westcott and Brandon 2000).

Clearly, the use of geo-information science tools is a prerequisite for sophisticated applied research on the history and the present situation of the area concerned. As Gillings and Goodrick (1996, p. 1) put it: "GIS is increasingly being seen as much as a place to think as a simple data management and mapping tool".

Our paper is organized as follows: "Dynamic Urban Spaces and Their Historico-Cultural Heritage" explains the importance of understanding the dynamics of change in urban spaces and the need to develop sustainable policies while preserving the historico-cultural heritage. Next, "Geo-Science Tools" discusses the recent possibilities of geo-science and their diverse capabilities of coping accurately with regional management. In "Cellular Automata, GIS and Cultural Heritage", we describe recent technological developments in GIS that can lead to a better understanding of the usefulness of CA and spatial data analysis as research tools for dealing with spatial sustainability. "Algarve: AGIS Laboratory for cultural Heritage" will then describe the Algarve as a laboratory of interesting possibilities for analysing cultural heritage ventures in a European context in combination with the application of GIS technology. On the basis of GIS data, we next develop a scenario of urban growth in the Faro-Olhão area in the Algarve, recognizing the current state of endangerment with a practical emphasis on the possibilities of GIS analysis and cognition. Finally, we will outline future directions and challenges of GIS as a toolbox for monitoring urban growth from a spatial and cultural resource perspective.

Geo-Science Tools

GIS technology was originally developed as a set of sophisticated digital mapping tools, but has gradually moved into a real scientific discipline, namely geo-science, which forms an integrated set of Information and Communication Technology (ICT)-based methods and tools (including satellite information, remote sensing and CA) which lies at the heart of modern detailed spatial and dynamic analysis of objects of all kinds.[1] Its user-friendliness and polyvalence makes geo-science an appropriate methodology for a wide variety of dynamic spatial analyses, e.g., objects in urban planning, traffic management, archaeological investigations, architecture and cultural heritage (see, e.g. Wheatley and Gillings 2002, Conolly and Lake 2006). Geo-science has derived its current popularity not only from its advanced representational possibilities in space and time but also – and in particular – from its high predictive potential (see, e.g., Syphard et al. 2004, Al-Kheder and Shan 2005, Cabral 2006). This also holds for cultural heritage and archaeological site management (see, e.g., Sebastian and Judge 1988, Kvamme 1999, Warren and Asch 2000, Ebert 2004, Verhagen 2007, Box 1999, Pontius and Chen 2006).

Since the Malta Convention on the management of cultural heritage resources, geo-science has assumed a prominent position in presenting, mapping and analysing cultural and archaeological assets, a tendency which in recent years has in fact been strengthened as a result of the policy need for sustainable local development. The overall idea is that cultural assets should not lose their scientific relevance in the case of urban or infrastructural development, so a balance has to be found between archaeological or historico-cultural interest one the one hand, and socio-economic and spatial development on the one hand, an intention also clearly outlined in the Valetta Treaty. The use of satellite information, in order to uncover spatial land use and land cover, has proven to be extremely fruitful for our in-depth analysis of the problems concerned here. The technologies involved are manifold and include such applications as Landsat, Thematic Mapper, SPOT or Corona. The various applications were summarized by Montufo as follows:

The results obtained by using satellite imagery for a survey of ancient rural land use patterns are highly dependent on three factors:
1. The existence of the remains for former land-use patterns in the study area.
2. The existence of other patterns that can be confused with ancient land use patterns.
3. The ability of the system to record and discriminate between patterns (Montufo 1997, p. 81).

The usage of satellite imagery for GIS is evident. Satellite imagery is of extreme importance to help locate and understand the dynamics of land use/land cover, as well as to represent and have a clear and as sharp as possible notion of space and morphological surroundings. Hence, one could consider satellite images as the principal asset used in a GIS for spatial understanding and relevant spatial analysis that can provide support for later decision-making. Thus, remote sensing in archaeology anchors itself in the very essence and usage of GIS in archaeology – it can be used either for research, to answer questions regarding past human activity or for management, to support in a proactive way decision-making and cultural heritage preservation.

It is generally recognized that the increasingly intensive use and modification of the landscape resulting from modern demands for efficient infrastructure and land use (agricultural production, mining, energy sources and leisure/tourism facilities) exerts growing pressure on cultural heritage in the landscape

(Grøn and Loska 2002, p. 4).

Satellite monitoring for cultural heritage management is an important issue that has been a very important tool in a rapidly changing world, helping better and more sustainable governance. "Satellite images are an excellent tool to monitor change in large natural and/or cultural sites" (Hernandez 2002, p. 104), in which the quick perception of the ongoing reality and the state of the site can easily be assessed at low cost and with no specific restrictions or boundaries. Hence, size and limit of observations do not depend as much on politics, but rather on scientific intuition. Not only does satellite imagery represent a tool that on a periodic basis can monitor any change and occurrence but it can also be seen as a dataset that allows predictive modelling which may be an asset for regional and local planning. The advantages of satellite remote sensing can be synthesized as follows (Hernandez 2002, p. 103):

– It offers a valuable tool to assist conservation activities;
– All information is exactly localized and gathered in one tool;
– Information can be updated continuously;
– Better decision-making by spatial analysis;
– Possibility of direct extraction of topographic and thematic maps for use on the actual terrain.

The "Cultural Cycle", as explained by the Department for Culture, Media and Sports of the United Kingdom,[2] can very well be adapted to the circumstances of monitoring cultural heritage via remote sensing satellite imagery. The Cultural Cycle has six key dimensions of action: creation, making, dissemination, exhibition/reception, archiving/preservation and education/understanding. Satellite remote sensing, used to monitor cultural heritage, can have an impact on the last three dimensions, in which the objectives could be understood as follows:

- Reception: reception of the satellite data with cultural heritage information for analysis;
- Archiving/preservation: importing results of imagery in a GIS, land cover/land use analysis to monitor change and actively preserve;
- Education/understanding: dissemination of results to create social awareness of the importance of cultural identity.

The importance of monitoring cultural heritage sites with satellite imagery is crucial, as it is a form of understanding ongoing change and has a direct impact on preservation issues, which is so important in a very quickly changing world. Thus, strategies can be taken more reliably and more systematically. Remote sensing via satellites and its growing technology is a tool for change.

It is clear that quite substantial investments are required for cultural heritage and archaeological research in urban areas. As such, the available database is no more than a mere reference of what originally might have existed in a given area. The gap between the originally existing sites and the currently identified ones may change (Joukowsky 1980). One of the most interesting possibilities in Cultural Resource Management in a GIS context is after all the capacity to predict change or dynamic behaviour given a set of rules or parameters. In this sense, predictive modelling is of extreme importance and should be largely used to facilitate the stakeholders' decision-making process and has great potential as a tool for archaeologists working in cultural resource management (Hill et al. 2007).

Cellular Automata, GIS and Cultural Heritage

The human need to understand the environment has always been a constant in the endeavour to gather knowledge. Since the dawn of history, human beings' aspiration to go beyond the commonsense rules to understand patterns and interactions has brought them the capability to survive. Not only has population adapted to nature, but discovering technology has amazingly quickly developed it in such a way as to gradually allow the construction of a new kind of nature: that of virtual reality and the era of the machines. The origin of this new system is no more than yet another of the ongoing reflexes of nature and can be described according to Ludwig Von Bertalanffy's "General System Theory":

There exist models, principles, and laws that apply to generalized systems or their subclasses, irrespective of their particular kind, the nature of their component elements, and the relationships or "forces" between them. It seems legitimate to ask for a theory, not of systems of a more or less special kind, but of universal principles applying to systems in general (Von Bertalanffy 1950, p. 32).

Intrinsically, this statement calls out for a convergence of different areas, sculpting a new kind of science that finds its roots in biology, physics, geography, sociology, and many other areas, that together have contributed to the construction and fundamental notions of Systems Theory.

In fact, a system can be defined as an ongoing interaction of reciprocal influences between different agents (Legrand 1991). It becomes quite obvious that with the existing advances of technology and computer-aided processes, these agents can be *virtually* represented and their "behaviour" specified by a set of variables in such a way that one can create behaviourist non-linear approaches to estimate and predict patterns in an *in vitro* environment in the computer. In any recreation of any agent that simulates behaviour, time is a crucial variable that deals precisely with the dynamics of change of the agent in a temporal context. Thus, the models that allow the creation of such agents and the context that allows their patterns to be studied must be a consequence of what are called dynamic models, in which the temporal factor represents a crucial factor to allow the study of the dynamic and its motion. Hence, agent-based models are the logical step to combine dynamic models with intuitive agents that relying on a set of variables allow predictive behaviour. These specific kinds of models have their branches in areas of the computational sciences and find a vast utility in many related areas. As they are capable of reflecting quite clearly the behaviour of groups and biological variables, they have been used quite extensively in the social sciences. After all, in these circumstances "computers offer a solution to the problem of incorporating heterogeneous actors and environments, and nonlinear relationships (or effects)" (Lansing 2002, p. 284).

One of the sub-forms of exploring and modelling these systems that evolved as the consequence of understanding these agents was Von Neumann's first CA. CA are discrete mathematical models that consist of a grid of cells that allow interaction of variables within the designated system, involving the variable time, thus representing a dynamic system in which patterns of behaviour may be observed. The applications of CA are manifold and are often used in any area which studies a system that is inherently dynamic and wants to predict a set of behaviours given a number of rules with a temporal basis. Because of their intrinsic nature (a grid-based system with a specific number of cells) they are quite adaptable to a GIS environment. Given the necessary software and programming experience or attachable models, one can adapt CA easily to the context of a GIS and do predictive multi-temporal dynamics of change on a spatial basis.

An important task of GIS is to monitor ecological change, in order to make a direct impact on change and sustainability. The combination of GIS with CA allows change of land use to be precisely tracked and assessed and may be an important guide for regional policies and stakeholders. In this sense, one of the important uses of CA in a GIS context is the possibility to measure and predict urban growth in a given area. This context is not new, as it had originally become important in the 1960s (Wilson 1974). However, it is with the development of computer hardware and software that CA has finally provided the possibility of giving reliable results that can also explain dynamics visually, if interpreted in a GIS. Although it is obvious that urban growth and increase of land use cover is inevitable, nevertheless, the analysis and interpretation of results can have a direct impact on how best such change can be oriented. CA must be seen in this context as a positive tool for monitoring dynamics towards firm results which can answer a question such as "What if urban growth continues to evolve under unchangeable conditions?" This simple question and its complex answer may be assessed with Urban Growth CA and is a step towards the preservation of fauna, flora and cultural heritage resources. Artificial areas, like cities, will continue growing, but perhaps with the help of technology in a more humane and sustainable form.

Algarve: a GIS Laboratory for Cultural Heritage

The Algarve is a region with heterogeneous morphology, which can be divided into three distinct areas: littoral (the coastline of the Algarve, which as a result of the rise of the tourist industry since the 1960s has largely been transformed into a number of medium-sized urban areas); barrocal (the central area of the Algarve, often related to agriculture) and the interior (composed of mountains that separate the Algarve from the rest of Portugal to the north).

Rapid urban growth took place in the Algarve from the mid-1960s with the explosion of the mass tourism industry in the area. At that time, the bewildering choice of tourist activities immediately endangered important natural and cultural assets, which consequently deprived the Algarve of some of its once natural charm, transforming the littoral areas into landscapes of bricks and mortar. This new landscape, characterized by hotels, towering over a once ecological scenario is still visible today, as tall buildings extend along the shores of the Atlantic Ocean.

While the tourist industry continues to flourish in the Algarve area, many important ecological topographic characteristics were lost forever in the chaotic 1960s and 1970s that the Algarve experienced. Now, almost 40 years later, in an integrated European context where sustainability has become an important issue, stakeholders are trying as best they can to manage the still important ecological and cultural assets in order to preserve the important landscape characteristics that have made the Algarve special since the time of the Phoenicians. A good example of this endeavour is PROTAL (Programa Regional de Ocupação do Território do Algarve – Regional Programme of Territorial Occupation in the Algarve), which was reviewed in 2006. This programme is in effect a manifesto of the willingness to provide sustainable land use organization and its needs in this region.

Europe's natural tendency of population growth threatens a dire scenario for small regions such as the Algarve: as much as initiatives such as PROTAL may try, urban growth is an unavoidable consequence, and sustainability has to cope further with larger and more complex urban sprawl which, if not monitored accordingly, obviously jeopardizes the landscape.

This seems to be the case in the vicinity of the Algarve's district capital, the city of Faro, which, with a population of slightly over 58,000 according to CENSUS 2001, experienced a total tourist population for the municipality of Faro of 204,344 individuals (INE 2006), that is, an increase of 3.5 times during its summer months. Even though tourism may be beneficial for the region's growth and has proved to be the main source of employment, if it is not correctly managed such a seasonal swelling of population may be detrimental for sustainable development.

Furthermore, not only seasonality but also employment opportunities are contributing directly to city growth, and this may clearly be seen on the periphery of the district capital Faro. An example of such growth is the city of Olhão, just 5 km from Faro, which is increasingly becoming the capital's dormitory city, as a result of more affordable prices as well as recent building opportunities.

This, as well as easy access to Faro and other important cities such as Portimão, Albufeira and Vila Real de Santo António, has made Olhão a booming city which is extending mainly along the main roads on Faro's periphery.

GIS tools and spatial data inventories such as (CORINE) Coordination of Information on the Environment land cover (CLC) may be important tools to analyse with some accuracy the urban growth phenomena, as data inventories reveal with CLC90 and CLC2000 the important dates of growth between Faro and Olhão, which may be dynamically assessed because of the existence of two distinct moments in time.

Homer's *Odyssey* is proof that his Heroes already knew the west of the Mediterranean (Maia 1987). "But the other cliff, thou wilt note, Odysseus, is lower – they are close to each other; thou couldst even shoot an arrow across – and on it is a great fig tree with rich foliage, but beneath this divine Charybdis sucks down the black water" (Homer 1984 XII, 102). This unique region, extending over almost half of the Iberian Peninsula from as far as the southern lands of the river Tagus to Spanish Andalusia, was settled by many civilizations.

The region of the Algarve belonged to the Tartessos region and was described by the geographer Strabo (63 BC–24 AD) in his renowned work *Geographica,* which gives an accurate historical and social description of the Ancient World. The existence of different civilizations is manifold and archaeological evidence remains from as early as the times of the Celts (Maia 1987) as well as abundant Palaeolithic remains, are visible (Veiga 1887). During the Roman occupation, Augustus redrew the administrative boundaries in the first century, and the region became a part of the province of Lusitania. It was only much later, at the beginning of the twelfth century that Lusitania became segmented into a number of different provinces. One of those provinces was the Al-Garb, a name from the Moorish, meaning "The Occident". Later, in 1250 the Al-Garb province was conquered by the Christians and became the region of the *Algarbe* and was incorporated in the sovereignty of Portugal. The heterogeneous morphology of the present-day Algarve was quite similar in the times of the ancient Algarve.

Turdetanium is a prosperous country with all kinds of products and in large quantity. This richness is doubled by exports. The existing estuaries serve as routes of transportation which is carried out by tiny boats that enable the connections from the river deltas to the open sea. The abundance of rivers and estuaries makes almost the entire region navigable

(Strabo 2007, *Hispania Antiqua*, II, 1).

Strabo also gives us a clear idea of the inhabitants' behaviour in Roman times, mentioning also some of the major cities at that time:

The inhabitants built their cities with great proximity to their rivers and estuaries. Those cities are Asta, Nabrissa, Onuba, Ossonoba, Mainoba and a few others. The existing channels that connect those cities also ease the already abundant commerce. Commerce is carried out with the entire Italy and Rome being quite accessible by boat (Strabo 2007, *Hispania Antiqua*, II, 5).

The city of Faro, formerly known as Ossonoba, dates back to the fourth century BC. Regarding Ossonoba, in the last 100 years, an archaeological debate has taken place concerning its exact location. No one knows for sure whether this ancient city was located on the existing urban area of Faro or rather on the outskirts of the current city.

This dilemma deserves special attention from the archaeological and scientific community, as Ossonoba with already pre-Roman influence became the capital of the Roman *civitas* (vast Roman administrative region). This rich multicultural background of the Algarve, as a heterogeneous region of the Mediterranean, bestows on it a richness of cultural heritage, intertwined with Phoenician, Roman, Moorish and early Christian archaeological history.

The region as a whole, with its multi-cultural identity, has in itself become a very interesting study: European policies and urban growth characteristics apply easily, and its cultural heritage is a very visible attraction which should be protected actively as otherwise it may be endangered.

Foci of Algarve Sustainability Challenges

Nowadays the Algarve area faces many sustainability challenges, which call for solid GIS-based research. The literature (Clarke and Hoppens 1997, Syphard 2004, Al-Kheder 2005, Cabral 2006) strongly recommends the usage of Euclidian distance factors (urban proximity and road proximity), as well as morphological characteristics (slope and land use) for predicting urban growth which is stochastically assessed. As tourism seems to be a key growth factor in the Algarve region, distance from the International Airport of Faro was taken into account, as well as proximity to the University campus. Social leverage was analysed using CENSUS data per parish (*freguesia*).

Table 1 illustrates the data inventories used for the creation of our urban growth model. It is this combination of different important geographic inputs that will enable an accurate assessment of urban change in the studied area. Road information was digitized from the Portuguese Digital Map at 1:500,000 and georeferenced as polyline shapefile layers in ArcGIS. Figure 1 explains the overall methodological process used, showing that the multiple data chosen for urban growth assessment will constitute our suitability map that, with linear information of growth change between CLC90 and CLC2000, will lead us to a first estimation of urban growth towards a known temporal frame: the year 2008. This prediction is done using CA iterations based on a Markovian transition matrix as will be explained later. Should the projection for 2008 prove to be accurate, assemblage of data will allow estimation for 2038. "Urban Growth Trends for the Faro-Olhão Area" describes the underlying database for our study.

Table 1 Data chosen for urban growth model

Data layer	Source	Original projection	Used for
Environmental data			
Algarve DEM 90 m resolution	SRTM (Shuttle Radar Topography Mission – NASA)	UTM	For creation of slope
Slope	SRTM (secondary data)	Lisbon Hayford-Gauss	Significant layer for APM
Portuguese administrative chart	Portuguese Geographic Institute	Lisbon Hayford-Gauss	Definition of municipality and freguesias boundaries
Land use for Portugal	Requested from Portuguese Environmental Institute, belonging to CORINE land cover 1990 and 2000 Project.	Lisbon Hayford-Gauss	Significant layer to understand land use/land change between CLC90 and CLC2000
Roads	Digitized on screen from carta de Portugal digital 1:500,000 scale – Portuguese Geographic Institute	Lisbon Hayford-Gauss	Road distance is critically analysed as an important factor for network proximity between Faro and Olhão
Social data			
Census 1991 and Census 2001	National Institute of Statistics (INE)	No projection	Used to balance weight factors among freguesias and tendencies of growth

Spatial Data Inventories and Urban Growth

The CLC project started on 27th June 1985 as a programme that would address the following issues: state of individual environments; geographical distribution and state of natural areas; geographical distribution and abundance of wild fauna and flora; quality and abundance of water resources; land cover structure and the state of the soil; quantities of toxic substances discharged into the environment and a list of natural hazards (EEA) (Fig. 1).

In this sense, CLC can be summarized as "an experimental project for gathering, coordinating and ensuring the consistency of information on the state of the environment and natural resources in the Community".[3] With the mapping of CLC2000, besides the already manifold usage of CLC, we have the advantage of assessing two distinct moments in time and, thus, an evaluation of changes in landscape and land use can be obtained by the analysis of multi-temporal images (Prol-Ledesma et al. 2002). Following the very important notion that dynamic modelling needs time-based support and that CLC usage was a standardized opportunity to assess change, we could not think of a more convenient method of assessing the change of urban areas than comparing the urban areas of Faro-Olhão in the CLC90 with the CLC2000 series. CLC has a general nomenclature which can be divided into five distinct types, namely: urban, agriculture, forest, wetlands and water bodies. All of these five types are present in the Algarve area.

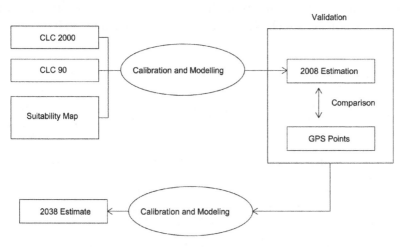

Fig. 1 Methodological approach for projecting urban growth prospecting

Creating a cross-tabulation matrix for both CLCs, we could compare CLC90 and CLC2000 at a glance and understand the possible changes within both time frames. From this comparison we drew the following conclusions:

1. Most of the agricultural areas have changed to urban areas;
2. A lesser quantity of forest areas have changed to urban areas;
3. Some forest areas have changed to agriculture areas;
4. A few agriculture areas have changed to forest.

Therefore, the matrix results indicate some clear and simple conclusions which are considered quite typical in an actual environmental context: urban areas expand on man-made soils, while unploughed land becomes ploughed and normally changes from forest to agricultural. Agricultural changes to forest may be related to abandonment or to governmental incentives for forest preservation. As no such incentives were planned for the Algarve region, the most probable reason for the change is related to agricultural abandonment. This information is of crucial significance to support a linear notion of urban growth tendency. It is this tendency that will manifest itself as a propensity of change which can be applied as a rule for our urban growth. Table 2 shows a cross-tabulation matrix for assessing changes in the different land use classes between CLC90 and CLC2000 (the columns represent CLC90, while the rows represent CLC2000).

On the other hand, Table 3 suggests the possibilities of conditional change to different land use types based on Markovian transition rules for an 8-year estimate, which allows us to estimate how much will be changed in 2008.

Table 2 Cross-tabulation matrix between CLC90 and CLC2000

	Urban	Agricultural	Forest	Wetlands	Water bodies	Land use change (%)
Urban	100.00	1.07	0.29	0.10	0.00	1.46
Agricultural	0.00	98.69	0.85	0.00	0.00	0.85
Forest	0.00	0.15	97.87	0.00	2.58	2.73
Wetlands	0.00	0.09	0.39	99.90	1.25	1.73
Water bodies	0.00	0.00	0.59	0.00	96.17	0.59

Table 3 Markovian transition probability matrix

	Urban (%)	Agricultural (%)	Forest (%)	Wetlands (%)	Water bodies (%)
Urban	85.00	3.75	3.75	3.75	3.75
Agricultural	13.21	83.89	1.79	1.11	0.00
Forest	2.28	6.75	83.19	3.10	4.67
Wetlands	15.08	0.00	0.00	84.92	0.00
Water bodies	0.00	0.00	12.31	5.94	81.75

Urban Growth Trends for the Faro-Olhão Area

A suitability map may be understood, as a consequence of present spatial interpretation, to recognize possible future land use scenarios. An initial rehearsal regarding urban growth tendencies was done by generating a comparison of CLC90 and CLC2000 with respect to urban growth change which allowed us to assess the existing growth for the area linearly. The insertion of further variables, such as recovered population data, distance weights to roads, urban centres, as well as international airport distance and university location, prove to be key economic drivers for future urban growth in the Algarve region. This may be seen in Fig. 2, where a suitability map results from the selection of the variables and consequently, the addition of the different layers, arriving at a conclusion about the propensity for urban growth in the studied area.

This weighted and normalized information, as shown in the Annex, allowed us to create a suitability map for the most probable urban growth tendencies in the forthcoming years. It is thus an example of prospective planning regarding existing urban growth, anticipating, as well as coping with, the natural tendencies of important factors that govern urban sprawl.

It can be clearly seen that a tendency for further growth around the periphery of Faro is likely to happen. As CENSUS data have pointed out, the most probable districts of further growth are on the outskirts of the district capital. In recent decades, proximity to the National Road 125 and to the University of the Algarve campus have been shown to be important factors for continuing urban growth. The overall trend appears to be a continuing growth of Faro-Olhão, as well as the possible growth of other urban nuclei such as Estoi and Quelfes.

Using IDRISI as a software tool with easily usable CA, linear CLC cognition, and the calculated suitability map will all allow us to assess the tendency of urban growth more accurately and thus understand the necessity for commitment towards the preservation of the cultural landscape which may occur in the near future.

Clark Labs – IDRISI comprises the perfect tool for accurate assessment for CA. CA transition rules are related to a set of possibilities constituted by iterations of Markovian probability matrices (if the CA_Markov module is used, as is the case in our study). The advantages of using Markovian probability matrices related to CA mainly concern the possibility of measuring different land use changes that are supported in the initially generated matrices (Table 3). This is a considerable advantage, as it shows the capacity of these matrices to cope with different kinds of land use trends and their transformation (Fig. 2).

Four important principles will allow cells to iterate, thus originating a CA. These principles (Batty 2007) create the concept of a CA for our region of study. Firstly, the land use of the region of the Algarve is represented in raster format with a specific dimension of equal-sized cells that relate to others by a given proximity or adjacency. Secondly, our cells can only take one state at a time, that is, one cell can only change into urban, agricultural, wetlands or water bodies and never into two of the classes simultaneously. Thirdly, changes in a cell depend on the existing *neighbourhood* of the particular cell, influenced by our fourth condition, the propensity to change previously calculated on our suitability map. The basic cell thus relates to its local *neighbourhood* and gains a spatial dimension which may be perfectly adequate for land use prediction and urban growth. An example of CA neighbourhoods may be observed in Fig. 3.

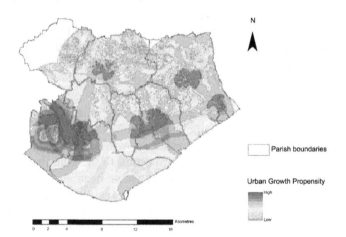

Fig. 2 Suitability map for urban growth

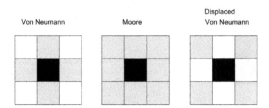

Fig. 3 Example of cellular automata neighbourhoods

Our urban growth model forecasts urban growth based on CLC90 and CLC00 information for two distinct time frames: 2008 and 2038. The reason for projecting the 2008 land use is related to the importance of validating the assumptions and choice of variables in our initial input. In this sense, two hypotheses occur: (i) our model shows enough accuracy and we are thus prompted to model the 2038 land use situation and urban growth tendencies or (ii) inaccuracy leads us to reframe our pool of variables and their choice in order to better grasp the tendencies of urban growth in the Algarve.

The validation of the 2008 urban growth was done on the actual terrain, using 100 surveyed points to target urban and non-urban areas. As a result, producer and user accuracy were tested, showing us the overall accuracy of our modelled 2008 land use for urban areas. Our 2008 forecast generated a result of global exactitude of 93% and a kappa statistic of 86%. These encouraging results allowed us to continue with our forecast of the 2038 land use/land change panorama. User accuracy is a result of the division of the number of correctly classified pixels in each category by the total number of pixels that are classified and indicates the probability that a pixel classified in a given category actually represents that category on the ground (Lillesand et al. 2004).

A clear tendency of urban growth around the periphery of existing urban centres seems to exist (Fig. 4). Thus, rather than the appearance of new urban centres in the Faro-Olhão area, growth seems to occur depending on attractiveness factors such as proximity to the University and to the International Airport. Those reasons seem to be the explanation for extended growth particularly along the west side of the Faro perimeter. Previously small and almost inexistent agglomerations at the beginning of the 1990s will inevitably form larger areas with some endangerment of the natural and historic landscape.

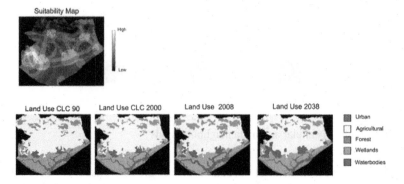

Fig. 4 Expected urban growth

Assessing the Historico-Cultural Heritage in the Faro-Olhão Area

In the mid-nineteenth century, Estácio da Veiga actively studied the heritage which remained from prehistory in the Algarve. Later he founded the first Archaeological Museum, which could be considered as the first academic initiative of archaeology in the Algarve. Prehistory and protohistory had already gained some relevance as archaeological records, but the clearly visible Roman and Moorish influence seemed to gain weight due to the growth of archaeological Romanticism which was important at the time when Estácio da Veiga was gathering information and continuing an, alas unfinished, fifth volume to his *Antiguidades Monumentais do Algarve* (Veiga 2006).

It was the initiative of the Instituto Português do Património Arquitectónico (IPPAR) in 1989 that for the first time resulted in an archaeological map of Portugal, which summarized some of the important archaeological remains in the region. Based on the *Carta Arqueológica de Portugal,* as well as on other bibliographical research, we were able to compare a total of 43 archaeological sites regarding their proximity to urban growth. The results were obvious: of our 43-site sample, 72% were located within a radius of less than 1 km from urban areas, while 26% were located within a maximum of 2 km radius, against only 2% which are located within 3 km of the urban perimeter. This indeed is an alarming scenario, as our comparison was based on the generated land use for 2008. As illustrated in Fig. 5, regarding the proximity of our archaeological remains to the urban area in our 2038 projection, the average expansion of up to 1 km in the next 30 years is endangering and could destroy 72% of the region's archaeological sites if no monitoring and planning takes place. Among the analysed sites, prehistoric site locations, Roman necropolises, Roman villas and Moorish artefacts were taken into account.

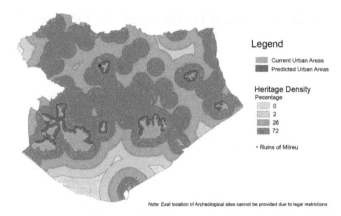

Fig. 5 Site propensity to change to urban use and urban growth prediction

One of the sites directly targeted for eminent endangerment are the ruins of Milreu, which were classified as a National Monument in 1910 and are considered to be one of the largest Roman Villas in Portugal.

Figure 5 represents a combination of site propensity to change to urban use and urban growth prediction in an attempt to visualize the possible endangerment of the cultural heritage.

Policy Lessons and Conclusions

It has become clear that the Algarve is an area of the utmost importance regarding a long tradition of historico-cultural heritage. GIS tools with their capability to assess spatial information and cope with large enough databases from various sources seem to be an important pillar for strategic decision-making support, as well as for regional planning and monitoring heritage endangerment (Fig. 5).

Urban growth, an unavoidable reality, may jeopardize a fragile cultural background which shares valued patrimony. The spatial cognition of such archaeological sites and better notions of urban growth and sprawl based on urban growth models and spatial analytical processes have proved to be important tools for an ongoing research agenda of historic and socio-cultural heritage protection in the Faro-Olhão area.

It is our hope that, with the increasing accuracy of urban growth models, the historico-cultural heritage endangered by the growth of urban peripheries may be better analysed, leading to sounder and more sustainable cities which would never lose the asset of their cultural identity, but pass it on to future generations to cherish.

Annex: Normalization and Tendency of UGM Variables

(a)   (b)

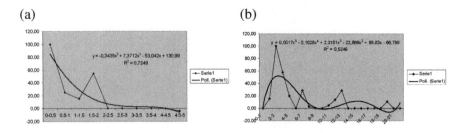

Fig. 6 a Road distance weight (x =kilometres; y = percentage);
       b Airport distance weight (x = kilometres; y = percentage)

(a)   (b)

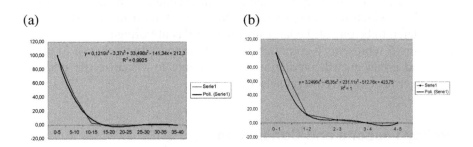

Fig. 7 a Slope distance weight (x = percentage rise; y = percentage);
       b Distance from CLC90 weight (x = kilometres; y = percentage)

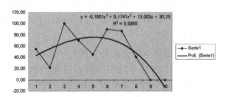

Fig. 8 University distance weight (x = kilometres; y = percentage)

Notes

[1]   See, e.g., Clarke and Hoppens 1997, Engelen et al. 1999.
[2]   http://www.culture.gov.uk/NR/rdonlyres/50E5EC89=7A5E-4B33-8CFA
[3]   Official Journal L 176, 6.7.1985 - European Environment Agency.

References

Al-Kheder S, Shan J (2005) *Cellular Automata, Urban Growth Simulation and Evaluation – A Case Study of Indianapolis*. GeoComputation 2005, University of Michigan, Michigan.

Batty M (2007) *Cities and Complexity: Understanding Cities with Cellular Automata, Agent-Based Models, and Fractals*, The MIT Press, Cambridge MA.

Box P (1999) *GIS and Cultural Resource Management: A Manual for Heritage Mangers*. Bangkok, UNESCO.

Cabral P (2006) *Étude de la Intersection Urbaine par Télédétection, sig et Modélisation, Mathématiques et Applications aux Sciences Sociales*, École des Hautes Études en Sciences Sociales, Paris.

Clarke KC, Hoppens S (1997) *A self-modifying cellular automation model of historical urbanization in the San Francisco bay area*. Environment & Planning B n. 24, pp. 247–261.

Conolly K, Lake M (2006) *Geographical Information Systems in Archaeology, Manuals in Archaeology*, Cambridge University Press, Cambridge, UK.

Ebert D (2004) *Predictive Modeling and the Ecology of Hunter Gatherers of the Boral Forest of Manitoba*. BAR S1221, Archaeopress, Oxford.

Engelen G, Geertman S, Smits P, Wessels C (1999) *Dynamic GIS and strategic physical planning support: A practical application*. In: Stilwell J, Geertman S and Openshaw S (eds) *Geografical Information and Planning*, Springer-Verlag, Berlin, Heidelberg, New York, pp. 87–111.

Gillings M, Goodrick G T (1996) *Sensuous and Reflexive GIS; Exploring Visualization and VRML*. Internet Archaeology I, http://intarch.ac.uk

Grøn O, Loska A (2002) *Development of Methods for Satellite Monitoring of Cultural Heritage Sites*, Technical Report NIKU, Norwegian Space Centre, Oslo.

Hernandez M (2002) *Use of Satellite Imagery and Geographical Information Systems to Monitor World Heritage Sites*. World Heritage Paper 10, UNESCO, pp. 98–104.

Hill B, Devitt M, Sergeyeva S (2007) *Understanding Past and Future Land Use, ArcUser Online*, http://www.esri.com/news/arcuser/0507/pastlanduse.html, April–June, ESRI.

Homer (1984) *The Odyssey*, trans. by Murray AT, Loeb Classics – Harvard University Press, Norwich.

INE (2006) *Anuário Estatístico da Região do Algarve – Statistical Yearbook of the Algarve Region*, Instituto Nacional de Estatística, Lisboa.

Joukowski M (1980) *A Complete Manual of Field Archaeology: Tools and Techniques of Field Work for Archaeologists*, Prentice Hall, Englewood Cliffs.

Kwamme KL (1999) *Recent direction and developments in geographical information systems*. Journal of Archaeological Research n. 7(2), pp. 153–185.

Lansing JS (2002) *Artificial societies and the social sciences*. Artificial Life n. 8, pp. 279–292.

Legrand G (1991) *Dicionário de Filosofia*, Edições 70, Lisboa.

Lillesand TM, Kiefer RW, Chipman JW (2004) *Remote Sensing and Image Interpretation*, 5th Edition, John Wiley and Sons, New York.

Maia MA (1987) *Romanização do território hoje português a sul do Tejo – Contribuição para a análise do processo de assimilação e interacção socio-cultural 218 a.C – 14 d.C*, PhD Thesis in Prehistory and Archaeology, Faculdade de Letras, Universidade de Lisboa.

Montufo A (1997) *The use of satellite imagery and digital image processing in landscape archaeology. A case study from the island of Mallorca, Spain*. Geoarchaeology n. 12(1), pp. 71–85.

Pontius GR, Chen H (2006) *GEOMOD modeling*. In: Eastman JR (ed) *Idrisi 15: The Andes Edition*, Clark Labs, Worcester MA.

Prol-Ledesma RM, Uribe-Alcántara EM, Diaz-Molina O (2002) *Use of cartographic data and Landsat TM images to determine land use change in the vicinity of Mexico City*. International Journal of Remote Sensing n. 23(9), pp. 1927–1933.

Renfrew C, Bahn P (2004) *Archaeology: Theories, Methods and Practice*, Thames and Hudson, London.

Sassen S (1998) *Globalization and its Discontent: Essays on the New Mobility of People and Money*, the New Press, New York.

Schiffer MB (2004) *Studying technological Change: A behavioural perspective*. World Archaeology n. 36(4), pp. 579–585.

Sebastian L, Judge J (1988) *Predicting the past: Correlation, explanation and the use of archaeological models*. In: Judge WJ, Sebastian L (eds) *Quantifying the Present and Predicting the Past: Theory, Method and Application of Archaeological Predictive Modelin*, Government Printing Office, Verlag, Washington DC, pp. 1–18.

Strabo (2007) *Geographica*, trans. by Forbiger A, Marix Verlag. Wiesbaden.

Syphard AD, Clarke KC, Franklin J (2004) *Using a cellular automaton model to forecast the effect of urban growth on habitat pattern in Southern California*. Ecological n. 2(2), pp. 185–203.

Veiga SPME (1887) *Antiguidades monumentaes do Algarve. II*, Imprensa Nacional, Lisboa.

Veiga SPME from (2006) *Antiguidades monumentaes do Algarve – Tempos Históricos,* vol. 5, Câmara Municipal de Silves, Museu Nacional de Arqueologia, Loulé.

Verhagen P (2007) *Case Studies in Archaeological Predictive Modelling.* ASLU 14, Leiden University Press, Leiden.

Von Bertalanffy L (1950) *An outline of general systems theory.* Philosophy of Science n. 1(2), pp. 134–165.

Warren RE, Asch DL (2000) *A predictive model of archaeological site location in the eastern Prairie Peninsula.* In: Wescott KL, Brandon RJ (eds) *Practical Applications of GIS for Archaeologists: A Predictive Modeling Toolkit,* Taylor and Francis, London, pp. 90–111.

Westcott KL (2000) Brandon RJ *Practical Application of GIS for Archaeologists: A Predicative Modelling Kit,* Taylor and Francis, London.

Wheatley D, Gillings M (2002) *Spatial Technology and Archaeology: The Archaeological Applications of GIS,* Taylor and Francis, London.

Wilson AG (1974) *Urban and Regional Models in Geography and Planning,* John Wiley and Sons, Chichester.

4. Leisure and Privatisation of Public Space

Leisure activities are tied to the evolution of consumer and shopping models. The reproduction of traditional urban forms inside leisure and consumer containers has drained the city of its public dimension. Bringing to mind worlds no longer real, creating generic spaces that imitate the city: these are the premises for the process of privatisation of contemporary public space that create entertainment-oriented themed environments. But in places unexpectedly released from standardisation, a different urban perspective can be developed, in which public space may be reconfigured as the space of accessibility and interaction.

Spaces of Consumption

Xavier Costa

Place as a Commodity

Contemporary processes of turning living spaces into a commodity are a decisive factor to properly understand the phenomenon of present-day cities. The ongoing redefinition of our environments as spaces of consumption includes strategies that permit their incorporation into the dynamics of advertising and commodification.

Our cities are increasingly defined by the dynamics of space transformation in a world of consumption, including strategies of publicity and commodification. The traditional notion of *contextualization* – which defined spatial design as a process of adjustment to "local" traits – is being replaced by *thematization* processes linking architecture to de-localized meanings, thus participating in a growing, universal visual culture. As a consequence, thematization tends to be emphasized when architecture and urbanism are connected with cultural and historical consumption, mass tourism and leisure and entertainment, in a general sense.

Spaces of consumption also refer to the consumption of places and spaces. It is increasingly difficult to distinguish those strategies that aim at defining spaces destined to promote consumption from those which favour the consumption of the spaces themselves. The British sociologist John Urry has studied space consumption phenomena within the framework of mass culture, as in the case of contemporary tourism. In his book *Consuming Places* Urry (1995, p. 2) Urry states, as regards *literal* consumption of places in our culture: "what people take to be significant about a place (...) is over time depleted, exhausted by its very use". One of the main forms of space consumption is based on its *visual* consumption – which can be performed from a distance, given the potential offered by present-day telecommunications. The "tourist gaze", as Urry says, is characteristic of this new relationship with spaces. The "tourist gaze" becomes visually objectified and captured through photographs, films and other kinds of images which allow the gaze to be infinitely reproduced. From this point of view, space consumption becomes inseparable from contemporary visual culture.

G. Maciocco, S. Serreli (eds.), *Enhancing the City*, Urban and Landscape Perspectives 6, DOI 10.1007/978-90-481-2419-0_9, © Springer Science+Business Media B.V. 2009

Archaeology and Consumption

Since the early modern period, in particular since the European Enlightenment, archaeological projects have transformed places of daily use into entities of exceptional significance – receptacles of traces and signs which could become mobile, removable and therefore exchangeable, collectionable.

Once the past became reified in the form of archaeological finds, these in turn could be marketed and could thus become commodified. This phenomenon makes reference to that "disenchantment" of the past, of history, which Max Weber and Walter Benjamin wrote about during the early decades of the twentieth century – the past presenting itself as an infinite accumulation of disconnected fragments. This landscape of desolation serves as a backdrop to strategies of consumption and collecting.

Parallel to these processes of reification, one can certify the transcription of the experience of places in terms of pure visual perception. This ocularcentrism which determines the experience of cities and spaces takes on a decisive definition in the work of John Ruskin, especially in his book *The Stones of Venice*, one of the most significant and influential architectural writings of the nineteenth century, published in three volumes during the 1850s.

In this extensive treatise on the city of Venice and its architectural and artistic heritage, Ruskin was able to codify the complexities of the historical city in a language and a series of descriptions. These were based firstly on visual perception of them, and secondly, on the subsequent transmission of this experience. Ruskin established a new language, as well as a new repertoire of diagrams and graphic descriptions, a prototype of later literature of incipient mass tourism. After extensive reception and success of this work, in the late 1870s Ruskin published an abbreviated version entitled *Traveller's edition*, conceived to be used *in situ*, as a portable guide while visiting the city. Together with its immediate precedent, *The Seven Lamps of Architecture* (1849), Ruskin's architectural text is for the first time addressed to the traveller, who is able to observe through direct experience what is being described. As a result, Ruskin established a new form of describing architecture and places which was to give way to the popular genre of *Baedekers* and other guidebooks for travellers, a phenomenon that anticipated twentieth-century culture.

Consumption and Public Space

Starting in the period immediately following World War II, a reflexive discourse on the relationship between architecture and mass culture was progressively defined. In the London-based Independent Group's writings and ideas of the 1950s, especially those by their critic Reyner Banham, as well as in the Paris-based urban reflections of Henri Lefebvre (1996) and Guy Debord (1967), we find the emergence of new questions that have persisted throughout these past decades.

In *La société du spectacle* (1967) Debord diagnosed the sublimation of the industrially produced commodity into an *image*. This defining trait of the society of the spectacle is particularly appropriate to understand the progressive transformation of places into sets of images. Once this transformation is produced, the qualities of places become apt to circulate and to be incorporated into wider structures within the global phenomenon of contemporary visual culture. Such an observation was emphasized by Ignasi de Solà-Morales' writings about the relationship between architecture, city and photography. Solà-Morales described how photography became a valuable instrument to take possession of spaces which are not familiar or known to us. Travellers who take a photograph of a place upon arrival for the first time are not only registering a new visual experience, but are also projecting the codes and meanings of the visual culture they carry within themselves onto a space that is still to be "interpreted". As Debord noted, a place can become "sublimated" into a pure image – and as a result can be consumed more easily. In fact, our dependency on images when it comes to establishing a relationship with places turns us into "permanent tourists" – as Urry would say – even when physical mobility is not taking place, as images themselves ensure virtual mobility.

Therefore, what do we mean by public space today, when most collective spaces and their meanings belong to consumption and entertainment? In the context of the exhibition organized in Bordeaux by the *arc en rêve centre d'architecture, Mutations* (2001), Rem Koolhaas suggested that the latest public activity is *shopping*. To paraphrase Koolhaas (2000), the mechanisms and spaces of shopping are shaping our cities' historic centres, our peripheries, streets and more recently our train stations, museums, hospitals, schools, internet, even the army. Airports have seen their benefits soar thanks to the transformation of travellers into shoppers – the end of the twentieth century will be remembered as the time when it became impossible to understand the city without the phenomenon of shopping.

Consequently, the consumption of spaces favours the proliferation, the universalization of generic spaces *par excellence*.

We find ourselves with the problem of considering architecture as a container for commercial activities, but at the same time as possible content to be incorporated into the dynamics of consumption. Marie Christine Boyer's article *Cities for Sale: Merchandising History at South Street Seaport*, published in 1992, offers an eloquent example of this fusion between container and content. In the transformation of the South Street Seaport area in New York City, based on an interest to preserve a historic district of Manhattan threatened by the urban development of Wall Street's financial district, the historical value of the area was used to introduce spaces of leisure activities and commerce. As proposed by Boyer, in the South Street case, we find a perfect coincidence between heritage protectionism and the introduction of new spaces of consumption. The formerly described historical cycle, which stemmed from the archaeological project and culminated in the commodification of architecture, is reproduced simultaneously in a project like the South Street Seaport one.

City Museum

Antoni Muntadas' artwork *City Museum,* presented in 1992, offered a reflection on this process of commodifying cities and all kinds of urban spaces. With a series of images dealing with the visual appropriation of places, especially by the "tourist gaze" described by John Urry (2000), *City Museum* displayed the dominant role of visual perception, as well as the projection of visual culture through the universal use of mediation techniques such as photography. In her essay on photography and its everyday use, Susan Sontag described how taking photographs constitutes a strategy of appropriating places through the projection of iconographies and visual affiliations – which allow us to incorporate the place we are visiting into a familiar visual culture. Through travellers' and tourists' anonymous *snapshots*, Muntadas pointed out the progressive colonization of spaces by the universe of images – as well as the phenomenon of a contemporary voyeurism which is increasingly framing our relationship with public spaces.

Both the configuration of spaces of consumption and the consumption of spaces are part of a parallel, inseparable process. Ever since Walter Benjamin identified the first contemporary commercial spaces in the *passages* of the *fin de siècle* European metropolis, a typological and cultural evolution has developed. From the *passage* to the boulevard, from Parisian *grands magasins* to North American department stores, from *hypermarchés* to theme parks, one finds the same process in which consumption and architectural space develop jointly. However, they also reveal that those public spaces which emerged during the modern period are progressively inseparable from modern strategies of shopping. Is it possible today to think of a public space that is not linked to consumption – whether it be a direct or visually related link? As Benjamin (1987) argued in "Paris, Capital of the Nineteenth Century", is our appreciation of heritage and historical culture inseparable from its commercialisation and eventual commodification?

As a conclusive point, the evolution of spaces of consumption described has triggered the development of new strategies of *space consumption*, a phenomenon without precedent. Spaces thus become realities that may be progressively "emptied" or "exhausted" with regard to their contents. Ranging from the present-day notion of historic heritage to the thematization of all types of spaces – natural, urban and domestic – there is one unstoppable process of transformation lying at the heart of the cultural project in which we all find ourselves immersed.

References

Benjamin W (1987) *Paris (ed) Capital of the nineteenth-century*, In: Benjamin W *Reflections*, Schoken, New York, pp 146–162.

Boyer C (1992) *Cities for sale: Merchandising history at South Street Seaport*, In: Sorkin M (ed) *Variations on a Theme Park: The New American City and the End of Public Space*, Noonday, New York.

Debord G (1967) *La société du spectacle*, Buchet-Chastel, Paris.

Koolhaas R et al. (2000) *Mutations, arc en rêve centre d'architecture*, Actar, Barcelona-Burdeus.

Lefebvre H (1996) *Writings on Cities*, translated and edited by Kofman E and Lebas E, Blackwell, Oxford.

Ruskin J (1849), *The Seven Lamps of Architecture*, Smith Elder and Co., London.

Ruskin J (1853) *The Stones of Venice*, 3 vol., Smith Elder and Co., London.

Urry J (1995) *Consuming Places*, Routledge, London, New York.

Urry J (2002) *The Tourist Gaze,* Second edition, Sage, London, Thousands Oaks, New Delhi.

Shopping as an Urban Leisure Activity

Laura Lutzoni

Simulation of the City and Evolution of Consumer Models

Leisure activities cannot be evaluated without taking into consideration the strong tie established between them and the spatial forms of shopping. Places of consumption have changed from areas that tended just to sell all manner of goods, to authentic areas of entertainment, their main characteristic being to simulate the urban centre, reproducing both its spaces and its functions. Whereas in the past leisure activities were localised in particular urban areas and practised only at specific times of day, there is currently a complete mixture of leisure and consumer phenomena in a single place, where there is total merging and equivalence of space for shopping and for entertainment. To understand better the way the shopping activity has become an integral part of leisure practices, we need to analyse the change in the bond between trade and urban space organisation.

Trading has constituted one of the main cornerstones into which the history of the city has ramified, and has contributed since it came into existence to characterising spaces and places destined for particular experiences of public and social life. Mass consumerism, the spreading of shopping malls, the thematisation of urban spaces and urban islands dedicated to leisure activities are phenomena that show the cultural and physical transformation of the contemporary city contributing in an important way to placing consumption at the centre of attention. Over the course of the centuries an indissoluble relationship had been established between trade and public space, so that trade could not exist without the presence of public space. In modern times the balanced, lasting pair has altered and we have seen a rapid change in the relationship. Commercial activities in particular, which in the past revolved like satellites round the public space fulcrum, currently create new commercial and entertainment spaces, emptying the city of its original, authentic functions.

In the contemporary age, within the urban structure the spaces destined for consumption are those that have mostly undergone transformation: in a few decades we have passed from a *spatial* model – characterised by the spontaneous aggregation of commercial activities, circumscribed and enclosed in a well-defined area, usually identified with the historic centre

G. Maciocco, S. Serreli (eds.), *Enhancing the City*, Urban and Landscape Perspectives 6,
DOI 10.1007/978-90-481-2419-0_10, © Springer Science+Business Media B.V. 2009

of the city – to an *a-spatial* model that has nowadays materialised in the figure of the urban island dedicated to commercial and entertainment activities, within which human activities are represented in the form of a *simulacrum*. Shopping centres fit into the urban fabric like shopping sanctuaries, temples where shopping loses its functional worth to become an experience of life and a leisure practice made up of gestures and codified rituals (Ritzer 1999). The new trading forms appear as models of a new social space, in which a show is put on daily with products and consumers as protagonists. Shopping centres impose themselves as local surrogates of centrality and evoke urban lifestyles, offering an artificial alternative to the traditional places of encounter, like town squares.

This phenomenon does not prove to be limited and circumscribed to shopping centres alone, but the progressive *standardisation urban space* has undergone has led to a negation of the city in the plural in favour of continuous "recycling" of what has already been seen and tried, the so-called *generic city* (Koolhaas and Mau 1998; Chung et al. 2001; Maciocco 2008). This is all to be interpreted in the light of the importance of consumption raised to its extreme consequences. The "generic city" is the city of shopping and leisure which has increasingly claimed in modern cities to simulate reality. And indeed this phenomenon of intense mercification of society has dissolved the relationship between *urbs,* the city meant as a physical place, and *civitas*, the city as the society inhabiting it. The idea according to which the improvement and growth of the *urbs* would be a driving force for the entire *civitas* has come up against a quite different reality. In effect, the *urbs* has sunk into an involutive spiral, for the obvious reason that – *civitas* being subordinate to *urbs* – the vital relationship between these two components, which had always been indissolubly linked to the destiny of the spatial organisation of the territory, was missing. The separation of *urbs* and *civitas* involves the loss of the relationship with place: men are no longer able to see and understand the city (Costa 1996). The loss of the capacity to represent the city corresponds to the disappearance of the city as a conceptual unit, in the sense that the contemporary city cannot be represented as it has become a *simulacrum* of a city (De Azua 2003), a copy of the copy of cities that never existed, were never inhabited by anyone, but were functional for mass consumption (Maciocco and Pittaluga 2006). This difficulty in representing the city materialises in projectuality indifferent to contexts and places (Ibelings 2001); the contemporary city may be defined as an "ageographic" entity for it tends to lose its relations with the physical and cultural geography of the place (Sorkin 1992). The territory tends to alienate itself to favour an urban image adopted as such, which completely disregards a social, public dimension to press more and more towards standardised representations (Koolhaas and Mau 1998).

The concept of thematisation of the city, with the consequent creation of urban islands devoted to leisure and consumer activities, cannot be understood without a brief analysis of the evolution of the spaces of trade. A reconstruction of the development of the first urban agglomerates makes clear how the city has revealed itself, from the very beginning, as a structure in which all the principal functions of the community were organised in the urban centre (Mumford 1961). The first forms of trade were situated in local markets, subsequently in medieval fairs, to arrive at the construction of authentic urban spaces, like squares and streets. From the nineteenth century onwards, in town planning development, vehicular traffic demand could no longer be underestimated, and found in the *commercial road* the answer to the new demands of society. New commercial activities were located in the streets of the commercial city and a preferential relationship became established for vehicular traffic, with little consideration given to pedestrians. With the advent of capitalism some of the old forms of market survived but, generally speaking, urban organisation did not leave room for the market square. The artisan's shop was replaced by a new type of *shop*, featuring a glass front where goods for sale were displayed. In this context the display of goods, characterised by sleekness and showiness, supported commercial activities with economic benefits and advantages (Sombart 1915). During the course of the nineteenth century the *gallery* structure spread, which very quickly appeared in each commercial city. This enclosed a series of businesses: shops, cafés and restaurants; its merit was basically that of keeping the shops at a distance from the streets. In the *passages* vehicular traffic disappeared and space presented as a road of commerce, created only to awaken desire (Benjamin 1986). The gallery, nevertheless, ran counter to the canons of the commercial city; its careful functionality was antithetical to the principle of transformability, which urban development, however, needed at that time. The heirs to the markets and fairs were the *universal expositions*, which created periodic spaces in the metropolises destined to spread and stage the arts, science and goods. The important functions of socialisation and modernisation carried out by the expositions reached their highest cultural significance in the period from halfway through the nineteenth century to the early decades of the twentieth. The urban space used by the exposition was a symbolic place, where progress was celebrated. After half a century the surface area destined for the universal expositions was multiplied fivefold and they became the mirror in which society could admire its progress. The precursors of department stores were the Paris *passages*, which from 1822 constituted trade centres specialised in luxury goods. In these spaces the literary figure of the *flâneur* became established, an individual swallowed up by the traffic, who, with an alienated gaze, walks aimlessly, observing the city through the veil of the crowd. His route is a labyrinth that changes shape at each step, and the department store is identified by the *flâneur* as the place where his fantasies materialise (Benjamin 1986). The "department store" was born in Paris in 1852; innovative features for those times were the chance to enter free, fixed prices, as well as a continuous turnover of stock. In the department store everything tended towards promoting the sale of goods. In this scenario shopping came into being, a ritual with the ultimate aim of purchasing the goods on sale. From its beginning, department store organisation and functioning manifested its superiority compared with the forms of retail selling, by mechanised operations, in which diversification of supply was entwined with the management unit.

During the course of history the definition of the term consumption has undoubtedly evolved. The concept was born under the influx of the Protestant Reform between the fifteenth and the sixteenth centuries. The Protestant cultural world had fundamental importance in formulating the original consumer models, in that dedication to work and saving facilitated the increase in personal wealth (Campbell 1989). But the consumer behaviours of the society we live in go back largely to the period of the industrial revolution. Departing from the nineteenth century, in effect, great economic expansion began which gave rise to today's consumer society. Only in the twentieth century did consumerism, as a mass phenomenon, become an essential, fundamental feature of society (Corrigan 1997). In Europe we can begin to speak of the development of consumerism from the end of the Second World War, when the model of life based on the myth of success and the quest for individual wealth was imported from America, which in the course of the early sixties was to create an authentic mass consumer society. The large quantity of goods put into circulation appeared to bring added meanings; to possess certain goods was a means that indicated belonging to a particular social class: the urban middle class. The department store became a sort of large "label handbook" and concepts were worked out from which the prototype emerged, in its entirety, of the middle class. A cultural requirement thus took shape, based on the satisfaction of needs from an individualistic viewpoint, in which consumption played a role of primary importance (Codeluppi 1992). The goods one wishes to purchase are charged with subjective meanings to satisfy the needs for security within contemporary society. Today's consumer culture has as its foundation the commercial manipulation of images and human desires, which are continually reprocessed through advertising, signs and shows.

The Society of the Spectacle and the Space of Containers

Shopping is a phenomenon typical of the affluent society, the key element of which is the spare time available of the individuals interested in buying. Shopping becomes a moment of immersion in an oneiric dimension: the spectacle begins – much earlier than the purchase – the moment the goods are presented. The depiction of goods that precedes the authentic purchase currently has a fundamental role and finds in shop-windows its primary element of attraction for the multitude of people immersed in the crowd and vehicular traffic. The mechanisms of purchasing products are always less justified by the intrinsic qualities of these and more linked with recognition, favoured above all by advertising. George Simmel describes the modern world as a stage that welcomes the economically developed society in which money has become the ultimate aim of every human activity (Simmel 1900, 1903). The author offers a portrait of modern man, alone in the crowd, who identifies other people exclusively on the basis of social role. This individual is subject to an alienation process and is continually bombarded by numerous offers of goods to be purchased. Moreover, consumption does not consider single subjective desires, but must be accessible and attractive for an ever greater number of people. For this reason the consumer society produces impersonal and non-subjective goods.

Shopping centres and theme parks, preceded by department stores and universal expositions, have fitted into urban space-like places that bring to mind elements of carnival tradition in their simulations and prodigious spectacles (Featherstone 1991). The spectacularisation of commodities gives life to a new type of sensitivity in our relations with goods, which are no longer sold and used for utilitarian purposes, but transformed into objects to admire. The space in which the modern consumer is immersed appears as a place without dimensions and out of time. Shopping centres may be revisited as liminal and transitory places, where it is pleasant to lose oneself in a timeless dimension, a space that isolates one from the outside world reproducing a man-size world inside, where one can wander, window-shop and meet other people (Codeluppi 1989). Like shopping centres, theme parks are spaces that do not belong to the local situation, but respond to a model used and explored by consumers who, by their presence, endorse its existential dimension. In the shopping centre one is absorbed from the moment one steps over the threshold and these public spaces have the aim of making non-identity possible (Augé 1995). In urban islands of leisure and consumerism the concept of public loses its meaning of collectivity and the new spaces replace the spaces of encounter and socialisation, once localised in the city. Ever larger and more frenetic, the city has become a victim of the society of the spectacle, which has brought it to a condition of urban disorientation (Debord 1970).

The first shopping centres were born in the USA in the thirties; the American nation, hit by the serious financial crash coined – as an urgent response to consumer stimuli and society's expectations of economic revival – a new lifestyle characterised by the growing spread of the automobile, the new American symbol, with which the shopping centre facility is strictly connected. The first buildings, called *selling centers*, were structures that developed along the main roads of the city and carried out the function of joining together different sales units along open-air routes, with a complete mixture of vehicular and pedestrian traffic. Between 1940 and 1950 the shopping centre took the place of the selling centre. In effect, the development of the automobile made greater mobility of citizens possible and commercial buildings proliferated more and more in the outskirts, surrounded by vast car-park areas (Carr et al. 1992).

Victor Gruen proposed a new model in 1940: the *regional shopping centre*, based on a clear-cut separation between automobile and pedestrian traffic and on the complete closure and air-conditioning of the building, inside which entertainment and recreational activities also began to be added (Wall 2005). The proliferation of regional shopping centres located in extra-urban areas gave origin to the crisis, still present today, between shopping centre and urban centre. In order to solve the critical aspects of the problem, at first facilities were reintroduced into central areas that reproduced the models conceived for and already existing in the outskirts, which inevitably had difficulty fitting into the urban fabric. The first malls were buildings linked with public transport infrastructures and surrounded by spaces destined for various functions, such as conference halls, accommodation, multifunctional complexes and offices. Commercial spaces took on more and more city features outside the city; they tried to offer services that responded to the demands of a society in which the importance of spare time was growing and in which the consumer sought virtual paradises, having by now become a habitual user of "non-places" (Augé 1995). The model of life of individuals shifted from ethico-moral values to new sentiments permeated with the pleasure of consumption and personal well-being. The process of standardisation of consumption led the individual to recognise himself in commodities, an identification completely ephemeral and temporary (Ilardi 1990).

The first shopping centre models attempted to reproduce the complex reality of an urban commercial area inside a container, ensuring at the same time the accessibility the historic centre lacked. Regional shopping centres, located at junctions with large arterial roads on the urban outskirts, became, in the first half of the twentieth century, authentic "commercial cities". In 1954 the Northland Centre was inaugurated in Detroit, the first centre designed by Gruen, a type consisting of the construction of a pedestrian area surrounded by shops and stores, the separation of vehicular traffic from pedestrian, and the creation of two attractive sales poles, around which all the remaining shops were situated. Roughly halfway through the twentieth century a strong tie between consumption and various leisure activities clearly began to be outlined, its origin going back to the nineteenth century with the first *passages*. The year after the creation of Northland, Disneyland was inaugurated. What the shopping centre has in common with the theme park, and in general with all leisure activities, is the close link these short-lived structures have with the city. In effect, precisely because they were born as "unreal shelters" from the pollution, inefficiency and disorganisation of cities, they would not have any reason to exist without the city whose spaces and functions they copy. The shopping centre, like the theme park, tries to reproduce the main streets of the city; the copy is perceived as reassuring since it is placed out of time, in a far-off, dreamlike dimension (Codeluppi 2005).[1]

From the sixties onwards the suburban shopping centre system determined impoverishment and decay of commercial activities in the urban areas. The model of the regional shopping centre attempted in the seventies to re-establish a relationship with the urban centre. The attempt encountered many problems in that the logic on which the choices of shopping centres were based ran counter to that of the city. To remedy this situation multifunctional buildings were created in which commercial space was integrated with towers for offices, conference rooms and accommodation; a solution that proved however inefficient.

Gruen presented an identikit of the typical consumer that crowded into the first shopping centres and defined the meaning of the shopping activity, completely opposite from the activity of merely purchasing, for a purpose exists which is an objective to be reached (Gruen 1973). Shopping is also a tiring activity, so it is important to create places of rest, refreshment and entertainment inside shopping centres. In the spaces for collective use in a shopping centre the activities previously carried out in cities are simulated: walking and strolling. The realisation of rest and entertainment areas, alongside the shop-fronts, produces a pleasant atmosphere, so that all the senses are involved, thus creating a particular psychological state in the consumer, so as to persuade him to buy.

The history of shopping centres from the seventies onwards saw an increase in the multiplicity and diversity of types. Most of the merit should be attributed to a renewed conception of shopping: those who go shopping devote themselves largely to discovering new objects and refining their capacities and talent in comparing products and they experience this activity as recreation. The development is therefore asserted of types of container that are more and more attentive to the internal environment and the supply of leisure and entertainment. Since the eighties all shopping centres have been regularly subjected to renovation operations, which consist of adding new attractions to the shopping centre, such as restaurants and multiplexes.

The Urban Land Institute in Washington has set down some useful guidelines to define the shopping centre: it is characterised, first of all, by the integration of *the traditional retail outlet* with large distribution (supermarkets or hypermarkets); secondly, by the presence of *para-commercial activities* (travel agencies, banks, medical centres, etc.); finally, by the presence of *extra-commercial* attractions (leisure and meeting-places, public offices, etc.). It is important to emphasise that the entertainment element now has an important function inside these spaces (Punter 1990; Crawford 1992). Each shopping centre, as well as taking care of surveys concerning the needs of users, localises the assortment of commodities available, picks out the architectural type that responds best to the demands of clients and carefully arranges the internal *lay-out* of shops and transit spaces.[2] In distributing the goods inside the supermarket it was found that sales increased if the client's route was directed in a certain way; thus, from a simple survey lay-out studies came into existence. In the field of shopping centre design, shops for essential goods, namely those that have the function to attract, take the name of "key unit" and are generally identifiable in department stores or hypermarkets. "Key units" are usually those that occupy a greater area than the other businesses, with the purpose of drawing clients into the centre. In lay-out organisation these elements are the first to be placed and planning of these spaces avoids the creation of so-called cold points, which would mean a crisis for a whole branch of the structure.

As has already been pointed out, the antithetical relationship with the city is one of the most important factors in the history of the evolution of spatial forms of shopping. The origin of the first shopping centres was based on a clear-cut spatial separation from the city and they were designed as containers that had no relations with the surrounding space. The new models tend to imitate and replicate urban space: buildings are designed to appear characteristic and generate sensorial experiences that induce the visitor to spend as much time as possible inside an urban island featuring consumer and leisure activities. All this aims at creating an environment that will replace the urban centre as a place of encounter, sociality and leisure. The new consumer centres tend, in effect, to encompass within them all modalities of spare time and leisure.

Consumer and Gratification Rituals

The activity of shopping should be framed in a much wider context than that in which we usually place it. Those who undertake this activity are driven by motivation that does not concern material needs and necessities, but rather the quest for new lifestyles, new tendencies and new identities. The shopping activity unites indissolubly with human activities, it being no longer possible to make a simple distinction between the concept of spending – meant as an act aimed at survival itself – and the notion of shopping as expression of the human personality. In this process the consumer is transported not by need but by desire, a self-produced force that has itself as its constant object and precisely for this reason is destined to remain insatiable. Currently we need to refer to an impulse stronger than a simple desire to keep the demand of consumers up to the levels of supply. The whim results in the purchase of a commodity becoming casual or unexpected, since the consumer's only worry is to buy goods and develop new desires (Bauman 2000).

Consumers seek pleasant sensations in shopping. It represents a way of evading insecurity, in that all objects on sale, and what they stand for, are accompanied by the promise of certainties. Indeed the conviction that one can express one's freedom by the simple fact of having chosen to buy one good rather than another, is enough to charge this act with meanings. The current consumer society is distinguished by a general dependence on shopping, a condition without which we have the impression we are being deprived of individual freedom. The item purchased is the instrument of differentiation between individuals, but at the same time an inescapable element that endorses belonging to a specific group. The possibility of buying goods expresses a form of freedom, in that the consumer's choice and potential right to choose count more than what is chosen. Consumer goods are products that do not last over time, but are subject to rapid changes due mainly to the changing models offered by the external world. We currently live in a culture in which satisfying our needs has to be immediate and at the same time short-lived. The desire to purchase that pervades the consumer is determined by a continuous search for gratification. The individual is aware that the objective of his total appeasement may never be reached, since it would entail the end of desire itself.

Shopping centres are places that do not aim at facilitating and promoting relations between individuals; to share physical space with other actors engaged in similar activities increases the importance of that activity, but any interaction between the actors would distract their attention from the actions they are individually engaged in (Bauman 2000). The main objective is to consume, so it is a phenomenon experienced in an individual manner only. In effect, however crowded places of consumption and entertainment may be, they do not constitute spaces of the collectivity. Anyone going into these spaces has the experience concentrating on his own objective; social relations, considered an interference, cannot but be brief and superficial. Anything that might happen inside a shopping centre will not affect the events that happen outside; within this space one has the feeling of being somewhere else. The shopping centre is a "place without place", that exists for itself, is enclosed within itself and keeps its due distance from the city surrounding it. Shopping places prove to be really attractive, especially for the great variety of sensations they are able to give, but also manage to offer elements that no real space can supply: a perfect balance between reality and safety (Celik et al. 1994). He who finds himself in a "non-place" (Augé 1995) should feel at ease as if he were in his own home, but no one should behave as he does at home, since a behaviour should be adopted that is totally projected towards consumption. "Non-places" colonise increasingly larger areas of public space and appear as spaces without identity, relations or ties with the context in which they are placed.

Urban Leisure and Public Space

The constant repetition of spatial forms of the city inside places linked with leisure and consumption drives an increasingly large number of individuals to search for experiences of an identitary type there and consider them as new forms of public space (Amendola 1997). These places are more and more subject to homologation phenomena, so much so that theme parks look more and more like shopping centres, which in turn resemble more and more museums and airports. The relationship nowadays between urban leisure and public space is so strong that we tend to speak of trade and city merging, with a consequent, progressive reduction of the world to a shopping mall (Crawford 1992, 2002; Zukin 2004). The process of diffusion and affirmation of places of leisure and consumption has reached fulfilment; it began at the beginning of the nineteenth century in Paris with the *passages*, continued in the second half of the nineteenth century with the department stores and reached a peak in the second half of the twentieth century (Amendola 2006), with the container type of activities linked with trade and leisure. The growing success of leisure and consumerism impresses a mark on urban space and the identity itself of the city, which is deprived of its traditional public space rich in relational functions and those of aggregation. It may be stated that these places realise the transformation of space through architectures that can be totally manipulated *a priori* and are bereft of unusual elements. Leisure spaces are different if compared with others, only because of localisation and not for particular features. Currently, projects are being worked on for places of leisure and trade with the objective of creating phantasmagoric spaces in which reality and illusion merge in a single sensorial perception. Inside the malls the purchaser is attracted by a large quantity of goods and undergoes a total loss of orientation within the space, accompanied by the incapacity to carry out objective assessments on purchasing a commodity. A significant role is played daily by advertising, which through the many media channels, makes the desire to purchase prevail over all forms of rationality. Advertisements actually carry out the function of attraction initially, then subsequently of disorientation in individuals, for the physical shape alone of the place would not manage to trigger loss of orientation.

From the point of view of space organisation, mall design takes on the configuration of the labyrinth; in actual fact, a false labyrinth is created in which the fear of getting lost does not really arise. In planning commercial spaces the creation of points of refreshment, leisure and entertainment need to be taken into consideration. The form of the commercial container is represented by a closed box with no windows, where the only openings are the entrances that regulate people's access. The condition of confinement of the containers is not just connected, however, with their walled form, but with the concept from which these spaces derive. In the containers there is an attempt to promote a condition of tranquillity and comfort, so as to encourage the purchasing of goods: everything is constantly monitored and checked with the aim of eliminating possible difficulties and forms of insecurity. Shopping centres and theme parks can indeed be compared with a labyrinth due to the perception they generate in the individual, but are different from the labyrinth in that it is possible to leave this place rapidly and at any moment.

Leisure spaces are increasingly taking on the typical features of urban space. The demand for entertainment and socialisation is directed nowadays at spaces of consumption and leisure, which offer themselves as simulacra of the city, attracting the visitor with an intense variety of urban experiences. The city of Las Vegas, for example, is distinguished by being inspired by the real shopping streets of contemporary cities, for it imitates them; but in these cities everything is both false and authentic. False because organised *a priori* by the designer, authentic because it reintroduces, worsening them, the features of urban centres. In a scenario in which environments become more and more fake, Las Vegas constitutes the extreme case of a process of simulation permeating contemporary space organisation (Ritzer 2001). In these places the traditional spaces of the city are recalled and anonymously imitated. Current leisure spaces offer the consumer the chance to have particular experiences, thanks to the simulation of other worlds, with the illusion of being in a public space (Ferraresi and Parmiggiani 2007). Simulation becomes the instrument that triggers a process of identification and makes the act of purchasing apparent (Amendola 2006). The new multifunctional areas imitate the urban centre and try to reproduce its spaces and functions. They are places of attraction and entertainment, with spectacles, games, encounters and events. The areas of pleasure and commerce try to evoke the city, but it is an unreal city, revived in a fantasy dimension.

The urban islands where consumer and entertainment activities take place are taking on growing importance in the sphere of the spare time productive system. As far as their period of origin and organisational principles are concerned, theme parks may be associated with shopping centres. The large funfairs, like Disneyland, are also "closed" places where the rite of consumption is celebrated. Disneyland park in Los Angeles, born in 1955, the year following the creation of the first shopping centre designed by the architect Gruen, gave origin to the affirmation of the urban island spatial type, an authentic architectural genre which has now spread all over the world. A significant example is certainly that of Dubailand, the largest theme park in the world, located in Dubai, in the Arab Emirates, and still being built, with completion anticipated between 2015 and 2018. The fundamental characteristic of this facility is the inclusion of a whole series of tourist accommodation systems, places of leisure and refreshment, as well as shopping centres, with the objective of creating an authentic simulated city. Dubailand park, the emblem of an urban island of leisure, constitutes the celebration of the *simulacrum*, reproducible *ad infinitum* in its forms and functions, the ultimate aim of which is to recreate within itself the typical spaces of urban sociality.

Nowadays a strong tie has been established between spaces of consumption and those of leisure: this relationship is implemented through projects that aim at uniting the traditional functional form of the mall with the entertainment model typical of the theme park. Namba Parks in Osaka, Japan, a complex designed by Jon Jerde, follows precisely these fundamental principles. It consists of a facility split on various levels of terraces and numerous routes, the main feature of which is to enable visitors to combine shopping with enjoyment of natural elements (Giovannetti 2004). At Namba Parks trade is one of the many elements that, together with the natural environment and possibilities for recreation, aims at giving life to a place where it is possible to "lose oneself". Namba Parks is, first and foremost, a leisure place, which becomes the spectacle of an imaginary vision in which one finds oneself immersed, like an actor on a stage which is continuously being renewed (Dell'Aira 2005). Jerde tackles the theme of consumerism, linking it with implications of a social type, and designs shopping centres imagining these places as spaces of entertainment. In this project can clearly be glimpsed the perspective of restoring to trade its spatial dimension, and doing so by "opening" the container and projecting its functions onto a wider space. We are therefore taking part in a development of spatial organisation: the traditional formula of the closed container has been surpassed, with the proposal as an alternative of a space characterised by a group of commercial activities, linked between them by a system of pedestrian routes and green areas. But Namba Parks possesses many features indeed of the malls and theme parks, first of all the creation within it of an authentic simulation of city-specific human and social activities (Fig. 1).

Leisure epicentres are in some cases located in marginal urban areas, inside abandoned industrial buildings, with the objective of setting in motion renovation and urban transformation processes, as in the case of Barcelona and Reading.

Fig. 1 Commercial perspectives in the contemporary city: Namba Parks in Osaka, Japan. Photo by Hiroyuki Kawano [3]

From the urbanistic point of view the case of Barcelona proves to be particularly interesting for it takes notable steps forward compared with the container type: shopping centres are integrated in the urban fabric and efficiently linked with the rest of the city. In the seventies, the city began a process of reconversion of large areas, from the industrial production sector to the tertiary industry. Discarded industrial areas located in strategic positions near to transportation infrastructures left spaces suitable for building inside the city. During the nineties trade became an element of fundamental importance for the development and economic growth of Barcelona.

At the same time the concept of spare time and personal well-being became founding elements of a new culture. In this period numerous shopping centres were inaugurated, which were fitted into the urban fabric, becoming instruments of regeneration for quarters that had markedly deteriorated and for the whole city in general. Thanks to their integration within the urban mesh and their being located near transport systems, the shopping centres do not produce negative effects on trade in the historic centre (Infusino 2005). In Barcelona the street is still currently perceived as a place with strong relations. Shopping centres fit into the existing urban space, often upgrading abandoned industrial areas: places once linked with production become symbols of urban leisure *par excellence*. In such a social and economic context it has been possible to avoid commercial decline and the deterioration of central areas of the city, and to start off a process of urban regeneration with the creation of consumer and spare time epicentres (Fig. 2).

The case study of the city of Reading is an example of urban regeneration in which transformation processes of urban areas were set in motion strictly linked with the industrial activities, with the objective of creating new consumer and entertainment poles.

Fig. 2 Attempt to integrate consumer containers into the urban fabric of Barcelona

The city is considered the Thames Valley regional capital and proves important for its strategic position in terms of London's Heathrow Airport. In this respect it is useful to recall how the valley mentioned has in recent years become one of the most rapidly expanding areas of the European Union. Such prosperity should be attributed to a whole series of factors, among which the role of prime interest has been played by the highly specialised workforce in certain key sectors of the economy, such as information technology, telecommunications, distribution and manufacture. Reading belongs, therefore, to this positive context from which a flourishing tertiary sector emerges. The site originated, moreover, as a prevalently industrial area. Up to 1960 the main sources of income and wealth came from the industrial economy. From the first half of the sixties Reading experienced a deindustrialisation phenomenon which caused an inevitable crisis. From the early eighties onwards, following closure of the principal industries, the city was involved in a general transformation, which led it to become in recent decades the most important economic presence of the Thames Valley. The industrial buildings have been converted into innovative structures in which spaces linked with consumption and leisure have been inserted, becoming essential elements and integrated into the various processes of urban regeneration. The departure point was the reconversion of the abandoned places, located at strategic points, the realisation of infrastructures linked with the marginal areas and creation at the same time of new forms of public space (Morandi 2003). The Reading phenomenon constitutes an example of urban redevelopment: the city with an industrial past and subsequent deindustrialisation phenomenon had an urban centre poor in attractions and a decayed urban landscape. A fundamental role was played by the will to give life to functional integration of certain aspects considered essential such as quality of life, trade, tourism, spare time and culture.

As these experiences emphasise, contemporary cities, increasingly projected towards the modern frontiers of consumerism, seem marked by a process of standardisation and spectacularisation and are spatially organised on the basis of the theme park and shopping centre model. An analysis of the spaces of trade in the strict sense, like shopping and leisure centres, as well as those places apparently far from trading activities, such as theme parks, has enabled us to understand how the process of consumption, raised to its extreme consequences, has given origin to phenomena like, indeed, the generic city, based on the principle of simulation of reality (Koolhaas and Mau 1998; Chung et al. 2001; Maciocco 2008).

In this perspective, edge areas, areas with great environmental worth and abandoned areas show their value as places rich in elements unexpectedly released from the inexorable process of standardisation. The need is asserted to depart precisely from these edge areas to design places able to oppose the mutation the contemporary city has come up against (Maciocco and Pittaluga 2006). These areas, precisely because of their features of indefiniteness and continuous transformation, are emerging as spaces from which to depart to design and construct a new urban perspective.

Notes

[1] The concept of Disneyisation of society (Bryman 2004) enables us to know the actual systems work, dominated by a wide range of choices for the consumer, where the principles regulating the operation of theme parks are reproposed in the organisational nets of the shopping centres, perfect, efficient places but bereft of authenticity and realism.

[2] Hence basic necessities were set apart in places far from each other and not very accessible spots; bulky products were put at the end of the route to avoid the client filling his trolley right from the start. Products with which the supermarket earned more were placed at the client's eye-level, and so on.

[3] Source: Giovanetti L (2004) *Namba Parks a Osaka, Giappone*. L'industria delle costruzioni, Rivista tecnica dell'Ance n. 379 September-October, Edilstampa pp. 65–66.

References

Amendola G (1997) *La città postmoderna. Magie e paure della metropoli contemporanea*, Laterza, Roma-Bari.

Amendola G (2006) *La città vetrina*, Liguori Editore, Napoli.

Augé M (1995) *Non place. Introduction to an Anthropology of Supermodernity*, Verso, London.

Bauman Z (2000) *Liquid Modernity*, Polity Press, Oxford.

Benjamin W (1986) *Paris, Capital of the Nineteenth Century*, Schocken Books, New York.

Bryman A (2004) *The Disneyzation of Society*, Sage, London.

Campbell C (1989), *The Romantic Ethic And The Spirit Of Modern Consumerism*, Basil Blackwell, Oxford.

Carr S, Francis M, Rivlin LG, Stone AM (1992) *Public Space*, Cambridge University Press, Cambridge, UK.

Celik Z, Favro D, Ingersol R (1994), *Streets and the urban process*. In: Celik Z, Favro D, Ingersoll R Streets (eds) *Critical Perspectives on Public Space*, University of California Press, California, pp. 1–8.

Chung CJ et al. (2001) *Harvard Design School Guide to Shopping*, Taschen, Cologne.

Codeluppi V (1989) *Consumo e comunicazione. Merci messaggi e pubblicità nella società contemporanea*, FrancoAngeli, Milano.

Codeluppi V (1992) *I consumatori. Storia, tendenze, modelli*, FrancoAngeli, Milano.

Codeluppi V (2005) *Rivista dell'Associazione Italiana degli Studi Semiotici on-line* http://www.associazionesemiotica.it/ec/pdf/codeluppi_31_12_05.pdf

Corrigan P (1997) *The Sociology of Consumption*, Sage, London.

Costa X (1996) *Ciudad distraìda, ciudad informe*. In: de Solà-Morales I et al. *Presente y Futuros: arquitectura en las ciudades*, Actar, Barcelona, pp. 184–189.

Crawford M (1992) *The World in a Shopping Mall in Variations on a theme park. The new American city and the end of public space*, Hill and Wang, New York, pp. 3–30.

Crawford M (2002) *Suburban life and public space*. In: Smiley DJ (ed) *Sprawl and Public Space*, Redressing the Mall, National Endowment for the Arts, Boston, pp. 21–30.

De Azua F (2003) *La necessidad y el deseo*. ns. 14–15, pp. 13–21.

Debord G (1970) *Society of the Spectacle*, Black & Red, Detroit.

Dell'Aira PV (2005), *Architettura per il commercio*, Edil Stampa, Roma.

Featherstone M (1991) *Consumer culture and postmodernism*, Sage, London.

Ferraresi M, Parmiggiani P (2007) *L'esperienza degli spazi di consumo. Il coinvolgimento del consumatore nella città contemporanea*, FrancoAngeli, Milano.

Giovannetti L (2004) *Namba Parks a Osaka, Giappone*. L'industria delle Costruzioni n. 379 September–October, pp. 58–65.

Gruen V (1973) *Centers for the Urban Environment, Survival of the Cities*, Van Nostrand Reinhold, New York.

Ibelings H (2001) Supermo*dernism: architecture in the age of globalization*, Netherlands Architecture Institute, Rotterdam.

Ilardi M (1990) *La città senza luoghi, Individuo, conflitto, consumo nella metropoli*, Costa & Nolan, Genova.

Infusino S (2005) *Commercio e centralità urbane: il caso di Barcellona*. In: Mela A (ed) *Città, commercio e grandi eventi*, Celid, Torino, pp. 95–110.

Koolhaas R, Mau B (1998) *S, M, L, XL*, The Monacelli Press, New York.

Maciocco G, Pittaluga P (eds) (2006) *Il progetto ambientale in aree di bordo*, FrancoAngeli, Milano.

Maciocco G (2008), *Fundamental trends in city development*, Springer-Verlag, Heidelberg, Berlin, New York.

Morandi C (2003) *Il commercio urbano. Esperienze di valorizzazione in Europa*, Libreria Clup, Milano.

Mumford L (1961) The *City in History. Its Origins, its Transformations and its prospects*, Harcourt, Brace & World, New York.

Punter JV (1990) *The Privatisation of public realm*. Planning, Practice and Research n. 5(3), pp. 9–16.

Ritzer G (1999) *Enchanting the Disenchanted World: Revolutionizing the Means of Consumption*, Pine Forge Press, Thousand Oaks.

Ritzer G (2001) *Explorations in the Sociology of Consumption. Fast Food, Credit Cards and Casinos*, Sage, London.

Simmel G (1900) *The philosophy of money,* Routledge, London.

Simmel G (1903) *The Metropolis and Mental Life*, Free Press, New York.

Sombart W (1915) *The Quintessence of Modern Capitalism*, Howard Fertig, New York.

Sorkin M (1992) *See you in Disneyland.* In: Sorkin M (ed) *Variations on a Theme Park. The New American City and the End of Public Space*, Hill and Wang, New York, pp. 205–232.

Wall A (2005) *Victor Gruen: From Urban Shop to New City,* Actar, Barcelona.

Zukin S (2004) *Point of Purchase – How Shopping Changed American Culture,* Routledge, New York.

5. Urban Tourism and Hybrid Spaces

Leisure and tourism activities cannot be dissociated from city activities. Tourism is not only a key aspect of local economies: city promotion cannot simply be aimed at influencing potential visitors but must involve the inhabitants and their cultural world. In this sense, tourism is urban if the "production" of the holiday occurs through forms and modalities aware of "self-production" by citizens. In the hybrid spaces generated by tourism, the project may thus favour going beyond passive fruition of holiday places to move towards aware fruition of the city as a significant inner experience.

Questioning the Urban in Urban Tourism

Gregory Ashworth

What is the Relationship between Cities and Tourism?

The relationships between cities and tourism are much wider than the scope of this chapter. Much tourism clearly occurs outside cities, but the importance of cities is easily argued and only the most relevant aspects of these interactions will be considered here. Most tourists originate from cities and most either seek out cities as holiday destinations in themselves or use services or visit attractions located in cities while staying on holiday elsewhere (Page 1992, 1995; Berg et al. 1995; Borg et al. 1996; Law 1993, 1995). However, more directly relevant for the purpose here is to specify those aspects of cities that contribute towards a tourism that not only occurs in cities but is also distinctly urban. It is these characteristics that relate the specific activity of urban tourism to the distinctive forms and functions of cities and underpin much of the discussion of policy.

The urban central place occupies a pivotal position within the functional hierarchies in the wider regional hinterland. Furthermore, and to an extent contradictorily, cities exist within functional networks with each other often regardless of, and separate from, their regional or national context. This is particularly marked in tourism where a mixture of inter-urban co-operation and competition can create various sorts of national or inter-urban and often international tourism circuits. Finally, urban tourism is characterised by variety in two senses. The variety of facilities on offer to visitors, and thus the variety of types of holiday experience, is in itself one of the main attractions of cities to tourists. Equally, these facilities are rarely produced for, or used exclusively by, tourists but are shared by many different types of users: in short, the multifunctional city serves the multi-motivated user.

It is clear that the relationship between cities, their forms and functions, on the one side, and tourist activity, on the other, has been so close and longstanding that the difficulty has been to separate the two rather than find links between them. Therefore, while tourism exists to an extent in all cities (there is no city that does not receive a single visitor), the importance of its impact varies not only with the magnitude of the tourism flow but more significantly with the type of city that accommodates it. There are

G. Maciocco, S. Serreli (eds.), *Enhancing the City*, Urban and Landscape Perspectives 6,
DOI 10.1007/978-90-481-2419-0_11, © Springer Science+Business Media B.V. 2009

simply many forms of urban tourism and many types of tourism city, and even adding the adjective "heritage" to both tourism and urban does little to reduce the variety. Finally, it should be remembered that although it will be demonstrated that cities are clearly important to tourism, this does not automatically imply that tourism is important to cities.

What is Urban Tourism?

Urban tourism is best defined as the overlap area between a number of adjectival tourisms (Fig. 1). In particular it contributes to two large general categories of tourism that have been labelled "special-interest" and "place-specific" (Ashworth 1995). Special-interest tourism is the pursuit while on holiday of interests that most probably are also pursued outside the holiday. The interest of people on holiday in what the city has to offer is only an extension of the same interest that they commonly express when not on holiday: these urban tourists are not therefore engaging in some strange obsessive holiday behaviour explainable in terms of tourism. Similarly, the supply of urban attractions is usually a response less to tourism demand than to much wider social needs and is not, therefore, explicable within tourism either. Place-specific tourism is where the tourism attraction is the sense of place itself, which may be composed of many broadly defined cultural attributes, structures and atmospheres. Although all tourism occurs somewhere and all places are unique, this form of tourism specifically uses this unique quality, rather than the generic characteristics of a place, as the tourism product.

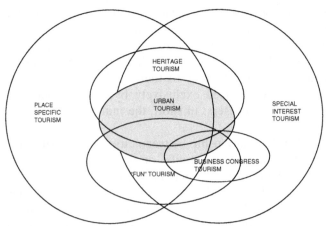

Fig. 1 Types of tourism

The motives of tourists who visit cities are so enormously diverse as to defy any attempt at comprehensive listing. Pleasure and entertainment in discretionary time makes use of the equally diverse facilities of cities. Similarly, heritage tourism is essentially both special-interest and place-specific, but only accounts for a part of each of those categories. It overlaps strongly with cultural tourism, which quite clearly encompasses, although is wider than, heritage tourism. More narrowly, art tourism can be defined as the tourism consumption of the artistic products and performances of a culture (though the original creativity presented need not be indigenous to the place of performance). Not all culture, heritage or art originates in cities, has been assembled in cities or is expressed by them. Most, however, are and only cities have the critical mass of such resources to attract and satisfy tourism demands. Many visitors to cities are motivated by some form of business rather than pleasure, although the two usually overlap to a large extent, either with pleasure being supplementary or, as in much congress tourism, with the unique place-specific characteristics being an integral part of the attraction for the visitor.

Questions About the Urban Tourist

Why Do Tourists Visit Cities?

Travel in general has grown continuously over the past 30 years and travel to cities could be viewed as just a reflection of that reality. Most gateways, largely airports, are located in or near cities as is most of the infrastructure for the support of travellers. In an increasingly urbanised world it is not surprising that cities account for an increasing proportion of visitors. An explanation of the growth in urban tourism would need to look more closely at the words "tourism" and "urban" here.

Cities are accumulations and concentrations of economic and political power, organisations and activity, as well as of cultural, entertainment and leisure activities. A large part of travel to cities is motivated by the first rather than the second set of attributes. Cultural centres such as Florence may accommodate 4.2 million visitor-nights and Salzburg 1.9 million, mostly motivated by leisure demands but cities with far fewer cultural pretensions, such as Hamburg (4.1 million visitor-nights), Lyon (2.9 million) or Zurich (2.0 million), have also benefited from the general growth in travel (Berg et al. 1995; Borg et al. 1996). We just travel more and not only for tourism.

Equally, even if the traveller can be designated as a tourist because of the discretionary nature of the motive to travel, the question can be posed, "are all tourists in cities urban tourists?" The use of an adjective before the noun tourism usually indicates a specific type of tourism experience (as in for example "cultural tourism" "gastronomic tourism", "sport tourism" and even the urban antithesis "rural tourism"). To what extent, therefore, is tourism in cities a similarly distinctive experience derived from the urban nature of cities? Here we can distinguish between tourism in cities, that is tourism to facilities that happen to be located in urban areas but would be equally satisfying to the visitor in a different non-urban milieu, and urban tourism *sui generis* in which it is urbanicity itself that is the primary motive of the tourist. What is this urbanicity, which we could contrast, for example, with its antonym rurality? Louis Wirth's famous essay on *Urbanism as a way of life* (1938) identified the essential defining characteristics of cities as density, heterogeneity and impersonal social interaction that Tönnies (1887) called *Gesellschaft,* leading among other things to freedom and anonymity. Cities are certainly characterised by density and diversity, whether of functions, facilities, cultures or peoples, which distinguish the urban from the rural. It is these characteristics that must be central to the urban nature of cities and thus define urban tourism, whether the tourism activities principally engaged in are classified as culture, entertainment or even shopping. It is notable that visitor surveys asking tourists in cities about what they actually do constantly reveal the dominance of very vaguely formulated activities such as "sightseeing", "wandering about", "taking in the city" and "getting among the people" (*onder de mensen* in Dutch). The serendipitous *flâneur* prevails over the determinedly directed tourist. This seems to get close to defining the significance of the urban in urban tourism.

How Do Tourists Consume Cities?

A number of generalisations, amounting to conventional wisdom, can be made about the way tourists consume the urban product (see for example Pearce 2005). First, tourists consume cities selectively. The tourist will experience only a very small proportion of all that the city has to offer. This is unsurprising and would apply also to almost any urban user, whether tourist or not. It could be argued that the tourist has more limited time, as argued below, and more limited, or perhaps only different, knowledge than locals. For whatever reason, there is plenty of empirical evidence of the consequences of these limitations. The spatial range of tourists, as bounded by their individual space-time budgets (Dietvorst

1994), results in the well-documented compact and spatially delimited tourist urban region (Ashworth and Tunbridge 1990, 2000), normally confined to one or a number of compact tourist "islands" of interest, leaving most of the city ostensibly tourist-free.

Secondly, tourists consume cities rapidly. The length of stay at urban tourism destinations is much shorter than in beach resorts. The average length of stay of beach resort holidaymakers is around 10 days, this being an average of two-week bookings (in most resorts around 50%) and one-week and shorter excursionists. The length of stay in even major urban destinations is rarely more than 2 days. This is not just that the motives for travel to cities are more varied and include many short stays not primarily motivated by holidaymaking (Berg et al. 1995). Even the world's most renowned cultural tourism centres such as Florence, Venice or Bath cannot generate long stays in any single centre (e.g. Salzburg, 2.0 days; Venice, 2.3); major world cities do little better (Paris, 2.2; Berlin 2.5; London 5.6) (Borg et al. 1996). Centuries of historical experience and cultural productivity are consumed in a few days. In smaller cities the stay is better measured in hours and any single urban feature, however renowned as a "must-see" attraction, will generate stays better measured in minutes than in hours.

Thirdly, tourists consuming urban experiences cannot be relied upon to return repeatedly. Beach tourism is well known for repeatedly attracting regular visitors to the same place and indeed often to the same hotel. However, it cannot be assumed that because cities offer varied attractions they will automatically generate similar repeated visits. Although urban tourists are quite likely to continue to patronise cities in general, there are various intrinsic reasons why specific cities may tend not to foster such a loyal clientele and generate return visits. First much urban tourism could be labelled Michelin/Baedeker collecting. Tourists have pre-marked sites and artefacts that must be visited if the place is to be authentically experienced. Once "collected" a repeat is superfluous and the collection must be expanded elsewhere. Ironically, the more unique the heritage experience, the less likely it is to be repeated. A generalised place product (London's *Covent Garden*, Paris' *Champs-Élysées*, Barcelona's *Ramblas* and the like) is far more likely to be consumed repeatedly than an original and specific place product (Luxor, Pisa or Niagara Falls find that their spectacular historical, natural or architectural attraction will tend to be a once-in-a-life-time experience). Equally, the more renowned and unique the urban product the more difficult it is to renew and extend the range of tourism products on offer. Places can become imprisoned in their immutable uniqueness as expressed through the unvarying but stringent expectations of visitors. Cities such as Bath, Florence or Weimar are so strongly focussed, especially in the imagination of the visitor, on a specific tourism product that change is difficult and an attempt to sell industrial Bath, modernist Florence or medieval Weimar would have little success. Cities with a more varied and diffuse range of possible products, such as London or Paris, have fewer such difficulties in extending or changing the product line.

Finally tourists consume cities capriciously. Many of those concerned with the management of cities may assume that their city has an assured and permanent tourist allure. Although all tourism, being a discretionary activity deeply embedded in psychological and social contexts (Pearce 2005), is influenced by inevitable changes in these contexts, there is reason to believe that urban tourism is especially vulnerable to quite rapid shifts in fashion and changes in consumer taste. The choice of urban tourism destination is a fashion-driven activity and like much cultural consumption, part of contemporary lifestyles are constantly being redefined. Even such seemingly immutable values as those derived from heritage and cultural expression cannot be relied upon to generate an unchanging tourist interest as the popularity of historical periods and artistic styles waxes and wanes. Thus what, where and who, is currently popular, and, in terms of the time span of developmental investment, will still be as popular in 10 years, will depend upon a fickle and fashion-conscious market.

Questions About the Urban Tourism Industry

The initial problem with posing questions about those who might be described as the tourism industry is to identify the subject. The "urban tourism industry" is characterised by diversity and extreme organisational disintegration. It would include those delivering various accommodation, catering, travel or entertainment services directly to the tourist, those assembling and marketing tourism packages, those managing the resources from which such packages might be composed and even public sector agencies with an interest in the impacts of tourism rather than its direct management. Not only are these various agencies diverse, often operating with quite different objectives and working methods, most of them also serve non-tourism markets, such as those providing mundane retailing, public transport or public utilities, or are mandated to prioritise non-tourism objectives such as those providing most heritage and cultural services. Many such agencies may not even be aware that they form part of a tourism industry and if they were made aware could be indifferent or even hostile to such knowledge.

Do You Know Who Your Market Is?

There is a widespread assumption that we can distinguish, isolate and identify a distinctive urban tourism market, and, by derivation, an equally distinctive urban tourist, and urban tourism product located in an urban tourism space. For if we cannot so distinguish a market, it becomes next to impossible to examine and manage it. There is a stereotypical average urban cultural tourist, who has been described with a remarkable degree of unanimity by many academic observers (Prentice 1993; Ashworth and Tunbridge 1990, 2000; Boniface and Fowler 1993; Page and Hall 2003; Pearce 2005) and is embedded as axiomatic by most tourism practitioners and policy makers. The almost universal caricature of the stereotypical "Baedeker/Michelin tourist" is 45–65 years of age, with a higher than average income available, education, and travel experience, holidaymaking independently in a group of two and staying in hotel accommodation. However, like all such stereotypes, this conceals both a large variety within the identified group and the existence of many other categories of urban tourist.

Any attempt to list urban tourism markets is doomed by diversity to be incomplete. The back-pack "Lonely Planet"/"Rough Guide" market may be as numerous, although not so profitable as the Michelin/Baedecker market. The cruise-stop market, the bachelor "stag-night"/discount airline market, the professional conference market, the health care market and the various niche activity markets for *aficionados* pursuing hobbies ranging from gastronomy to war-gaming, are only examples of urban tourism markets, which could easily be extended. However, this is not to suggest that because cities cater for a wide variety of tourist demands markets need not be segmented, separated and targeted as with any other product. The questions, "do you know enough about the tourists you are trying to attract to entice them to visit your city and, once they are there, do you know enough to manage their experience?" are however rarely satisfactorily answered.

Who Is Paying your Costs and Contributing towards your Benefits?

To the tourism industry many of the resources of the city appear to be zero-priced, freely accessible public goods. Public places and public facilities are either completely free (as public space) or usable well below cost (as with most museums, historic buildings and many public services). Such a fortuitous windfall resource may appear ideal to the tourism industry. It has however two dangers. First, freely accessible public goods tend to be over-used to the point of depletion as the interests of the individual and of the public are contradictory, a general condition known as the "tragedy of the commons" (Hardin 1968). Secondly, the urban resources utilised by the tourism industry are not freely provided in that they are paid for by other users or by the community as a whole. The tourism industry therefore becomes a parasitical free-rider on the facilities that someone else is paying for. This is probably an untenable situation in the long term with a number of national and local disadvantageous consequences. The solution is the very familiar one of reconciling costs with benefits between individuals, economic and social objectives and between the public and the private sectors. In economic terms, this means internalising the externalities, usually fiscally, and in spatial terms, balancing costs and benefits at different spatial scale jurisdictions. In short, cities are not cheap to run and maintain and someone has to pay but there are many ways of deciding who, how much and how.

Can You Change Fast Enough?

Many of the characteristics of urban tourist behaviour described above have implications for the management of the urban tourism product. A rapidly consumed, fashion-driven activity can only be effectively managed by an organisation capable of either constantly discovering and attracting new markets or continuously changing or extending the product range on offer. The very fragmentation of the urban tourism industry may make such longer term strategic planning less likely and more difficult.

Questions about the Tourism City

What Is the Tourism City?

In one sense the phrase "tourism city" is without meaning. All cities to a greater or lesser degree receive tourists and there is no "tourism city", at least outside the purpose-built tourism resort developments, which hardly count as cities, that does not also serve other urban functions. Therefore, it can be argued that either all or none of the world's cities are tourism cities. Nor is it possible to select some arbitrary level of economic dependence at which a city becomes a tourism, as opposed to a non-tourism, city. Indeed, as will be argued later, the cities with the most value to tourism and attracting the largest number of tourists are generally those in which tourism has the least relative significance.

That said, it is possible to identify many different types of tourism city determined not only by the motives and expectations of the majority of visitors but also by the way the city, or at least its policy makers, sees itself (Fig. 2). Again this is best expressed as a series of overlapping, changeable categories rather than discrete and stable types. Even the broad category of "tourist-historic city" (Ashworth and Tunbridge 1990, 2000) has many variants. The large show-case capitals for example, with their imperial and national collections, symbols and associations, are quantitatively the most important attractors of cultural tourists but at the same time have many other important, usually far more important, non-tourist and non-heritage functions. Conversely, the almost perfectly and completely preserved heritage "gem" cities are indisputably tourist-historic but form only a small, and in many ways unrepresentative, proportion of tourist-historic cities. The designation "art city" has been given to places which were not only the physical locations associated with artists and their products but where the place itself, including usually its physical structures, becomes inseparable from the creative works. Salzburg is Mozart and Memphis is Presley. But the category "art" and its celebration in festivals can be so widely drawn that clearly not all art or festival cities are necessarily tourist-historic.

Cities are also more than centres of commodifiable culture and heritage. They are centres of complex economic, retailing, educational, entertainment, sports and many more activities, all of which can provide either the principal or the secondary motive for a visit. It is worth noting here that almost all these functions of cities exist in the service of both external and internal markets, and from the viewpoint of the facility it is rarely necessary or even possible to separate the two.

Which Urban Problem Are You Trying to Solve with Tourism?

A city creating policies for tourism or embarking upon marketing campaigns targeted at tourists needs to be clear about which urban problem tourism is being recruited to solve. Tourism may be seen as contributing jobs and incomes to a lagging economy, extra direct and indirect taxes to hard-pressed local authorities, animation to area regeneration if only by putting people on the street, especially when other facilities are closed, and creating a liveliness that is itself an attraction (Burgers 1995); it can give critical support to local services and facilities which would otherwise be uneconomic, enhance and promote local place identity, civic consciousness and local self-esteem through the flattering attention of visitors to local attributes and contribute to many more objectives of urban policy.

Tourism facilities that are themselves not economically viable are often included in multi-functional projects (Snedcof 1985) because of the positive externalities they contribute to developments and districts. The point is that each of these is possible but, equally, a failure to define which of these is intended is likely to result in none of these goals being satisfactorily achieved.

Likewise, of course tourism brings local costs, whether economic, such as bidding up the price of scarce factors of production, the foregoing of development opportunities elsewhere and the free use of public facilities financed locally; social, such as undesirable demonstration effects, social change or disruption of a social balance; or just physical through congestion and a crowing out of locals. Ultimately, the fundamental questions, especially for the public agencies involved, are "does our city need tourism and if so, to what extent, of what sort and, above all, for which purposes?"

Have You the Management Philosophies and Structures to Do It?

Tourism can play many roles in the city but at the same time little of the city was actually created by, or is managed principally for, tourism. Tourism is generally only one use of urban facilities and urban space and is in competition with other uses that will often be prioritised, if only for reasons of local political accountability.

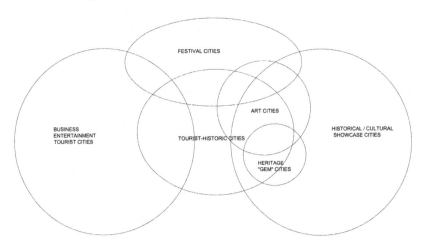

Fig. 2 Types of tourism city

This has many practical implications for the management of resources that were created for, and dominantly serve, other multiple uses. Few cities have the management structures in existence that can manage diverse multiple uses.

The dilemma facing urban tourism development is that while each place is in, at least potential, competition with every other place, success or survival will largely depend upon cooperation between places. Networking and packaging, joint promotions and the regionalisation of place brands are among the usually recommended policy solutions to many of the weaknesses of urban tourism outlined above. If competition is unavoidable, so also is cooperation and both may occur in the same places. An application of this concept of "coopetition" is essential and requires skilled and sensitive management.

Whose City Is It?

The tourist is in one sense consuming a different place product than the local users, even if this product is created from the same resources and even co-exists in the same physical space. Therefore there is always an underlying question, "whose place is it?"

Conventional wisdom in tourism studies has generally separated tourists from residents. In simple terms, the important distinction has been that one is on holiday and the other not and many consequences are seen as stemming from this dichotomy. Local residents are generally accorded primacy in the claim to the city, and this assumption underlies much local management policy. Additionally local uses are often accorded a higher intrinsic moral or even aesthetic value than outside uses, especially tourism.

In many instances, however, the tourist and the local resident cannot usefully be distinguished in terms of motivation or behaviour. Much urban tourism is a "special-interest" activity, which is by definition only a continuance on holiday of accustomed interests and activities. Tourism consumption occurs for such a wide variety of reasons, within varied behavioural patterns and in diverse forms, as to render the separation of tourist from local not only impossible but also often quite irrelevant. The tourist is just the resident on holiday: the resident just the tourist between trips. Secondly, the nature of urban tourism leads to a convergence between local and tourist consumption which can only be understood through creolisation and social convergence/divergence models (Ashworth 2003). Thirdly, the globalisation/localisation debate, which is quite central to considerations of tourism at the destination, is best conflated within "glocalisation" models rather than any spurious idea of insider community against outsider tourist. Fourthly, the shaping and management through policy of place image, place identities and socio-political cohesion or inclusion/exclusion generally precludes any distinctive tourism policy or management being shaped.

Thus it is likely that tourism does not exist in the city as a discrete set of resources, motivations of individuals, activities or field of management policy. The tourist, the industry and the local policies are all too embedded in other, much wider considerations for a successful isolation (Fig. 3). Indeed the pretence that the tourist actually exists in a discrete sense comparable to other product consumers, is a major obstacle to the furtherance of both the theory and the practice of tourism, not least but not only in cities.

Paradoxical Answers

The idea that there exists an automatic and universal harmonious symbiosis or, conversely, just as inevitable and inherent a contradiction of goals and behaviours, between cities and tourism, is assumed rather than questioned or explained. The relationship poses more questions than can currently be answered with confidence.

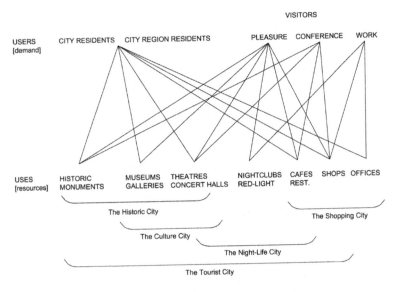

Fig. 3 The tourist city and other cities (from Burtenshaw et al. 1990)

We are left to reconcile a series of paradoxes:

Urban tourism is important: but we know little about it. This imbalance in attention was noted by Ashworth in 1989 and reiterated in 2002.

Cities are very important to tourism: tourism is not very important to cities or at least to most cities, most parts of cities, most of the time (Ashworth 1989).

Tourism can contribute substantial economic benefits to cities: but the cities whose economies most need the contribution of tourism are likely to benefit the least. It is the cities with a large and varied economic base that gain the most from tourism but need it the least.

Many tourists visit cities: but tourists are largely invisible in cities. The cities that accommodate most tourists are large multifunctional entities into which tourists can be effortlessly absorbed and are thus largely economically and physically invisible.

Tourists make an intensive use of cities: but little of the city has been created for tourist use. Ultimately from a number of directions we arrive at the asymmetrical relationship between the tourist and the city, which has many implications for policy and management.

Tourism needs cities: but cities do not need tourism.

References

Ashworth GJ (1989) *Urban tourism an imbalance in attention*. In: Cooper C (ed) *Progress in tourism*, Belhaven, London, pp. 55–64.

Ashworth GJ (1992) *Planning for sustainable tourism*. Town Planning Review n. 63(3), pp. 325–330.

Ashworth GJ (1995) *Managing the cultural tourist*. In: Ashworth GJ and Dietvorst AGJ (eds) *Tourism and spatial transformations: implications for policy and planning*, Cab international, Wallingford, pp. 265–284.

Ashworth GJ (2003) *Urban tourism: still an imbalance in attention?* In: Cooper C (ed) *Classic reviews in tourism*, Channel view, Clevedon, pp. 143–63.

Ashworth GJ, Tunbridge JE (1990) *The tourist-historic City*, Belhaven, London.

Ashworth GJ, Tunbridge JE (2000) *Retrospect and prospect on the tourist-historic City*, Elsevier, London.

Berg L et al. (1995) *Urban tourism: performance and strategies in eight European cities*, Avebury, London.

Borg van der J (1990) *Tourism and urban development faculty of economics*, Erasmus University of Rotterdam, Rotterdam.

Borg J van der, Costa P, Gotti G (1996) *Tourism in European heritage cities*. Annals of Tourism Research n. 23(2), pp. 306–321.

Boniface P, Fowler P (1993) *Heritage and tourism*, Routledge, London.

Burgers J (1995) *Public space in the post-industrial city*. In: Ashworth GJ, Dietvorst AGJ (eds) *Tourism and spatial transformation: implications for policy and planning*, CAB international, Wallingford, pp. 147–158.

Burtenshaw D, Bateman M, Ashworth GJ (1990) *The European city*, Fulton, London.

Dietvorst AGJ (1994) *Cultural tourism and time-space behaviour*. In: Ashworth GJ, Larkham PJ (eds) *Building a new heritage: tourism, culture and identity in the new Europe*, Routledge, London, pp. 69–89.

Hardin G (1968) *The tragedy of the commons*. Science n. 162, pp. 1243–1248.

Law CM (1993) *Urban tourism: attracting visitors to large cities*, Mansell, London.

Law CM (1995) *Urban tourism*, Routledge, London.

Page SJ (1992) *Managing tourism in a small historic town*. Town and country planning n. 61, pp. 208–11.

Page SJ (1995) *Urban tourism*, Routledge, London.

Page SJ, Hall CM (2003) *Managing urban tourism*, Prentice Hall, London.

Pearce PL (2005) *Tourist behaviour: themes and conceptual schemes*, Channel View, Bristol.

Prentice R (1993) *Tourism and heritage attractions*, Routledge, London.

Snedcof H (1985) *Cultural facilities in multi-use developments*, Urban land, Washington.

Tönnies F (1887) *Gesellschaft und Gemeinschaft und*, Fues's Verlag, Leipzig.

Wirth L (1938) *Urbanism as a way of life*. American Journal of Sociology n. 44, pp. 1–24.

The Ambivalent Space(s) of Tourism in Italian Colonial Libya

Brian L. McLaren

Tourist Space

In the Italian colony of Libya during the course of the 1920s and 1930s there developed an extensive and quite elaborate tourist system that facilitated travel through the Mediterranean coastal region as well as deep into the pre-Saharan interior. This system combined what was among the most advanced networks of transportation and accommodation of any Western colony – providing a level of service that was coincident with or even superior to the standards that could be expected in Italy – along with a number of "authentic" local settings that brought tourists in relatively direct contact with the indigenous populations – in this case offering a vicarious, though entirely safe, experience of the local culture. The liminality of this tourist experience – being both continuous with the metropole and deeply immersed in the indigenous culture – is entirely coincident with Italian colonial politics in Libya, which sought to incorporate this colony into the larger Italy at the same time as it attempted to preserve its cultural heritage. The alternating and sometimes even simultaneous experience of the modern West and the indigenous East placed the colonial tourist in an ambivalent space in which the tensions between these seemingly incommensurable realities were articulated. Even though the goal of the foreign tourist in Libya was to escape their moral and cultural boundaries in favor of the experience of an "Other" culture, that culture was entirely framed by Italian colonial politics and in that sense was already a part of Western modernity.

This essay investigates the ambivalent spaces of tourism in the Italian colony of Libya through its combining modern tourist infrastructures with carefully preserved (and even invented) indigenous environments. What will emerge from this discussion is the sense that these ambivalent spaces, like all contemporary tourist environments, navigate between the need to provide basic amenities in a simple and efficient manner and the demand to produce a new and unfamiliar cultural experience. The carefully devised intermingling of these realities in the colonial context produces something similar to what sociologist Dean MacCannell describes as the "staged

G. Maciocco, S. Serreli (eds.), *Enhancing the City*, Urban and Landscape Perspectives 6,
DOI 10.1007/978-90-481-2419-0_12, © Springer Science+Business Media B.V. 2009

authenticity" that arises from the interaction between front and back regions of contemporary tourist environments (MacCannell 1999, pp. 91–107). However, not only are these ambivalent spaces a product of a tourist discourse that calls for a carefully staged presentation of authentic environments, they are also a product of colonial discourse. As postcolonial theorist Homi Bhabha has argued, this discourse takes place in a "Third Space of enunciation" – that is, a hybrid space in which the supposedly opposed forces of modernity and tradition are seen to coexist in all of their differences (Bhabha 1994, pp. 36–38). These hybrid tourist spaces are also ultimately the product of modernity – seen as a volatile and progressive cultural force that combines radically conflicting realities.[1] Following an initial discussion of the connection between tourism and colonization in Libya, this paper will proceed through an examination of first the modern and then the indigenous tourist spaces and conclude with a selective presentation of the intermixing of these spaces under the auspices of colonial tourism. Through this investigation, a better sense will emerge of the interaction between the experience of the modern and the native under the colonial system of the Fascist government and more broadly of the ambivalence of all (modern) tourist spaces.

Tourism and Colonization

The intricate relationship between the colonization of Libya by the Italian government and the tourist development of this same colony was the central argument of a book published in 1934 under the title *Colonizzazione e turismo in Libia*. The author of this book, Giuseppe Vedovato, was a student of colonial studies at the Cesare Alfieri Royal Institute of Higher Studies in the Social and Political Sciences in Florence who took part in an instructional trip to Libya that led to this research project and its eventual publication.[2] The joint sponsorship of the book by the Colonial Studies Center in Florence and the Fascist University Group underscores the fact that, during the 1930s, tourism stood at the intersection of Italian fascist politics and the economic development of its colonies. The publication of this book during the first year of the Governorship of Italo Balbo is a further indication of its significance. Libya enjoyed a substantial resurgence under the direction of Balbo, who was Minister of the Italian Air Force under Mussolini between 1929 and 1933 and a member of the *quadrumvirato* that organized the so-called March on Rome which precipitated Mussolini's rise to power in 1922 (Segrè 1987, pp. 91–113). This book is a reflection of the colonial politics of Balbo in Libya, whose revival was closely aligned with its tourist development.

In more specific terms, Vedovato traces the relation between the Fascist attempts to populate Libya for the purpose of agricultural development and the improvement of the tourist system. While no literal connections were seen to exist between these two systems – such as attempts in the late 1930s to encourage tourist excursions to the recently settled agricultural towns – their interests were seen to be coincident at both an economic and a political level.[3] The book argues that the conditions necessary for a viable tourist system in Libya, such as the establishment of lines of communication, and the creation of population centers along these itineraries, would open up the colony for the movement of goods and the settlement of people for the purposes of agriculture. It is in this regard that tourism is referred to as the "catalyzing agent for the economic process" (Vedovato 1934, p. 8). Tourism was also viewed as a civilizing and modernizing force. Not only did Vedovato argue that the exposure of the products of these agricultural activities to a tourist audience would potentially create new markets back in Italy, he asserted that "more frequent contact with interests and ideals carried by foreign and national tourist caravans" would create "a more elevated civil and economic level" in the colonies (Vedovato 1934, p. 9).

Although the close relationship between tourism and colonization in Libya is most clearly evident in the mid-to-latter part of the 1930s, this was by no means the beginning of this connection. During the governorship of Giuseppe Volpi (1921–1925), the tourist system in Tripolitania was considered an important part of the colonial development. Indeed, the creation of a tourist system was one of the four main components of the program of rebirth of Tripolitania along with the reoccupation of land, the organization of an agricultural economy and the construction of a suitable image to mark the Italian presence (Talamona 1992, p. 69). On the one hand, tourism was seen as an integral part of the "politics of transportation" within the colony (Queirolo 1926, p. 260). On the other, it was viewed as a separate industry with its own issues and concerns. In taking stock of the wide range of attractions that tourism in Tripolitania offered the foreign visitor – from hotels and modes of transportation to historic sites and special events – one commentator argued that it had the potential to be an industry of considerable importance, particularly with the help of an aggressive propaganda campaign (Niccoli 1926, pp. 511–512).

The ambivalence of tourist spaces in Tripolitania during the Volpi era was a fairly direct product of its negotiation between modernizing and preservation forces that were an integral part of the emerging tourist system. In the first case, the foundation of a network of transportation and accommodations was largely the result of a series of government policies that were linked to modernizing the region and carefully organizing its experience for foreign tourists. These initiatives included the improvement of maritime connections between Italy and Tripolitania for both commercial and tourist purposes.[4] The colonial authorities worked closely with the local Chamber of Commerce and the National Association of Tourist Industries (ENIT) to produce tourist publicity and guide books and stage a number of tourist events.[5] It also made a substantial investment in the tourist facilities, such as the luxurious Grand Hotel in Tripoli which began construction in 1925. Despite these efforts, the tourist infrastructure during the Volpi era was still quite modest, with only three hotels in Tripoli – the Grand Hotel Savoia, the Hotel Moderno and the Hotel Commercio – and few forms of public entertainment, which at that time comprised two theaters, some small movie houses and three clubs.[6]

The tourist system during the Volpi era was also linked with a relatively systematic program for the preservation of the indigenous culture – a resource that quite obviously was the primary motivation for visiting the region. These preservation initiatives, however, dated back to the initial days of Italian occupation in 1912 when the engineer Luigi Luiggi prepared a master plan for Tripoli which stated that the character of the old city should be preserved without any change. Notably, one of the motivations behind this conservation effort was "the local imprint that the aesthete and the tourist seek" (Luiggi 1912, p. 124). During the early 1920s, this program was supported by a government commission that identified buildings and objects of historic interest and eventually called for their preservation (Bartoccini 1926, pp. 350–352). An equally significant initiative was undertaken related to the native artisanal industries of Tripolitania – a program that was aimed at improving the indigenous economy. The Government Office of Indigenous Applied Arts was founded in January of 1925, with the mission to study these industries, make proposals for their expansion and promote their sales through exhibitions and displays (Rossi 1926, p. 517). In attempting to improve the artistic production of local craftsmen according to a Western conception of these industries this office brought in indigenous master craftsmen from Algeria, Tunisia and Morocco, whose production was regulated by the French colonial authorities (Rossi 1926, p. 518).

The Italian intervention in the indigenous arts and its connection to the tourist experience is particularly evident when looking at the suqs and marketplaces of the cities and towns in Tripolitania. In the guide book

Guida di Tripoli e dintorni of 1925, the area of the Suq al-Turk was presented as "the most characteristic of indigenous life". This covered market space contained two rows of shops where "Arab and Jewish merchants in their picturesque costumes sell the most varying goods".[7] Another area of the old city that was presented as being of significant tourist interest was the fabric and carpet market of the Suq al-Mushir adjacent to the Karamanli mosque, where a series of small workshops of indigenous craftsmen both produced and sold their wares (Fig. 1a). Of considerable importance is the fact that these were the same artisanal industries that were in the process of being restructured by the Government Office of Indigenous Applied Arts. The workshops and markets of the Suq al-Mushir in Tripoli thus were not an authentic experience of the indigenous culture so much as they were a self-conscious presentation of that culture under the aegis of a preservation program.

This government office was also active in improving the organizational and economic systems of these industries. The improvements involved, among other things, financial support for acquiring more traditional raw materials. The enhancement of the distribution system for native artisanal products was largely connected with regional and national fairs and exhibitions in Italy, Europe and the colonies. One such display included the creation of a permanent exhibition in Corso Vittorio Emanuele III in Tripoli which was organized along with the local Chamber of Commerce. While the primary appearance of this permanent display is that of a metropolitan shopfront, one cannot miss the subtle use of arabising motifs in the surrounding wooden frame (Fig. 1b). Like the preservation to program of Volpi – which aimed at creating more authentic artisanal products within a more efficient distribution system – this permanent exhibition is a perfect expression of the unresolved tension between metropolitan influences and native culture in the tourist system.

The indigenous artisanal industries in Tripolitania enjoyed a significant amount of attention in the years following the governorship of Volpi. The increasing interest in the native products was at least in part due to the participation of the Government Office of Indigenous Applied Arts in exhibitions and fairs (Rossi 1927, pp. 67–70). There were numerous public displays of the Libyan craft industries, such as the "Tripoli Village" at the Turin International Exposition of 1928. This representation of an indigenous village included what was called the Tripolitanian suq – which was a fragment of the old city of Tripoli complete with vendors and their typical wares[8] (Fig. 2a).

Fig. 1 a Workshop and stall, Suq al-Mushir, Tripoli, ca. 1925;
b Window display, Corso Vittorio Emanuele III, Tripoli, ca. 1925

With the appearance of a literal re-enactment of the indigenous marketplace, this display is an example of the importance of a sense of authenticity to the value of native artisanal objects. However, not unlike the workshops in the Suq al-Mushir, it offered more than a mere image of the indigenous landscape and culture. It was a hybrid space which presented native culture in a manner that screened out all contradictory aspects. In respecting and preserving the cultural practices of the Libyan populations, the colonial administration was at the same time redefining those practices according to the demands of modern Italian society. The ambivalence of Italy's colonial politics is, in this case, perfectly matched with the ambivalence of the tourist experience. In fact, in sharing this common conceptual basis it can be argued that the tourist encounter – wherein the foreign visitor experiences the indigenous culture through the modern frame of metropolitan society – is fundamentally a colonial encounter. Conversely, it can be asserted that in their negotiation between the metropole and the colonial context the colonist is, in essence, a tourist.

Constructing a Tourist System

Being returned to our uncontested rule, Tripolitania has become an important proving ground of the maturity of our colonization. The Fascist Regime has completed an unprecedented work. It knows how to give the natives – in the dignity of their active struggle – the sense of a will to rule that is not limited to only affirm the reality of the occupation, but to also construct and assure it for our time and for all time... The Government begins this work with a clear vision of all of the political, moral and economic needs and above all with the intention to make Tripoli into a truly modern city (Piccioli 1929, pp. 250–251).

The organization of the tourist system in Libya reached its highest level of development under the aegis of the modernization program of Italo Balbo. The construction of an infrastructure of roads and public services undertaken during this period provided the necessary preconditions for the development of a well-organized and efficient tourist system. The intersection of the tourist discourse with the more general improvement of the colonial context was symbolically expressed in the "National excursion" organized by the Italian Touring Club (TCI) in Libya in April of 1937. One group of participants began in Tripoli heading east to Benghazi while a second took an equal and opposite itinerary, visiting virtually all of the significant historical sites from the Tunisian border to Egypt. As a gesture of colonial propaganda not unlike the recent inauguration by Benito Mussolini of the *strada litoranea* or coastal artery, this excursion was meant to assert that with this new road, Libya was being organized for its future tourist demands. As was rhetorically stated in the TCI magazine *Le Vie d'Italia* in June 1937, this tourist experience "offered a concrete demonstration of the great importance that the new imperial artery also assumes for tourist purposes" (Bonardi 1937, p. 434).

The considerable financial investment that the Balbo administration made in the improvement of the road network was not an isolated gesture. The creation of a paved system of highways designed according to the most modern standards was undertaken in conjunction with a substantial program for the construction of new tourist facilities that was initiated in the first days of Balbo's Governorship, when he created a commission to centralize all building activities (Bucciante 1937, pp. 4–5). In so doing, the tourist architecture during the Balbo era participated quite directly in the broader political discourse within architectural culture that called for the creation of a more uniform appearance proper to both Libya's colonial status and its Mediterranean setting. Indeed, in 1934 four new hotels began construction and four others were substantially renovated, all in a relatively consistent Mediterranean vocabulary and all under the direction of the colonial administration.[9] This initiative, in conjunction with the construction of the *strada litoranea*, resulted in the creation of a coordinated system of modern roads and hotels that described two basic itineraries that soon comprised the most common and desirable tourist experiences in this colony. The first of these reinforced Libya's Mediterranean status, stretching from Zuwarah on the west to Tobruk on the east, linking Libya's largest cities of Tripoli and Benghazi and the major archeological sites of Sabrata, Leptis Magna, Cyrene and Apollonia. The second route explored Libya's African and Saharan setting, traveling south from Tripoli past the agricultural estates in Gharyan, passing through Yifran and Nalut and ending in the oasis settlement of Ghadames.

The most crucial initiative that the Balbo administration pursued for the creation of an organized tourist system was the foundation of a centralized authority for the control of all tourist-related activities. This ambition was realized with the creation of the Libyan Tourism and Hotel Association (ETAL) in May of 1935. As a state-sponsored corporation, the formation of this group can be understood in relation to the increasingly centralized efforts at coordinating and directing the Libyan economy. It provided the services of a travel agency, organizing tourist itineraries involving all forms of travel. It acted as tour operator, providing car and motor coach transportation throughout the region.[10] The ETAL was also responsible for the management of the eighteen hotels that belonged to the Libyan government and the municipality, and for supervising a network of entertainment facilities that included a theater and casino. Finally, this group handled its own publicity campaigns, producing publications like brochures, guide books, and postcards and organizing displays at exhibitions and fairs. This combination of activities and resources not only allowed the ETAL to provide an inclusive package of services for the tourist audience, it was able to conduct these activities with a unity of purpose that was not possible prior to its inception, providing "a solution that without exaggeration can be called totalitarian".[11] Through the supervision of this network by a centralized authority whose point of reference was clearly metropolitan, a certain standard of services and amenities were almost universally available throughout this colony.[12]

Indeed, the experience of modernity was found throughout the tourist system of the Libyan Tourism and Hotel Association, which attempted to provide a network of modern travel services that met the expectations of the Italian and foreign traveler. While one of those expectations was, naturally, providing a well-organized system, of equal importance was creating an atmosphere that was familiar to the tourist. The idea of creating a metropolitan standard of comfort was particularly evident in the network of hotel facilities, which had a consistent level of amenity in centers of secondary tourist importance as well as the major cities of Tripoli and Benghazi. All of the ETAL hotels provided first- or second-class lodging, the only exception being the luxury accommodation of the Uaddan Hotel and Casino in Tripoli. Moreover, all of the hotels had modern bathroom facilities, and all except the Tripolitania Hotel in Tripoli offered the option of three meals with a room. Their publicity photographs are particularly imbued with the desire to convey an image of metropolitan comfort. One such example is an image of the dining room at the Hotel of the Gazelle in Zliten, where the contemporary furnishings and tableware set within a spare and elegant interior space present an image of modern hospitality and comfort that elides any specific references to the colonial context (Fig. 2b).

The Libyan Tourism and Hotel Association also provided a series of modern amenities and tourist-related activities that effectively transported the metropolitan context to Libya. Among the most compelling sources of the experience of the metropole in the colonies were the activities organized by the Theater and Performance Service. One of their main venues was the Uaddan Theater, which offered a confluence of modern event and modern setting. This group brought in actors and musicians from Italy to provide forms of entertainment that principally appealed to a highly cultured Western audience. During the 1938–1939 tourist season this program included bringing in nine different drama companies and sponsoring four orchestral concerts (Vicari 1942, p. 971). The metropolitan aspect of this theater is similarly evident in the architectural expression of the interior. Designed by the Architect Florestano Di Fausto in conjunction with Stefano Gatti-Casazza, its highly polished wood surfaces and dramatic lighting provided a luxurious and highly appropriate context for these metropolitan performances. In its relatively conventional appearance as well as in the Western content of the events themselves, the tourist was effectively transported back to the streets of Italy.

a   b

Fig. 2 a Tripolitanian suq, colonial exhibition, Turin, 1928;
b Dining room, hotel of the Gazelle, Zliten, 1935

While an important part of the tourist experience in Libya was the desire to experience an "other" culture, it was also closely tied to the political program in Libya during the latter part of the 1930s, which aimed to modernize this region in order to incorporate it into the larger Italy. The tourist system in Libya was a projection of these modern standards of travel onto the colonial context, creating a tourist experience that was continuous with that found in Italy. In so doing, tourism was a kind of propelling mechanism for the modernization process that was at this same time satisfying the expectation of metropolitan standards in the civic life of Libya. However, in creating an efficient system of travel and accommodation throughout Libya, the Libyan Tourism and Hotel Association – through participating in the modernizing and colonizing program of the Fascist colonial authorities – provided a means for the foreign traveler to escape the sometimes difficult reality of the colony for an experience of metropolitan "comfort".

Re-presentations of the Native

For its Oriental, indigenous and primitive fascination, Tripolitania holds a preeminence over all of the regions of the African Mediterranean, being less profoundly penetrated by the cosmopolitanism that radiates from the cities of Egypt, Tunisia, Algeria and Morocco. The Arab, devoted to his traditions, lives in his psychological and social climate, without mystifications and contaminations. Moreover, the faith that the Italians inspire in the natives permits us to experience their way of living (Ravagli 1929, p. 269).

Just as the modernization program in Libya was necessary for the establishment of an efficient tourist network, the efforts of the colonial authorities relative to the preservation of Libyan culture were instrumental to the form and presentation of indigenous culture within the tourist system. The most important distinguishing feature of colonial tourism – as opposed to tourism within the metropole – is the conjunction of a modern tourist system with a strange and exotic setting. The tension between this "other" culture and the necessary level of organization and comfort produced an ambivalent experience for the modern traveler. In its support of the culture of the Libyans the indigenous politics in Libya under Balbo would seem to be the equal and opposite of the modernization program, which called for Libya to be Italy's fourth shore and thus an extension of Italian soil in North Africa. However, a policy of respect for the Libyans – including the preservation and reinforcement of their indigenous cultural institutions and practices – was, in fact, carefully coordinated with the incorporation of this region into metropolitan Italy. Just like the modernization program that was at this same time introducing a system of roads and public services, the indigenous politics were motivated by the desire to bring that culture in alignment with the standards of the metropole.

The indigenous politics of Balbo involved a combination of firm rule and carefully conceived gestures of reconciliation. The colonial authorities in Libya maintained strict control of these populations, which were punished for infractions that were regarded as either morally dangerous or contemptuous of colonial rule. In order to create a climate of mutual respect, Balbo met with leaders of various indigenous groups on matters of education, public assistance and religion. He also attempted to appease former dissidents through a 1936 program for the restitution of personal goods and property that were confiscated during the period of "reconquest".[13] These political tactics were reinforced by a systematic propaganda effort – a campaign that included pamphlets and flyers written in Arabic that quite obviously were aimed at the image of Italy in the larger Muslim world.[14] At the same time the colonial administration exercised a considerable amount of control over the native populations. Although recognizing the need for defending the religious and cultural traditions of the Libyans, Balbo did not hesitate to speak of the eradication of "those old retrograde customs that oppose themselves to the social evolution of these same populations" (Balbo 1939, p. 746). This meant that while the Libyans were allowed to practice according to their traditions – though these were within the prescribed confines of religion and the family – all broader forms of social and political organization were conceived according to the dictates, and ultimately the moral standards, of the colonial administration.[15]

The experience of the foreign tourist in Libya during the Balbo era was thus a constant negotiation between the relatively direct projection of Fascist modernity onto the colonial context and the re-presentation of the indigenous culture. While this presentation of the native element was no less important for the creation of a successful tourist system in Italy, there was a simple but significant difference in the colonies – that is, the culture being presented was not Italian. One trajectory of this discourse, based on the influence of contemporary colonial literature, suggests that the tourist would encounter Libyan culture through a mysterious and even dangerous adventure. A second and seemingly opposite vehicle for the appropriation of local culture was through the filter of scientific research and representation. In this case, the knowledge of the indigenous culture by the tourist was an analog to its objective study, which leads to a manner of experiencing the Libyans and their culture as objects in a living museum.

Although both of these representations are clearly Orientalist ones – establishing the local populations and their culture as primitive and backward in relation to the West – there are some important distinctions. They place the Western subject in a specific relationship to the object of study – the first being romantic and literary, the second objective and scientific.

The first of these interpretive mechanisms, colonial literature, was a form of writing that emerged in conjunction with the increased attention given to the colonies after Mussolini's first visit to Tripolitania in 1926. Although many of the experiences recounted in the earliest of these publications were from the period following the initial Italian invasion of this region, it was not until the colonies enjoyed broad popular appeal – and the support of the Fascist government – that such writings were both conceived and published. One of the most significant influences on this form of writing are the travel accounts of Italian and foreign explorers who traveled to Africa in the late nineteenth and early twentieth centuries (Del Boca 1992, pp. 7–22). Equally formative to Italian colonial literature of the mid-1920s was the work of poet, novelist, and political agitator Gabriele D'Annunzio which provided a sensuous and descriptive prose and initiated themes of heroism and social transgression. The writing style and literary devices of colonial novels enjoyed a broad dissemination in published material related to colonial travel during the late 1920s as well as having a fairly direct influence on the iconography of this tourist propaganda. In giving visual form to these well-established literary devices, these publications participated in an Orientalist discourse which was aimed at fueling the desire to travel in what was presented as an unfamiliar and even perilous land.

The second mechanism through which the indigenous culture of Libya was appropriated and disseminated was under the aegis of scientific research and study – an activity that both motivated and benefited from the colonization process. The most significant research expeditions took place during the Fascist era, and in particular after the military reconquest of Libya in 1932. It was not until the early 1930s that areas of interest to researchers, other than those in the coastal regions, were under firm military control. Prior to this time these efforts had been limited to the travels of Italian explorers during the nineteenth century, which produced little in the way of serious research. This work eventually encompassed a number of separate disciplinary fields, including anthropology, archeology, ethnography, folklore studies, geography and geology (Del Boca 1991, p. 271). Not surprisingly the scientific research in Libya during the Fascist period was a form of validation of the politics of Italian colonial rule. The politicization of this research is due to the fact that many of the organizations involved had long been supporters of Italy's colonies (Surdich 1991, pp. 449–451 and 460–461). Much of this scientific work can thus be seen as a literal extension of the Italian control over these regions.

One of the most interesting results of the intersection of tourism and scientific study is that the research expedition became an important conceptual model for structuring the tourist experience. In some cases, tourism so thoroughly assumed the procedures of anthropology that it became a form of analogous research. An example of this phenomenon can be found in the "National Excursion" to the Fezzan in the southwestern desert region of Libya held by the Italian Touring Club (TCI) in April of 1935. One of the significant aspects of this excursion is that it followed an itinerary that was almost identical to that of an anthropological and ethnographic mission led by Lidio Cipriani and Antonio Mordini in 1933. In fact, the research from this mission, which was sponsored by the Italian Geographic Society, was even published in the official TCI magazine in September of 1933 (Cipriani 1933, pp. 679–691). In looking at the subsequent report of the National excursion in the same journal it is quite apparent that not only was this tourist itinerary inspired by and followed the route of a scientific one, it was clearly organized to support the same kind of "systematic and patient inquiry" (Bonardi 1935, pp. 485–496).

The influence of the preservation programs of the colonial government and ongoing scientific study of the region can be seen quite directly in a number of the publicity efforts of the Libyan Tourism and Hotel Association, such as the 1938 book *Itinerario Tripoli-Gadames*. This guide-book was published to advertise the route that would take tourists from Tripoli to Ghadames and back as part of a five-day excursion. The organization and content of this publication is decidedly hybrid. The text is divided into a series of sections that describe the basic itinerary of the trip. This structure is overlaid with a separate narrative created by a series of water color images of the excursion. These sensuous images prominently feature the system of hotels and amenities provided by the ETAL as well as the tourist experience of the indigenous culture – which is depicted through a decidedly romantic filter (Fig. 3). While this approach would suggest the exotic literary model prominent in the representation of indigenous culture in tourist literature, this tendency is counteracted with a series of black and white images that provide objective documentation of the direct experience of the native environment and culture.

The parallel between this text and contemporary scientific discourse is most clearly evident in the approach taken to the writing style. Despite the

Fig. 3 Berber castle, Nalut, from *Itinerario Tripoli-Gadames*, 1938

detailed and descriptive nature of the text, *Itinerario Tripoli-Gadames* contains the kind of dispassionate prose that is employed in more objective tourist aids. Moreover, its portrayal of the indigenous culture provides a historical, cultural and racial understanding of these people in the manner of an anthropologist or ethnographer. One such example in the text is a presentation of the Berber populations, who were described for both their appearance – being "predominantly blond, with light colored eyes, and a tall and thin stature" – and their customs – being "more severe, more rigid, more bound to the observance of law".[16] This publication, like the larger system of accommodation, entertainment and transportation services, adopts the objective means through which contemporary scientific discourse re-presented the indigenous populations to a metropolitan audience. Under the guise of this "science", this publication theorizes the tourist experience as a form of objective research that allows the traveler to view the native environment and culture in a manner that seems without any interference by the modern West.

This scientific mode of representation of indigenous culture can also be seen quite directly in the tourist facilities of the Libyan Tourism and Hotel Association, and in particular in the pre-Saharan hotels of Yifran, Nalut and Ghadames. In the design of the Hotel Nalut, the architect Florestano

Di Fausto located a low horizontal building on the edge of a large plain, with the restaurant and guest rooms overlooking an immense and rugged valley (Fig. 4). The relationship between the building and the adjacent town can be found in its representation in the publication *Itinerario Tripoli-Gadames*, where the discussion of its facilities is accompanied by a historical and ethnographic description of its people. This publication is an important illustration of the intersection between the tourist discourse in the colonies and contemporary activities in various fields of scientific research – studies in which this region and the Berber people were important subjects.[17] It is also quite apparent that, in this presentation, an analogy is being made between the "heroic resistance" of these people against the Ottoman invaders and the rugged forms of their ancient castle, which was referred to as "a sort of petrified myth".[18] Through re-enacting these indigenous forms, the Hotel Nalut was participating in a contemporary ethnographic discourse – the unadorned and primitive lines of its building masses suggesting the unyielding resistance of the Berber people and the perceived unchanging character of their culture.

The connection between the pre-Saharan hotel in Nalut and Berber cultural traditions offered in *Itinerario-Tripoli Gadames* reveals an important aspect of the tourist discourse in Libya under Italian colonialism, where the re-presentation of the native was closely tied to and part of a "modern" and "objective" conception of the primitive qualities of Libyan culture. Despite the desire for authenticity that is part of any tourist

Fig. 4 Hotel Nalut, Nalut, 1935

environment – and that this tourist system was clearly feeding – that authenticity was entirely constructed to be in accordance with the views of the Italian colonial authorities. Notwithstanding the fact that it allowed the foreign traveler to immerse themselves in an unfamiliar cultural experience, colonial tourism – through the influence of the unbiased practices of scientific research – placed the foreign traveler in a detached and objective relationship to the native environment and culture.

The Ambivalent Spaces of Tourism

The tourist experience of the Hotel Nalut, like that of most of the facilities of the Libyan Tourism and Hotel Association, provided the foreign visitor with an index of the larger political project of Italian colonialism in Libya. Through these facilities the tourist was presented with an experience that alternated between the comforts of the modern West and the shock of the primitive East. Significantly, this "primitive" East was itself a product of Western culture and in that sense was also a modern experience – framed as it was by scientific research in the fields of anthropology and ethnography. The ambivalent spaces of tourism thus placed the foreign tourist in an in-between realm – neither completely immersed in the local culture nor safely contained within the metropolitan systems of political and social control. It is in this regard – in the relationship between ongoing political and social change and long-standing cultural traditions – that we can think of the tourist experience as a fundamentally modern one. Indeed, it is perhaps under the auspices of tourism that the inherent tensions between modern conceptions of space and the evolving attitudes to the past – which were themselves largely redefined during the modern period – were exposed and ultimately left unresolved.

A particularly compelling example of the ambivalence of the tourist experience in Libya can be found in the contrast between two facilities that were owned and operated by the Libyan Tourism and Hotel Association (ETAL). The first is a travel agency in Tripoli, where the tourist – despite being fully immersed in the colonial context – was presented with an image of metropolitan efficiency with few, if any, references to the colonial context (Fig. 5a). From the sleek wooden countertop to the carefully ordered filing systems containing the maps and brochures needed for an efficient travel experience, this shop is a projection of the spatial and organizational ideals of the metropole onto the colonial context – a mirror of the aspirations of the modernization program of the colonial authorities under Italo Balbo. The Libyan Tourism and Hotel Association also had a shop in Rome that sold cigarettes, tobacco and products of Libyan artisanry[19] (Fig. 5b).

In a setting that was suggestive of a dark and mysterious "Oriental" interior, the products of the indigenous artisans of Libya seem mere commodities for sale to a metropolitan audience. However, given the location of this shop in Rome, it was, in fact, an inducement to travel – the artisanal products having the status of ethnographic objects through which the Libyan culture could be experienced and understood. The ambivalence of the tourist experience in Libya is perhaps most powerfully expressed in the interregnum between metropolitan and colonial as expressed by these two tourist facilities – the first projecting metropolitan efficiency onto the colonial context and the second exposing the metropolitan traveler to a strange and unfamiliar culture.

A final example of a tourist facility that perhaps best shows the nature of the tourist experience in Libya, is an Arab café that was constructed at the Suq al-Mushir in Tripoli. This project, designed by the architect Florestano Di Fausto, was located in the Artisanal Quarter that this architect executed under the mandate of the Building Commission of Tripoli. This larger building complex was one of the most important restoration works carried out during the Balbo administration due to its location within the nineteenth-century Suq al-Mushir just inside the walls of the Medina and adjacent to the castle and the Karamanli mosque (Bucciante 1937, p. 4). This is, of course, the same indigenous marketplace that was the subject of the preservation program of the Volpi administration in the mid-1920s. This educational and entertainment facility was important because of its close connection with the Balbo administration's reorganization of the indigenous craft industries of Libya.

a   b

Fig. 5 a Libyan tourism and hotel association travel agency, Tripoli, 1935;
b Libyan tourism and hotel association tobacco shop, Rome, 1935

The program of the larger project accommodated the new facilities for the Muslim School of Arts and Crafts, which required a combination of classrooms and workshops and some small shops for selling artisanal goods (Bucciante 1937, pp. 10–11). As with previous administrations, the challenge was to improve techniques in the interest of recuperating past traditions that had been lost or abandoned. This emphasis was related to two areas of concern in the indigenous arts; the impact of mass-produced goods and the potential loss of traditional techniques – something for which a considerable research effort was made in all regions of this colony (Quadrotta 1937a, pp. 6–8 and 16–24). The dilemma was that, while there was a desire to improve the indigenous industries according to modern and Fascist exigencies, this could not be conducted at the expense of the perceived function that they performed as a register for the authentic traditions of each region.

The Artisanal Quarter at the Suq al-Mushir provided a tourist experience in which the indigenous architecture and culture of Libya was presented in an "authentic" environment. This was in part due to the fact that the facility was so carefully interwoven into the existing context so as to create a continuous relationship with the historic architecture of the castle and the surrounding fabric of the old city. This connection was also more figurative. The aesthetic expression of this project, described as exhibiting a "modern sense of architecture associated with eastern Mediterranean motifs", shows a careful assimilation of traditional spaces like the Karamanli courtyard in the nearby castle.[20] The new courtyard of the Muslim School of Arts and Crafts, which was surrounded by the workshops and classrooms, contained a large reflecting pool and was decorated by ceramic tile produced by the students (Fig. 6a). This approach seems to be in stark contrast with the educational spaces, which presented the indigenous culture of Libya in an objective "modern" environment (Fig. 6b).

However, the decoration of the courtyard with the products of Balbo's restoration program connects the historical reference to the castle with the contemporary program of redefining the native culture of Libya. The conflation of the historical past with attempts to re-enact it in the present applies more broadly to the tourist experience of this facility. Such a seamless relationship is created between the existing context and associated restoration work and the new intervention so as to make them impossible to be separated. Just like the artisanal wares that were being offered in the shops of this new tourist facility, the forms of the building so closely follow contemporary research into traditional forms that they are themselves part of a "modern" program of historic preservation.

In a similar manner, the Arab Café offered the metropolitan traveler an experience of native culture in an environment that suggested the indigenous building traditions. Operated by the Theater and Performance Service of

a   b

Fig. 6 a Courtyard at Suq al-Mushir, Tripoli, 1935;
   b Muslim School of Arts and Crafts, Suq al-Mushir, Tripoli, 1935

the ETAL, this facility presented Arab musical and dance performances in a setting that one commentator argued "fully reproduces the suggestive local environment" (Vicari 1942, p. 971). Just like the larger project for the Artisanal Quarter, the café space is a carefully studied reinterpretation of the local forms, expressed through a restrained and simplified architectural vocabulary. The sense of authenticity of the design was reinforced through the use of decorative tile produced in the adjacent Muslim School of Arts and Crafts – which themselves re-enacted traditional forms and patterns – and through the furnishings – which also attempted to re-create historical forms and techniques. The interest in creating an experience for the tourists that was faithful to the Libyan traditions extended to the music and dance performances, which included the eroticism of traditional oriental dance.

However, this "authentic" experience was assembled according to the same set of values that pervaded the broader preservation project of Balbo in Libya. Not only were the traditional dances and costumes determined by demands of the Western traveler, the musicians and dancers were trained to perform in accordance with the colonial administration's sense of the correct Libyan traditions.[21]

While the appeal of the indigenous culture of Libya in the tourist system was in its exotic qualities, it is also clear that this presentation had to conform to a contemporary Western understanding. The ethnographic discourse related to the production of native artisanal objects and the rational logic with which the indigenous events in the tourist network were planned and staged underscores the fact that in the tourist system in Libya the tensions between the modern and the indigenous produced an ambivalent space that was neither entirely modern nor entirely traditional. Indeed, the experiences provided by these tourist facilities rightly suggest the need to question just what is indigenous or native to a region or culture in the modern context. The spaces of tourism in Italian colonial Libya – perhaps like all contemporary tourist spaces – are more than a carefully balanced alternation between the organizational mechanisms of tourism and the indigenous culture that foreign travelers sought to experience. They are an instantiation of the tensions inherent in modernity, wherein political and social change and indigenous or regional expressions seem in a constant state of negotiation. However, in this case rather than to see the forces of modernity as the crucial frame for this discourse it is perhaps more interesting to see it from the opposite side – that is, from the point of view of tradition. The tourist spaces in Italian colonial Libya offer a "third space", an "Other" modernity that not only elides the pure expression of the smooth surfaces of the metropole, it challenges the notion of authenticity and of the stable cultural traditions that were themselves in the process of being invented during the modern period.

Notes

[1]   This kind of description of modernity is found in Berman (1982).
[2]   Vedovato (1934), p. 3. In the introduction to the book, Armando Maugini, director of the Istituto Agricolo Coloniale Italiano, provides a brief description of the terms of this research project.
[3]   Vedovato (1934), pp. 6–7. In this part of the book, Vedovato argues that it is not so much that agriculture or industry would create landscapes of touristic interest, nor that tourism is a call for agriculturalists to visit the colonies, as it is that, in reality, the relationship between them is integrated and complementary at an economic level.
[4]   "Il Governatore invia lettera dell'Istituto Coloniale Italiano (sez. Tripoli) sul trattamento che sarebbe usato a Siracusa ai viaggiatori ed alle merci da e per la Libia". ACS-PCM 1921 13-3-1707.
[5]   *Il Convegno archeologico di Tripoli.* Rivista della Tripolitania I, (6) May–June 1925, pp. 417–423.
[6]   *Guida di Tripoli e dintorni* (1925) Fratelli Treves Editori , Milan, pp. vii–xii.
[7]   *Ibidem*, p. ix.
[8]   *La Mostra delle Tripolitania.* L'Italia Coloniale (5) 11, November 1928, pp. 226–227.
[9]   Bucciante (1937), p. 5. The new hotels constructed during the Balbo era were eight in total; the Berenice in Benghazi (1935); the Cussabat (1936); the Derna (1937); the Rumia in Yifran (1934); the Nalut (1934–1935); the Tobruk (1937); and the Uaddan (1934–1935) and the Mehari (1934–1935) in Tripoli. The

renovation projects were the Ain-el Fras in Ghadames (1934–1935); the Sirt (1934–1937); and the Gazelle in Zliten (1935).

[10] ETAL, *Realizzazioni fasciste. Gli sviluppi del Turismo Libico*, ASMAE-MAI 5-5, Fascicolo 18.

[11] ETAL *Report of the Ente turistico ed alberghiero della Libia*, ASMAE-MAI.4.29, Fascicolo 210.

[12] ETAL (1939) *Annuario Alberghi in d'Italia*, Turati Lombardi E.C., Milano.

[13] A meeting between Balbo and forty prominent leaders among the local populations was held in the Palazzo del Governo on September 13, 1935. As reported in *Agence d'Egypte et d'Orient*, 2,34 (September 12, 1935), p. 2, this meeting was to "study important problems in favor of the Arab population". The decree of Balbo that allowed for the return of this property, from October 10, 1936, was published in *La Voix Indigène* December 17, 1936. This policy was continued into 1937, in part due to Mussolini's visit to Libya in March of 1937. Ferrini G *Disposition du clémence du Gouvernement Italien en Libyie en faveur de trente-cinq familles Arabes resortissantes des colonies Italiennes*, La Voix Indigène (December 17, 1936). This policy was continued into 1937, in part due to Mussolini's visit to Libya in March of 1937.

[14] One such publication is *What Italy has done for Islam in its Colonies,* Istituto Grafico Tiberino, Istituto Grafico Tiberino, Roma 1937, found in ASMAE-Affari Politici, 17, 1937.

[15] Italo Balbo, La *politica sociale fascista verso gli arabi della Libia*. In: Reale Accademia d'Italia, Fondazione Alessandro Volta, *Convegno di scienze morali e storiche* 4–11 ottobre 1938-XVI. Tema: l'Africa, Vol. 1 (Reale Accademia d'Italia, Roma, 1939, pp. 738–739). The qualified support of native customs was particularly true for religious practices, which were tolerated "as much as they are vital and derive from the laws of the Prophet", and prohibited if they were understood as "deviations of religious fanaticism".

[16] ETAL (1938) *Itinerario Tripoli-Gadames* Tipo-Litografia Turati Lombardi Milano, p. 13.

[17] Scarin (1940) and Corso (1940).

[18] *Ibidem*, p. 36.

[19] *Relazione tecnica del Direttore Generale al bilancio dell'esercizio 1936-37,* ASMAE-MAI.4–29. Fascicolo 210.

[20] Quadrotta 1937b, p. 955. The entrance hall further illustrates this connection, containing a Byzantine fragment found at the archeological site at Sabrata.

[21] "Relazione tecnica del Direttore Generale al bilancio dell'esercizio, 1936–1937", p. 23. In response to a lack of qualified local musicians and dancers – the initial performers largely being from Tunisia – the ETAL created an Arab music school to train the Libyans.

References

Balbo I (1939) *La politica sociale fascista verso gli arabi della Libia*. In: Reale Accademia d'Italia, Fondazione Alessandro Volta, *Convegno di scienze morali e storiche. 4–11 ottobre 1938-XVI. Tema: l'Africa*, Vol. 1, Reale Accademia d'Italia, Roma, pp. 733–749.

Bartoccini R (1926) *Gli edifici di interesse storico, artistico ed archeologico di Tripoli e dintorni*. In: Piccioli A (ed) *La rinascita della Tripolitania. Memorie e studi sui quattro anni di governo del Conte Giuseppe Volpi di Misurata*, Mondadori, Milano, pp. 350–352.

Berman M (1982) *All That is Solid Melts into Air: The Experience of Modernity*, Simon and Schuster, New York.

Bhabha H (1994) *The Commitment to Theory*. In: Bhabha H *The Location of Culture* Routledge, London, New York, pp. 18–38.

Bonardi C (1935) *Col touring nel Fezzan*. Le Vie d'Italia n. 45(7), July, pp. 485–496.

Bonardi C (1937) *L'avvenire turistico della Libia*. Le Vie d'Italia n. 43(6), June, pp. 434–437.

Bucciante G (1937) *Lo sviluppo edilizio della Libia*. In: *Viaggio del Duce in Libia per l'inaugurazione della litoranea. Anno XV. Orientamenti e note ad uso dei giornalisti* Stabilmento Tipografico Il Lavoro Fascista, Roma.

Cipriani L (1933) *Una missione scientifica italiana nel Fezzan*. Le Vie d'Italia n. 39(9), September, pp. 679–691.

Corso R (1940) *Africa Italiana, Genti e costumi*, Pironti, Napoli.

Del Boca A (1991) *Gli italiani in Libia. Dal fascismo a Gheddafi*, Laterza, Roma-Bari.

Del Boca A (1992) *L'Italia e la spartizione dell'Africa. In nome della scienza*. In: Del Boca A *L'Africa nella coscienza degli Italiani*, Laterza, Roma-Bari, pp. 7–22.

MacCannell D (1999) *The Tourist: A New Theory of the Leisure Class*, University of California Press, Berkeley.

Niccoli E (1926) *Il problema industriale in Tripolitania*. In: Piccioli A (ed) *La rinascita della Tripolitania. Memorie e studi sui quattro anni di governo del Conte Giuseppe Volpi di Misurata*, Mondadori, Milano, pp. 487–512.

Piccioli A (1929) *Tripolitania: La Rinascita della Tripolitania*. In: *Guida d'Italia del Touring Club Italiano. Possedimenti e colonie*, Touring club Italiano, Milano, pp. 250–269.

Quadrotta G (1937a) *Appunti sull'Artigianato Libico*. In: *Viaggio del Duce in Libia per l'inaugurazione della litoranea. Anno XV. Orientamenti e note ad uso dei giornalisti*, Stabilimento Tipografico Il Lavoro Fascista, Roma.

Quadrotta G (1937b) *Sviluppo e realizzazioni dell'artigianato in Libia*. Rassegna Economica dell' Africa Italiana n. 25(7), July, pp. 925–967.

Queirolo E (1926) *La politica delle comunicazioni.* In: A Piccioli (ed) *La rinascita della Tripolitania. Memorie e studi sui quattro anni di governo del Conte Giuseppe Volpi di Misurata,* Mondadori, Milano.

Ravagli F (1929) *Tripolitania: il Turismo.* In: Bertarelli LV (ed) *Guida d'Italia del Touring Club Italiano. Possedimenti e colonie,* Touring club Italiano, Milano, pp. 269–272.

Rossi FM (1926) *Le Piccole industrie indigene.* In: Piccioli A (ed) *La rinascita della Tripolitania. Memorie e studi sui quattro anni di governo del Conte Giuseppe Volpi di Misurata,* Mondadori, Milano, pp. 513–519.

Rossi FM (1927) *La Fiera e le piccole industrie tripolitane.* L'Italia Coloniale n. 4(4), April, pp. 67–70.

Scarin E (1940) *L'insediamento umano nella Libia occidentale,* Ufficio Studi del Ministero dell'Africa Italiana, Roma.

Segrè C (1987) *Italo Balbo: A Fascist Life,* University of California Press, Berkeley CA.

Surdich F (1991) *Le spedizioni scientifiche italiane in Africa Orientale e in Libia durante il periodo fascista.* In: Del Boca A (ed) *Le guerre coloniali del fascismo,* Laterza, Roma-Bari, pp. 449–461.

Talamona M (1992) *Libya: An architectural workshop.* Rassegna n. 51, September, pp. 62–79.

Vedovato G (1934) *Colonizzazione e turismo in Libia,* Prem. Stamperia Raffaello Beraglia, Salerno.

Vicari E (1942) *L'Ente turistico ed alberghiero della Libia (ETAL).* Gli Annali dell'Africa Italiana n. 5(4), December, pp. 955–975.

Waterfront Retrieved: Buenos Aires' Contrasting Leisure Experience

Agustina Martire

Public Space on the Buenos Aires' Waterfront

The southern waterfront of the city of Buenos Aires has been recovered. Now that more than 20 years have passed since the projects began, we are able to get some perspective on these developments and can confront them with the integral history of this area. The areas of Puerto Madero, Costanera Sur, Reserva Ecológica and Santa María del Plata have distinctive characteristics and these are reflected in urban landscape, architecture and especially through the use of these spaces. Real estate developments cohabit with public space, tourism with local leisure facilities, and the most expensive office floors with local choripan[1] stands, all of these in a development in which the state, the municipality, international corporations and real estate companies have collaborated and discussed to produce a hybrid *new* space for the city.

These projects for reuse of a peculiar urban space have been influenced not only by urban ideas but also by leisure practices and by economic interests in conflict with the social needs of the city. The development of the Buenos Aires waterfront, like many other such developments in the world, has given answers to leisure activities and to the needs of the market as well as those of the public. What is interesting about this particular case is the diversity of functions and meaning of different spaces in the same location, starting from the reuse of old infrastructures such as the stock houses of the old port, passing through the reuse of public parks and promenades to the *ex novo* projects of new urban and real estate development.

What we can observe in this development throughout the twentieth century is that there has been a process of differentiation of spaces, starting from a local perspective in the realisation of public space to current standardisation and homogenisation of urban space. The first projects for waterfront parks, such as Costanera Sur, by Benito Carrasco, of the 1910s were indeed inspired by urban ideas imported from abroad, but these were interpreted and realised at a much faster and more efficient pace than those proposed in Europe at the time. As the end of the century approached there

G. Maciocco, S. Serreli (eds.), *Enhancing the City*, Urban and Landscape Perspectives 6,
DOI 10.1007/978-90-481-2419-0_13, © Springer Science+Business Media B.V. 2009

was a tendency to copy a model that has been internationally "successful" but tends to provide a standardised space without local identity.

In this paper[2], we will look at the current situation of the Buenos Aires waterfront and refer to each of the areas analysing their meaning, use, morphology and identity to provide a critical view of these spaces of leisure. We will start by giving an account of current leisure theory to understand the scope of its influence on leisure spatial development. Then we will look at the current state of waterfront leisure developments worldwide to understand the hypothesis of the standardisation of these spaces. Later, we will describe the history of the analysed spaces on the Buenos Aires waterfront, so as to understand the complex influences that have shaped the harbour and public spaces of the waterfront. That will lead to the analysis of the current situation, where we will try to focus on diversity and the positive and negative aspects of each of these spaces.

Leisure Perspectives

In the past 40 years, in the Western world, leisure has not only increased as time free from work, but it has also gained ground in all kinds of research fields. Studies on tourism, urban leisure and recreation are being developed in the sciences, from economic to social and from political to spatial. However, culture has been one of the main issues addressed within leisure studies.

Ian P. Henry (2001) provides a deep analysis into the leisure policies of Britain, but despite its local condition, it sheds light on processes that are happening at a global level, especially in Europe and the United States, but not disregarding Asian and Latin American countries. His main hypothesis is that at the end of the twentieth century, leisure was a relevant source of identity in terms of production function. Henry rejects the discussion about the definition of leisure itself. To support the content of his work, Henry uses the definition of leisure given by Kaplan in 1975:

> leisure consists of relatively self determined activity/experience that falls into one's economically free time roles, that is seen as leisure by participants, that is psychologically pleasant in anticipation or recollection, that potentially covers the whole range of commitment and intensity, that contains characteristic norms and constraints, and that provides opportunities for recreation, personal growth and service to others (Kaplan 1975, p. 26).

Henry writes from the perspective of policy making and it is true that, nowadays, leisure as cultural development has become part of most urban policies; culture is used as a way to enrich the lives of citizens, to increase tourism up to the point of turning culture into a commodity. It is difficult then to separate the concepts of cultural and commercial leisure.

Even though the debate about the definition of leisure might be sterile, it is important to analyse the different applications of these concepts on activities, to be able to give a wider insight into the implementation of space for leisure purposes. Other perspectives on leisure activities and their purpose provide a wider view of their significance. James Murphy (1987), for example, states a clear subdivision of interpretation of leisure as behaviour. In the structural–functional approach, leisure is a residual instead of an integral part of life. On the other hand, the social-action approach views individual behaviour as fulfilment through leisure experience. Then he observes two dominant views: the objective and the subjective. Within the objective view, leisure is seen as quantitative, residual or discretionary time; as a form of activity; a symbol of social class; a social instrument and a function of social groups and lifestyles. On the subjective side, we find the philosophical and psychological perspectives. From the philosophical viewpoint, the author goes back to the concept of leisure described by Aristotle, as the basis of culture and the end towards which all action is directed. All these concepts are usable and applicable to the construction of leisure space currently.

Glasser adds to the debate, describing the shift from earlier ideas about culture, pointing out that mass culture became prominent from the second half of the twentieth century. "Mass media emphasis on the interpretation of popularisation of cultural matters indicates a ready enough market for an effort on the middle section of the social diamond to be consciously preoccupied in its leisure with the pursuit of enlightenment and culture" (Glasser 1970, p. 156).

Audio visual reproduction systems have influenced not only industrialisation, production and work but also leisure activities, especially in the last three decades, the commercialisation of literature, music, cinema and sport, widening the reach of a standardised culture to the population. However, the pursuit of enlightenment and culture loses part of its appeal and value, transforming the appreciation of these matters and the way of using them.

From another perspective, Johan Huizinga (1950) introduces the idea of *Homo Ludens* as the natural evolution from *Homo Sapiens* through *Homo Faber*. According to Huizinga, Man the Player had to be brought to the spotlight, for social sciences had not given the concept of play the supreme importance it should have. In Huizinga's opinion play was older than culture, being one of the main bases of civilisation.

Commercial development of recreation and leisure has, as much as cultural development, been extremely relevant in the urban context of recent decades. Planning is at the top of the list in the discussion, and guides most of the development of leisure spaces, to provide city dwellers with the *optimal* leisure conditions. The issues of standardisation and commodification are of great concern in the academic context.[3]

For Glasser (1970), social activities are considered a source of release, which at the present time have to be paid for. Clubs, restaurants, dance halls, drinks, drugs and gambling are just some of these activities. Through these he observes that there is a universal tendency of people to adjust to problems by isolating themselves from them. Sport, even though it has been incorporated into urban daily life since the nineteenth century, appears as a rising leisure phenomenon; in the first stages of life, a person's participation is active, which leads to subsequent passive participation that is more centred on the urge for emotional identification. Indulgence recreation brought new activities into the picture in the 1970s when the cult of the body became essential. Glasser's study concludes that within Western cultural disintegration, leisure has become almost purely commercial despite the fact that some minorities use their leisure time for more significant purposes. His work can also be called *holistic* for he tries to find a link between the purely theoretical meanings of leisure and its actual applications. For him "Culture is the outward manifestation of man's attempt to understand himself in relation to his environment" (Glasser 1970, Chapter 4) and leisure activities should reflect this uncertainty.

If we compare the theoretical view of leisure and the application of it to practice, a big gap is to be found. When it comes to a practical way of applying leisure to commerce, management and planning, the quest for the significance of leisure for the individual practically disappears. Leisure becomes almost an exact science and it is mostly called recreation. The aim of most studies in this field is the effectiveness of planning leisure spaces with a profit goal.

In the planning sphere, Pat Farrell (Farrell and Lundgren 1983) approaches the subject in a purely pragmatic way. She proposes three areas of planning process: (1) organisational patterns, (2) segments of the programme service unit and (3) activity clustering. This categorisation is simply a tool for leisure planners; the consideration of management and marketing for leisure planning is used as the instrument for providing leisure events and activities in a format that can be used, disregarding the location or type of activity. In management, leisure is considered as a service that can be provided either by the state or by private investment. This approach is shared by most management professionals. Most literature about management and planning aims at specific cases and activities within leisure, predominantly in the United States. This gives an insight mainly into the ways leisure is used in planned activities. These are the arts, coastal recreation, camping, commercial recreation, mass media, play, sport, religion, travel and tourism. Gold (1975, 1980) gives a supply and demand analysis, plus goals, needs and design aspects at the time of leisure planning.

Bannon (1976) makes a thorough comprehensive study of leisure planning in a completely pragmatic way. His process requires step-by-step action that consists of analysis, establishment of goals, strategy, programme, implementation and evaluation. His whole study is the development of this model. Bannon's view of the situation of leisure is also quite pragmatic. In his view "in the past people found satisfaction in their work" (Bannon 1976, p. 22) but they do not anymore and personal guilt produced by increased leisure calls for a need of productivity. He states that "Planning is political, it determines who gets what when and how" (Bannon 1976, p. 28). In a position that also seems too determined to approach the subject he affirms that "Any procedural or theoretical model is useful only for defining major tasks to be performed (...) Most social models rely on a simple problem solving approach" (Bannon 1976, p. 35).

His book may be very useful in the case of directly planning recreation facilities (not leisure), for he gives a practical and safe process of application of a recreation project. Nevertheless, even though he goes through all the details possible in the process of planning, there seems to be no questioning whatsoever into the quality of space and life of the individuals who would be using this recreational space.

From the economic perspective of Clawson and Knetch (1966), economic interest falls into four main areas within this sphere: the work/leisure choice, allocation of time between leisure activities, demand for specific leisure activities and evaluation of projects through cost-benefit analyses. The two broad questions for them are efficiency and equity. "By and large, leisure and work are competitors for time. If one increases, the other decreases. This is so for the individual and for society as a whole" (Clawson and Knetch 1966, p. 7).

Clawson and Knetch seem to simplify the question of leisure and to reduce it to its basically practical terms. This is a perfectly useful tool, like those for management, especially in the quest for profit of these activities. It does leave aside any hints of social significance of leisure or any open questions about the benefits of these activities and projects besides the cost and financial success of them.

From a philosophical perspective, Lefebvre (1990, Chapter 1 par. 2) develops a new sociology of leisure. He mainly states that leisure ideas and practices are part of a larger apparatus of ideological reproduction that serves to maintain capitalist social relations. Lefebvre calls our urban society a "bureaucratic society of controlled consumption"; he also states in acid criticism of urban society that "Never has the relationship of the human being with the world experienced such profound misery as during the reign of habitat and so-called 'urbanistic rationality'" (Lefebvre 1990, Chapter 4 par 4). This position sheds some light on the real processes of consumption and what we mentioned earlier about the commodification of leisure activities. Lefebvre goes as far as criticising the whole of urban society, which is not our opinion, but we share the idea that commodification of leisure can only lead to standardisation and the loss of local identity and sense of place of each specific urban centre.

Leisure space in the urban context has constantly been addressed in recent years. New parks, squares, cultural facilities, harbours, waterfronts, malls, festival markets and promenades have all been developed in the last decades and are growing and taking over spaces of the city. There have been particular studies on the development of leisure and recreation space especially in the United States. The methods of zoning from the 1960s were harshly criticised in the 1970s. "The predilection of the city planner for sorting land use by functions and putting all like uses together has segregated residential areas into compounds which include only houses" (Van Doren et al. 1974, p. 11).

The authors of this book focus on the human element as a crucial one in the provision of public space, leaving form and programme in the background. The role of the city planner was also questioned in the 1970s, for:

having no direct mechanism, such as market indication, to inform him about what people want has led him to make assumptions about objectives. This condition, in which he has only limited responsibility for the services produced, and few direct and intimate links with what people want and need, has impelled him to rest his case on what people ought to want, such as the orderly, the efficient, the beautiful (Perloff and Lowdon 1974, p. 38).

In this publication, the authors intend to give a wide description of what outdoor recreation is and try to provide methods for the subsequent planning of these spaces. One of the main issues in this book, which is touched upon by most of the authors, is related to the importance of recreation as an economic value that cannot be measured for it is not market priced. This issue is discussed thoroughly, but there is little mention of the real significance of urban public space for the dweller.

Cranz (1980) finds from a historical point of view four steps in the development of park environments during the last century. Before the 1900s there was the pleasure ground era, an attempt to create a rural area in the middle of a city. Between 1900 and 1930 this was focused on children and their play needs. From 1930 to 1965 park planning was driven by demand. Finally, in recent years, the Open Space Era has arrived, which is a time of experimentation and a new concern with involving citizens in the urban parks.

We agree with this categorisation, having studied particular projects, especially of the first two periods explained by Cranz. There have been numerous studies and projects for open space development in the last four decades, with different characters and pointing out their human and economic significance. Many different typologies of public space development have been introduced. These have mainly been provided by governments and authorities in a top-down manner. However, a few new methods of cooperation and participation have arisen in the past decades, involving citizens and private firms. These projects have proved more difficult to implement, but some of them have been successful in providing a diverse and participative urban leisure space.

The waterfronts have been a crucial space in the city for these kinds of developments. The abandoned harbours and technical facilities of the nineteenth century have been restructured and adapted to new uses and programmes combining passive and active, cultural and commercial leisure practices. The following chapters on the specific case studies will investigate this subject further.

Current Waterfront Situation Worldwide

Many studies are being developed and published on the current state of waterfront urban spaces and fewer on the history of these developments. A problem of standardisation has been found in the recent development of waterfront leisure areas, and the study of past cases might be helpful for the diversification of these projects. The thorough studies on the different types of leisure activities and applications shed light on the narrowness of its application to urban planning, especially on urban waterfronts.

Currently, in the world, we can find various typologies of use of the waterfront. Use has mainly been made, on the one hand, of the harbour – generally located on the outskirts of the city – as the old infrastructures became obsolete; and on the other hand, of urban waterfront space, which has been used for different functions, such as residential, commercial, leisure or a mixed use of these. The case of American cities, which have tended to homogenise space, can also be applied to certain Asian and Middle Eastern cities, given the effects of globalisation. Cities such as Osaka, Cape Town, Dubai, Hamilton, Miami, New York and Seattle, to name but a few, have developed or are developing areas of their waterfront in a very similar way, with an international typology of building on the one hand or with a constructed theme-like historical image.

Sorkin, Jacobs and Boyer have observed this phenomenon in cities as a whole and have criticised this tendency. "American cities are being rapidly transformed by sinister and homogeneous design. A new kind of urbanism – manipulative, dispersed, and hostile to traditional public space – is emerging both at the heart and at the edge of town in megamalls, corporate enclaves, gentrified zones and pseudo historic marketplaces" (Sorkin 1992, back cover).

Sorkin appeals to the standardisation of space as a reproduction of the theme park, a space of simulacra of constructed identity. Christine Boyer also describes these spaces as constructed identities for the eye:

Places like Battery Park City and South Street Seaport are sustained not only by the pleasures of picture writing, but by the expansion of historical tourism, the desire to "just-look" at the replicated and re-valued artefacts and architecture of another time. Yet to historicise is to estrange, to make different, so that a gap continually widens between then and now, between an authentic and a simulated experience (Boyer 1992, p. 199).

The inconvenience of these spaces as internationalised and standardised lies in the fact that identity of place is lost and there is little difference between a project in Asia, Africa or Latin America. One such case is the Wynyard project in Auckland, New Zealand, where, even though the programme is varied, with parks, offices and dwellings, the entire existing structures are disposed of and a series of buildings with the same dimensions and image are projected. The parks are well located facing the water, using a maximum of waterfront perimeter, but the distribution of green space is homogeneous and there are few changes in the distribution of vegetation. The parks are mainly just open space with grass and some rows of trees, lacking diversity.

In South Africa, for example, the case of the Victoria and Alfred waterfront in Cape Town is different in the sense that it tries to keep some of the identity the space used to have as a harbour. In this way, as happened with Battery Park City in New York, explained by Boyer, we can see this will for historicising space, which estranges the place and develops into a basically "just-look" but also just-buy commercial district. Something that is also worrying is the fact that the V&A Waterfront Company proposes to develop waterfront areas in this way throughout the world, which adds to the possibility of having a single manner of developing these areas worldwide.

One of the most significant cases of a standardised waterfront is that of Dubai. This is a city that has only existed for some decades and has been created completely from scratch, in the desert, but in an area with a very strong cultural identity, as is the Middle East. However, it has developed into a homogeneous city, with all necessary services and uses, but without any sort of local identity. The waterfront has been thought of and developed with exactly the same type of perspective. Malls, residential and business centres, hotels and beaches are all cut out in an international style, resembling more a theme park than a city. The paradigmatic example of the space of simulacra named by Sorkin can be found in International City in Dubai, where pieces of different towns and countries of the world are reproduced in the form of residential areas copying styles that are "representative" of the "essence" of these European and Mediterranean countries.

To add one more case, we can look at the Sakishima development in Osaka, Japan. This is another characteristic waterfront project of the 2000s where a variety of functions is proposed, but the design lines and the use of space are limited and lack any of the issues that identify Japanese culture, giving an image of space that could be found elsewhere in the world.

European cases do not escape standardisation. Even though European cities have the value – though not always exploited – of traditional urban space, new projects for the waterfront tend towards standardisation. With the sprawl of business parks on the waterfronts such as those in Amsterdam, Bilbao, Hamburg, Liverpool or Vigo, we can see a tendency to build large open spaces, with little park design and either standard commercial buildings or landmark buildings, in a quest to identify the image of a city.

To elaborate with some examples, we can pick out Llano Amarillo in Algeciras, Spain, an area in Europe with a strong local identity that is home to another of these leisure space projects. Even though some design issues are addressed for the area, such as the palm trees that recreate the geometrical layout of Arab designs, the space is homogeneous; the proposal for commercial areas does not differ from others in Europe and the open space has no differentiation of areas.

The restructuring of Barcelona's waterfront has been said to be a success story by critics, by the public and by the tourists. However, this success was more due to the recovery of the beach and the cleaning of the waters than to the urban and architectural interventions that were carried out. The main criticism of this project did not concern the projects for the Olympic Games but what happened later, namely the Forum 2004 project. The area of the forum was planned near Besós, where numerous projects for parks had been presented since Cerdá's plan of 1859. In the end this was not developed as a park, which the zone of the city really needed, but as a dry open area, with great open spaces lacking any sort of identity or function. Once the forum was over, the place was used for events and concerts, but when it is not being used in this way the space is left barren and empty.

In Hamburg, Germany, Hafen City has been redeveloped as a "cultural and art district". However, this space does not reflect any sort of local identity. Instead, the sculptures and urban furniture are as homogeneous as the urban layout and architecture.

The case of Bilbao is a typical case of city branding. This has proved to be successful in attracting foreigners, but the elements used for this strategy have been the importation of signature architecture such as the Guggenheim museum by Frank Gehry. We do not question the architectural value of this building, but this has led the way to the reproduction of these types of spaces all over Europe and the world.

These are just some examples of this approach to redesigning the urban waterfront, and this phenomenon is finally starting to be noticed and criticised further from theory and closer to practice. In the competition for Hong Kong's waterfront,[4] it was especially stated that the "standardised designs over long stretches of waterfront should be avoided". Even in some UK cases the commercial success of these developments has been questioned. Such was the case of Bristol, where, according to Mark Jones "(the projects) have recently been significantly affected by lack of visitor numbers leading to the closure of former flagship projects – those of Wildwalk and the IMAX".[5]

And we can close with a quotation from Jane Jacobs:

Well I think that it's a more dangerous situation – the standardisation of what is being produced or reproduced everywhere, where you can see it in the malls, in every city, the same chains, the same products are to be found. This goes even deeper with the trouble with import replacing because it means that new things are not being produced locally that can be improvements or anyway different. There is a sameness – this is one of the things that is boring people – this sameness. This sameness has economic implications. You don't get new products and services out of sameness.[6]

If we bring past cases together, especially those formulated in the last decades of the nineteenth century and the early decades of the twentieth, we can observe that the programme for these projects was much wider, that different types of leisure were considered and that waterfront parks were much more present than in contemporary projects. Moreover, architectural morphology and local species of plants were much more varied than in current projects.

The *Centro Internazionale Città d'Acqua*,[7] located in Venice, is the only European institution that brings together information and analysis of waterfront developments. However, this institution is focused on current projects and has no historical perspective on them. Moreover, more than half of the worldwide projects presented by them in their catalogue refer to harbour projects and technical facilities that have little or nothing to do with the urban condition. This is why it would be interesting and productive to study a greater and more varied number of these cases, to develop research that might serve to enhance the local identities of waterfront urban spaces and recover ideas that have been left unnoticed for further development of these particular urban areas.

Translation and Transference

We wish to compare the differences between the earlier – early twentieth century – approach to the exportation/importation of urban ideas and the current globalising and homogenising operations of the latest decades. For this purpose, we will analyse the processes of translation and *trans-culturation* addressed by current literature.

The concept of *transculturación* was coined by Fernando Ortiz (1940) in the 1940s, in his description of the cultural complexity of Cuba. Even though this concept refers to a different cultural reality than that of the cases studied, his description of the re-territorialisation of ideas can be used in this case. For the first time, Ortiz analysed the process of a mixed culture from a different perspective, not talking about *acculturation* but about *trans-culturation*, putting local culture in a more prominent position than the one it had occupied until then.

In the field of urbanism, this kind of analysis was re-addressed more recently by Joe Nasr and Mercedes Volait (2003) in their compendium of articles with the premise of the importation-exportation of urbanism, which placed cases in America, Africa and Asia in a central position. The authors point out the lack of awareness of the complexity of these processes in recent specialised literature. In particular, they draw attention to the under-representation of *peripheral* cases compared to the *central* ones that established urban planning models. They highlight the fact that most of the literature regarding the international exchange of urbanist ideas in *developing* countries was focalised on colonial and post-colonial situations (King 1976). Nasr and Volait do not deal with the colonial cases but focus on another perspective, one in which the complex combination of exchange of ideas, models and the visit of urbanist professionals shaped the international scope of city planning. In a more specific analysis, Jean-Louis Cohen (1997) also addresses this process of exchange, dealing with the influence of North American urbanism and architecture on Europe. He considers the translation of the American model or *Americanism* as Europe's subconscious, in a process of passing from horizontal to vertical urban planning. The studies of George Collins and Christiane Crasemann Collins on Camillo Sitte (Collins and Collins 1986) and Werner Hegemann (Crasemann 2005) address the process of translation, especially of texts and the way they are interpreted by translators, as transference and retro-transference. In the book on Hegemann, for example, the authors point out the way the urban planner, on his visit to Buenos Aires, was not only influenced by local urbanism, but also took with him some ideas he developed, inspired by the city he visited for the first time.

All of this literature deals with the complexity of the circulation of ideas and the construction of knowledge in the specificity of certain contexts. These theories will be used as a framework for the analysis of the case of Buenos Aires and the first projects for the leisure waterfront.

History of Puerto Madero

With the purpose of understanding the processes of transformation of the waterfront area of Buenos Aires, we should look at the origins of the harbour and leisure places in this space.

During the nineteenth century the urban condition of Buenos Aires experienced problems. One of the most serious conflicts concerned the harbour, which led to commercial and projectual problems.

The subject of the development of Buenos Aires harbour has been recently analysed by commentators (Silvestri 1993; Pando 1989; Lucchini 1981; Longo 1989) and evolution towards a more urban perspective been observed, especially in the work of Graciela Silvestri. It is not the intention of this text to question these approaches but their views are necessary to understand the processes of the conflict between harbour development and the need for provision of leisure areas, especially at a time of radical economic, social and urban transformation.

There was hardly any construction done in the harbour until 1852, when there was a competition called for by the government. The two main projects presented were those by John Coghlan (1857–1887) and Carlos Enrique Pellegrini (1800–1875). These two professionals were engineers, Irish and Italian, respectively. They belonged to a group of engineers that were connected with the army, and this fact partly conditioned the design of their projects. According to Silvestri (1993), the reason why these initial projects completely cut off relations between the city and the river was not the technical need of defence from river tides but more a matter of military defence.

The two main projects, those of Luis Huergo (1837–1913) and Eduardo Madero (1833–1893) have been subjected to analysis and considerations throughout the last decades of the twentieth century as well as 100 years ago. The reason for this discussion has to do with the fact that the destiny of the whole Buenos Aires waterfront lay in the decision to implement one of the two projects proposed. To sum it up, Huergo and Madero's projects differed formally in one main aspect. Madero's was a closed harbour of docks connected by a canal comparable to that of Liverpool or Montevideo, with only two entrances. Whereas Huergo's project, in exactly the same location, consisted of a series of parallel docks, a dented harbour, a structure that had recently been introduced in the United States and Australia.

Huergo's project was much more innovative in that the typology used for the comb-shaped harbour was the latest advance in port technology. Huergo proposed a regional harbour that could be continued up to the mouth of Paraná River, therefore providing an integral solution to the trade issues of the region. This was a rather ambitious project but the limited project for the city did not depend on the regional proposal. In his project, Huergo kept the existing image of Buenos Aires, the traditional centre as the neuralgic point of the whole country. Madero's image of the city, on the other hand, was focused on services and production being sent to the hinterland. He proposed an almost inland harbour, limited in space and with no possibility of expansion.

After serious conflicts of interest between government and investors, the choice for the project to be built was taken in 1882. This took place during the process of capitalisation of Buenos Aires and Madero's project was chosen under these circumstances. The harbour was built in a short lapse of time, between 1889 and 1897 (Fig. 1).

The harbour was placed on the southern shore of the city, adjacent to the Government building and the whole central area of Buenos Aires. It consisted of a 21-foot deep canal, an outer embankment, an outer dock and four interconnected 21-foot deep docks for the loading and unloading of merchandise. On the sides of the docks a series of warehouses with cranes were built to receive the loads from the ships. A great amount of money was invested in the harbour. It boasted 17,000 m of dock perimeter, 134.4 ha of water, 219,000 m² of warehouses and 97 km of railways.

Once Madero's harbour was chosen and building was begun in 1885, a fraction of the land gained from the river ended up in the hands of the harbour authorities.

Fig. 1 Puerto Madero.1890 – *Archivo general de la Nación. Archivo fotográfico. Caja 865*

These lands were supposed to be sold at a public auction to private entities for the expansion of the city and to be made into 100 by 100-m blocks, like the rest of Buenos Aires.

In this respect, the newspaper La Prensa accused Madero of the speculative sale of land and of occupying an accessory and not a main role in the construction of the harbour. He was even accused of being an agent of the Baring Brothers. This real estate operation could not be carried out for, due to the crisis of 1890, the price of land rose and the foreign investors bailed out from the operation. In his own defence Madero said: "if the government had accepted one of the proposals when they were made, the harbour would have cost nothing".

The conditions in which this project was chosen and then built have been a matter of discussion for years, but we will not dwell on this conflict on this occasion. We will stick to the consequences that the building of Madero's project brought to the evolution of the leisure coast. The technical problem of Madero's design anticipated by Huergo arose in Puerto Madero a few years after it was built. By the beginning of the twentieth century the weight of ships had grown in a few years from 4 to 10 thousand tons and would soon grow to 20 tons. This circumstance, added to the increase in commercial activity, showed how soon Madero's project would be obsolete and this called for the design and building of the new harbour.

In 1907 the National Government decided to tackle the decision of building a new harbour. The project consisted of a series of docks, comb-shaped harbour, similar to Huergo's project but located in the northern area of the waterfront north of Puerto Madero. The project proposed six open docks and two jetties to protect them. The building of the harbour took place between 1911 and 1919 and the harbour created another material barrier between the city and the waterfront.

On the whole, Buenos Aires can be considered a peripheral harbour in the historical period studied, not belonging to the traditional network of European and Mediterranean harbours. As is correctly observed by Silvestri (1993, pp. 104–105), peripheral harbours like the North and South American ones were outstanding for several reasons. One of the main reasons was that Mediterranean harbours, having a long tradition and a long past were a "cumulus of interventions throughout time where no coherence could be found". Examples such as Naples and the old harbour of Genoa showed contradictions in their structure. Cases like that of Marseille would be an exception, for this was a systematised harbour that had been built after abandoning the old one.

Another issue that allowed the building of the harbour *ex-novo* to be ahead of the traditional harbours of Europe was that there was a lack of pre-existing heavy weight cultural elements. Or rather, these pre-existing elements were already in a process of transformation that allowed the flexibility it was not possible to achieve on the European continent.

This hypothesis coincides with the one we are attempting to illustrate in this paper regarding the leisure waterfront areas. The open space for leisure on the urban waterfront had development potential due to the flexibility that these new urban centres, such as Buenos Aires, offered. Besides, even the exception for this case given by Silvestri, the case of Marseille, coincides with the exception as a leisure waterfront in a European harbour city, due to the harbour being moved; Marseille was a pioneer in proposing a leisure area at the waterfront.

Regarding the space contested by leisure needs and harbour facilities, the discussion about the port takes a different angle. We have to admit that, despite the problems of spatial segregation caused by the building of Puerto Madero and the whole railway network that came with it, Madero's project was much more successful than Huergo's would have been. Madero's project left a new waterfront available, which was a land of experimentation, and later the main waterfront promenade of the city. As regards the new port built from 1911, this caused a real barrier between the city and the river, not allowing any further development of leisure practices of any kind.

History of Costanera Sur

The project for Costanera Sur proposed by Benito Javier Carrasco (1877–1958) took place between 1916 and 1919, with the intention of building a bathing resort. It was located on the landfill behind Puerto Madero, between Brazil and Belgrano streets. This location, as we saw before in projects for the harbour, had been disputed between port authorities and municipal ones, for once Puerto Madero was built, the triangle of land that separated the harbour from the waterfront remained barren land.

Benito Carrasco was an agronomy engineer dedicated to urban issues between 1916 and 1919 with the role of Director of Parks and Promenades of the city of Buenos Aires. He studied agronomy engineering at the Faculty of Agronomy and Veterinary of the province of Buenos Aires. Carrasco shared ideas about landscape and urbanism such as the *garden city*, with his mentor Carlos Thays. Ebenezer Howard's *garden city* underwent a series of translations from its origin to its arrival in Buenos Aires that reached a very different concept, especially in its application to specific projects. French urbanism had been influential in Buenos Aires, and the texts that arrived from abroad came frequently in their French translation. Architects such as Léon Jaussely had translated English texts such as Unwin's *Town Planning in Practice* (Unwin 1922). The way in which Howard's *garden city* was translated into the *cité-jardin* of French urbanism influenced the use of this concept in Buenos Aires, transforming it from the garden city as an ideal independent element to the residential area named *ciudad jardín*. However, Buenos Aires did not have as many problems of lack of hygiene, congestion and lack of space as some cities in England had, but the steady, fast growth of population and industry allowed reflection on potential solutions to these problems. Therefore the problem was considered before it became unmanageable. Carrasco considered it an important issue to develop workers' neighbourhoods guided by the ideas of the *barrio parque* (park neighbourhood), probably also derived from the translation of the original concept of *garden city*.

There is no written evidence of this but the ideas of Josef Stübben (1845–1936), illustrated at the Chicago International Engineering Congress of 1893, also seem to have been influential in Carrasco's ideas of park design and suburban neighbourhoods. The need for air and open space for hygienic reasons that had been present at most of the gatherings of urbanists at the turn of the century were present in Carrasco's discourse. Issues like the dimensions of streets, sidewalks and other lanes within boulevards were also similar in Carrasco's and Stübben's treatises.

An important document is left from Carrasco's years as a Director of Municipal Parks: "*La Memoria de los trabajos realizados en los Parques y*

Paseos Públicos de la Ciudad de Buenos Aires. Años 1914, 15 y 16". In this text he describes in detail his position on park design and planning and expresses many considerations about the function of parks in different fields of urban environment. Some of these issues refer not just to the aesthetic but also to the social functions of parks, saying that parks and gardens have to fulfil their social *mission*. Children would also be highly considered in the principles of park design. "A piece of culture, driving away and separating bad habits, forbidden games to a great amount of children that until a short time ago did not know the benefits nor the joy of the healthy practices" (Carrasco 1916, p. 91).

This reminds us of the rational recreation movement that developed in Britain and the United States during the nineteenth century. Most interesting within this movement is the remark that Cross made: "Park commissioners also believed it their duty to reform leisure time as well as space" (Cross 1990, p. 98). This caused the first mass cultural centres to become the hallmark of the rational recreational movement. "These trends, along with regulated sport contributed to cultural uniformity and reduced the disorder associated with both rural popular leisure and the degrading pleasures of the new industrial cities" (Cross 1990, p. 99).

The subject of the baths would not be mentioned in the city council until it was recommended that the waterfront avenue and baths be built in 1917. In 1916 the Secretary for Public Works, the engineer Aguirre, under Intendente Gramajo's administration, entrusted the *Dirección de Paseos*, led then by Benito Carrasco, with the elaboration of a project to transform the abandoned lands of the waterfront. The idea was to build a swimming – pool taking advantage of the thermal waters that were supposed to lie at the site.

One of the main inconveniences found by Carrasco in realising this project was that public access for the numerous railways arriving at the harbour would cut off accessibility to the area. The railways on the bridges would especially narrow the access streets.

The first section of the project from Estados Unidos to Belgrano consisted of a 10-m wide path on the river "destined for pedestrians and a stretch of gardens where places for diversions and rest would be established". Football fields and tennis courts, separated from the path by a curtain of elm-poplars would cover the anti-aesthetic docks of the harbour.

In this section of the project, we can see a very austere and reduced version of similar elements used in the project for the northern part of the city. Two great stretches of park, grass lawns with some bushes located on the southern part provide a more natural landscape.

The section closer to avenida Belgrano included a pier very similar to that in his previous project for a northern avenue, with a pavilion or lighthouse at the end of the pier. Apart from the sports fields we can also see a large pavilion just before the entrance to the pier, which could be meant as a Casino or other leisure building proposed.

Every terrace leading from the waterfront avenue to the beach seems to have a staircase descending to the beach, despite the fact that this is not explicitly explained by Carrasco in his texts. The second section of the project, that going from Belgrano to the north was mainly destined for the circulation of vehicles. As seen in the plan, the street in that area runs parallel to the river, as it reaches Belgrano it runs diagonally and leads the way to the whole section of park and baths programme. In the southern part the promenade for pedestrians is parallel to the river.

This section between Belgrano and Darsena Norte consisted of an ample sidewalk 10-m wide with a stretch of gardens on both sides so as to avoid the monotony of a wide monochromatic sidewalk. At the Cangallo intersection a semicircular *plazoleta* with gardens and pavilions would be built. The end of the avenue was situated at the Córdoba roundabout intersection, which would also serve as a parking lot for automobiles.

The outline of the avenue, streets and roundabouts was realised in the early years after the project was approved in 1917. So was the pier, built by the *Centro Nacional de Ingenieros* (Fig. 2). Despite Carrasco's criticism of this project, judging it anti-aesthetic and expensive, it received good public response. But before going into that it is relevant to describe the programme for the pier and surroundings. The document[8] was written some months after the inauguration of the pier. The first section of the article was dedicated to explaining the need of a space of hygiene and entertainment for the urban population.

The recent inauguration of the Municipal Baths and the city council incidents involving it, have kept the attention of the public alive about this establishment created by the municipal government for the entertainment and hygiene of a section of the urban population. This population was lacking these services as well as a waterfront park destined to those who, not being able to afford it, were not able or keen to move to Mar del Plata or other Argentine or Uruguayan bathing resorts.[9]

This shows once more a will to provide public leisure space for all kinds of city dwellers, especially the less economically fortunate. Accessibility and nearness to the city centre is a key element in the discourse and in the facts.

Fig. 2 Construction pier. Costanera Sur. 1919 – *Archivo de la Nación. Archivo Fotográfico. Caja 3234*

Regarding the situation, it is clear that proximity to the urban population is the undeniable advantage for the public. However, it presents the inconvenience – unavoidable in the whole southern waterfront up to the Riachuelo – of forcing the people to use the turning bridges linking the regions east and west of the capital's harbour. Therefore, the flow of the people will be interrupted by that of the harbour. Fortunately, in the holidays, when public attendance is greater, the harbour is not at work, or hardly. Then, given its location facing the harbour in the southern part of the city, the situation is suitable.[10]

Problems of accessibility created by the city harbour are mentioned but no apparent solution is given to the problem of the south, whereas the prediction of a solution to the problem of the works anticipated in the northern part of the city is stated.

The pier had little to do with the European continental and British piers, such as those of Eugenius Birch. Those pleasure piers were light structures of wood and iron, rising high over the ocean, and possibly with jetties for small ships. This one was a heavy concrete structure with integrated changing cabins that were part of the pier itself. This whole project took some years to be built and was realised by different entities, but throughout it was faithful to Carrasco's original design.

The waterfront area built for the inauguration of the project in December 1918 was apparently very well received by the public. It is relevant to say that his project for the southern baths, especially its pier, fulfilled the need for leisure space close to the city. This can be read in the articles on the inauguration day. The result of the design and building of the avenue and baths was stunning. The city dwellers were evidently welcoming the recovery of the shore.

Today the south zone of the capital receives, in equal proportion to that of the north, the benefits of municipal action. This new bathing zone, built on the sand banks that until recently were deserted, is a clear demonstration of the new order of things opening up for the neighbourhoods of the south. The proud promenade shows its elegant silhouette to the horizon of the Rio de la Plata. (...) What a great spectacle the waterfront promenade will provide, with its thousands of souls strolling along the wide avenue that borders the estuary![11]

Finally, one project using the entire waterfront as leisure space could be implemented, close to the city (Fig. 3). Though social reform was not an intention, the project nevertheless provided, because of its geographical location, a meeting space for different social classes at the picturesque waterfront landscape. From a financial perspective, the investment made in the building of the pier and baths was justified by the benefits of the project and was to be recovered in four years from the rents for spaces in the area.

Regarding the necessity of baths for recreation and hygiene for the people, it was a conviction that floated in the environment, for which reason its realisation, not only did not generate one single protest, but received general applause. So much so that the desire has been heard to build another bath on the northern side of the waterfront, as was the idea of doctor Le Breton, and we still believe that the government of the city is already busy with its project, which we approve without claims.[12]

Fig. 3 Costanera Sur. 1930 – *Archivo de la Nación. Archivo Fotográfico. Caja 3234*

The work of Carrasco in the parks and promenades of Buenos Aires is essential. This is even more relevant in the case of the waterfront projects. This man, a local professional, with strong, determined ideas and a sensitive feel for the needs of his city, was able to develop projects despite the criticism and lack of recognition of the authorities and his peers.

His solutions for the problems of his city were complete and detailed. The variables he considered and the processes he used were complex and elaborate. In his book *Parques y Jardines,* for example, he explains his process of design as follows. He would consider the preliminary operations for the formation of the park, and gather all relevant information about the site, the project, the influence of the weather and seasons, perspectives, elements that compose a garden, placing of statues, water as an ornamental element, different kinds of trees, bushes, foliage, grass, paths, floral decorations and so on.

History of Reserva Ecológica

In the early 1970s, during the military government, a new landfill project was created on the southern side, in front of the Costanera Sur promenade. This was an addition to those that had been developed in the northern part of the city. They consisted of gaining land from the river to expand the urban areas. The northern landfills had been done initially to provide park space, but they were finally used to build the municipal airport, that would be another element to separate the city from its riverfront.

Land-filling on the southern side, proposed in 1978, was meant to provide an administrative centre for the city, on the lines of Le Corbusier's project for Buenos Aires of 1937. The landfills were built using the Dutch "polder" system. An extended motorway was being built around the city, to limit and connect it with the metropolitan area. For this purpose, the buildings located on this fringe were expropriated and subsequently demolished. The debris from the demolished buildings was deposited in the river, building embankments. As the zone within the embankments filled with silt from the river, the water confined inside was drained, though this work was not fully achieved.

The initial project for the administrative district was not carried out, though the work of depositing debris on the river continued until 1984, when it was finally suspended. From then on, spontaneously, a series of vegetation communities began to sprawl onto the landfill area. These plants provided refuge and food for various animal species and they began to reproduce in the area. From dumping ground the place turned into a self-built nature reserve, which was finally recognised as such by the government in June 1986, when the *Concejo Deliberante* sanctioned a law to protect the area (Fig. 4).

The *Parque Natural y Zona de Reserva Ecológica Costanera Sur* comes under the office of the Under Secretary for the Environment of the City Government of Buenos Aires.

Real Estate Development and Standardised Leisure Space

Like many other waterfront cities in all corners of the world, Buenos Aires was one of those that chose the waterfront area as a main space of investment and urban development at the end of the 1980s.

The area had changed profoundly since the harbour had fallen into disuse and a new one been built in the 1920s. As Puerto Madero was closed, access to the promenade and bathing facilities of Costanera Sur became more restricted. Problems of jurisdiction between the state and the city and a lack of cohesion in administrative intent left the area empty and useless for decades.

There were plans for restructuring the area in 1940, 1960, 1969, 1971, 1981 and 1985, but none of them were carried out.

Fig. 4 *Reserva Ecológica*. Google Earth 2008

In the 1980s one of the first institutional intentions to redevelop the area of the harbour and the space around it arose when the city of Buenos Aires contracted *Consultores Europeos Asociados* (CEA), an entity associated with the city of Barcelona, Spain, to develop a plan for the area. The following attempt for intervention in Puerto Madero was an international competition held in 1987. The *Comunidad de Madrid* and the *Municipalidad de Buenos Aires*, through the *Instituto de Cooperación Iberoamericana*, announced a competition of ideas for urban development in different parts of the city. One of them was the area of Puerto Madero. Many architects participated in this competition, but it did not lead to a recommendation and building.

1989 was a pivotal year in Argentine economy. While the country had historically been one of the strongest in South America, it had gone through a period of economic instability that had led to the hyper-inflation of 5,000% for that year. A new president was elected in 1989, Carlos Menem, and his neo-liberal policies were directed at the privatisation of public companies and private real estate development in the city and country.

In November 1989, in a deal between the national and municipal governments, the law was signed for the creation of the *Corporación Antiguo Puerto Madero*. This corporation was to be a public-private entity whose task was to develop a financial, regulatory and physical plan that would control and develop the area and would provide an inviting entry point for global capital and corporations. The 170 hectares of land would be exclusively in the hands of the *Corporación*, which had worked through public competitions and private projects for the design and development of the whole area.

The original project for Puerto Madero consisted of a great real estate development, to be mostly occupied by offices and dwellings. When this project was presented, the *Sociedad Central de Arquitectos* protested and following negotiations it was agreed that only 30% of the land would be destined for buildings, and the rest would be left as public space. This decision made the whole development of Puerto Madero very peculiar. The real estate development included the restoration of the old stock houses for high-quality offices and dwellings and the new construction of high-rise buildings also for the purposes of dwellings and offices.

This distribution of land led to the current condition of the place, where despite the fact that a large part of the area is dedicated exclusively to the top end of society both in dwellings and offices, public space for the use of all citizens is present as well, showing a contrast that is peculiar to the city of Buenos Aires. To strengthen this idea, Carlos Corach, the former minister of the interior stated that "Puerto Madero is much more than real-estate development: it is the new course announced by the future city…and it is the design of urban space that emphasizes the public good" (Lariviere 1999, p. 13). This success story is arguable, for the development of the area has led to the image of a city that is standardised and homogenised to the point of being almost unrecognisable as a part of the city of Buenos Aires.

Now there are four distinctive spaces in the area, all with different spatial qualities. First of all, closest to the city centre, there is the area of the old harbour. It has 16 brick stock houses from the original project for Madero harbour built in the early 1900s. These buildings have been restored and are mainly offices and dwellings, with the ground floor occupied by restaurants facing the dikes. They were the first buildings to enter a public competition and were built between 1991 and 1998. This space has a certain identity to it, even though the buildings were constructed following typology and materials brought from Britain. It looks strangely similar to the London docklands and its public space mainly has a tourist function. The other target of this open space is basically office workers from the area and some from downtown, who have lunch and dinner on the terraces facing the water.

On the other side of the dikes there is the greatest real estate development of the country. In 1996 the *Corporación Antiguo Puerto Madero* set up the second part of the plan to develop the eastern section of the area. With a much more extensive area than the one occupied by the stock houses, it required large infrastructure works with the creation of streets and services. Only three buildings were kept in their original shape and the rest of the stock area was demolished. It was finally decided to destine the area for mixed uses, both office and dwelling. High-rise buildings and consolidated dwelling blocks configure the space of this area. Great towers have been built and the area has been exploited for tourist purposes as well, with some of the most renowned hotels being built in the area, such as the Hilton and other local hotels becoming established. The Faena Hotel + Universe, built in 2004, must be one of the most ambitious projects in Puerto Madero; built in a restored grain stock house it had the collaboration of Philip Stark to give a signature to the building. This is only one of the signatures that we find in Puerto Madero, as in many other cities, be they on the waterfront or elsewhere. Another of these is the bridge of Calatrava, which crosses one of the dikes from the old, restored Puerto Madero to the new developments. This is a clear case of branding that affects this city and many others, where the paraphernalia of architecture and design invades urban space to make it uniform and standardised.

The New Green Areas: Local Leisure Space and Identity

The development and restoration of Costanera Sur and the green areas of Puerto Madero was parallel and contemporary to that of the real estate development. A competition was announced by the *Corporación Antiguo Puerto Madero* in 1996 for the development of the green spaces and restoration of the waterfront promenade. We have to point out that by this time the waterfront promenade no longer faced the river but a lagoon created by the landfill, which gave a completely different character to the development.

The competition was won by the Novoa, Garay, Magariños, Sebastián, Vila, Verdecchi y Cajide group. The group focused on the development of green areas that would coexist with the high-rise buildings surrounding them. The project was divided into three parts. First of all there are two great parks between the real estate developments. These have different sorts of native species of vegetation and different sections for activities such as sports and games for children. One of them, Parque Micaela Bastidas, with more than 72 ha, is designed on two levels and has different options of pathways for strolling and a square for children's games. The Mujeres Argentinas park was inaugurated in 2007 and has as a centrepiece a great green amphitheatre area and this is also equipped with restrooms, which adds an important facility to the park area.

The third part is the Costanera Sur, which was already listed as a heritage site in current legislation. Therefore it was restored to its original condition, keeping the access points to the water. The avenue, sidewalks and the elms have been set up in the original position giving a restful and nostalgic image to the place.

These park projects (Fig. 5), which were fortunately realised and are still kept and maintained, have been a social success for the city. Buenos Aires, with its high density and social inequality, has been provided with a large amount of green open space for the public, with facilitated accessibility and continuous maintenance, in an area that had been derelict for more than 30 years.

The projects for the parks have followed the spirit of Carrasco's projects, embracing a vast plan and focusing on accessibility from the city. This is considered a successful project for it responds more to local necessities than to the forces within the market and the need to brand the city.

Fig. 5 Puerto Madero and New Parks 2006– *Archive Alicia Novick*

Open Space by Chance

It is ironic how a development can turn out to move so far from its original plan. The main aim of the planning of the 1970s was to provide an efficient type of transportation following the North American model, using the car as the main means of transport. This led to the building of the ring road around the capital, producing the debris that was deposited in the river, and created the ecological reserve. Very far from the expected plan of an administrative district, the area turned out to be a protected landmark of the city. This reserve has all types of vegetation and animals of the area, providing a strange nature zone just steps away from the noise and pollution of the city. This was never planned, but it turned out to be a peculiar space, where very different types of people enjoy walking and bicycle rides along the paths that cross the reserve.

Unfortunately, the reserve blocks the view of the river from Costanera Sur, the view of the horizon that was so valued by the urban planners of the beginning of the twentieth century, but it does add a new space of leisure, of active leisure, and a new frontier, and a new horizon, next to the still eroding pieces of brick and metal left from the debris of the old fringe of the city.

Gated Community Steps away from Central Area

The project for Santa Maria del Plata, located on the southern side of the *reserva ecológica* must be one of the most worrying of the Buenos Aires waterfront.

The area was full of water by the time the national government awarded it to the Boca Juniors Club to construct a landfill to expand the Club's premises. The landfills were done, but urbanisation of the area was not carried out by the club. Instead it was bought by a private company called Santa María del Plata. This company organised a competition to plan an Olympic village with the possibility that the 2004 Olympic Games be held in Buenos Aires. The competition was won by three different groups of architects, and the company executives decided that the three studios should come up with a single project. The project proposal was made, with difficulty by the three studios, but once the news arrived that the games would not be held in Buenos Aires, the whole project was discarded.

The lands were then bought by Inversiones y Representaciones Sociedad Anonima (IRSA), which was already developing part of Puerto Madero. This company hired the winning group of the previous competition, then Baudizzone, Lestard, Varas to draw up a completely different sort of project, a basically private development for dwellings, very similar to a gated community, but only steps away from the centre of Buenos Aires. This project is now being developed, and it is worrying that it will be carried out. For the time being one of the most complicated situations is that a great slum has developed in the area, and neither the municipality nor the national government have decided what to do about it.

Closing Notes

We have examined the projects and realisation of the Buenos Aires waterfront recognising four distinctive areas. They each have a different structure, function and use. Some of these areas, namely old Puerto Madero and new Puerto Madero are observed as homogenised, internationalised space, where identity is scarce and morphology presents an area that could be found in many other cities in the world.

On the contrary, when we look at the area of Costanera Sur and the new parks projected next to it, we observe another approach, one that relates more to the local identity of place and needs of the city dwellers and was first approached by Benito Carrasco.

Benito Carrasco proves to be extremely concerned, not only with the aesthetic improvement of the city, but also and especially with the needs of the dwellers. The presence of such a wide range of leisure activities in his projects shows a deep interest in the development of human behaviour. He considered all these new forms of leisure as contemplation, activity, entertainment, spectacle and a didactic tool for the enhancement of the behaviour of citizens. Added to this is the fact that he proposed this type of programme on the waterfront, and managed to have his project realised, which was quite an achievement. The inclusion of sports facilities showed an early interest in the fact that in Europe, as Corbin (1990) states, gymnastics were becoming a civic duty. As regards the international influence on his projects, it is evident that he received and studied the foreign examples of his discipline, but was able to combine this with his own capacities and his knowledge of the local scene.

There have been countless discussions about the development of Puerto Madero from all perspectives, from authorities, the press and the public. However, the actual situation is one of contrast between the public space of the parks, used mostly by the dwellers of the southern end of the city, and the real estate development, with its international offices, high-standard apartments, commercial and gastronomic areas, where the built-up square metre costs as much as it does in European or North American cities.

Having seen all the possible approaches to leisure in general, and leisure space in particular, it seems that the current development in waterfront spaces worldwide is simplistic and reductive. It seems necessary to cross the boundaries of disciplines to be able to approach the design and projection of these areas with a wider perspective, not limited to the universalising ideas of urban design.

Notes

[1] This paper is based on research done by the author for the PhD thesis: *Leisure Coast City. A comparative history of the urban leisure waterfront.* The focus of the thesis lies mainly in historical research. The content referring to contemporary projects and developments has been researched exclusively for this paper, attempting to compare historical issues with current ones. The thesis was discussed in Delft in May 2008.

[2] Local type of sausage sandwich.

[3] Among others: Horne 2001.

[4] http://www.pland.gov.hk/p_study/comp_s/harbour/harbour_finalreport/ch5.htm

[5] GTE Conference 2008 – Geography for Weekenders Mark Jones, University of the West of England.
http://www.geography.org.uk/download/GA_PRGTEConf08Jones.doc

[6] http://curbed.com/archives/2006/04/25/jane_jacobs_19162006.php

[7] http://www.citiesonwater.com/public/index.php

[8] Revista de Ingeniería. *Planes Balneario 1919*, n. 503 Año 23 n. 9 Semestre 1 pp. 568–578; n. 504 Año 23 n. 10 Semestre 1 pp. 672–677; n. 505 Año 23 n. 11 Semestre 1 pp. 729–738.

[9] *Ibidem.*

[10] *Ibidem.*

[11] "Balneario Municipal". La Razón, 24 de Diciembre 1926, p. 8.

[12] Revista de Ingeniería. *Planes Balneario 1919*, n. 503 Año 23 n. 9 Semestre 1, pp. 568–578, n. 504 Año 23, n. 10 Semestre 1 pp. 672–677, n. 505 Año 23 n. 11 Semestre 1 pp. 729–738.

References

Bannon J (1976) *Leisure resources, its comprehensive planning*, Prentice Hall, Englewood Cliffs NJ.

Boyer C (1992) *Cities for sale: Merchandising history at South Street Seaport*. In: Sorkin M *Variations on a theme park*, Hill and Wang, New York, pp. 181–204.

Carrasco BJ (1916) *La Memoria de los trabajos realizados en los Parques y Paseos Públicos de la Ciudad de Buenos Aires. Años 1914, 15 y 16*, Talleres Graficos Weiss y Preusche, Buenos Aires.

Clawson M, Knetsch JL, (1966) *Economics of outdoor recreation*, John Hopkins Press, Baltimore.

Cohen JL (1997) *Scènes de la vie future*, Flammarion, Paris.

Collins GR, Crasemann Collins C (1986) *Camillo Sitte, the birth of Modern City Planning*, Rizzoli, New York.

Corbin A (1990) *'Backstage'*. In: Aries P, Duby G (eds) *A history of private life, from the fires of the revolution to the Great War*, Harvard University Press, Cambridge MA.

Cranz G (1980) *The politics of park design: A history of urban parks in America*, The MIT Press, Cambridge MA.

Crasemann Collins C (2005) *Werner Hegemann and the search for universal urbanism*, Norton, New York.

Cross G (1990) *A social history of leisure since 1600*, Venture Publishing, State College PA.

Farrell P, Lundgren H (1983) *The process of recreation programming, theory and practice*, John Wiley and Sons, New York.

Glasser R (1970) *Leisure; penalty or prize?*, Macmillan, London.

Gold S (1975) *Urban recreation planning*, Lea and Febiger, Philadelphia.

Gold S (1980) *Recreation planning and design*, McGraw Hill, New York.

Henry I (2001) *The politics of leisure policy*, Palgrave, London.

Horne J (ed) (2001) *Leisure cultures, consumption and commodification*, Leisure Studies Association, University of Brighton, Eastbourne.

Huizinga J (1950) *Homo Ludens: A Study of the play element in culture*, Beacon Press, Boston.

Kaplan M (1975) *Leisure: Theory and policy*, John Wiley and Sons, New York.

King AD (1976) *Colonial urban development, culture, social power and environment*, Routledge and Kegan Paul, London.

Lariviere F (1999) *Corporación Antiguo Puerto Madero S.A.: Un Modelo de Gestión Urbana 1989–1999*, Ediciones Lariviere, Buenos Aires.

Lefebvre H (1990–1970) *The urban revolution*, University of Minnesota Press, Minnesota.

Longo R E (1989) *Historia del Puerto de Buenos Aires*, Fernandez Blanco, Buenos Aires.

Lucchini P (1981) *Historia de la Ingeniería Argentina*, CAI, Buenos Aires.

Murphy J (1987) *Concept of leisure*. In: Murphy J (ed) *Recreation and leisure: An Introductory handbook*, Venture, Oxford.

Nasr J, Volait M (eds) (2003) *Urbanism, imported or exported? Native aspirations and foreign plans*, Wiley Academy, West Sussex.

Ortiz F (1940) *Contrapunteo cubano del Tabaco y elAzúcar*, Editorial de Ciencias Sociales, Habana.

Pando HJ (1989) *El Puerto de Buenos Aires*, Fadu, UBA.

Perloff H, Lowdon W Ir, (1974) *Urban growth and planning of outdoor recreation*. In: Van Doren C, Priddle G, Lewis J (eds) *Land and leisure, Concepts and methods in outdoor recreation*, Maaroufa Press, Chicago.

Silvestri G (1993) *La ciudad y el río, Un estudio de las relaciones entre técnica y naturaleza a través del caso del puerto de Buenos Aires*. In: Liernur J, Silvestri G (eds) *El Umbral de la Metrópolis, transformaciones técnicas y cultura en la modernización de Buenos Aires 1870–1930*, Editorial Sudamericana, Buenos Aires.

Sorkin M (1992) *Variations on a theme park*, Hill and Wang, New York.

Unwin R (1922) *L' Etude Pratique des Plans de Villes (Introduction a l' Art de Dessiner les Plans d' Aménagement et d' Extension)*, Librairie Centrale des Beaux-Arts, Paris.

Van Doren C, Priddle G, Lewis J (1974) *Land and leisure, concepts and methods in outdoor recreation*, Maaroufa Press, Chicago.

6. Urban Populations and Rights of Citizenship

The spatial experience of the various urban populations creates situations of union and conflict, but populations competing in the city are also therefore elements of urban vitality. In cities where tourism has an important economic role, it is thus necessary to reflect on the relationship between tourist populations and their respective attitudes to places, exploring in particular the ways in which certain tourist population profiles draw near to the figure of resident inhabitant and how they activate "fidelisation" processes. From this viewpoint, tourism, too, though seeming to be an activity aimed at the exclusive dimension of the holiday and play, may constitute the preconditions for creating new citizenships.

Which Tourisms? Which Territories?

Arnaldo Cecchini

> *The man who finds his country sweet is only a raw beginner; the man for whom each country is as his own is already strong, but only the man for whom the whole world is as a foreign country is perfect*
> (Ugo di San Vittore).[1]

In Praise of Mass Tourism

I would like to begin with a commonplace idea that has a rather classist component (I should say very classist): the idea that mass tourism is "bad" in itself and therefore an enemy to fight in the name of the rights and prerogatives of quality, intelligent, cultured, rich, elite, tourists.

There has been an elite tourism (actually for some time it was all that there was), but we certainly should not have regrets over it. Rather than feel nostalgic about the *Viaggi in Italia* of the *Grand Tour*, the sensual, sweet life of English princes and nobles in Capri or Taormina (Littlewood 2004) or the ambiguous sex play in Venice (Symonds 1985) or of intellectuals from all over the world in Tangier,[2] or the middle class holidays of the late nineteenth and early twentieth centuries, as the gold epoch that never was, we prefer to recall that one of the first laws of the Blum government in 1936 was two weeks' paid holiday for all workers.

And we like to remember that the socialist Leo Lagrange, the first head of the newborn *Sous-secrétariat d'Etat aux Sports et à l'Organisation des loisirs,* took concrete initiatives to enable workers, on holiday for the first time, to give a meaning to this measure: return train tickets with a 40% discount, a census of camp sites, preferential tariffs at hotels and special trains. In spite of the fact that two weeks' paid holiday were a measure voted for unanimously by the French Parliament,[3] this choice infuriated the employers and right-wing public opinion, whose newspapers spoke of *salopards* who would be invading the beaches.

Nevertheless, complaints of the elite apart, the fact that the masses were able to have access to enjoying their spare time, travelling, holidays, is a positive fact, a positive achievement. Organising holiday time to build up discipline and check the urges and claims and desires of the popular masses was the objective of the totalitarian states. But there was a difference between the proletariat holidays of France and Germany (which

G. Maciocco, S. Serreli (eds.), *Enhancing the City*, Urban and Landscape Perspectives 6, DOI 10.1007/978-90-481-2419-0_14, © Springer Science+Business Media B.V. 2009

it is useful to emphasise as it serves for our reflection): in 1942 in Nazi-occupied France, Léon Blum explained to the Riom Tribunal when they accused him of not having prepared France for war, the effect and distinctiveness of his paid holidays.

Lagrange, Blum's Vice-Minister of *leisure*, had immediately clarified that in a democratic society it is not a case of "corporalising" the fun and pleasures of the masses as happens in dictatorships, where organisations responsible for managing the pastimes of people exist so that they do not think, do not reflect. Each person has to be able to choose ("in joy and dignity") how to use his spare time.

There is also a different settlement modality behind this oscillation between the regimented holiday and the spontaneous one. On the one hand, the great Nazi tourist complex was presented at the Paris International Exposition of 1937 where it received a *Grand Prix* – a resort situated on the island of Rügen in the Baltic Sea for the *Kraft durch Freude* (Strength through joy), the Nazi leisure association that became the greatest tourist agency in the world. The facility would accommodate up to 20,000 tourists simultaneously in hotel rooms realised in a simple but modern, functionalist style, in light colours, and above all, each room would have sea view guaranteed, the hotel buildings would be narrow and would extend for several miles along the coast. The enormous hotel complex would have all manner of services enclosed within it: cinemas, cafés and restaurants with wide panoramic windows, a small harbour, enormous swimming pool, covered in case of bad weather, reading/writing rooms, billiard rooms and so on. The style could be defined "modern classic", with a clear influence of modernist architects. It was a modernist utopia, an authentic amusement town of glass and cement, which made use of the latest innovations such as central heating for all rooms and a series of attractions in the latest fashion (Löfgren 2001, pp. 242–246). The totalitarian conception of holidays was not only reflected in the organisation of spaces but also in that of times and destinations: the beneficiaries of these trips could not choose their destination, and the programme of activities was completely planned.

And here is the other extreme described by the anarchical urbanist Colin Ward: one of the causes of the construction of cottages and small second homes in the country and along the English coasts was the spread among the lowest social strata, too, of the habit of having holidays and weekends out of town. In effect, the law on paid holidays (*Holidays With Pay Act*) of 1938 involved 18.5 million employees, 11 million of whom enjoyed this benefit for the first time; the spreading of places to inhabit was "wild", eyed with horror by urbanists and architects, but it is fair to remember that not all land is so precious as to be destined for growing mountains of

European grain, or worse, left unproductive at the expense of contributors, and not all urbanistic principles are so precious that they cannot occasionally be put aside (Ward 1998, pp. 44–54).

The will to control and regiment has, however, to tackle the spontaneous urges of the "will to enjoy" of people and their bodies (without forgetting – as we will see – that the Great Other[4] of constituted power is dialectically able to take over transgression, too, in fact to "order us to transgress"). The will to enjoy departs from plebeian dreams of "sweet idleness", the binge, the dirty joke, based on body functions (Bachtin 1995).

The spontaneous urge to occupy spaces and repropose autonomous modalities of time management espouses in these new holiday makers the pleasure of doing the same things as the others, repetitiveness, seriality and conformism. A dual urge that is at the basis of a second feature of the "plebeian" character of popular amusements: the pleasure gained from sweet idleness (Richez and Strass 1996).

The second reverse side of the coin is the great strength of the Market. The regimentation or construction of holidays on the Fordist model,[5] and the institutionalisation of transgression was obtained by the organisation of consumption; what had been the joyful, dignified fun, a little anarchical and greatly self-managed, of the French working class women and men and their daughters and sons was transformed into an homologised and homologising industry, in the extension of Fordism and seriality to spare time and holidays.

But during the course of the 1960s, the latter changed into goods. Social tourism militants all referred, some more some less, to the "three Ds", "fundamental functions of leisure" according to Joffre Dumazedier, "relaxation that frees from tiredness", fun that frees from boredom and development of the personality that "frees from the automatism of thought and daily action". The consumer society has replaced them with the "three Ss", *Sea, Sex* and *Sun*. The "summer revolution" has made the militant dream of a holiday period that should contribute to the regeneration of the "tireless little worker" disappear and has eliminated free consumption of the traditional activities to the advantage of commercialised consumption (Richez and Strass 1996, p. 437).

The great epoch of Fordist tourism was born, that of mass consumption, which can be despised also by the left, as consumerist and conformist.

And yet "the old Mole" continued to dig; La Cecla meanwhile noted that to speak badly of tourism is fashionable, but it is often forgotten that residents have almost always stopped "seeing" what only strangers notice. In this sense, tourism is a marvellous school of "detachment" from the place for its inhabitants. Through the eyes of tourists, inhabitants can be re-educated to appreciate the place they live in, not always with the nuisance and inconvenience tourism brings with it. Instead of getting annoyed with tourists, it would be better to think about the faults of our Ministers of Tourism: no one has managed so badly such an immense patrimony and potentially huge source of wealth (La Cecla 2001, p. XV).

And thus tourist populations imposed to a certain extent a new point of view on places and then, little by little, the paradigm of the Fordist holidays lost its "charm" in the various components of mass tourism (which is not only popular tourism, but also small and medium middle class, and with certain different details, a slice of the rich, too), the young people first and foremost (the history of the effect of the "great revolution" of 1968 on the evolution of holidays needs to be written).[6]

Let us return to the thread proposed by Urry:

Mass consumption: purchase of commodities produced under conditions of mass production; a high and growing rate of expenditure on consumer products; individual producers tending to dominate particular industrial markets; producer rather than consumer as dominant; commodities little differentiated from each other by fashion, season, and specific market segments; relatively limited choice – what there is tends to reflect producer interests whether private or public.

Post-Fordist consumption: consumption rather than production dominant as consumer expenditure further increases as a proportion of national income; new forms of credit permitting consumer expenditure to rise, so producing high levels of indebtedness; almost all aspects of social life become commodified, even charity; much greater differentiation of purchasing patterns by different market segments; greater volatility of consumer preferences; the growth of a consumers movement and the "politicizing" of consumption; reaction of consumers against being part of a "mass" and the need for producers to be much more consumer-driven, especially in the case of service industries and those publicly owned; the development of many more products each of which has a shorter life; the emergence of new kinds of commodity which are more specialised and based on raw materials that imply non-mass forms of production ("natural" products for example) (Urry 2002, p. 14).

It is unquestionable that next to a model of mass consumption that is maintaining itself and probably growing with the entry of new potential tourists from the large rapidly developing countries, a post-Fordist tourism is becoming more and more substantial, and not only has growing dimensions but also a sort of cultural hegemony that to a certain extent is a reference point, too, for the prevalent consumer models of mass tourism.

Tourisms and Populations

As we were saying, the Fordist epoch did not just end in the factory. The "mass" tourism epoch managed by and like an assembly line exceeded maturity and no longer worked like an exclusive or preponderant system of mass tourism: as in production, also for the spare time market, Fordism did not disappear, it remained quantitatively relevant and perhaps prevalent, but no longer the dominant paradigm; mass tourism also appears to have been symbolically de-qualified; It had negative connotations, and mass tourists no longer wanted to be called "mass tourists" either. Clearly, we can no longer speak of tourism *tout court* also for mass tourism. In the meantime, a separate circuit for luxury tourism, sometimes with unpleasant intersections, was left continuously in search of privacy and exclusivity, far from the proletariat *salopards*. But more and more, in the tourism of large numbers, the flows, interests and ways of fruition differentiate are ramified (Mazzette 2002, p. 12).

These are then the classifications: seaside, rural, cultural, health, ludic, sexual, religious, gastronomic, congress, ethnic, historic, sports, study, business, ecological, mountain, cinema, television, scholastic and recreational tourism[7]; obviously these types of tourism interweave, but that does not mean that specialist areas do not exist (Mazzette 2002, p. 13).

And yet the approach I would like to propose is not based on this functional, slightly essentialist, classification, which we might use at some moment, but I wish to refer to the approach we might call "the population approach" following the trend of Martinotti (1993), Mela (1996) and Nuvolati (2007), which, if appropriately articulated with respect to the modalities of use of territories and cities by tourists, may be of great help in identifying the different kinds of tourism and possibly defining policies to manage them.

These days, there is a great desire for new tourism, as a discovery of the self and others, as freedom from differences and comparison of plural experiences. Contact with diversities not as recognition of varieties to satisfy seasonal fashions along the itinerary of precodified places but as the integral perception of an environment, as an existential, alternative space (Bandinu 1996, p. 21).

As Ciaffi and Mela (2009) recalls, in modern urban development and that of the contemporary epoch for Martinotti (1993), the populations that "inhabit the city" have ramified in different ways: in the traditional city there was only one population, with substantial equivalence between those who inhabited it at night and those who inhabited it during the day (and worked there), the *inhabitants,* whereas in that of the *first generation* there is a population of *commuters* added to the day population of inhabitants from the peri-urban areas, in the *second* generation – apart from the fact that the flow of commuters is also exiting – a third population is added, the so-called *city users*, who include tourists, too, as well as the users of the various urban services; in the *contemporary* city, a third population appears, which may in a slightly improper way be defined as *businessmen*[8]: women and men who work, consume, enjoy themselves in the city, coming from other places, perhaps very far.

It goes without saying that an individual will not be considered to "rigidly" belong to these groups: we belong to different groups in different places (it is not impossible to belong to all four) and sometimes in the same place (e.g. in different districts of the same city). The ways space is used are well exemplified by these diagrams, taken from Nuvolati (2007, pp. 100–101) (Figs. 1–3).

This classification, to which Nuvolati proposes a fifth group be added, that of the *flâneurs*,[9] poses various problems for our purposes.

First of all, it is not easy to place the immigrant population within this diagram (it is true that to a certain extent each of them belongs to one or more of the categories proposed, but often with full qualifications).

Secondly, it may seem reductive to consider only three activities for characterising the behaviour of the inhabitants, considering them, moreover, only on a dichotomous yes/no scale.

Finally, of particular importance for our reflection, there is the "reduction" of the figure of the tourist within the *city users* category, which if it appears justified for large cities, where tourism in the proper sense is a component not predominated by flows, is more problematic for situations in which this component is the determining one within those flows, or even predominant from the economic point of view or almost exclusive.

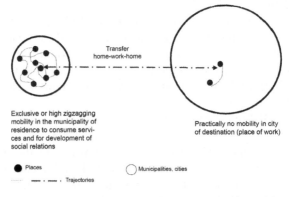

Fig. 1 First industrialisation phase: the large city as a predominant place of work

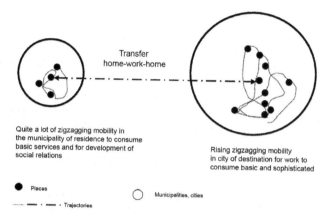

Fig. 2 Modernisation phase of productive models and lifestyles: the large city as a place of work, consumption and fruition of services

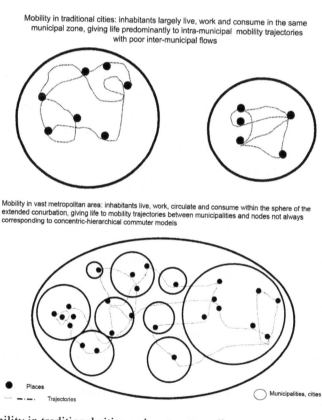

Fig. 3 Mobility in traditional cities and vast metropolitan areas

The following classification, taken from Nuvolati (2007, p. 164), may give us some better tools, though this, too, is suitable above all for metropolitan situations (Table 1).

A similar approach is that of Ciaffi and Mela (2009), also proposed in this book.

The population approach we have re-proposed seems very useful for it enables the phenomenon "use" of places on the part of each population to be defined and characterised. As Nuvolati maintains, some areas marked by continuous, homogeneous use are defined *incessant areas*. Others, which witness evacuation processes during the night hours, are *empty at night*, yet others, which on the contrary show an invasion beginning with the evening hours, are *active especially at night* and, finally, others, which witness continuous use but of a heterogeneous nature, are said to be *shifting from day to night*. This typology may be applicable to many contemporary urban realities that tend to become structured and transformed with respect to several functions.

Table 1 Metropolitan populations typology based on certain characteristics[10]

	Place of residence	Prevalent relationship with territory of origin	Prevalent activity in destination territory
Residents (wealthy ranks)	Historic centre Residential quarters	High identification	Home, work, consumption
Commuter residents	Farthest suburbs or metropolitan area	Medium–low identification	Work (consumption)
Commuters	Municipalities in other neighbouring provinces	High identification	Work (consumption)
City users and tourists	Farthest suburbs or metropolitan area	Medium–low identification	Consumption
	Municipalities in other neighbouring provinces	High identification	Consumption
	Other cities/nations	Various levels	Consumption
Businessmen	Other cities/nations	Various levels	Work (consumption)
Flâneurs	Other cities/nations	Various levels	Home, work

Nuvolati also affirms that the image of the city that ensues is that of a meeting place of various populations – inhabitants, commuters, *city users* and businessmen – who at different times of the day cross paths, exchange services, but also clash and enter into conflict, be it in a metaphorical sense, in controlling resources that are not endless (Nuvolati 2007, p. 22).

For our purposes, it is worth defining better what we mean by "tourist population". I would like to look again at Martinotti's diagram and try to extend it in two ways; on the one hand, adding another activity to the three he envisages (for simplicity's sake, I will call it "spending time", meaning pleasure activities, or *leisure*), and on the other passing from a dichotomous scale to one with three values: yes, no, partly; we would thus have 81 description boxes, instead of the eight possible ones in Martinotti's diagram (Table 2).

Limiting ourselves to extending the table to the fourth characteristic and keeping the dichotomous scale of Yes/No, we will have a table with 16 possible populations that we will try to classify and name[11] (Table 3).

The classification could be further divided if we were to use three instead of two values, adding Partially (P) to Yes, No: for example, the box P N Y Y would define a person who lives for a part of the year in one place, does not work there, consumes there and "spends time" there and could therefore stand, for example, for a retired person who lives for some months in his home in the Canaries (taking for granted that he would also be a P N Y Y at his first home in Tradate, a small town in Lombardy, Italy), while the Turin holiday maker who spends a month in the Piedmont Alps would be the classic holiday maker (at home he might be a P Y Y Y if he works where he lives and spends his leisure time there or a P Y Y N if he goes to spend his leisure time elsewhere or a P N Y N if, as well as spending his leisure time away, he is also a commuter).

Table 2 Table of possible combinations[12]

Population	Inhabit, I	Work, W	Consume, C	Spend Time, S
	Yes/No/Partly	Yes/No/Partly	Yes/No/Partly	Yes/No/Partly
	Yes/No/Partly	Yes/No/Partly	Yes/No/Partly	Yes/No/Partly
	Yes/No/Partly	Yes/No/Partly	Yes / No /Partly	Yes/No/Partly
	Yes/No/Partly	Yes/No/Partly	Yes / No /Partly	Yes/No/Partly

Table 3 Classification of urban populations

	I	W	C	S	Population
1	Y	Y	Y	Y	Traditional residents
2	Y	Y	Y	N	Young residents
3	Y	Y	N	Y	Shopping mall residents
4	Y	Y	N	N	Non-local residents
5	Y	N	Y	Y	Traditional commuters
6	Y	N	Y	N	Young commuters
7	Y	N	N	Y	Shopping mall commuters
8	Y	N	N	N	Uprooted commuters
9	N	Y	Y	Y	Businessmen tourists/study tourists
10	N	Y	Y	N	Traditional businessmen
11	N	Y	Y	N	International hotel tourists/International businessmen
12	N	Y	N	N	Goal-oriented businessmen
13	N	N	Y	Y	Classic tourists/City Users
14	N	N	Y	N	Buyer City Users
15	N	N	Y	N	Trippers City Users *Voyeurists*
16	N	N	N	N	Office City Users

We like this approach not only because of our craving for taxonomies ("nothing is more wonderful than the list") but also because it reminds us that one of the characteristics of the post-modern condition is that of being able to be classified in a "multiple" way, or in our case belonging to different populations. Moreover, if we try to "play" a little with the tables, we ought to define properly what work is (Who are the unemployed? And the housewives? And the pensioners? Easier for the students). We might consider as ascribable to the tourist category those who do not live in a place, but look for recreation there, or rather "pleasure" (*leisure*); the definition the World Tourism Organisation gives of a tourist is he who moves from his own place of residence to go to another place, for a period of time greater than 24 hours and less than 1 year, for reasons different from carrying out an activity remunerated at the place of destination; he who travels for a shorter time is a tripper. In effect, according to Cohen, we might say that the tourist is a voluntary traveller (he chooses to do it or thinks he does), a temporary one (he has a habitual place of residence and often works), he travels expecting pleasure (not to earn from it) derived from novelty and change (it is supposed that there be a component of discovery or change from normal life) experienced in a circular trip (he returns home) that is relatively long (not an occasional break) and not recurrent (he does not always go to the same place); a debatable definition, but useful (Cohen 1974, pp. 527–555).

In this sense, we might (non-recurrence of the journey apart) consider as "tourists" those belonging to groups 9, 11, 13 and 15; of these 13 would belong to the *city users* category and 9 to that of *businessmen* according to Martinotti, while 15 would be the category of *city users* in an extended sense and 10 that of *businessmen* in an extended sense. Let us consider the possible cases. In effect, if we take a person who, though not living in a place, works, spends leisure time and also consumes there (by consuming we mean that he spends on activities different from the services that he – perhaps – went to buy), we have the classic figure of the person who goes on a business trip but does not give up "being a tourist". Whereas if we take the person who, though he does not live in a place, works and spends leisure time there, but does not consume, we have a person such as perhaps a University Professor, though not specially *sui generis*, who maybe stays at Mogliano Veneto and purchases at the local shopping mall but goes to give his lectures and seminars at Ca' Foscari in Venice and visits the Galleries of the *Accademia* and the *Biennale* (and here we interpret him with respect to Venice, as, in terms of Mogliano, he is nothing more than a traditional commuter). If we then take one who, though not residing in a place, does not work there but consumes and spends leisure time there, he is – we might say – a *city user* who is an authentic tourist. As opposed to the person who, though not residing in a place, spends leisure time there but does not consume, who is a (not very well considered) *city user* of the type often called a tripper. If, then, one does not live in a place, does not work there, does not consume nor spend leisure time there, one is there for a hospital appointment. As can be seen, this proposed classification leads trippers back to the category of tourists, as is not usually done, but they have, nevertheless, to be put somewhere; for various reasons it would not be a bad idea to let them be considered part of the family of "tourists": on the one hand, at the origins of mass tourism there was also the excursion; on the other, in the social, economic and environmental impact of tourism, of which we will speak, the imprint of trippers should be anything but underestimated; for simplicity's sake we will call them tourists, too, the term commonly used, visitors, seeming less useful in this context. We also note in passing that another variable to be taken into consideration might be that relating to the possibility of those belonging to the various populations to decide in respect of local policy choices, which would give us other useful clues and might reveal surprises, if by deciding we were to not limit ourselves to meaning the mere fact of being able to vote or be elected.[13] As we have said, the reasons for which we go to a place also count a lot and could enrich the population sub-groups with details, as elements precious for managing tourist policies; thus, just as the tourist's attitude counts, so that the birth of so-called ethical tourism (Pattullo and Ollery 2007) and the battle against *low-cost* flights and the environmental impact of fast holiday tourism (Hickman 2007) will not seem irrelevant to the decision maker, similarly, it would also be better not to neglect the concept of sustainable tourism due to the abuse made of it (Williams et al. 2002; Bizzarri and Querini 2006). This rather risky classification will be useful for us to define what "good" tourism is and for enabling us to assess the territorial policies tied to tourism, but let us leave this combinatory dizziness aside for now and move on to other things.

Income and the Conflict between Populations

Scaramuzzi (2000, p. 237) rightly remarks that "tourism" is becoming the great consumer and transformer of territories, precious or barren, and also the great substitute for other economies at the edges of the more canonical industries. She maintains that in some cases the presence of tourism has not reached the devastating capacity of the other urbanisations and, apart from the effective capacity of "multiplying development" and/or integrating with indigenous qualities, guests have been accommodated "with care" from the architectural and landscape point of view (Scaramuzzi 2000). We do not want to underestimate here the role that the tourist industry has had in upsetting the Italian coastal zones, but it has not always gone better in non-tourist zones; the poorest zones have been saved somewhat, where neither industry nor speculation had any interest in building.

A heavy industry, then, tourism, no worse than other industries, but no better. And above all, not the first or only one responsible for "plundering the territory".

The decisive aspect of plundering the territory and the tourist industry's responsibility in this plundering lies in the role of revenue in city and territory development. This fact is shown also by the population approach. The populations competing in the city (and in every place where homes or services can be located) are linked with each other but are also in conflict. For our analysis, we will refer in particular to the "tourist cities", i.e. to cities (therefore entities inhabited by a consistent number of residents, with at least one urban function) of the tourist type (namely in which, or in important, identifiable portions of which, tourism has a prevalent or very significant economic role: we might say that it is the main, even if not involving the majority, economic activity). Let me explain better: Venice belongs to this classification of tourist city, both if considered as a municipality (tourism is the most important economic activity, though not of the majority) and as an insular historic centre (with some doubts in this case as to whether it has still remained a city), Cortina less (it is hardly a city: the residents' part is not consistent), Rimini is (there is a city that continues to live in summer, too), Porto Cervo in Sardinia is certainly not, and so on; in this classification Florence is a "tourist city", Rome much less. A marker measuring tourist "dependency" of a city is not difficult to construct. In actual fact, any good policy (including urbanistic, economic and territorial economic policy, as tourist policies are or should be) ought to have accurate, reliable data available; it is quite strange that – in spite of the importance tourism has in world economy – the information systems on tourism give such poor, unreliable data. For example, there is no systematic, rigorous evaluation of actual presences: official data do not permit knowledge of how many visitors stay in private houses and even if the various reports on Italian tourism try to estimate the consistency of the true supply of beds compared with that registered, reliable disaggregated and spatialised data do not exist. All this occurs in spite of the fact that the non-official consistency is almost double: we can estimate actual presences as almost a billion, a fact that tells us that on average, for each day of the year, something like 5% of Italians are "on holiday". It seems strange that the second home phenomenon in Italy or the homes rented for holidays are not the subject of greater attention, if we think of the enormity of the impact that the over 20,000,000 (twenty million!)-bed potential, in over 5,500,000 houses not occupied in Italy, has on the environmental, social, economic, cultural, aesthetic, lifestyle, fiscal and urbanistic fields. And yet, as many studies demonstrate – conducted by the Faculty of Architecture at the University of Sassari and Alghero Municipality in Sardinia – and in particular the Reports on Tourism of the city of Alghero, an efficient estimate of presences in second homes is not impossible and may prove very reliable.[14] But the issue is another: to handle the question of "second homes" means to think the unthinkable, namely to pose the problem of contrasting the weight of the revenue in the economy and the advantages that many gain.[15] I believe that this issue of unoccupied houses is at the centre of the field of conflict between populations (obviously not only between the field of residents and that of tourists). Taking the cue from Nuvolati, we may identify five types of conflict between urban populations, which, *mutatis mutandis*, also hold for "our" tourist cities.

- Economic conflict [in cities there is polarisation between the international *upper* class and their "servers", with the other classes localised in suburban areas or in small–medium municipalities (Sassen 1997); also with respect to tourist cities the tendency may be that of conflict between visitors and "waiters" with the "others elsewhere"].
- Cultural conflict (the cultural contrast between tourist populations and residents can in some cases be very bitter; even when the natives are forced to spontaneously be themselves).
- Fiscal conflict (often in tourist cities the balance between fiscal revenue and tourism management expenses can be very negative, at least for the municipality's coffers).
- Conflict over space occupation (this is the principal conflict: bad cash chases away good: nothing can resist against the Venice mask shops or Florence *jeanseries*, no resident will ever have access to residence if, with residence, there is undisturbed tourist use: from bed and breakfasts to second homes).
- Conflict over access to goods and services (suffice it to think of the transport system and mobility or even healthcare services, as well as those few bakeries left or the many restaurants that "adjust" prices and – low – quality on tourists).

As for any other form of organisation and differentiation of urban spaces that is not explicitly, programmatically and radically governed by the public sector,[16] revenue calls the tune and all the others can do is dance. Naturally, some processes can be controlled by far-sighted entrepreneurs, who can "venture" because they have gained revenue themselves, but they have not been content with speculative profit (as was, for example, the experience of Karim Aga Khan's invention of the Costa Smeralda in Sardinia, not praiseworthy but not evil either), but usually the plunder perspective prevails – especially in tourism. In this sense, there is a kind of infamous pact between predators: on the one hand, speculators with short-term interests, contrasting substantially with those of the resident populations and local entrepreneurs, on the other "ready to go" tourists. In tourist cities, the risk of rapid decline is very great, especially if places are not "unique": the life cycle of these tourist areas becomes very rapid in many cases and rejuvenation impossible; for "unique" cities tourism lasts, but the city disappears, in other cases both disappear. We could consider replacing this wicked pact with a virtuous one, between the "good" parts of the populations, but it is not a simple issue. Let us try to make some observations before proposing a possible work instrument. It is not only tourists that cause urban devastation, as we have said. Of course, Fordist mass tourism, managed like an assembly line, with the same logics of seriality, efficiency and time compression, as well as being paradoxical, was devastating. But if for a long time (and still today) many tourists "have bought" this product, might it not be that it gives an answer (however distorted and banal) to a real demand (rest, health, beauty, discovery, evasion and transgression)? And therefore makes it possible for many to satisfy (or believe they satisfy, which is almost the same)[17] this requirement?

And is the break in the "Fordist" paradigm of tourism organization, which recently occurred involving many consumers, really such a fundamental "step ahead"? Does the "toyotism" of "à la carte" journeys make the illusion less deceptive? "Smeralda" tourism was not Fordist, but was it very different (purchasing power apart) from the mass tourism from which it wanted to be separated? And was it, as intended, really beneficial? It is actually very difficult to determine the economic effect of tourism; as Urry maintains, it is difficult to estimate the economic impact of any tourist initiative, also because it is a problem to assess the so-called multiplier. And even more difficult is the evaluation of such multipliers within a local economy, for various reasons: relations between businesses are particularly complex and confused due to the large number of small businesses involved; the losses in economy are often very difficult to evaluate; there is not a clear, accepted definition of "tourist" and therefore of what tourist expense is; the definition of "local economy" is in any case controversial, so the greater the territorial unit, the greater the apparent multiplier (Urry 2002; Candela and Figini 2003, 2005). As a matter of fact, tourists consume a rather special "good". As Urry highlights, almost all services supplied to tourists have to be delivered at the same time and place in which they are produced, and the quality of social interaction between the provider of the service and the consumers is part of the "product" purchased by the tourist. The problem arises from the fact that the production of services for the consumer cannot be carried out entirely behind the curtains, far from the tourist's gaze (Urry 2002). The tourist good is almost always (also) a "relational good", that is, an immaterial good, of which relations between people are an essential component[18]; this is something more than the relational component that has still continued to be important in some services. Then, the tourist good is often (or claims to be) also a "positional good",[19] and we will return to this aspect when we speak of "luxury tourism", one of those private goods subject to a bond of social scarcity, rather than a bond of a material nature; altogether, those goods whose utility for a person depends on the fact that it is only for the few; by their nature these goods will never be able to be "mass", for the degree of satisfaction they give is due to being the showcase of the few, in fact they constitute the sign, the demonstration of a *status*: it is a case of what is called the *Veblen effect*,[20] by which purchasing a certain good serves to certify belonging to a social group of high *status*. In fact the "miracle" of the contemporary economy was the invention of pseudo-positional goods (Bruni and Zarri 2007), that is "mass positional goods" (a true oxymoron), namely goods for wide consumption, thus only apparently a vehicle of positionality. On the other hand, actually the conquest of a particular relative position, the high "relative position" that these goods promise, inevitably proves to be ephemeral indeed in the light of the widespread nature of this modality of consumption, a little like in the oxymoronic slogan *Exclusively* for *Everyone.*

Together with the invention of "pseudo-relational" goods (from the forced smile of shop assistants to the happy voice of the *call centre* employee, to the role of animator at a tourist village), pseudo-positional goods constitute one of the main effects of "corruption" of the tourist industry and characterise its social impact.

It is also difficult to estimate the social impact of tourism; to this issue John Urry dedicates some shrewd observations:

There are complex relationships between tourists and the indigenous populations of the places at which those tourists gaze (...)

1. The *number* of tourists visiting a place in relationship to the size of the host population and to scale of the objects being gazed upon (...)

2. The predominant *object* of the tourist gaze (...) Those tourist activities that involve observation of physical objects are less intrusive than those that involve observing individuals and groups. Moreover, within the latter category, the observation of the private lives of host groups will produce the greatest social stress (...)

3. The *character* of the gaze involved and the resulting spatial and temporal "packing" of visitors (...)

4. The *organisation* of the industry that develops to service the mass gaze (...)

5. The effects of tourism upon the *pre-existing agricultural and industrial activities* (...)

6. The economic and social differences between the visitors and the majority of the hosts (...)

7. The degree to which the mass of visitors demand *particular standards of accommodation and service* (...)

8. The degree to which the *state* in a given country actively seeks to promote tourist developments or alternatively endeavours to prevent them (...)

9. The extent to which *tourists can be identified and blamed* for supposedly undesirable economic and social developments (...) (Urry 2002, pp. 51–53).

Four phases of the life cycle of the tourist resort have been recognised on the grounds of the relationship between tourists and local communities, which take up Butler's cycle again[21] namely the *Tourism Area Life Cycle* (TALC):

– an idyllic (or Gauguin) phase when a few lucky tourists pacifically immersed in the host society share its style of life and infrastructures;
– a competition/conflict phase when the tourists, already more abundant, share the existing infrastructures with the local people; the two groups are still in contact but observe each other with diffidence;
– a separation phase, when the tourists, often more numerous than the hosts, have their own infrastructures available and come into contact with the local people only via codified channels (guides, agencies, hotel porters, etc.); the tourists take on the role of "chickens" to be plucked;
– assimilation/genocide when, with a total reversal of roles, the interests of the tourist community prevail over those of the local one and this is reduced to an empty shell at the service of forces foreign to its own past and tradition (Butler 1980).

In each of the phases, the quality of relations between the different populations is not irrelevant, i.e. understanding whether the relationship is of a predatory nature: predatoriness is usually reciprocal, even if power relations may be unbalanced in favour of one of these, and are usually – for economic reasons – unbalanced in favour of the tourist populations; but – as we have said – there is not only one population either among the tourists or the residents.

As for the other cycle, for this one, too, the possible variations are several and some go in the post-Fordist direction we have spoken of (or even post-tourist).

And the picture may also become more complicated if we remember the environmental impact (Berardi 2007) of tourism, an impact that is tied, too, to the fact that one of the characteristics of a part of the goods needed to attract tourists to a place, namely the condition necessary to be able to sell them services, is "common goods" (Ricoveri 2005), i.e. goods with the characteristic of being rivals, it is true, but which to some extent are not excludable. A good is a rival if its consumption by an individual reduces its availability for consumption on the part of other individuals; it is excludable if it is possible to prevent someone from consuming it. These two characteristics are not "incorporated" in the good and, in particular excludability, are to some extent dependent on technological development and political, cultural, religious choices. Combining these characteristics of goods we obtain the pattern (see Table 4).

Table 4 Characteristics of goods

	Excludability	Non-excludability
Rivalry	Pure private goods	Common property goods (common or better common pool resources)
Non-rivalry	Spurious public goods (club goods)	Pure public goods

It is worth saying something on the subject.[22] Goods that are really "market" goods are only those that are rivals and excludable, which are basically goods in the proper sense, whereas all others are to be treated with the appropriate good sense; a few details may be necessary to understand this. A rival, non-excludable good may be, for example, a public space, like a square; no one can be prevented from being in the square, but beyond a certain limit, fruition of this good may be made impossible by overcrowding. We speak of commonly owned goods or indeed "common goods" and among them we may include water or information; a clearer case is that of fishing in international seas.

A non-rival but excludable good may be, for example, a musical passage in digital form, given that the reproduction of digital support, which is basically a file, is virtually unlimited but may be limited by *copyright,* even though here excludability is only a legal possibility, since all forms of piracy make it a *de facto* good with low excludability; clearer cases might be collective transport when access control systems work; an interesting example is also university education. Examples of non-rival, non-excludable goods are, for instance, national defence (and in this case the *free rider* is one who does not contribute to expenses for defence by not paying taxes, but enjoys the benefits from which he clearly cannot be excluded), the trade union (*free rider* is the worker not enrolled in the trade union who nevertheless enjoys the contractual benefits obtained by the trade union) and public illumination. It is easy to understand how the four categories, though useful from a conceptual point of view, do not always have rigid, stable limits: if, for example, the pastures of a community are rendered excludable by being attributed to individual owners and enclosed (as were the famous *enclosures* of the eighteenth century),[23] a common good is transformed into a private good. In general, when we refer to non-excludability, we mean in practice not so much that it is impossible, but very expensive or complicated, to exclude and prevent consumption or use of the good.

It can easily be understood why *free riding* arises only in the two categories of non-excludable goods: in the others, the ticket has to be paid before there is access! If we return for a moment to relational goods (or to the relational components of a good), it would seem that these exclude *free riding* (in a relationship reciprocity is needed), but these behaviours make themselves possible again if we are dealing with pseudo-relational goods that enable and accentuate the predatory nature of tourist consumption (predatory in both directions: towards tourists and on the part of tourists). In a good, recent book (*Lo sguardo vagabondo*), Nuvolati analyses one of the figures he had introduced, in a slight deviation, in his study of *Mobilità quotidiana e complessità urbana*, the figure of the *flâneur* and briefly that of the *choraster* (Table 5).

I do not want to show favour towards Romantic, elitary conceptions but remain faithful to the idea of the "right to tourism", I do not think everyone should always be curious urban time wasters, I think that the multiplication of careful, detachedly participant walkers would not be sustainable. But we cannot rule out the thought that some *flânerie* component may accompany the tourist experiences of many. And neither do I want to think that everyone should have the same love and identification with places attributed to the *choraster*.[24]

And nevertheless we may not rule out the thought that some component of caring for places may accompany the tourist experiences of many and that a gender-based gaze may exist on holiday, too. Or the critical, law-breaking gaze of the *stalker*.[25] And yet we cannot rule out the thought that some component of non-homologated gazes may accompany the tourist experiences of many. Or the tenacious will to reveal of the *dérive* psychogeographers.[26]

Table 5 Male and female conceptions of tourism

	Male conception	Female conception
Tourist	*Flâneur*	*Choraster*
	Observer	Actor
Tourist destination	Destination	Chora
	Resort	Space
	Object	Interaction
	Image	Social values
Tourism	Activity	Experience
	Visit	Process

And why not believe that the thought cannot be ruled out that some component of deconstruction of given itineraries may accompany the tourist experiences of many? Or the capacity to reconstruct routes at different levels of those practising *parkour*,[27] though we cannot rule out that it is thinkable that some component of verticality and invention may accompany many people's tourist experiences.

But these practices, and many others, perhaps more traditional, also tied just to familiarity and empathy, might be present in the experiences of those who travel because those who travel should have time to "waste time", to do many things that are of no use, to lose themselves (La Cecla 2001). In these attitudes resides the seed that makes possible, not always everywhere or forever, "good" tourism.

A Model and a Dashboard

The Bases of the Model

The network of concepts we use to try to define "good" tourism refers to a model of classification of tourist populations that I have elaborated and named with the acronym FDMP (faithfulness, duration, mobility, period). The conceptual base of the model is that of characterising tourists on the grounds of four parameters, all linked with the quantity and quality of the time spent by the tourist on the territory, which when combined give rise to at least 16 potential profiles (if we decide to give only the value yes or no to each feature).

The features are as follows:

Faithfulness: which determines to what extent the tourist habitually frequents the place (e.g. a reference marker could be linked with the number of consecutive years of presence; for example, we could define a tourist as faithful if he has come for three consecutive years or four times during the last six years).

Duration: which measures the time the tourist spends on the territory in a year (it could be "adjusted" with respect to the regional average).

Mobility: which measures the desire to get to know the territory on the part of the tourist; a tourist who travels over the territory compared with one who stays in a single resort (a holiday village) will certainly have a different relationship with places: mobility accentuates awareness and knowledge of the territory on the part of tourists (we could measure this aspect counting the number of sites he/she visits during a holiday).

Period: which measures a tourist's willingness to have his holiday at different times of year (it might also contain an estimate of willingness to change the period in which he comes). Obviously the determination of these features implies a rigorous definition of markers and collection of adequate data.

By the FDMP model, we can thus attempt to "measure" how near a certain typology of tourist comes to the figure of resident inhabitant, basing ourselves on an examination of all the 16 classes that arise from this model. It immediately appears clear that the tourist nearest to being an inhabitant is the one whose FDMP features have high values; using the FDMP abbreviation to define the various classes, followed by a plus or minus sign, we will have, for example: F+D+M+P+ (abbreviated FDMP) which we have called *citoyen* to point out the fact that – basically – a tourist who always comes stays for a long time, moves around on the territory and who comes in different seasons is not much different from a resident; whereas a F–D–M–P– (abbreviated as an empty space shown with the symbol []) is a *voyeur*, one who has happened to be in a place just to have a quick look which he will not repeat; or a F+D+M+P– (abbreviated FDM) is a tied *citoyen,* who probably for professional reasons, though having a relationship of identification with the place, may frequent it only in particular seasons and so on.

The FDMP Model

If we place ourselves on an axis whose unit of measurement we suggest be the quantity (and quality) of the time spent by the tourist on the territory, we will have as extremes the FDMP tourist (the *citoyen*) and the [] (the *voyeur*). All the other classes are in between. Obviously, within a given territory, the number of people belonging to a particular profile can vary both because new people are added to the flows and because a tourist can pass from one profile to another; this variation can depend on external factors (let us say, the dollar/euro relationship) or internal factors (realisation of policies favourable for establishing virtuous relations with the territory). Note that the dichotomous division is very arbitrary; we ought rather to operate with "hazy" values. If we could get the information necessary to measure FDMP features and to weigh them up showing them on a graph with an origin and four axes with their units of measurement representing the FDMP weight, the area of the graph would represent the tourist and his position on the [] – FDMP axis.

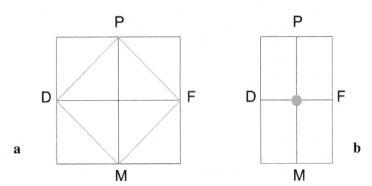

Fig. 4 Details of the model **a**. *citoyen*, **b**. *voyeur*

Figure 4 shows the graphic equivalent of an FDMP tourist with all features judged at maximum potential and the graphic equivalent of the [] tourist.

An interesting aspect of this description is that it may be very useful (might be useful, I ought to say, considering the poor availability and reliability of the data) to define objectives governing the tourist flows brought in line with the context.

The FDMP Model for Imagining Scenarios

The model we are proposing is based on the use of *software*[28] for constructing and assessing scenarios that at its origin, some years ago, we called *The Time Machine* (MDT).[29] With this model, an action may be chosen[30] or sub-groups of actions selected to implement (strategies) and therefore to estimate, with an approximation technique, the consequent value of the probabilities that will be obtained following activation or the strategy of single events or groups of events (*scenarios*) or the values of single variables or groups of variables. Numerous problems exist in defining the model: in particular the choice of the entities, the definition of the time "lapse", the probabilities, efforts and influences between entities. This process of model definition may be carried out by "experts" directly or using suitable estimate techniques or may be the fruit of collective discussion between experts, clients, users and interested parties; in the latter case, this same process is useful for common understanding of the problem and solutions.

In the case in point, with respect to the actions and strategies to be set up to "categorise" the composition of the tourist populations departing from the 16 categories we have proposed, we have tried to construct a reasonable example which could be used as a first phase of construction of a conceptual map between public decision makers and operators. We have considered 19 events, 16 of which linked with the possible absolute consistent increment (this is an intentionally vague indication) of each of our categories

Categories of tourist

FDMP *citoyen* [probability=20]
FD summer habitué [probability=70]
Voyeur [probability=90]
Busy FMP *citoyen* [probability=30]
Habitual FDP visitor [probability=30]
Bound FDM *citoyen* [probability=50]
Passionate but disloyal DMP [probability=30]
FM territorial habitué [probability=30]
Occasional FP habitué [probability=30]
Summer DM traveller [probability=70]
Loyal DP pensioner [probability=40]
MP hunter [probability=30]
F fixed guest [probability=80]
Una tantum D [probability=60]
Greedy M [probability=40]
"Where I get I get" P [probability=70]

Possible actions in relation to tourist categories

Rights of citizenship [effort[31]=1]
Integrated town of Olbia [effort=10]
Loyalty cards with strongly dissuasive effects [effort=1]
Support for increase in low-cost flights [effort=2]
Innovative transportation [effort=5]
Non-summer events network [effort=4]
Support for agriculture [effort=4]
Redevelopment of residential patrimony [effort=9]
Integrated town of Arzachena [effort=7]
Conquest of Porto Cervo [effort=7] environmental policies [effort=7]

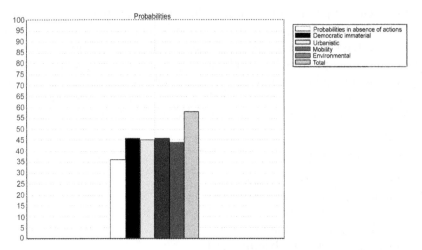

Fig. 5 Output of model: deseasonalisation and fidelisation scenario

It may be of some interest that on the basis of the model we have constructed, and making reference to a scenario we have called *Deseasonalisation and fidelisation* (Fig. 5*)*, the best result is obtained with a "frugal" strategy, namely of low effort that aims at reinforcing the sense of belonging of visitors; in particular the combination of Actions 1, 3, and 6 with six total efforts proves to be the most effective (apart from that entailing the use of all actions, which nevertheless has a very high "cost" (effort = 57), as the figure shows (Fig. 6).

As is obvious, the model I am presenting is only a rough indication; to be able to use it, data, markers and a more meditated construction of the probabilities and relations would be needed, but it can give the idea of how, even in a context under public discussion, we can face in a coherent, systematic way the definition of tourist policies linked with the territory.

Tourists as Agents: Another Simulation

The model we propose also serves to evaluate territorial and tourist policy choices; it is an authentic instrument of simulation and gives quantitative results, but since it is an "agent-based" simulation, it can describe the results of actions describing the possible subjective behaviour of individuals, in this case individuals who have to organise their holidays.

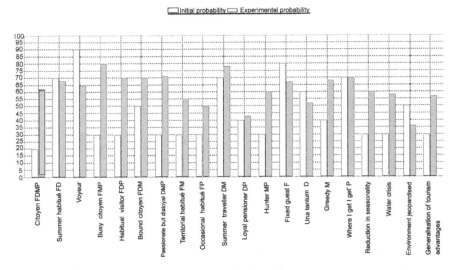

Fig. 6 Table output of model: probability of events[32]

"Agent" simulation models, *multi-agent systems (MAS)* or *agent-based* models (Wooldridge 2002) have the objective of reproducing a system's behaviour departing from the interaction between "individual" entities equipped with certain properties which interact with each other (Fig. 7).
In particular, in the case of territorial models (also called *Multiagent-based geosimulations*) operations are carried out with

– entities that represent human beings and infrastructures
  (houses, urban services, roads, etc.);
– properties and behaviours of the entities;
– relations between entities;
– external influences.

Our tourist model constructed with an MAS[33] has the following basic hypotheses:

– tourists try to maximise the usefulness of their holiday;
– a tourist satisfied with his destination is more likely to return than one who has obtained less usefulness;
– a satisfied tourist can influence other individuals "similar" to him in choosing the same destination, while a dissatisfied tourist does the opposite.

The entities considered are tourists, tour operators, accommodation services and "attractions" present at each of the possible destinations.

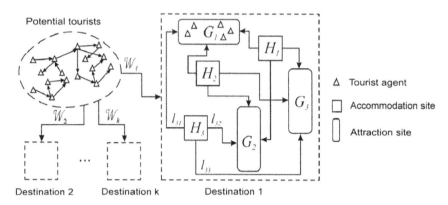

Potential tourists

Destination 2   Destination k   Destination 1

Δ   Tourist agent

☐   Accommodation site

▯   Attraction site

Fig. 7 The general model

Destinations are characterised by accessibility, accommodation, attractions and internal links – accessibility depends on price, time and capacity; accommodation on type, quality, price and capacity; attractions on type, quality, price and capacity and internal links on type, price and capacity. Each tourist is characterised by his/her *profile,* memory of the experience, set of links with other agents, information on destinations and possible actions. During simulation, agents have to make decisions regarding their actions; these decisions will be made in a probabilistic way on the grounds of the agent's features: at each possible alternative, the agent associates usefulness, usefulness features are transformed by the model into probabilities.

Agents' properties are as shown in Table 6.

The possible actions are

Action B1: Choice of holidays

– B1.1: Choice of period
– B1.2: Choice of duration
– B1.3: Choice of destination, accommodation, transport means
– B1.4: Decision on departure date

Action B2: Experience of holiday

– B2.1: Choice of attraction
– B2.2: Evaluation and memorisation

Action B3: Influence of other agents

Table 6 Properties of agents

Property	Set definition
Age	<15, 16–24, 25–44, 45–65, >65
Gender	M – F
Family size	1, 2, 3, >3
Income	Low, medium, high
Education	Basic, diploma, degree
Occupation	Employed, retired, unemployed, student

In our model, there are 100,000 potential tourists with features distributed in a casual manner, five destinations with various modalities of access, accommodation and attractions; the time "lapse" is 12 hours.

The accommodation, attractions and accessibility features are as the figure shows (Fig. 8).

Implementation of the model enables the results of actions to be verified, which modify the accessibility, quality and price of accommodation, and so on. An empirical verification and refinement of the model would necessitate precise data referring to a group of resorts in "competition".

A "Dashboard" for Tourist Policies

The combination of an instrument to define scenarios able to be assessed publicly, in a simple manner and varying in depth, in relation to the combination of political choices and a more *hard* simulation technique, able to propose quantitative results but bearing in mind concrete, "subjective" modalities of fruition of goods connected with tourism, could be a consistent part of what I like to define as the "dashboard" that could be made available for those who have to make decisions. Obviously, we are speaking in the first place of the group of public decision makers (at the different scales), but this dashboard may also be useful for private decision makers, operators in the sector, resident citizens and even tourists to understand how the system works, to reason also on the medium and long term, take into account the whole group of interests in the field and the public features of many of the "goods" put at stake by tourism.

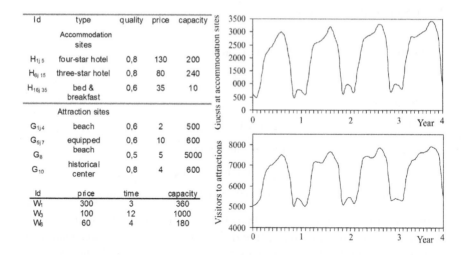

Id	type	quality	price	capacity
	Accommodation sites			
H$_{1j\,5}$	four-star hotel	0,8	130	200
H$_{6j\,15}$	three-star hotel	0,8	80	240
H$_{16j\,35}$	bed & breakfast	0,6	35	10
	Attraction sites			
G$_{1j\,4}$	beach	0,6	2	500
G$_{5j\,7}$	equipped beach	0,6	10	600
G$_8$		0,5	5	5000
G$_{10}$	historical center	0,8	4	600

Id	price	time	capacity
W$_1$	300	3	360
W$_3$	100	12	1000
W$_6$	60	4	180

Fig. 8 Accommodation, attractions and accessibility

What should the dashboard contain? We have already said that one of the principal defects in the definition of tourist policies is that of information bases; thus an observatory is needed to manage and control an *informative system* structured on an updated database which puts together information of various types, spatialising these data, linking them to direct regular and scheduled surveys, and which is able to produce both a general report and specific studies. Then instruments are needed that facilitate the construction and evaluation of policies with strategic value in a public, participated dimension, enabling alternative scenarios to be faced. Moreover, effective models are needed, sophisticated and simulation-friendly, that enable quantitative answers and forecasts "in the proper sense" to be given, with respect to certain specific, detailed choices. Finally, a set of instruments is needed for communication and sensitisation involving the whole of the populations concerned in the definition and implementation of choices, to make everyone, in some way, a "citizen" of the territory.

Conclusions

To go into more concrete detail, we wish to refer to research work we have carried out in recent years to understand which are the elements that can be used to define a group of actions for a reasonable tourist policy.

In the report on tourism of one of the tourist towns of Sardinia, Alghero, an analysis carried out on interviews with certain "protagonists"[34] pinpointed some objectives-desires, which confirm the data of the questionnaires addressed to a vast sample of operators:

deseasonalisation,
developed tourist policies,
synergies with the territory,
welcoming policies,
improving mobility.

To understand what these objectives-desires are teaching us, let us try to summarise some of the concepts:

– There are many types (segments) of tourism, with different types of impact and different advantages and problems; with a great deal of simplification we may say that some segments are "better" than others in a particular context.
– In each of these segments, there is competition at an international level and also for the better tourisms there are many possible alternatives.
– The different segments do not always get on with each other, therefore different types of supply may clash.
– "Good" typologies of tourist are those that have affection and care for the places they visit: for urban places and those with cultural-historic dimensions as well environmental, "good" tourism is that which is faithful, stays for quite a long period of time (not necessarily consecutively), lives and moves on the territory (also in an extended way) and is willing to come at different times of year.
– "Good" tourists are therefore basically nothing but "temporary citizens": there is a *continuum* between tourists of this type and residents, which means that a "beautiful" city "rich in facilities" for the resident is so for tourists, too (a city that belongs to one as it does to the other).
– For a city, a "healthy" or resilient (adaptable) and not fragile economy cannot be based only on tourism (including that conceived in the extensive way).
– Nevertheless, some types of tourism can have the role of pivot for integrated economies and actions for enhancing and rediscovering the historic and cultural patrimony.

To give an example, a crucial question is that of mobility, but it is so for residents before tourists; intelligent policies for intelligent mobility (the repetition is intentional) improve the quality of life of citizens, girls and boys, old and young, and tourists and are good for the environment, for those who are studying, working and enjoying themselves (be they tourists or not). The most relevant issue continues to be that of the "waiter population", fundamentally only he who produces richness attracts it ("developed" places are needed to draw important developed tourist flows). When I maintain that we need to avoid the monoculture of tourism, I am stating a principle that should be described in different ways depending on the circumstances and situations at the outset. Already "mature" situations in which tourism is already predominant or exclusive and has been for some time and has actually "governed" building development and territorial and social organisation are to be treated in a different way from "nascent" situations or those in which the phenomenon is recent or in which the impacts are not so great. But in any case, it is a question of constructing "social capital" (Putnam 2004; Cartocci 2007) and building cities, creating other activities beside tourism, which perhaps complement it, or which tourism complements, diversifying and picking out and governing the various flows, mixing populations, creating good employment and quality professions. Beyond the "formulas" (such as that of the three "T"s proposed by Richard Florida)[35] which are also still useful at least as a departure point for reflection or as a memento, even if they cannot be used as a litany, a territory without quality for those who live there is not a hospitable territory: those who visit can only contribute to ravaging it with the complicity of some of its residents. Formulas are always to be taken with great attention also because the new creative class (admitted that it exists and is definable) is not always distinguished by its careful attention to the social and cultural devastation that globalisation leaves behind it and for a true search for the quality of the territories it crosses. And by quality, we must understand at the same time environmental quality, urban quality, quality of relations, diversity in ways of life and equity in the distribution of advantages. We do not mean to say that it is easy, but the elements we have proposed can to some extent give indications for delivering ourselves from the mortal embrace of tourism as a monoculture, as an elitary or pseudo-elitary good, as consumption that is doubly predatory. This makes us think that the dashboard we have proposed to govern tourism dynamics really does have some use. And may tourists be less foreign and a few more foreigners be residents.

Notes

[1] These words of Ugo San Vittore going back to the twelfth century are taken from a Bulgarian living in France, Tzvetan Todorov, who found them, thanks to a quotation by Edward Said, a Palestinian who lives in the United States "who had found it, in his turn, in Erich Auerbach, a German exile in Turkey" (Todorov 1992, p. 250).

[2] See on this and other "stories" Aldrich (1993).

[3] Blum announced on June 6 that he would present the law; it was presented to the Chamber on June 9 and voted on the 11th of June votes against 1; the Senate confirmed the law with 295 votes against 2: since 1913 there had been draft laws, all rejected or discarded (see Richez and Strass 1996).

[4] I refer here to two texts by the Slovenian philosopher Zizek; Zizek's distinction between enjoyment and pleasure should be looked at again (Zizek 1999, 2001).

[5] This is the constant reference in Urry's text to which we will return (Urry 2002).

[6] And I am not referring simply to the great phenomenon of the *hippie* trips and life *on the road* (see Maclean 2007), which links up with the vagabond phenomenon of the *hobos* (see Anderson 1994).

[7] Some classifications are less babelic than this, which is similar to the *Emporio celeste di conoscimenti benevoli* Borges speaks of; Smith (1989) makes a distinction between ethnic, historic, cultural, environmental and recreational tourism and Pollini (2002) makes a distinction between explorative tourism, elite tourism, "off-the-beaten-track" tourism, unusual tourism, initial mass tourism, mass tourism and *charter* tourism, trying to assess the impact of tourism.

[8] The masculine form does not support the fact that – as Nuvolati's surveys show – in some places many of these people are often women: for example in the world of fashion in Milan.

[9] Nuvolati from a *gendre* viewpoint, perhaps the *choraster* figure proposed by Wearing B and Wearing S (1996) should be introduced, but this would imply reconsidering the whole table; in any case we will return to this point.

[10] Source: Nuvolati (2007, p. 164).

[11] The populations we can classify to some extent as tourists are highlighted.

[12] Source: revised from Nuvolati (2007, p. 22)

[13] One of the characteristics of the current phase of the democratic model (and its crisis) is the role that non-democratic entities have in determining political choices at a local level and at a government level; for example, the rating agencies often "vote" for economic choices before parliaments and sometimes instead of them; in our case the choices of the large tour operators often have the effects of first greatness on territorial policies in tourist resorts. See, for example, Crouch (2003).

[14] Data exist that can in an indirect way give elements for estimating presences and occupation of second homes (from the production of refuse, zone by zone,

to the degree of occupation of parking-lots, data on the sales of certain products, electricity consumption, zone by zone, the number of calls from mobile phones); these data, checked by some direct surveys, can provide very reasonable indications for understanding what is happening in the tourist presence area, including also an evaluation of excursionists.

[15] If I were to think of something that approaches the neo-liberal political genius, I would think that a system that makes the payment of pensions depend on financial speculation, including – in the front line – building speculation, would be very close; as is obvious, when the need arises, it will be the small savers who will pay for the pensioners and the pensioners for the small savers, and when the pensioners, savers, workers and contributors have to pay: whichever way you turn the wheel, the speculators win.

[16] Which does not mean directly controlled.

[17] And what do we want to do: take the red or the blue pill? "Blue pill, end of story. Tomorrow you will wake up in your room and believe in what you want. Red pill, you stay in a wonderland … and you'll see how deep the den of the White Rabbit is …" this is the alternative Morpheus proposes to Neo in The Matrix (film by Andy and Larry Wachowsky 1999); for an interesting discussion on really living and imagining living, see Irwin (2006).

[18] On relational goods see Gui (2002).

[19] On the role of positional goods in contemporary economy, see the classic text by Hirsch (1981).

[20] The name derives from the American sociologist Veblen; see Veblen (1999).

[21] The cycle is divided into an initial *exploration* phase in which the resort is discovered by the first visitors but does not have equipment or services available to receive guests and is often not very accessible; visitors, rather than tourists, are more explorers or travellers and have numerous contacts with the local population. Immediately after this, the presence of these first tourists gives a boost to the investment of capital in services, facilities and accessibility; there is involvement of the local *society,* economy and resources. The tourist *development* phase, in the proper sense of the term, follows: the tourist population increases to the point of exceeding, at some periods of the year, the resident one, the resort enters a tourist circuit of much larger dimensions, investments often arrive from outside. A possible consequence of success is the dizziness it determines: interventions on facilities and infrastructures may impair or destroy the landscape, environmental, cultural or social resources that had initially produced the tourist attraction, undermining survival in the long term; in this phase, the existence of far-sighted planning and strong public control is decisive; this is the *consolidation* phase in which the tourist flows stabilise and often become loyal. But consolidation gives origin to *stagnation,* due to the loss of the "special" attractiveness of the area, which is then subjected to competition from new destinations, more fashionable, less expensive, which steal visitors to these resorts that have now become traditional and everyday. The consequence is usually a gradual *decline* in the local tourist economy, which may sometimes be maintained at a local dimension, with weekend and excursionist tourism. Or *rejuvenation* of tourism

itself may occur, thanks to the discovery or creation of new factors of attraction, able to activate a new life cycle of the tourist economy. See Butler (1980) and Pearce (1989).

[22] For more complete treatment, see Varian (1998).

[23] On the *enclosures* see Cameron R, Neal L (1993). The historic/economic model is owed to Slicher Van Bath (1972), pp. 230, et seq.

[24] See Wearing 1996; *choraster* derives from the Greek term *"chora"* (place, space) which, as well as the series of meanings it has in Greek and in Plato's Timaeus, has found many new ones following reinterpretation by Jacques Derrida, Julia Kristeva and Elizabeth A. Grosz; see Grosz (1995).

[25] See http://www.stalkerlab.it/; the *stalker* is he who "furtively pursues his prey", but *Stalker* was also the protagonist of the film of the same name of 1979 by Andreï Tarkovski.

[26] Psychogeography is a Letterist invention, developed as an architectural and urbanistic practice by the Situationists; in Debord (1958), the *dérive* technique is defined as the hurried moving through various environments: the concept is closely linked with recognizing psychogeographical effects and asserting a ludic-constructive behaviour, thus countering any classical notion of journey or walk; and again in Debord (1958): "To experience a *dérive*, go around on foot with no time constraint or destination. Choose your route as you go not on the basis of what you KNOW, but on the basis of what you SEE around you. You should ALIENATE YOURSELF and look at each thing as if you are seeing it for the first time. A way to make this easier is to walk at a regular pace and glance slightly upwards, so that the ARCHITECTURE is brought into the centre of your visual field and leave the level of the street in the lower margins of your view. You should perceive space as a unified whole and let yourself be attracted by details".

[27] "*Parkour* is the art of knowing how to move around. The main objective of this discipline is to achieve control of the body and mind to overcome the obstacles surrounding us. Those who practise *Parkour,* called *traceurs* or 'route creators', aspire to overcome in a creative, fluid, athletic and aesthetically valid way the natural or artificial barriers that they find along their way". www.parkour.it. See also *Yamakasi – i nuovi samurai*, the film directed by David Belle.

[28] The functioning of this *software* is described in a detailed way in Blecic et al. (2007b).

[29] This *software,* realised by Giuseppe Andrea Trunfio and designed also by Ivan Blecic and Arnaldo Cecchini, was inspired by the game *Future* designed for the Kaiser Alluminium & Chemical Corp. by Theodore Gordon and Olaf Helmer in 1966; it can be downloaded from the site www.lampnet.org; see Blecic et al. (2007a) and Blecic and Cecchini (2008).

[30] The events may be *Internal events* of the system (the happening of which is considered possible within the time situation established, their definition including the probabilities of happening estimated within the time interval); *Exogenous events* (which influence other entities of the model, but are not affected in turn, their definition also including the probabilities of happening estimated within the time interval).

310   A. Cecchini

[31] *Effort* necessary to carry out an action: it may be modified by the occurrence of exogenous events.

[32] "Experimental probability" of an event, namely the frequency of occurrence in the various iterations or the efficacy of a strategy in modifying the total probability of a scenario defined as a mean of the probability of the positive and negative events composing it (occurring for the positive events and not occurring for the negatives ones).

[33] See details in Cecchini and Trunfio (2007).

[34] For the *Secondo rapporto sul turismo ad Alghero,* 80 questionnaires were proposed to operators (out of around 200) and 13 in-depth interviews: see http://atoss.lampnet.org.

[35] The three "T"s stand for talent, tolerance and technology; see Florida (2003).

References

Aldrich R (1993) *The Seduction of the Mediterranean. Writing, Art and the Homosexual Fantasy,* Routledge, London, New York.

Anderson N (1994) *Il vagabondo. Sociologia dell'uomo senza dimora,* Donzelli, Roma.

Bachtin M (1995) *L'opera di Rabelais e la cultura popolare. Riso, carnevale e festa nella tradizione medievale e rinascimentale,* Einaudi, Torino.

Bandinu B (1996) *Narciso in vacanza,* AM&D, Cagliari.

Berardi S (2007) *Principi economici ed ecologici per la pianificazione di uno sviluppo turistico sostenibile,* FrancoAngeli, Milano.

Bizzarri C, Querini G (2006) *Economia del turismo sostenibile. Analisi teorica e casi studio,* FrancoAngeli, Milano.

Blecic I, Cecchini A, Trunfio GA (2007a) *A decision support tool coupling a causal model and a multi-objective genetic algorithm.* Journal of Applied Intelligence n. 26(2), pp. 125–137.

Blecic I, Cecchini A, Trunfio G A (2007b) *Two Complexities and Six Models.* In: Albeverio S, Andrey D, Giordano P, Vancheri A (eds) *The Dynamics of Complex Urban System: An Interdisciplinary Approach,* Springer-Verlag, Berlin, Heidelberg, New York, pp. 111–141.

Blecic I Cecchini A (2008) *Design Beyond Complexity: Possible Futures – Prediction or Design? (and Techniques and Tools to Make it Possible).* Futures n. 40(5) June, pp. 537–551.

Bruni L, Zarri L (2007) *La grande illusione false relazioni e felicità nelle economie di mercato contemporanee.* Working Paper n. 39, Faculty of Economy, Forlì – Degree Course in Economy of Cooperative Businesses and Non-Profit Organisations, Forlì - Bologna March, pp. 1–15.

Butler R (1980) *The concept of a tourist area cycle of evolution,* Canadian Geographer n. 24, pp. 5–12.

Cameron R, Neal L (1993) *Storia economica del mondo II. Dal XVIII secolo ai nostri giorni,* Il Mulino, Bologna.

Candela G, Figini P (2003) *Economia del turismo*, McGraw Hill, Milano.

Candela G, Figini P (2005) *Economia dei sistemi turistici*, McGraw Hill, Milano.

Cartocci R (2007) *Mappe del tesoro. Atlante del capitale sociale in Italia*, Il Mulino, Bologna.

Cecchini A, Trunfio G A (2007) *A Multiagent Model for Supporting Tourism Policy-Making by Market Simulation*. In: *Lecture Notes in Computer Science 4487. Proceedings of ICCS 2007 – International Conference of Computational Science*, Springer-Verlag, Berlin, Heidelberg, New York, pp. 567–574.

Ciaffi D, Mela A (2009), *Social analysis of populations: an application of the tourist-phenomenon*. In: Maciocco G, Serreli S (eds) *Enhancing the city: New Perspectives for Tourism and Leisure*, Springer-Verlag, Berlin, Heidelberg, New York, pp. 313–332.

Cohen E (1974) *Who is a tourist? A conceptual clarification*. Sociological Review n. 22, pp. 527–555.

Crouch C (2003) *Postdemocrazia*, Laterza, Roma-Bari.

Debord G (1958) *Théorie de la dérive*. Internationale Situationniste n. 2, December.

Florida R (2003) *L'ascesa della nuova classe creativa* Mondadori, Milano.

Grosz E A (1995) *Space, Time and Perversion. Essays on the Politics of Bodies*, London, New York.

Gui B (2002) *Più che scambi, incontri. La Teoria economica alle prese con i fenomeni interpersonali*. In: Sacco P, Zamagni S (eds) *Complessità relazionale e comportamento economico* Il Mulino, Bologna.

Hickman L (2007) *The Final Call. In Search of the True Cost of Our Holidays*, Eden Project Book, London.

Hirsch F (1981) *I limiti sociali dello sviluppo* Bompiani, Milano.

Irwin W(ed) (2006) *Pillole rosse. Matrix e la filosofia*, Bompiani, Milano.

La Cecla F (2001) *Turismo supponendo che sia una cosa divertente*. In: Löfgren O, *Storia delle vacanze*, Mondadori, Milano, [Introduction to].

Littlewood I (2004) *Climi Bollenti. Viaggi e sesso dall'Era del Gran Tour*, Le Lettere, Firenze.

Löfgren O (2001) *Storia delle vacanze*, Mondadori, Milano.

Maclean R (2007) *Magic Bus: On the Hippie Trail from Istanbul to India*, Penguin Books, London.

Martinotti G (1993) *Metropoli. La nuova morfologia sociale della città*, Il Mulino, Bologna.

Mazzette A (2002) *Studiare il turismo, un modo per capire come è cambiata la Sardegna*. In: Mazzette A (ed) *Modelli di turismo in Sardegna. Tra sviluppo locale e processi di globalizzazione*, FrancoAngeli, Milano, pp. 11–27.

Mela A (1996) *Sociologia delle città*, NIS, Roma.

Nuvolati G (2007) *Mobilità quotidiana e complessità urbana*, Firenze University Press, Firenze.

Pattullo P, Ollery M (2007) *Vacanze etiche. Guida a 300 luoghi di turismo responsabile*, Einaudi, Torino.

Pearce D (1989) *Tourist Development*, Harlow: Longman scientific & technical, London, New York.

Pollini G (2002) *Il sentimento di appartenenza socio-territoriale e l'impatto del turismo sulla comunità locale*. In: Pollini G, Gubert R *Turismo, fluidità relazionale e appartenenza territoriale*, FrancoAngeli, Milano.

Putnam RD (2004) *Capitale sociale ed individualismo*, Il Mulino, Bologna.

Richez JC, Strass L (1996) *Un tempo nuovo per gli operai: le ferie pagate (1930–1960)*. In: Corbin A *L'invenzione del tempo (1850–1960)*, Laterza, Roma-Bari, pp. 401–442.

Ricoveri G (ed) (2005) *Beni comuni tra tradizione e futuro*, EMI, Bologna.

Sassen S (1997) *Città globali*, Utet, Torino.

Scaramuzzi I (2000) *Turismo: un'industria pesante*. In: Indovina F, Savino M, Fregolent L (eds) *Millenocentocinquanta – Duemila. L'Italia è cambiata*, FrancoAngeli, Milano, pp. 235–250.

Slicher Van Bath BH (1972) *Storia agraria dell'Europa Occidentale*, Einaudi, Torino.

Smith VL (1989) (ed.) *Hosts and guests. The Anthropology of Tourism*, University of Pennsylvania, Philadelphia.

Symonds J A (1985) *Voglie diverse*, Frassinelli, Milano (the original was written in 1897).

Todorov T (1992) *The conquest of America: the question of the other*, Harper Perennial, New York.

Urry J (2002) *The Tourist Gaze*, Second edition, Sage, London, Thousands Oaks, New Delhi.

Varian H (1998) *Microeconomia*, Edizioni Cafoscarina, Venezia.

Veblen T (1999) *La Teoria della classe agiata*, Einaudi, Torino.

Ward Colin (1998) *La città dei ricchi e la città dei poveri*, E/O, Roma.

Wearing B, Wearing S (1996) *Refocussing the tourist experience: the flâneur and the chorister*. Leisure Studies n. 15(4) September, pp. 229–243.

Williams P, Griffin T, Harris R (2002) (eds) *Sustainable Tourism: A Global Perspective*, Elsevier, Amsterdam.

Wooldridge M (2002) *An Introduction to Multi-Agent Systems*, John Wiley & Sons, Chichester.

Zizek S (1999) *Il grande Altro: Nazionalismo, godimento, cultura di massa*, Feltrinelli, Milano.

Zizek S (2001) *Il godimento come fattore politico*, Cortina Editore, Milano.

Tourist Populations

Daniela Ciaffi and Alfredo Mela[1]

"Population" as a Sociological Concept

When we speak in everyday language of "population" of an area we use the term in the singular: the living conditions of the population, the welfare of the population and so on. But in the "ecological" vein of urban sociology – which originated in the Chicago School of the twenties – the term is often used in the plural, based on a transposition to socio/spatial analysis of concepts deriving from ecology, the science that studies the relations between organisms and their environment. If the anthropised environment in which human societies live can be compared with the habitat of the different animal and vegetable species, why not conceive of such an environment as an ecosystem[2] and refer, instead of to the human "population" as an indistinct group, to the "populations" that make up its different social subgroups? The human ecology approach, then, studies the city as a particular type of ecological system. This is a somewhat partial view, as it neglects many essential aspects of social interaction. Nevertheless, it can easily be traced back to our daily experience. Let us think, for example, of looking at some city images from the viewpoint of the environment/populations relationship. Costa Smeralda: hoteliers and tourists. Milan: white collars, businessmen and new immigrants. Venice: the tourist population beside that of residents and students away from home. Whereas the opposite exercise might be to wonder: what population is missing? In the streets of university campuses, for example, there are usually many fewer housewives than in other urban contexts. To give another example, often people coming from the crowded southern countries of the world, who visit Europe for the first time, ask: but where do you hide the children in your cities?!

By and large, the study of populations may suggest a specific way of analysing human presence on the territory: a way that does not clash with other more complex reflections on social interaction, but which, as we will see, offers some important advantages. Let us, then, describe this concept better, referring above all to the use that was proposed of it in the *Nineties* by Martinotti (1993), with reference to metropolitan populations and their "ways of using" the city.

G. Maciocco, S. Serreli (eds.), *Enhancing the City*, Urban and Landscape Perspectives 6, DOI 10.1007/978-90-481-2419-0_15, © Springer Science+Business Media B.V. 2009

Metropolitan Populations

The concept of "metropolitan populations", unlike other sociological terms referring to aggregates of subjects, is a social concept in which reference to space has a constituent role. In sociology many other concepts exist which refer to collective entities but do not inform us of their "whereabouts". We speak, for example, of "social strata" if we refer to a homogeneous income situation and if we wish to draw attention to "how much", or we speak of "rank" if attention is placed on lifestyles and, thus, the "how" dimension prevails. Some concepts only presuppose that forms of (economic, social and cultural) homogeneity exist among the subjects belonging to the same aggregate; others take for granted that the collective social entity is composed of subjects endowed with regular interaction, such as "organisations". Yet others place the accent on collective behaviour, such as in the case of certain types of social movement. Whereas, in the case of populations, the phenomenon that is put first and foremost is the occupation of a given space on the part of a group of subjects.

For the Zanichelli Encyclopaedia "population" is "the group of people who inhabit a place". In Wikipedia the biological meaning contaminates the first meaning and the definition expands: "the group of subjects or particular species who live in a given geographic area or space". In this article, however, we do not intend to refer to this generic concept, in which the reference to space arises in a static form, but to that of "metropolitan populations", introduced by Martinotti in 1993 in his text *Metropoli*, which departs from the idea of the increasingly essential role taken on by urban mobility. In this book, with its subtitle *La nuova morfologia sociale della citta* (New social morphology of the city), the analysis does not begin, as we might expect, by picking out urban territories occupied by groups of homogeneous subjects. Instead groups of individuals are singled out that simply have patterns of use of the city in common and, in particular, patterns of mobility. This departure point appears, in effect, more suitable for analysing contexts, like contemporary ones, for which it is no longer enough to identify the urban population with the resident one.

But in what way is the resident population different from the whole group of urban populations? According to Martinotti, in traditional cities the population used to be able to be described by a single verb: to inhabit. The fact of inhabiting the city indicated the latter as the general place of the social life of subjects. In contemporary cities, on the other hand, beside the population inhabiting the city, there are others who merely work there or use it as consumers.

Martinotti's schematisation, summarised in Table 1, replies with three verbs to the question: What do these populations do in the metropolitan space? Live? Work? Consume? (Table 1).

On the basis of the different responses to these three questions four types of urban population are singled out: inhabitants, commuters, city-users and metropolitan businessmen. This schematisation also leads us to split metropolises into four "generations" that have followed one another over time: the traditional city (distinguished solely by the presence of inhabitants); the first generation metropolis (inhabitants and commuters); the second generation (inhabitants, commuters and city users) and the third generation (inhabitants, commuters, city users and metropolitan businessmen).

In this paper we will not dwell on describing these categories. In relation, however, to the tourism theme – of which we will speak below – the singling out of *city users* and *metropolitan businessmen* should be emphasised, i.e. those who are city consumers but do not live there, as two types of population focused on for different reasons. On the one hand, they represent a precise commercial *target* pinpointed by tourist operators, together, for example, with leisure, cultural and environmental tourists; on the other, the singling out of these populations is at the basis of precise territorial management policies by public administrators, when they establish, for example, that non-residents pay an entrance ticket to some cities that are particularly frequented by tourists and/or bustle with traffic.

Mela et al. (2000) develop Martinotti's analysis distinguishing within the metropolis the internal compact part (*core*) from the outer rings (*ring*) and asking themselves into which of the two spatial ambits, respectively, residence, workplace and predominant place of fruition of services and free time fit.

Considering all the possible combinations, eight populations are picked out, summarised in Table 2: (i) urban residents, (ii) non-rooted periurban dwellers, who live in the *ring* but frequent the *core* both for work and in their free time, (iii) commuters, (iv) city users, (v) reverse commuters, or those who live in the centre and work outside, (vi) *ring users*, i.e. those who go out of the city centre only to consume services or leisure facilities, (vii) non-rooted urban dwellers, who use the *core* only as a place of residence and (viii) periurban residents, who do all kinds of work in the external rings.

As we have said, analysis by population merely considers patterns of "use" of the city. Nevertheless, is it possible to also link with these modalities of space fruition "attitudes" towards it (Mela 2006)?

Table 1 Populations[3]

Population	Live	Work	Consume
Inhabitants	Yes	Yes/No	Yes
Commuters	No	Yes	(Yes)
City users	No	No	Yes
Metro-businessmen	No	Yes	Yes

Table 2 Eight populations singled out on the basis of "core" and "ring" distinction[4]

Residence	Place of work	Services/free time	Population
Core	Core	Core	Urban residents
Ring	Core	Core	Non-rooted periurban dwellers
Ring	Core	Ring	Commuters
Ring	Ring	Core	City users
Core	Ring	Core	Reverse commuters
Core	Core	Ring	Ring users
Core	Ring	Ring	Non-rooted urban dwellers
Ring	Ring	Ring	Periurban residents

Consideration of such a connection would enable the analytical instrument to be enriched, adding a cultural dimension to the "ecological" analysis: it would, moreover, permit sub-types characterised by different attitudes towards space to be distinguished within a same population.

Thus, if we analyse, for example, the population of tourist users of the city or territory, we can pick out at least four types of attitude:

– "consumerist", in its extreme form of so-called "wild tourism" or very quick "touch and go" visits which preclude any form of exchange with the local populations (Cordero 2001), often considered the opposite of sustainable tourism;[5]
– functional, traceable back to the "industrial tourism" of the holiday organised on the basis of the number of stars one can allow oneself;
– aesthetic or observant: "cultured" tourism;[6]
– local "care", by which the challenge launched by globalisation to territories undergoing competitiveness is taken up by a tourist culture of "multiple belonging", able to be experienced individually (e.g. journeying along ancient pilgrim paths) or in groups (e.g. taking part in action-holidays on environmental, anthropological themes).

Literature is rich in reflections on these different types of tourist attitude. Some concern the definition of possible attitudes, including that of the *flâneur*, the over-refined traveller who enjoys losing himself in the city, or the "choraster", the active woman-traveller who empathises with the places she visits and gives her personal contribution to transforming reality (cf. Table 3). From a psychological point of view, for the "choraster" tourism becomes a growth process stimulated by the novelty of places and situations quite different from the activity of the *flâneur,* oriented towards the need to confirm himself and his image through travelling experiences.

The Population Approach for the Analysis of Tourism

As already revealed by the above remarks, tourism may be indicated as one of the most suitable social phenomena for an analysis using the concept of populations. This may be motivated above all bearing in mind the characteristics tourism presents in the current phase. In effect, as has on several occasions been observed in the literature on the subject, in contemporary societies the tourism phenomenon not only takes on a dimension of growing economic importance, but also gives rise to an ever sharper diversification between the ways it manifests itself, the organisational forms it adopts, the profiles of the social figures it addresses and the actual meanings tourists attribute to their own experience.

From an economic point of view, this diversification may be interpreted as the articulation of a tourist market into a plurality of niches, each of which represents a segment of an increasingly globalised tourist industry.

Such an industry consists, as far as supply is concerned, of operators at work who have different specialisations, while regarding demand, consumer figures are present who are diversified no longer just from the point of view of economic availability, but also from that of preferences expressed with regard to the modality of fruition of tourist consumption.

Table 3 Two particular tourist profiles[7]

Wearing and Wearing (1996)	Nuvolati (2002)
Flâneur	Choraster
Male conception	Female conception
Loses himself in the city with observant attitude	"Lives" urban experience with participant attitude
Is attentive to places and images	Is attentive to social values and interaction

From a socio-cultural point of view, this articulation of preferences may in its turn be interpreted by relating it with many features of the post-modern condition: for example, fragmentation of cultures and sub-cultures, emergence of requirements tied to post-materialist values (Inglehart 1977) and re-emergence of attention for the specificity of places and local ways of life that promotes the taste for exploration and *flânerie* (Nuvolati 2006). From an urbanistic point of view, then, the diversification of tourist phenomenon manifestations may be studied in the consequences it has on the organisation of the spaces aimed at accommodating a variety of forms of activity: such organisation is destined to interact with the shape of the built-up and the natural environment, with the landscape patrimony of the different areas, proposing transformations of them that sometimes risk destroying the resources they intend to enhance.

To use the population approach to further knowledge of this variety of ways of existing of current tourism means to construct an analytical instrument undoubtedly much more circumscribed with respect to each of the points of view just evoked, but which, to some extent, may be considered transversal with respect to them and, thus, fit to bring them into contact. In actual fact, to consider the different types of tourist as populations, though entailing a relatively "poor" categorisation from a sociological point of view, nonetheless enables their differences to be classified and the social groups with which tourists interact in a given area to be defined as populations in their turn, e.g. with the residents of tourist zones or with the subjects employed in them. Moreover, the approach in question, though presenting the disadvantage of requiring a simplified representation of behaviours and attitudes empirically verifiable, has the advantage of lending itself to a formalisation and use of modellistic instruments for analysing relations between populations.

A Classification of Populations of Tourist Areas

On the basis of a population approach tourists are a particular type of user that, in this case, are not necessarily *city* users but – at least as regards a specific act of fruition – are nevertheless users of a defined area, in which the artistic, environmental and landscape resources are concentrated that represent the primary object of interest for tourists. From here onwards, however, population analysis will not merely propose a classification of tourists but will also be extended to the other populations present, in a more or less stable way, in the areas in question. In effect, the tourist area is almost always (unless it is a case of a territory of purely naturalistic interest that the tourist merely explores) a space where residents are also present, a part of whom are employed in managing the service activities necessary for the development of tourism. Moreover, given that these activities do not operate throughout the whole year (or at least not with the same intensity), it is typical of many tourist areas to see workers present who come from external areas during the months of greatest tourist flow, whether they be commuters from surrounding areas or workers residing in the place itself for periods of varying length. We will therefore deal with the group of populations of a tourist area, trying to distinguish them – as is typical of this approach – on the basis of the spatial relations they set up with the territory and, in particular, the modalities by which the problems of residence, work and use of services are faced.

Compared with *city users*, tourists or at least the great majority of them, are distinguished by a different residential requirement; in effect, while *city users* are by definition resident elsewhere, with respect to the city whose services they use, tourists, though not having a stable residence in the area they are frequenting[8], stay there for a period of time long enough to require recourse to forms of temporary residence. For the purposes of the classification we intend to propose, this residence may be traced back to two modalities, each of which gives rise to a number of variants. The first might be defined a "periodic residence": it concerns those types of tourist who repeatedly frequent the same place, for example, migrating there in a particular season. In this case, the tourists themselves are the owners of second homes, or rent accommodation each year in the same place (and often the same accommodation). Although the social figures in the two cases have differentiated features (the owner of a second home is a borderline case of tourist and is more an intermediate figure between the latter and the resident), for the purpose of obtaining a sufficiently schematised representation of the populations of a tourist area, the fact of tracing them back to the same condition is acceptable. The second residential modality is of a more sporadic nature: it will be defined as an "occasional" residence. In this case, too, groups of subjects are considered the same who, on the basis of pre-chosen residential modalities (hotels, residences, boarding houses, accommodation rented for the season, camp-sites, etc.) highlight different economic possibilities and/or cultural preferences, linked, though, by the fact of having occasional relations – even if of varying length – with their place of tourist fruition.

Then as far as work activity is concerned, it has already been said that this does not simply concern residents, but also workers coming from abroad and that it is largely a case of work concentrated in some parts of the year only.[9] In this classification we will distinguish basically two types of work: that repeated in cycles based on the different seasons of the year and that with a more occasional nature, namely carried out by subjects who do not work seasonally at the same place. From the residential point of view, workers coming from outside employed in tourist services also have to solve their housing problem during the periods in which they are present in the area considered. From this point of view the solutions they have available are the same as those presenting themselves to tourists, i.e. a periodic residence is a possibility – in the case of workers who go to work for the season in a given place – or an occasional residence, which in some cases may also coincide with the place of work, in the case of workers with more casual work relations in this place. The problem of residence, vice versa, does not concern two types of subject: those who reside in the place itself and who presumably have a more continuous work relationship, and commuter workers who thus go home each day to their place of residence after work. While the latter will be considered a specific population, the former will be identified only by their condition as residents.

Then, as far as the services present in the area and their fruition are concerned, the main distinction to make is that which differentiates services specifically addressing tourists (like, for example, those aimed at offering tourist information) and ordinary services, which involve all populations present in a given area (like trade or health services). In this case, too, it is obviously a schematic distinction that – on further study – might give rise to additional remarks and the pinpointing of intermediate cases. Thus, it might be pointed out, for example, that services strictly for tourism can be used also by residents in some cases (e.g. renting umbrellas on a beach) or that there are ordinary services that it is unlikely will interest tourists (e.g. schools). Generally, however, this distinction between two types of service may prove sufficient for our purposes.

So, summarising, the variables that need to be taken into consideration to arrive at a classification of populations present in a tourist area are 7: three refer to residence, which may be "stable", "periodic" or "occasional", two to work, which may be "seasonal" or "occasional", and two to fruition of services, which may concern "tourist" services or "ordinary" ones. Each of these variables is treated here in a dichotomous form: each population – with regard to each variable – may find itself in a particular condition (yes) or not (no), for example, may use ordinary services or not, may use an occasional residence or not. In some cases, nevertheless, in order to not multiply populations unnecessarily, with regard to some conditions the dual possibilities "yes/no" are expressed. In this case, the use of the initial capital letter indicates the condition considered most frequent: thus Yes/no expresses the hypothesis according to which it is more common that in the subject population there be a majority of subjects who actually find themselves in that condition; No/yes indicates the opposite hypothesis.

Bearing this in mind, we thus see population classification corresponding to a consideration of the possible combinations of the variables enucleated before; a non-systematic consideration, however, in that not all combinations theoretically possible are judged significant (Table 4).

The "inhabitants" are the only population among those considered that are characterised by stable residence. Regarding work, they may be employed in the tourist sector of their place of residence, or they may not. In the first case, it is supposed that their work tend to have a stable or seasonal nature and only in some cases may have an occasional nature (for example, as a second casual job). Inhabitants are in any case interested in using ordinary services, whereas they are less likely to be interested in using specifically tourist services (with the due exceptions, as mentioned above). For simplicity's sake, in this table inhabitants are considered a single population: actually an important distinction that might be introduced – and which becomes essential when the attitudes and above all the relations between populations are considered, as will be seen below – is between inhabitants employed in the tourist sector of the area in question and those employed in other sectors.

Table 4 The populations present in a tourist area

Population	Stable residence	Periodic residence	Occasional residence	Seasonal work	Occasional work	Fruition ordinary services	Fruition tourist services
Inhabitants	Yes	no	no	Yes/no	No/yes	yes	No/yes
Loyal tourists	No	yes	no	no	no	yes	Yes/no
Tourists	No	no	yes	no	no	Yes/no	Yes
Visitors	No	no	no	no	no	No/yes	Yes
Commuter workers	No	no	no	Yes/no	No/yes	No/yes	no
Seasonal workers	No	yes	no	yes	no	yes	Yes/no
Occasional workers	No	no	yes	no	yes	yes	Yes/no

The former are, in effect, residents whose interests are, however, tied to the tourism phenomenon, while for the latter tourism is a phenomenon that only concerns them as the dominant activity of their place of residence, but is foreign to their direct interests.

In the scheme presented here tourists are divided into three different populations.

The first comprises "tourists that have become loyal clients". This means people who habitually frequent a particular place, where they are cyclically present each year, also for prolonged periods. They therefore have a periodic residence in this place, do not work there, are induced to use ordinary services – given the length of their stay and also the familiarity they acquire with the social environment of the zone – they tend to be interested in tourist services, even though in some cases, especially for people who have been frequenting the place for a longer period of years, they could do without it, similar to the inhabitants themselves.

The second population is that of "tourists" *tout court*. They do not frequent the same place in cycles, even though their stay may be relatively long. In any case their residence is occasional; they do not work in the area itself, tend to use ordinary services (except for residential solutions that provide an answer to all ordinary needs tied to residence, such as the case of tourist villages) and are interested in tourist services.

The third tourist population is composed of subjects we might label "visitors", in that their consumer activity takes place within the span of a day. It is therefore passing tourism, which reduces contact with the opportunities present in the zone to a minimum, except for those that are the reason for the visit. Obviously this population does not work in the area either and is interested above all in using tourist services, while, given the shortness of the stay, they can do without frequenting ordinary services.

Workers in the tourist sector can also be subdivided into three distinct populations:

"Commuter workers" do not need any type of home in the zone considered, they do work of a seasonal (or stable) nature, only in some cases occasional, they do not tend to use ordinary services (in that it is more likely they use them in their place of residence; but it is not to be excluded that some services are also used in the place where they work), they are not interested in tourist services.

"Seasonal workers" are characterised indeed by the cyclic nature of the work they do; they need a periodic residence in the place where they work; they also use the ordinary services of this same place and it is not to be excluded that, in choosing to do a seasonal job in a tourist resort there is also – as a secondary motive – the fact that they are able to use tourist services, for example on days off from work.

"Occasional workers" have a profile similar to that of the previous population; they are different from them due to the more casual nature of their work and, therefore, to the need to use a residence that is also more occasional.

Tourist Populations and Attitudes

As can be noted, the populations picked out here have a different way of using the territory and, in particular, the residential, employment and service resources present in a tourist area. If, as well as this way of use, we intend to also take into consideration the possible socio-cultural attitude towards the territory, the following observations can be made.

For the inhabitants of tourist areas the relationship with the territory will tend to take on the same characteristics (moreover highly variable depending on the socio-cultural characteristics of the different social groups) that each resident population has with regard to its own area of residence. Then, for those who also have a job linked with tourism, this type of activity will be perceived also as an economic resource of the area, to be enhanced and expanded; in some cases perhaps it will be favoured even to the detriment of conservation of landscape and cultural values.

Tourists that have become loyal clients often show attachment to places (Fenoglio and Vinardi 2001; Baroni 1998) as much as that of the inhabitants, which goes as far as developing a secondary sense of belonging, added to that concerning their city of residence. Sometimes the "care" attitude is even more accentuated compared with that of inhabitants, in that these tourists are keen to conserve the landscape and artistic values that for them constitute the factor of attraction of that location, while they do not share with the inhabitants employed in the tourist sector the conception of this sector as an economic resource to be maximised. Furthermore, this attitude of care extends in rarer cases to the point of pressing them to be active in the protection and expansion of ordinary services that they do not use (e.g. schools).

For those who have been simply labelled "tourists" it is more difficult to pinpoint a standard attitude: it varies, rather, depending on a group of variables that distinguish the different niches of the tourist market from each other. Thus, for mass tourists, for example, it is possible that their attitude towards the territory be of a principally functional nature, whereas for those seeking forms of responsible or environmental tourism, an attitude of care develops which, nevertheless, in this case depends on a basic cultural inclination of the tourist, rather than the recurrent nature of his/her relationship with that territory.

The attitudes of visitors may also be of strongly differentiated types. In this case, in fact, it is possible that the short visit be motivated, in the variety of cases, by diametrically opposed attitudes: on the one hand, there is the figure of the "touch and go" tourist, for whom an attitude of rapid consumption of the tourist experience prevails, regardless of the conservation of the places he or she leaves behind; on the other hand, the rapid visit may just be a stage in a *flânerie* route, carried out by subjects who have an aesthetic, observant attitude towards the territory.

For workers the basic attitude might be that of a functional, instrumental nature, given that the relationship with the territory is above all a work situation. As already mentioned, however, it is not uncommon for a seasonal job to be carried out by particular subjects, too (such as, for example, university students during holiday periods), for whom motivation linked with the environmental and/or socio-cultural specificity of the places where they go to work is added. In these cases, the instrumental attitude might be integrated, or even substituted, by an attitude of aesthetic fruition and curiosity.

Ecological Relations between Tourist Populations

The use of an approach based on population analysis – however much strong standardisation is needed of the social features considered to single them out – presents an important advantage: it actually allows the analytical categories that may be useful for classifying relations between the populations themselves, to be transposed from the sphere of animal and vegetable ecology. As is known, this type of transposition is also recurrent in the sphere of research tradition originating in the School of Chicago of the twenties and its subsequent developments in the middle decades of the twentieth century (Gottdiener 1994). More recently – especially from the eighties onwards – still based on a use of concepts of biological origin in the social and territorial field, mathematical models were developed which permit an analysis formalised on the relations between human populations (Mela 2006). In this paper it might be useful to briefly mention one of these, worked out by two American geographers, Dendrinos and Mulally, experts in the urban planning field (1985).

This model has its origins in a tradition of biological studies going back to the works of Lotka (1924) and Volterra, aimed at studying the dynamics of two or more animal populations in a given environment (for example, two species of fish in a marine environment) by simulation using a mathematical model. A similar model, in the study by the two American geographers quoted above, is used to analyse the relations between social groups present in the urban environment. The model assumes that the increase or decrease in numerosity of two populations cohabiting the same city is produced, on the one hand, as a function of the rates of growth pertaining to each of them and, on the other, on ecological relations that are established between the one and the other. In mathematical terms the model is expressed by the following equations:

$$dx/dt = x\,(k + ax + by)$$

$$dy/dt = y\,(l + cx + dy),$$

in which

x and y are the two populations under consideration;

dx/dt and dy/dt are the derivates with respect to time of the two populations, from which the tendency to increase or decrease their numerosity over time can be obtained;

k, l, a, b, c and d are parameters.

In particular, among the parameters above, k, l, a and d always have a positive sign and stand for the rates of "reproduction" of the population, or the dynamics that depend on its intrinsic features. Vice versa, parameters b and c may have a positive sign, or nothing or negative, and, depending on this sign, define the way in which the dynamics of a species conditions those of the other.

Summarising, therefore, the ecological relations possible between the two populations are those indicated in Table 5.

Table 5 Ecological relations between populations

B	c	Type of relation between populations x and y
+	+	Symbiotic relation
0	+	Commensalistic relations
+	0	
+	–	Predator-prey relations
–	+	
–	0	Amensalistic relations
0	–	
0	0	Isolation relation
–	–	Competitive relation

The sociological interpretation that can be attributed to each of these relationships will obviously depend on the specific applications of the model and, above all, on the way in which the populations have been defined and the advantages and disadvantages of reciprocal cohabitation conjectured, in the context the application refers to. Here we will try to highlight the meaning that the relations in question could take on if the model were used to study relations between the populations of a tourist area, classified according to the scheme illustrated above.

On the basis of this scheme, relations between two populations are "symbiotic" when a synergy exists between them, or when both gain advantage from their co-presence in a given area. In the case of a tourist area symbiotic relations can be established above all between the tourists and that part of the inhabitants directly involved in tourist activity. Similar symbiotic relations may be further established also between tourists and that share of workers (in particular commuters or seasonal workers) that are part of tourist activity in a relatively continuous way, so as to obtain advantages for themselves linked with the intense frequenting of a place by tourists.

Relations are defined as "commensalistic" by which one of the two populations gains advantages from the presence of the other, while the second gains no advantage, but is not damaged either. An example of relations of this type concerns the relationship between inhabitants and tourists (in particular tourists that have become loyal clients) as regards the use of ordinary services. Those who intensively frequent a tourist resort also need to use some of the ordinary services set up above all to satisfy the needs of residents. Strong development of these services is an advantage to the tourists who use them, with this fruition – if the services are of an adequate size – causing no damage to the inhabitants.

The "predator-prey" relationship is established when a population takes advantage of the presence of the other and the latter suffers damage. In a social ambit, typical examples of relations of this type are those based on a relationship of exploitation (namely a relationship in which the sharing out of advantages and disadvantages between the two parties is particularly unbalanced): the exploiting population gains advantage from the presence of the exploited, while the latter only receives damage. In a tourist resort predator-prey relations can be determined between the share of inhabitants who organise tourist activity and the workers (in particular casual or seasonal ones) who operate in badly paid activities, devoid of guarantees and/or at high risk. It might be supposed that relations of the same type also exist between inhabitants who practise certain forms of tourist activity and the tourists themselves, if the activity is badly organised, excessively costly and/or risky for the tourists. For this hypothesis, however, particular conditions have to arise for it to be able to prove plausible. In effect, in a predator-prey relationship a tie has to exist that conditions the prey to damaging cohabitation with the predator: in the case of occasional workers it is economic necessity that presses the latter to sporadically accept forms of work that are not advantageous for them. In the case of tourists, on the other hand, it is more difficult to conjecture a similar condition of necessity: nevertheless, the lack of alternatives in tourist consumption might concur in pushing the prey towards co-presence with predators, or there might be deceptive forms of intermediation or advertising. Then there is a predator-prey relationship of a different nature that might become established between visitors who show an attitude of rapid consumption of the tourist experience and the inhabitants. The former do, however, gain a subjective advantage from this form of experience lived in the light of their cultural model, while the latter (and in particular those foreign to the tourist sector) only obtain damage.

The "amensalistic" relationship involves a population undergoing a disadvantage due to the presence of the other, without receiving either advantage or damage. Typical relations of this nature are those that can become established between tourists and that part of the population not engaged in tourist activity, in the case in which the presence of tourists creates strong conditioning in terms of use of services and modalities of fruition of urban spaces by the residents. In such a case, while the residents who have an active role in the tourist sector see the damage they suffer as citizens compensated by an economic advantage, those operating in other sectors receive only disadvantages. From their point of view, tourists are indifferent to the presence of a population of inhabitants with whom they do not have reason to enter into contact.

A relationship of "isolation" is spoken of in the case in which co-presence between two populations of no importance to either. In the tourist area a similar relationship may be established between the populations considered previously for the amensalistic case, if tourist pressure is not such as will generate damage to the inhabitants. A similar relationship of isolation is recognisable between the inhabitants not engaged in tourism, or the tourists that have become loyal clients, and workers who produce services not of interest to these populations.

Finally, a relationship is "competitive" if both populations suffer disadvantages from their reciprocal co-presence. This relationship becomes established within an area of tourist interest between two populations that express diametrically opposed requirements as regards fruition modalities or enhancement of the resources present on the territory. This is the case, for example, of the clashes that may be generated between tourists who have become loyal clients (in particular owners of second homes), who show themselves interested in a rigorous defence of environmental quality and inhabitants who own land and appear, vice versa, inclined towards greater exploitation of the opportunities of expanding the built-up zone (Jess and Massey 2001). A similar relationship may also become established between different tourist populations interested in tourist fruition modalities that are incompatible: e.g. between loyal tourists interested in elitist use of the territory and tourists (or visitors) who want intensely consumerist fruition.

Conclusive Remarks

What prospects are there for the development and application of the approach discussed in these pages? In short, we may reply to this question indicating three different veins of further study: the first at a theoretic level and the other two at that of empirical applications in a projectual and territorial planning sphere.

On the theoretic plane, it seems we can say that the approach based on population analysis requires further effort for effective consolidation of its conceptual apparatus. In actual fact, apart from its original matrix deriving from *human ecology*, it presents itself as a possible place of convergence between quite diversified sociological traditions: from the sociology of mobility (Urry 2000; Davico and Staricco 2006) to studies pertaining to the sociology of cultural processes, consumerism and lifestyles. In the case of applications to the tourist sphere, moreover, it is obvious that a further reference point may be constituted by the sociology and anthropology of the tourism phenomenon. All these traditions may contribute in a significant way to offering adequate foundations for the study of populations; nevertheless, this task requires a commitment that is anything but trivial to make heterogeneous concepts compatible that could enrich such an approach, but which – if not adequately harmonised – would risk making it "explode" in a variety of non-comparable directions.

On the plane of applications, a vein of further study is undoubtedly represented by the empirical verification of the approach; this means seeking adequate markers to render population classification criteria operative, as well as the definition of their ecological relations, etc. With reference to a specific tourist resort, this type of analytical undertaking would mean, for example, empirically verifying the presence of the above-proposed distinctive factors between the various types of tourist population, or those working in the sector, and picking out suitable markers of the different forms of relations envisaged by the model illustrated above. Along this vein of investigation it is very likely that we will have to clash with the problem of the lack of data already available and with the need to be able to carry out research in the field using direct survey methods. It is, however, also evident that only this task of verification (or, if preferred, falsification) of hypotheses can contribute to validating them, or making them evolve or replacing them with hypotheses that encounter greater empirical feedback. The effects of this activity might prove to be fertile for planning local development policies in tourist areas and also for preparing territorial plans that seek to pinpoint (albeit in a necessarily selective way) modalities of tourism promotion compatible with the needs of different populations, as well as with environmental sustainability criteria (Pieroni and Romita 2003).

There is a second line of application, on the other hand, using mathematical models, like that of Dendrinos-Mulally or others deriving from the same trend, to realise simulations using appropriate algorithms and informatics programmes.[10] With regard to the use of this type of model, nevertheless, it is important to specify the following: they present a dynamic character and can thus simulate the variation over time of the numeric consistency of the populations studied. Nevertheless, the purpose of a simulation is not that of formulating reliable forecasts on the potential dynamics of a tourist area, to be used directly as data for socio-economic programming or territorial planning. In effect, as has already been highlighted at several points, the degree of simplification of real processes, necessary to make a modellistic application possible, is such as to not render the results of a simulation immediately usable at the operative stage. This may in fact enable rigorous highlighting of the implications over time of each assumption formulated for implementation of the model, from the classification of the populations to the sign and value attributed to each of the parameters. From this point of view, then, the result we should expect is not so much that connected with the definition of the numeric value of the *output*, as that tied to the study of progress itself; in other words, the result of greater value consists of verifying that – given two populations and conjecturing for them certain types of ecological relation – both tend to find a point of equilibrium over time, namely one of them is destined to be cancelled out, or there will be oscillation of a cyclic character of the numerosity of the two populations. We might say it is a case of a result of a more qualitative than quantitative nature, even though this depends on the application of a formally rigorous model, based on numeric data. In any case, in spite of not being immediately translatable into projectual indications, this type of result can also prove to be of great use at the planning stage: it can actually highlight the coherent and incoherent elements of a tourist development programme destined to have particular types of population cohabit, taking – so to speak – the implications of plans with a variety of objectives to extreme consequences in the medium and long term, and thus evaluating their compatibility.

In short, for the development of the population-based approach, in-depth theoretic study, the study of empirical cases and modellistic simulation should proceed along parallel courses. Only if it is possible to make significant steps ahead along each of these lines will it be possible to know better both the potential and the limits of this research perspective.

Notes

[1]   The article was conceived jointly by the two authors; however, the final draft of points 1–3 was written by Daniela Ciaffi and the remainder by Alfredo Mela.

[2]   "The dimensions of ecosystems can vary greatly. A forest is an ecosystem but so is a small pond within it. A single farm is an ecosystem just as an entire rural territory is. Small villages, towns and great metropolises are ecosystems. A region of thousands of square kilometres is an ecosystem and planet Earth itself is an ecosystem. Even though people are part of an ecosystem, it may be useful to imagine man-environment interaction as relations between the human social system and the rest of the ecosystem. [...] 'Social system' is a cornerstone concept of human ecology, for anthropic activities that have an impact on ecosystems are strongly influenced by the type of human society". (Marten 2002).

[3]   Source: Martinotti (1993, p. 152).

[4]   Source: Mela et al. (2000, p. 28).

[5]   De Masi writes thus (2006): "'Alienated' tourism. Already today over 800 million people exist in the world who are entitled to 40 days' holiday. 90% of these 800 million tend towards a type of tourism that enables them to spend as little as possible; it often creates disorder, noise, pollution; it ends up chasing away quality tourists; it causes the entire socio-economic system to decay".

[6]   De Masi once more (2006): "'Aware' tourism. Around 10% of the 800 million citizens who have 40 days' annual holiday have an annual income greater than 150,000 dollars, with an inclination to spend around 500 dollars per day during their holidays. To them should be added at least another ten million wealthy pensioners. It is a case, therefore, of some 90 million people coinciding with the most cultured and most attentive segment in their choice of destination. [...] A 'post-industrial' tourism that lasts all year round and in which a multi-functional offer has to intercept a multi-motivated demand. A demand that is more and more identified with visitors of the inter-connected world, the frequent flyers, mature people endowed with desynchronised free time, young intellectualised globetrotters, single people, homosexuals and women bearing gender issues, businessmen/women, 'foodtrotters' seeking authenticity, new mass tourists sensitive to the environment and culture".

[7]   Source: revised from Nuvolati (2002, p. 157); summary of Wearing and Wearing's considerations (1996, p. 237).

[8]   In this paper we will leave out the case, in itself interesting, however, of forms of tourism practised by residents who rediscover the natural and socio-cultural

attractions of the area they live in, or who devote themselves to exploring hidden aspects of the city (e.g. underground spaces, abandoned buildings and infrastructures). In the first case this is a form of tourism that is taking on quite large dimensions and is often encouraged by municipal administrations, with events of the "doors open to the city" type, addressing residents but also tourists and visitors and aimed at improving the image of the city externally, too. In the second case, it is a question of niche tourism, which makes us reflect, however, on the variety of urban resources that open up to be used by non-conventional users.

[9] We are not considering here the case of places with a continuous presence of tourism, like the great cities of art. In any case, if we were to consider the stable work present in a tourist area, this would not lead to singling out new populations. In actual fact, it may only be residents or commuter workers who do stable work in a tourist resort. The first group of subjects will be identified *tout court* with the population of residents, the second with that of "commuters" (grouping it, therefore with the seasonal or occasional commuter condition).

[10] In this respect, see Monaco and Servente (2006).

References

Baroni MR (1998) *Psicologia ambientale*, Il Mulino, Bologna.

Cordero M (2001) *Trekking tribale*. Volontari per lo sviluppo, August – September 2001, http://www.volontariperlosviluppo.it/2001/2001_6/01_6_14.htm

Davico L, Staricco L (2006) *Trasporti e società*, Carocci, Roma.

De Masi D (2006) *Per un turismo made in Italy*, Genova, Palazzo Ducale, 20 September 2006, http://www.symbola.net/din/adminphp/doc/De%20Masi.pdf

Dendrinos D, Mulally H (1985) *Urban Evolution Studies in the Mathematical Ecology of Cities*, Oxford University Press, Oxford.

Fenoglio MT, Vinardi M (2001) *La prospettiva dell'attaccamento*. Appunti di Politica Territoriale n. 9, pp. 53–66.

Gottdiener M (1994) *The New Urban Sociology*, McGraw-Hill, New York-London.

Inglehart R (1977) *The Silent Revolution: Changing Values and Political Styles among Western Publics*, Princeton University Press, Princeton.

Jess P, Massey D (2001) *Luoghi contestati*. In: Massey D, Jess P (eds) *Luoghi, culture, globalizzazione*, Utet, Torino, pp. 97–143.

Lotka AJ (1924) *Elements of Physical Biology*, Williams and Wilkins, Baltimore.

Marten G (2002) *Ecologia umana. Sviluppo sociale e sistemi naturali*, Edizioni Ambiente, Chap.1, http://reteambiente.it/ra/sostenibilita/catalogo/3709.htm

Martinotti G (1993) *Metropoli. La nuova morfologia sociale della città*, Il Mulino, Bologna.

Mela A (2006) *Sociologia delle città*, Carocci, Roma.

Mela A, Davico L, Conforti L (2000) *La città, una e molte: Torino e le sue dimensioni spaziali*, Liguori, Napoli.

Monaco R, Servente G (2006) *Introduzione ai modelli matematici nelle scienze territoriali*, Celid, Torino.

Nuvolati G (2002) *Popolazioni in movimento, città in trasformazione*, Il Mulino, Bologna.

Nuvolati G (2006) *Lo sguardo vagabondo. Il flâneur e la città da Baudelaire ai postmoderni*, Il Mulino, Bologna.

Pieroni O, Romita T (2003) *Viaggiare, conoscere e rispettare l'ambiente. Verso il turismo sostenibile,* Rubbettino, Soveria Mannelli.

Urry J (2000) *Sociology Beyond Societies*, London, New York.

Wearing B, Wearing S (1996), *Refocusing the tourist experience: the flâneur and the choraster.* Leisure Studies, n. 15(4), pp. 229–243.

Tourism and Local Participation: What about the Citizens?

Monica Johansson

The Public Debate in Castelfalfi, Tuscany

This article examines one case of tourism development which is a clear example of a setting posing several palpable challenges to participative approaches and the development of a type of tourism which can be considered socially sustainable.

The theoretical framework will mainly build on the notions of deliberative democracy. Other alternative or complementary approaches to analyse planning processes and policy[1] will also be discussed.

The empirical section will explore one specific site, the village of Castelfalfi in the municipality of Montaione, Tuscany, Italy.[2] This specific site has been selected since it can be considered a good example of a process in which participation and social sustainability appear to be two important objectives.[3]

Anyone wanting to explore planning processes that will lead to enhancing the city, also the objective of this book, would most likely find it difficult to draw immediate parallels between a city context and Castelfalfi. Castelfalfi is, indeed, a limited context in terms of geographical area and number of residents. Today the village has about 15 inhabitants, the majority of whom are not permanent residents. The whole municipality, Montaione, has 3,700 inhabitants. The process in Castelfalfi does, however, throw light on challenges – difficulties as well as possibilities – facing tourism development processes. Findings and conclusions drawn from the Castelfalfi case may, therefore, be useful in other (tourism) planning processes in which social sustainability and participation are considered. As a matter of fact, urban planners as well as other scholars who study citizens' participation in programmes, policies and projects in cities, have limited the geographical scope of their research to the neighbourhood (Ciaffi et al. 2005; Attili and Sandercock 2009) or to a group of stakeholders, a so-called "partnership"[4] in order to deal with a part of the complex, manifold realities in cities.

G. Maciocco, S. Serreli (eds.), *Enhancing the City*, Urban and Landscape Perspectives 6,
DOI 10.1007/978-90-481-2419-0_16, © Springer Science+Business Media B.V. 2009

Fig. 1 Typical Tuscan landscape, view from Castelfalfi. Photo by Gaetano Ariti

Castelfalfi provides a good example of local governance as prescribed by the Regional Law emanated by the Regional Council of Tuscany.[5] The law includes measures for enhanced citizen participation. Much has been said about participation in the planning debate during the last decades, but this case is a rare instance of regulation for enhancing citizens' participation, perhaps the first case of "public debate" in Italy (Floridia 2008, p. 2).

A public debate has been activated in the municipality regarding the development of Castelfalfi, and a Communications Guarantor appointed to perform a number of tasks aimed at assuring citizen participation in all phases of the local planning process. The Guarantor himself, Massimo Morisi, refers to the process as "a classic case of deliberative democracy".[6]

The Turn towards Deliberative Practices

The reasons why participation and deliberation approaches have been adopted during the last decades are several. One of them is, without doubt, the fact that societies have become complex and difficult to govern. In the contemporary society, planners, politicians and other decision makers have faced and are still facing serious challenges related to steering, control, decision making, implementation and administration of public matters. These, in turn, are related to numerous, thorough societal changes. For example, it is becoming impossible to maintain centralised control of communication, power and economy, and increasingly difficult to foresee and plan action. There is no longer merely *one* power-center, that is, if *one* such power-center ever existed in the first place (Carlsson 1993).

Another characteristic of the contemporary society is that a multitude of activities and organisational processes are taking place also outside formal organisations and governments (Gjelstrup and Sörensen 2007). The demarcation line between state and civil society and private and public has become unclear in a web of interaction (Kooiman 2003). It is no longer as easy as it used to be to pinpoint crucial actors in implementation processes (Carlsson 1993). Power becomes dispersed in new organisations, exchanges, collaborations, networks and institutions that have become established alongside the old for several decades (Castells 1997; Carlsson 1993; Hajer 2003; Gjelstrup and Sörensen 2007).

Planners, politicians and decision makers are, of course, not unaware of these tendencies. In order to maintain equilibrium and adapt to social phenomena in the contemporary society, nation-states and central governments have created new institutions that canalise interests (Castells 1997). Steps have been taken in order to involve the surrounding society and groups that were not considered decision makers previously. New forms and methods of planning have emerged mainly during the last decades. Examples of such initiatives from the field of regional and local development policies have emphasised the participation of local and regional authorities, organisations, businesses and other actors in the planning, implementation and evaluation of programs, incentives and other measures taken to favour local and regional development such as the "partnerships" in the EU programs for structural development or the Italian model of *programmazione negoziata*.[7] One of the principal objectives of these initiatives is to encourage contacts between private and public institutions and spheres (Garofoli 2001). "Stakeholders" (potential beneficiaries) are being involved and consulted as they are expected to contribute to the development process with their knowledge and, claim critics, since they bring legitimacy to decisions (Donolo 2003).

Terms such as "decentralisation", "local decision making power" and "empowerment"[8] have been on the agenda since the 1970s, and a lively debate on who should participate and what instruments should be used to involve stakeholders is still going on (Timothy 2007).

According to Healey (1993, p. 233), old structures and techniques applied in planning, which Healey refers to as "based on a narrow and dominatory scientific rationalism" have hampered or, at worst, impeded the prospects for a more democratic, environmentally sustainable planning process which would possibly promote social justice.

The first cases of planning processes adopting a participative approach had appeared already in the 1950s, but during the end of the twentieth and the beginning of twenty-first centuries traditional, narrow-minded techniques and structures in planning clashed with the ever-changing society, and the need for a new planning paradigm became evident.

For Healey, the modern idea of planning focuses on "finding ways in which citizens acting together can manage their collective concerns with respect to the sharing of space and time" (Healey 1993, p. 234). She points out that, despite various errors committed and difficulties encountered along the way, considerable achievements have been reached by the introduction of new ideas and methods in planning. Healey refers to Habermas and the concept of communicative rationality as a possible way forward. Communicative rationality builds on a conception of reason which offers new prospects for planning through intersubjective communication. The Habermasian conception of communicative rationality constructs the basis for the more ambitious concept of "deliberative democracy", which has been referred to lately by planners and decision makers as they attempt to involve the local community in development processes. The public debate on Castelfalfi appears to be a good empirical example for comparison with theoretical aspects on deliberation.

Local Participation in Tourism Development

Citizen participation has, as we have seen, become crucial in various planning and development processes and tourism development processes are no exception.

A number of researchers (Davidson and Maitland 1999; Gow and Vansant 1983; Hatton 1999; Simmons 1994; Timothy and Tosun 2003) have indicated local participation as one of the important cornerstones of sustainable tourism. An approach which emphasises local participation aims at involving the stakeholders at the specific destinations as well as the community residents. Several of the negative impacts of tourism can, according to many scholars and planners, be avoided if citizens are given the opportunity to participate.

Participation is, furthermore, considered one of the important aspects possibly leading to the fulfilment of some important goals of sustainable development in tourism, such as social equity and the preservation of cultural and ecological integrity (Timothy 2007, p. 199). Participation thus not only concerns the social aspects of sustainability, but represents one of the cornerstones of sustainable development in general.

Tourism is, however, a complex phenomenon, and sustainable tourism involves more than the participative, social aspect. Ideally, a successful tourism development process is "economically, ecologically and socially sustainable, because it: has less impact on natural resources and the environment than most other industries; is based on enjoyment and appreciation of local culture, built heritage, and natural environment, as such that the industry has a direct and powerful motivation to protect these assets; can play a positive part in increasing consumer commitment to sustainable development principles through its unparalleled consumer distribution channels; and provides an economic incentive to conserve natural environments and habitats which might otherwise be allocated to more environmentally damaging land uses, thereby helping to maintain bio-diversity" (WTTC, Commission on Sustainable Development 1999, p. 1).

Citizen involvement can, hence, be expected to bring several advantages related to criteria of sustainability, but there are also other reasons why politicians and other decision makers involve people in planning for tourism.

Inhabitants communicate values and attribute meaning to the territory, which can be expected to appeal to and attract tourists. Professional "place-makers" and managers identify the values and the meanings generated by the inhabitants and use them commercially (Meethan 1997). In some cases, place-making does not come about through the identification and use of authentic values and meanings. Instead well-known brands (branding) or so-called *kitsch* attributes are used to help render the place recognisable and appealing for visitors as well as for inhabitants. This is especially true for city contexts, but it is possible to find examples also in more limited geographical settings. It should be mentioned here, though, that kitsch-attributes may not be promoted merely by "place-makers", neither do *all* locals contribute with exclusively *genuine* and *authentic* values and meanings. There exist examples of research which verify that inhabitants may prefer and even promote *kitsch* attributes (Atkinson 2007).

Difficulties Related to Tourism

Planners and inhabitants involved in a process for developing tourism are likely to run into challenges, and lessons can be learned by analysing previous and similar development processes. Some common examples of negative impacts of tourism are illustrated below.

Tourists compete with the local community in using and enjoying important natural resources such as water and electricity[9] and/or spaces for recreation like parks, museums or other sites. Furthermore, criteria for environmental sustainability and the possible impacts of tourism on nature and natural resources are not always correctly measured and interpreted.

The needs and demands of tourists may dominate the development of sites and attractions, while there is a risk that those of residents are neglected as the local community attempts to adapt to and serve mainly the visitors.

Planners and/or decision makers often do not know enough about the expectations and demands of tourism, which may lead to unwise investments with negative impacts on economic return, environment or clashes with the expectations of the local community. As a matter of fact, tourism development processes are often managed at a level and a speed involving considerable social disruption (McKercher 2003).

Furthermore, tourism development processes are likely to entail conflicts about how the equilibrium between development and preservation should be achieved, which values should be attributed to a place and how these values should be communicated, which natural resources must be protected and how, etc.

Unequal access to participation as well as to benefits generated by tourism and lack of information, resources and power are some of the problems mentioned by Scheyvens (2002). The same author also emphasises that in order to ensure local tourism development, communities "need to make informed decisions about whether to engage in tourism development, and if their answer is positive, how to engage in tourism development" (Scheyvens 2002, p. 9).

Deliberative Democracy

The scientific debate on deliberative democracy took off at the beginning of the 1970s. It developed as part of a vigorous discussion on how to offer an alternative or complement to representative democracy, the implementation of political decisions from the "top down" and to the "ever present, long-established" interests. The concept "deliberative democracy" derives from a radical democratic ideal which is typical for the contemporary occidental democratic systems characterised by the struggle to achieve equilibrium between principles for popular sovereignty on the one hand, and individual rights and constitutionalism on the other (Wiklund 2002, p. 44). Deliberative politics is a form of democracy that calls for a critical analysis of traditional and established forms of governance and organisations. Decisions presuppose the consensual legitimisation of efficient and just solutions, a kind of participative democracy through which public decisions are taken closer to the citizens. Theoretical models of deliberative democracy suggest the provision of new spaces (so-called *arenas*) where all individuals interested in a problem can discuss, suggest solutions and evaluate the advantages and disadvantages of different alternatives. Deliberative politics is to be regarded as a normative concept of democracy. Habermas refers to Dahl (1989) to define some conditions that are indispensable for permitting a "process capable of producing decisions that will serve as binding as well as advantageous for everyone" (Habermas 1996, p. 375). The "process must guarantee: (a) inclusion of all persons interested in the matter; (b) true and equally distributed opportunities to participate in the political process; (c) equal right to vote in decision making; (d) equal right concerning the choice and confirmation of the agenda and matters discussed; (e) a situation in which all actors interested – with sufficient information and good reasons – can form an opinion on the matters that are to be examined and of controversial interest" (Dahl 1985, p. 59 quoted in Habermas 1996, p. 375).

Deliberative democracy is discursive democracy, and can be described as "a reflective learning process" (Habermas 1987 quoted in Wiklund 2002). How can the concept of "discourse" be defined? It should not be interpreted as any or all kinds of communication, but as more specific and truly specialised discussions (Mazzoleni 1998). Discourse aims at guaranteeing individuals' self-reflectiveness in the communicative process, at interpretation and comprehension, i.e. the product of the process, being genuine and shared, and at normative, accepted rules being rational, and thus considered legitimate by all interested individuals. Hence, it is all about arriving at a normative interpretation and approach that is accepted by all interested actors (Wiklund 2002). Communicative processes, in a context of deliberative democracy, are decentralised. The means for reaching agreements and for carrying out public political action are networks of communication in the public political sphere, inside and outside the parliamentary complex (Habermas 1996).

In the conception of deliberative democracy, politics is not an end in itself (as is the case in liberal or republican approaches). The sovereignty has neither to be concretely concentrated in the people, nor must it be anonymously expressed in the juridical-constitutional competences (Habermas 1996). Conflicts and disputes are not solved through an aggregation of private interests that frame social choices (and laws), but through a process of deliberation on the relevant issue with the objective to arrive at a common judgement, that can be accepted by all interested parties concerning the organisation and regulation of collective action (Miller 2003).

Meanings and Values Are Socially Constructed

Habermas outlines the concept of *lifeworld* as a foundation for communicative action by thoroughly describing its nature and content. The concept of lifeworld or *Lebenswelt* was originally developed by Edmund Husserl, who can also be said to be the father of phenomenology. Lifeworld is to Husserl "the everyday common-sense world in which we live and work" (Gorman 1976, p. 491).[10] Another definition is that lifeworld is every individual's sense of consistency and meaning in his/her existence, which derives from the conception and knowledge of the context in which we live and thrive. Lifeworlds can, through communication, be explained to other individuals. This approach and this conception of the world and other individuals also entail a certain understanding of individuals' responses to things that happen to them or experiences they have. Individuals' reactions to things that happen or experiences lived are not to be conceived as objective, but as perceived and comprehended by the individuals.

Lifeworld provides the very foundations for agreement, while the formal concepts are systems of references that contribute to comprehension in that the participants in the communicative process can start out from their common lifeworld (objective, social or subjective) in order to attain comprehension and consensus. Interpersonal contact in the social world manifests itself as legitimisation. The subjective dimension of the lifeworld is also exposed in communicative action, since the individual expresses his/her personal experiences of an issue or an entity.

Individuals do, however, "not relate point-blank to something in a world but relativize their utterances against the chance that their validity will be contested by another actor" (Habermas 1987, p. 120).

Habermas explains the relevance of his theory as a means for analysing mechanisms of understanding and agreement. The lifeworld becomes one of the cornerstones of Habermas' theory of discourse and deliberative democracy. This theoretical construct of how lifeworlds are created and recreated in a continuous process of interaction and communication is important if we want to attempt to arrive at an understanding of how different individuals perceive the world, how they take sides in conflicts, how they justify their action and choose who they will collaborate with.

Politicians and other decision makers need, therefore, to take lifeworlds into account, and act in terms of deliberation if they wish to understand outcomes of decisions, policies and planning processes.

Bevir (2003, pp. 216–217) comes close to Habermas' perspective as he writes: "The fate of policies depends on the ways civil servants, citizens and others understand them and respond to them". The author continues:

"If policy-makers kept this firmly in mind, they still would not be able to predict the consequences of their policies but they might at least forestall some of their unintended consequences. More generally, they might accept that the management of networks is largely about trying to understand, and respond suitably to, the beliefs, traditions and practices of those they hope to influence".

"The relations between ideas and behaviour are mutual", Lundquist (2007, p. 163) asserts, as he attempts to describe how ideas in local self-governance in Sweden "functioned both as steering measures and steering goals". Lundquist's perspective is discursive, and he investigates the meanings of words and concepts. The author claims that "words are never neutral, but that they take on a crucial role in the construction of reality" (Lundquist 2007, p. 165).

Healey et al. (2003) adopt the same perspective in their study of policies and initiatives of deliberative governance in Newcastle. Healey et al. claim "that meanings and actions are actively constructed in social contexts through relational dynamics" (Healey et al. 2003, p. 64). In their piece of research on Newcastle, the authors analyse "how knowledge resources and relational resources are mobilized, and how this effects the frames of reference or discourses through which meanings are arrived at and mobilized"[11] and "the processes by which meanings are disseminated".[12] The authors attempt to render policy analysis operational by considering it a "deliberative, action-oriented practice in which meanings and values are socially constructed" (Healey et al. 2003, p. 64).

Background to Castelfalfi and the Public Debate

The village of Castelfalfi in the municipality of Montaione (province of Florence) in Tuscany, covering a total of 1100 hectares, is situated in a typical Tuscan landscape (Figs. 1 and 2) of rolling hills, grapevines, cypresses, olive trees, meadows and scattered buildings. People have lived here as far back as the Etruscan period. In the eleventh century, the first citadel was built on the premises. The territory came under the Bishop of Volterra; in 1475 Giovanni Francesco Gaetani and his wife Costanza de' Medici reinforced the citadel and constructed a villa. The Roman San Floriano church, which still exists, was reconstructed in 1511. During the Renaissance period, Castelfalfi developed from being a military fortress to a residential setting living off agriculture, and later, at the beginning of the nineteenth century, tobacco was cultivated. Today the old tobacco factory has become a hotel, and the citadel a restaurant. In the 1830s, as many as

600 inhabitants lived in Castelfalfi, while nowadays there are only 15 residents (the majority of them are not permanent residents).

During the nineteenth and twentieth centuries, Castelfalfi changed owners several times, and despite various suggestions and attempts initiated by the municipality, the owners, inhabitants or other actors, the village and its buildings gradually declined.

In 2007 one of the leading multinational tourist operators, Touristik Union International (TUI), bought Castelfalfi from the owners, a Milanese family, with the aim of developing it into a tourist village with hotel, resort, spa, congress centre, golf course (an extension to the already existing golf course) and other sports facilities. TUI has also expressed interest in resuming the cultivation of olives and vines, which has been dormant for several decades.

The TUI project was presented to the Municipal Council during spring 2007 but was rejected by the Council, since the intervention planned, which included considerable new construction, as well as the recuperation and restructuring of the remains of the old, medieval village, was considered too large-scale. In July 2007, TUI presented a new proposal, a feasibility study, which was approved by the Municipal Council.

Fig. 2 The village of Castelfalfi. Photo by Cristiano Nasta

Given the importance of the project, the Council also decided to launch a public debate and appoint a so-called Communications Guarantor, responsible for collecting and forwarding information related to the Castelfalfi project between the local community and Montaione Municipal Council. It should be mentioned, however, that the intervention could still be considered large scale. According to this plan, the total investment made by TUI will amount to approximately 295 million euro[13]; old buildings will be recuperated and restored, a new hotel, some additional new buildings and a so-called "Robinson club" will be constructed and Castelfalfi will have the capacity to host a total of over 700 guests contemporaneously.[14]

Castelfalfi is a case of local government as prescribed in the Regional Law 69/2007, emanated by the Regional Council of Tuscany. The law includes measures for enhanced citizen participation. A public debate has been activated in the municipality regarding the development of Castelfalfi, and the Guarantor will perform a number of tasks aimed at assuring citizen participation in all phases of the local planning process, which is the municipality's competence. The Guarantor has been responsible for producing and providing information and describing the development process in Montaione. Abundant material: a debate forum, a press archive, minutes from assemblies and a final report, etc. is available on the public debate website (www.dp-castelfalfi.it). This allows the process, by the Guarantor Prof. Massimo Morisi himself referred to as "a classic case of deliberative democracy",[15] to be explored and evaluated.

The public debate was initiated to provide complete and transparent information and, at the same time, to give any citizen (individuals and groups) the opportunity to express their opinion on the project. As we have seen, during the last decades, planners, politicians and other decision makers have referred to deliberation and made attempts to encourage inhabitants to become involved in planning processes. It can, however, be argued that specific regulations for enhanced citizen participation have been a fairly rare phenomenon up until this point. This fact, together with Morisi's reference to deliberative democracy, makes it an interesting empirical case to set against Habermas' theoretical models.[16]

Various modes and instruments of communication were used. The website www.dp-castelfalfi.it was (and still is) functioning as an archive for all relevant documentation, the expression of opinions by institutions, associations and committees, etc. The website hosts, furthermore, a press archive and an interactive forum available for anyone interested in expressing their opinion, asking questions, etc. The latter is still accessible on the Internet, in February 2009, although the forum has been closed.

Five assemblies were organised, open to all citizens of Montaione and neighbouring municipalities, and anyone else interested in the project. The assemblies aimed at providing a detailed description of the project and collecting all the various opinions expressed. Each assembly numbered 120–230 persons.

In addition, anyone interested in the project had the opportunity to pose questions via e-mail (or on the webforum). The Guarantor answered after having consulted the responsible body concerned (such as the Municipal Administration), the Mayor of Montaione or the TUI managers. It was also possible for associations and/or individuals to post a contribution to the debate on the website. All pertinent contributions have been published and can be downloaded from the website; they have also been displayed at the Town Hall and some of them have been discussed at the assemblies. A written report of the process was published on www.dp-castelfalfi.it by the Guarantor in December 2007. This final report provides a summary of the many activities of the process: the five assemblies; the Toscana Resort Castelfalfi Project Guide (printed in 2,500 copies); the website and all the documents posted there, including the interactive forum, the press archive with approximately 40 articles, a film about the Castelfalfi intervention; a campaign to encourage and broaden participation including personal invitations, flyers (5,000), posters (500) and a number of telephone calls to individuals, associations, enterprises, etc.; a guided tour of the village to explain the intervention planned; three specific assemblies with tourist operators, farmers and environmental associations.

The public debate was officially concluded on 14 December, 2007 with the last public assembly and the presentation of the final report.

At the end of the debate the webforum had received 66 messages, 20 written contributions had been published and 2,288 visits had been registered on the website.

As the reader might have expected, the debate was lively, sometimes outrageous, and convincing arguments in favour of, as well as fiercely repudiating, the project were presented. Many actors representing various interests were involved in the debate: the Municipality of Montaione, TUI, environmental associations, citizens in general, political parties, businesses and the daily press (Floridia 2008, pp. 7–23).[17]

Several challenges which could possibly be encountered by the citizens of Montaione and their territory have been debated. The problems discussed are principally those referred to in a previous section of this chapter as recurrent in instances of tourism development: unequal access to sites and attractions between tourists and citizens; the possible constraint on natural environment and energy resources, and the importance of finding adequate ways to evaluate and measure such impacts; the importance of economic return to the local community vs. the investors' ambitions, as well as the potential conflict between advocates of the *status quo* on the one hand and the promoters of progress and development on the other.

The loudest voices against the project have, perhaps, been raised by environmental associations such as Legambiente, WWF and Italia Nostra. These are also the actors remained in opposition to the project even in its somewhat limited form, after its modification and the agreement of July 2008. The criticism mainly regards aesthetic values, natural resources and water and energy supply.

Representatives speaking in favour of the project emphasise the opportunities for young people to find a job within the tourism industry and the possibilities for local firms to profit from the increased influx and presence of visitors. Another recurring comment is that Castelfalfi and the surrounding territory needs this action to survive and reawaken, after decades of gradual decline.

In December 2007, the Guarantor, Morisi, published a letter on the Internet. It was an answer to various criticisms expressed (mainly on the www.eddyburg.it website) against the public debate in Castelfalfi. Morisi wrote: "the public debate in Montaione on the TUI project has been a classic case of deliberative democracy. As such, it left anyone expecting the community of citizens to be sold out to the multinational company by a weak or corrupted Mayor and a servant Guarantor, disappointed". Morisi continued by explaining that the result of the process was that the citizens expressed their approval of the TUI project. The project has, furthermore, according to Morisi, made the citizens aware that they are in charge of their own destiny, and that the territory is the object of many interests.

The process resulted in a series of claims presented in eight paragraphs intended to summarise its outcome.

The first paragraph states that the inhabitants of Montaione are mostly in favour of realising the project, but – and this is the second but no less important paragraph – that the project must be re-dimensioned so that it is compatible with the context of which it is part. The third paragraph recalls the importance of assuring that the increased demand for energy and water supplies will be available, and that the resources utilised are renewable. The fourth refers to aesthetic and architectonic values, and the overall quality of the physical intervention on the landscape and emphasises the need to safeguard the environment also in this respect. Item number five calls for a limitation of the number of tourists, in order to render possible the development of a supply of high-quality tourism, using the local community and its natural and cultural environment as its principal resources. Yet another claim emphasised by the inhabitants during the process is that agricultural activity should be resumed, and that opportunities should be given for collaboration between TUI and local entrepreneurs. According to prospects presented by TUI, a few hundred new jobs will be created through the development of Castelfalfi. The inhabitants maintain that this opportunity is of the utmost importance for the territory. Opportunities for young people to gain experience and for schools and universities to benefit from the presence of a multinational tourist company are stressed. One final requisite, expressed in the last paragraph, is that the project and the development be monitored continuously.[18]

Morisi (2007) writes that the decision taken – to favour the project – is restricted by a number of taxing, precise conditions. The most important condition is "a considerable, very considerable, re-dimensioning of the project. Will TUI accept? We will see. Unfortunately the territory belongs to them, although not exclusively to them. And the participation has made them understand this".

Morisi refers in his letter to claims that had already been put forward in the public debate, but which later took the form of a Cooperation Protocol signed in July, 2008 by the Municipality and "Tenuta di Castelfalfi s.p.a", and entailed considerable amendments to the project. A document including all amendments to the original proposal was published on www.pd-castelfalfi.it. Some of the most important alterations are that: the total surface area of the resort must not exceed the present area by more than 10%; the number of new tourist beds must not exceed 430, and the number of new residential beds will be 40; no existing buildings may be demolished or enlarged; only two of the four planned new villages may be constructed adjacent to the previously existing buildings. For the other two villages, specific restrictive regulations will apply to safeguard respect for aesthetic and architectural norms; agricultural activity will be resumed (specific conditions will also apply to cultivation); energy must be generated using renewable resources as far as possible; a low-water-consuming type of grass will be selected for the golf-course, etc. Finally, the name of the new village will be Hotel Arte e Cultura instead of "Robinson Club" (the name suggested by TUI). Many additional regulations (for instance the number of swimming pools, the space allowed for use by commercial activities, etc.) are detailed in the document.

As the agreement was signed, a decision was also taken to establish a "monitoring committee", which would take on the task of monitoring the project and its progress.[19]

A few urban planners have been active in the debate. One of them is Edoardo Salzano, who is the editor of the website www.eddyburg.it, where several articles on Castelfalfi have been published. It is not possible to give a full account of the discussion taking place on www.eddyburg.it here. Some of the most important contributions have been made by Sandro Roggio, Alberto Magnaghi, Edoardo Salzano and Paolo Baldeschi (quoting Salzano). One argument discussed on eddyburg focuses on the unequal opportunity to set the agenda and be involved in the debate (Roggio 2007). Another criticism raised is that in order to make "better" decisions, the local inhabitants would need more information and knowledge. This criticism is mainly expressed by Magnaghi (2008), who writes that citizens are "bombarded by TV commercials", and that they are under the spell of "heterodirected imagination". A third line of argument is presented mainly by Salzano (2008) and Baldeschi (2008), who both argue that the intervention in Montaione is of such importance that the debate ought to be widened, and the discussion extended so as to involve actors at a national and international level in the debate and decisions made. Salzano questions the roles of politics and politicians as promoters of regional law. In particular, he mentions the Regional Council of Tuscany and President Claudio Martini, and emphasises the importance of considering and defining what the adequate administrative and political level/s of involvement should be in debates such as that in Montaione.

Giorgio Pizziolo is yet another scholar who participates in the debate on www.eddyburg.it. He criticises the role of the Guarantor, describing him as "a kind of plenipotentiary and judge of participation" and as a threat to transparency and democracy. Several of the contributions on www.eddyburg.it discuss Morisi's role and how it has been performed. Letters posted generally convey the message that the Guarantor, on the whole, has interpreted and performed his mission correctly. The discussion among the scholars and the exchange of letters between Morisi and a few of these scholars mainly regard the overall approach of the debate and the process, defended by Morisi and generally criticised by the rest of the scholars. Some of the scholars (Pizziolo 2008, Salzano 2008) criticise mainly the conclusions of the debate, the eight recommendations summarised and the concepts used by the Guarantor in the final report.

The fact that a law has been emanated with the objective to create participation processes has provoked reactions. One of the most articulate criticisms was expressed by Giorgio Pizziolo, who claims that the prospects for participation are hampered by the regulation, as he states that what are often referred to as "participation" are really evaluations of previously elaborated projects and proposals, participated consultation in authorities' decisions and the formulation of mandatory laws.

The law, according to Pizziolo, overlooks some of the most vital and open aspects of participation. Pizziolo mentions three forms of participation that are not likely to develop within the framework of the law: (1) extremely valid "bottom-up" processes existing regardless of constructed, formal settings; (2) the creative process, the most exciting element of participation, during which participants suggest and develop a project together; and (3) the dynamics of participants' acting and "doing" together.

Is the Public Debate in Montaione, a Case of Deliberative Democracy?

Earlier in this chapter, some cornerstones of deliberative democracy were presented. It is clear that the process that took place in Montaione is difficult to evaluate as a case of deliberative democracy if we use Habermas' theoretical framework. Habermas' model poses high demands on necessary conditions, and he does not lay down clear indications for how his theoretical framework is to be applied in empirical situations. Habermas' call for critical analysis, an alternative approach to the traditional models of democracy, reflective learning processes and socially constructed meanings, runs the risk of becoming too discursive and idealistic. As a matter of fact, these are some of the recurrent criticisms presented by Habermas' critics. Luckily the theoretical framework of deliberative democracy has developed and complementary approaches and tools have been added to Habermas' theory.

In his article about deliberative democracy in the Castelfalfi case Floridia (2008) refers to more recent, handbook-type literature, such as "The deliberative Democracy Handook" (Fung-Gastil-Levine 2005), which contains examples from the United States. Floridia uses parameters such as scale of deliberation, deliberative processes agenda, inclusiveness of deliberative processes, asymmetries of information and knowledge among involved individuals and cognitive schemes conditioning the quality of deliberation. Floridia (2008) presents an interesting report focusing mainly on (a) where decisions regarding the territory are taken, and by whom; (b) who actually has the right to participate (and decide) and (c) how it is possible to actually participate and influence decision making. In his final conclusion, Floridia (2008) claims that the case of Castelfalfi is an example which provides "a concrete example of how deliberative democracy, despite all its imperfections, can live, and efficiently, in the real world, – made of conflicts, contrasting interests, diverse visions and images of the world, inequalities in terms of power and knowledge – and can truly contribute to improving the quality of democracy and of our democratic institutions" (Floridia 2008, p. 39).

The scope of this chapter is somewhat different than that of Floridia's and therefore, even though the site and the phenomena analysed are the same, this account of the process is not as thorough, nor does it follow the same path. This chapter does not explore discourse *per se* at any considerable depth, but instead takes a step back and poses the question "Is the public debate in Castelfalfi really a case of deliberative democracy?" Let us go back to some of the prerequisites that Habermas indicates as crucial for deliberative democratic processes and use them as lenses as we explore the process in Castelfalfi. Habermas' theory, somewhat simplified, revolves around three issues: accessibility and inclusiveness, decentralised decision making and legitimate norms and rules.

Accessibility and inclusiveness. All persons interested must be included. Possibilities to participate and the right to vote in decision making must be authentic and equal. Furthermore, everyone must have the equal right to define the agenda. Matters discussed and sufficient information must be available for all, so that opinions can form.

Decentralised decision making. Communicative processes are decentralised and take place in communication networks of the public political sphere, inside and outside the parliamentary complex (Habermas 1996).

Legitimate norms and rules. Decisions should be binding and advantageous to everyone. One of the important outcomes are normative, accepted rules considered legitimate by all interested individuals (Wiklund 2002).

Accessibility and inclusiveness. The debate in Castelfalfi appears to have followed Habermas' framework in terms of inclusiveness, once it started. Many possibilities existed for individuals, as well as representatives of political, economic and environmental associations and interested parties to express themselves. The debate (at least the assemblies) was partly structured by the Guarantor and his team. The only assembly providing a more general introduction to the public debate was the first. The following revolved around: (2) The "Toscana resort Castelfalfi" Project, (3) Landscape and architectural quality, (4) Landscape, water and agriculture and (5) Energy, economic impacts and the Robinson Club. This was, however, possibly a necessary limitation. As observed by Floridia (2008), it contributed to keeping the discussion more stringent, and strong polarisation between advocates of the *status quo* and the "pro-development" could be avoided.

Decentralised decision making. According to Habermas' theory, communicative processes are decentralised and take part inside and outside the parliamentary complex. In the case of Castelfalfi, the public debate involved, activated and urged many individuals to intervene, but the initiative did not come through decentralised networks of citizens. Furthermore, a law established by the Regional Council delegated the municipalities to conduct the process. As observed by Salzano (2008) and Baldeschi (2008), there may be a risk that the debate become limited to the local level, and that important issues and decisions not receive the attention and deliberation they might deserve.

We cannot be sure of the Municipal Council's objectives for suggesting the public debate was mainly to legitimise the decisions that had already been taken or would have been taken with or without participation, nor will we ever find out whether politicians and decision makers intended to introduce truly alternative approaches to traditional forms of democracy.

The law on participation established by the Regional Council in Tuscany can hardly be considered one of the norms or regulations that Habermas is referring to as he calls for the importance of legitimate norms and regulation.[20] To Habermas legitimate norms are one of the outcomes of deliberation, and not primarily the activities carried out to enforce the law, which appears to be the case in Castelfalfi. Pizziolo's letter published on www.eddyburg.it previously referred to in this chapter expresses concern over the regularisation of processes which, according to him, ought to remain flexible and open for bottom-up initiatives and to enhance creativity.

Once again the topic of the debate was not suggested by the citizens. The Municipality suggested a public debate on Castelfalfi. As a matter of fact, and as also observed by Floridia (2008) as well as by Morisi (2007) the village had already been bought by TUI as the public debate started. The issue was therefore "a specific project and not a search among alternative solutions to a collective problem". It was, thus, a private rather than a public issue although it cannot be neglected that TUI had bought a part of a "collective heritage" (Floridia 2008, p. 37).

However, the final agreement made between the Municipality of Montaione and "Tenuta di Castelfalfi s.p.a" did become a kind of official regulation, which, as we have seen, entailed considerable limitations to the original plan presented in 2007. Furthermore, the future process will be monitored by the Committee (as detailed in the agreement), which can be considered a kind of control-mechanism that, if it works, fills the important function to evaluate whether the agreement is respected. The norm (if we choose to call the agreement a legitimate norm as intended by Habermas) has not, of course, been accepted by the entire collective of individuals, associations, business representatives, etc. Many critical voices were also expressed after the closure of the public debate, and the press archive at the dp-website includes several contributions to the debate also for 2008 which do not give the impression of a general will, as expressed in the final report and the eight recommendations for Castelfalfi previously referred to.

Conclusions

Some of the important prerequisites for a deliberative process appear to be lacking in the Castelfalfi debate. The village had already been bought, and the decisions to be taken were not selected by the citizens. The public debate (as well as the regional law on participation) appears to be a clear example of how the local (and regional) government, as well as TUI, involves citizens so as to render decisions taken legitimate.

It should be mentioned, though, that the issue appears to have involved a large number of individuals, and the minutes of the assemblies also provide good examples of interventions by representatives of associations, political parties and businesses as well as "ordinary citizens".

The outcome of the debate, the Guarantor's report and the agreement regarding amendments and delimitations to the original plan can possibly be seen as normative guidelines and/or rules. Decisions taken were, hence, legitimised (although not recognised as legitimate by all involved actors) through the public debate. Decisions taken can and will be monitored and evaluated, which, of course, is an important prerequisite for checking that decisions taken are respected.

As has been mentioned, the lenses we are using to analyse the process in Montaione are pretentious. Although politicians and decision makers are acquainted with the concept of deliberation and deliberative democracy and although they do refer to it, it should be mentioned that this has not been the case in the Castelfalfi debate. The only example of reference to "deliberative democracy" that can be found is the one previously referred to, made by the Guarantor, Morisi.

In the documents posted on the website, the concept generally referred to is "participation", which can be considered one of the important aspects of deliberation, yet is considerably less specific and, hence, less pretentious, if used as a theoretical frame for evaluation of a debate.

Is the framework of deliberative democracy adequate for an analysis of this kind? It is up to the reader to judge. Advocates of alternative approaches to planning and policy analysis often claim that the concept of deliberative democracy neglects important concepts such as power, conflict and values.

Flyvbjerg (2001) claims research in social and political science often lacks an adequate representation of the concept of power. He calls this a "general deficiency". Flyvbjerg refers to Habermas and Foucault, who both argue that the misuse of power is one of the most important problems of contemporary society. Flyvbjerg (2001) criticises Habermas for proposing institutional development and constitutions as solutions to problems in contemporary society, and advocating consensus rather than conflict. Flyvbjerg claims that if scientists and practitioners continue to resort to the chimera of communicative rationality, they will run the risk of getting lost in theoretical discourses and ignoring practical everyday contexts in which people are constantly involved in situations of power, interests and conflict rather than consensus. Conflict is, according to Flyvbjerg, a natural constitutive element of a strong democracy. This is the main reason why he places power and conflict at the centre of his analysis of society. Flyvbjerg eventually advocates Foucault, who: "focuses his efforts on the local and context-dependent and toward the analysis of strategies and tactics as a basis for power struggle" (Flyvbjerg 2001, p. 107). Conflicts and power relations can, for instance, be studied scientifically through an "analysis of discourse", which could possibly have been an alternative method for analysing the public debate in Montaione in this article.

John Forester (1993) refers to Majone (1989) and Stone (1988) as two of the representatives of a new movement in planning and policy analysis, which he calls "the argumentative turn". This approach sees values as central in planning processes. Analysing such processes therefore implies exploring and understanding the values shaping it. Stone (1997) brings contrasting values and meanings into focus as she depicts the world of policy (and politics, which for her is inseparable from policy) as a paradox. Stone describes how politics is about metaphors and analogy and about getting "others to see a situation as one thing rather than another" (Stone 1997, p. 9). Maynard-Moody and Stull (1987, p. 251) express a similar opinion as they contend that "the policymaking process involves framing issues so that conflicting views and values are brought together". These authors claim that consensus building is central to policymaking, and the articulation of values is at least as important as tangible results in understanding policy. It should be mentioned, though, that Forester's point is not to criticise Habermas. Forester emphasises words and arguments as carriers of values, and thus suggests the analysis of language and its meanings. He wants to contribute to the fields of planning and policy analysis by widening the scope of the analyst, so that studies of planning and policy processes also take aspects such as legitimacy, authority, responsibility, causality, interests, needs, obligations, preferences and values into account. The objective is to show how language not only depicts, but also constructs the issues at hand.

An approach which takes conflicting values into consideration is the advocacy coalition approach. The advocacy coalition approach (Sabatier 1986, 1999) focuses on strategic interests among actors, and their conflicting values. The analyst in such research plays "the role of an operating official rather than a critic of existing practice or a source of ideas" (Dryzek 1982, p. 317).

Yet another approach within the field of analysis of planning and policy would be to make a bottom-up analysis and use the "implementation structures" suggested by Hjern and Porter (1983). Hjern and Porter claim that formal organisations are no longer relevant as units of analysis. Formal organisations depart from the assumption that they are capable of coordinating and controlling action despite the fact that, in the contemporary period, programs are implemented in a set of organisational pools rather than by single organisations. Therefore, policy analysis aiming at identifying and exploring and/or evaluating program implementation and departing from the objective of formal programs and single organisations will not be very successful[21] (Hjern and Porter 1983, p. 217).

Instead Hjern and Porter (1983) suggest implementation structures as a new unit of analysis. Implementation structures are "bundles of program-related activities and parts of organisations" and "a group of persons with various organisational memberships" (Hjern and Porter 1983, p. 265). The formation of an implementation structure is most often a result of a process of self-organisation, thus the conduct and the rationale of the implementation structure cannot be explained by simply referring to the norms and rules of either the organisation or the formal hierarchy. Many rationales such as the expectations of mutual benefits, power, force or induction, individual self-interest, etc. may be the motives behind the formation of implementation structures.

The analyst would have needed to carry out interviews starting from "the bottom" to find the structures in the Castelfalfi case. Implementation structures always exist, but they can only be scarcely discerned in formal documents and minutes of assemblies, etc. Given the level of framing of the public debate in Montaione, the law on participation, the assemblies, the role of the Guarantor, etc., it can be assumed that it would have been difficult to find implementation structures in Montaione, outside the formal structures in any case.

Returning to the question considering the adequacy of using deliberative democracy as a theoretical framework for this chapter, the conclusions would, most likely, not have been very different even if the concept of "deliberative democracy" had been replaced by, for instance, "participation". As can be observed as we look back at the public debate, questions and doubts, often regarding accessibility and inclusiveness, decentralised decision making and legitimate norms and rules do appear. These are, as we know, also important cornerstones in Habermas' framework. Furthermore, it can be argued that the theoretical framework does not ignore either power or values, although the objective of paying close attention to these aspects is not addressed explicitly.

Will the debate in Montaione contribute to sustainable tourism? Only the future will tell. The plan is still to be implemented, and the agreement is to be respected and monitored. It is clear that many of the issues which needed to be discussed, for instance, water and energy supply, protection of existing buildings, cultural heritage and natural resources, maintenance and expansion of agriculture on the Castelfalfi estate, considerations concerning employment of locals, economic return for local businesses, etc., have been brought up and discussed. Despite the flaws of the process, the situation would, most likely, have been even worse if the public debate had not been activated at all.

It can, therefore, be concluded that the Castelfalfi process indicates that important steps are being taken towards enhanced participation and deliberation, which ought to lead to a more sustainable tourism.

On the other hand, Castelfalfi is not a case of deliberative democracy. One of the aspects which does not conform with Habermas' theory is that the initiative to start the public debate was not the outcome of a broad deliberative process. In actual fact, a *law* suggested, permitted and framed the deliberation.

Pizziolo criticises and repudiates the idea of a law on participation. In an attempt to be constructive, he suggests that if a law is considered as indispensable by politicians and other decision makers, it must be more flexible, and encourage activities from the bottom-up. Pizziolo also suggests that the law is monitored and, if needed, amended annually instead of every four years.[22] He expresses anxiety as he writes that there is a risk that the law "about rules for participation is transformed into a rule which eliminates active participation, from below, that aggregated spontaneous participation capable of producing creative outcomes". In other words, according to Pizziolo, creativity cannot be encouraged by regulation. Translated into other terms, aggregated spontaneous participation is the form of self-organisation that Hjern and Porter look for in their implementation structures. The degree of regularisation and organisation from above in the public debate in Montaione makes implementation structures of self-organisation difficult to detect.

The regional law on participation and how participation should be carried out provides, perhaps, the most palpable testimony that the debate in Montaione clearly deviates from the theoretical ideal of deliberative democracy.

Laws need legitimisation. Participation and deliberation are crucial for legitimisation to ensue, but regulation is not capable of generating participation and creative outcomes.

Notes

[1] Policy analysis is a kind of evaluation, an investigation into delivery, and aims at reaching a better understanding of the relation between policy and action, where two poles have generally discussed whether policy should be prescriptive or descriptive (cf. Barrett 2004; Lin 1998; Glemdal 2008). Another continuous debate among scholars has concerned how policy analysis should relate to state power (Hanberger 1997). Many factors combined make implementation research a complex, multifaceted and often contested field. The academic field of policy analysis experienced its heyday during the 1960s and 1970s as grand scientific research projects were carried out aiming at evaluating the effects welfare policies and organisations could deliver to society and its members (Rothstein 1998).

[2] All written material referred to in this chapter to describe the background, debate and process has been downloaded from www.dp-castelfalfi.it. The author has neither been present at any of the assemblies nor personally involved in the debate. The author alone is to be held responsible for interpretations made and conclusions drawn from the abundant material to be found on the website for the public debate.

[3] It should be mentioned that observations made and conclusions drawn by the author result from the study of written sources, mainly found on www.dp-castelfalfi.it and www.eddyburg.it. The author alone is responsible for possible misinterpretations or errors.

[4] See for instance Healey et al. (2003).

[5] Regional Law emanated by the Regional Council of Tuscany on 27 December 2007, Norms supporting participation in the formulation of regional and local policies.

[6] The letter in which Morisi refers to the process as a case of deliberative democracy was published on 28 December 2007 on the websites: www.casolenostra.org and www.eddyburg.it . It is also available on: www. dp-castelfalfi.it

[7] In English: negotiated planning

[8] Empowerment is a process as well as a condition. It implies the transfer of decisional power (authority to act, choice of actions, management and monitoring of decisions and resources) from central authorities and external investors to local communities and their stakeholders. As suggested by the term

itself, "empowerment" always competes for elements and relations of power, and the process, being a dynamic and not a static one, may result in less agency (disempowerment). Empowerment processes not only transfer authority and agency, but also responsibilities for outcomes (Timothy 2007).

[9] The reader may be led to think that these are problems mainly occurring in rural areas. It should be mentioned, however, that tourists compete with the local population over water also in cities such as Barcelona, Mexico City, Goa, Benidorm and Antalya (www.wbcsd and www.responsibletravelnews.com). As a matter of fact, measurements taken in Antalya, Turkey and in Mallorca, Spain show that tourists generally consume a much greater daily amount of water than the inhabitants of the tourist sites. In urban areas, in Mallorca a tourist consumes between 440 and 880 litres of water a day, while the average consumption of the inhabitants is approximately 250 litres per day per person. The corresponding figures for Antalya are 600 litres per day per visitor, compared to 250 litres per local inhabitant (www.biodiversity.ru).

[10] The concept of lifeworld had also been used by Durkheim, departing from the affirmation that traditional societies are characterized by a common order called "life world", in which collective mythical and religious values are intertwined and are important integrative forces in society (Wiklund 2002, p. 39). Durkheim, together with Husserl, and Wittgenstein originally coined, interpreted and developed the concept (Habermas, 1987). Habermas is one of the contemporary theorists who contributed with important developments and applications of the concept in his analysis of communicative action.

[11] Hajer (1995), Schön and Rein (1994) quoted by Healey et al. (2003).

[12] Latour (1987) quoted by Healey et al. (2003).

[13] *Guida al Progetto* Toscana Resort Castelfalfi (A Guide to the Project Toscana Resort Castelfalfi) p. 35 published on www. dp-castelfalfi.it

[14] On 31 July 2008 a Cooperation Protocol was signed between the Municipality and "Tenuta di Castelfalfi s.p.a". which modified and limited these measures.

[15] The letter in which Morisi refers to the process as a case of deliberative democracy was published on 28 December 2007 on the websites: www.casolenostra.org and www.eddyburg.it. It is also available on: www. dp-castelfalfi.it

[16] It should be mentioned that Floridia (2008) has carried out a study using an approach similar to mine, as he explores deliberative democracy, strategies for negotiation and argumentation and relates them to the public debate in Castelfalfi. The article, which was presented at the annual convention of the Italian Association of Political Science in September, 2008, has been published in Italian on the website: www.dp-castelfalfi.it, and provides excellent documentation on the debate, as well as an interesting analysis of the discourse, its various actors and the outcome.

[17] Floridia (2008) thoroughly analyses the roles and positions of each of these groups.

[18] www.primapagina.regione.toscana.it/indew.php?codice=25387&sott_c=63

[19] According to the agreement between the Municipality and TUI, the committee will consist of one representative of each of the two parties, to be assisted when necessary by other parties specifically chosen by them.

[20] It should be mentioned that Habermas does not ignore the importance of laws and the constitutional state. Instead, communication and deliberaton are indispensable for making laws acknowledged and respected by the public. The law and rights of the civil society are accompanied by the regulations of the "Rechtstaat" (state governed by law), the logic of division of powers, rationality of practices in court, etc. (Reese-Schäfer 1996, p. 81).

[21] It should be mentioned that formal organisations may be part of the structuring. What Hjern and Porter are suggesting is simply that formal organisations should no longer be treated as starting points and taken for granted as points of reference.

[22] According to the original suggestion, four years would be the standard period of validity of the law. It would therefore not be possible to revise it and make amendments before the end of the period. Pizziolo claims that a shorter period of time would be preferable, since that would permit gradual modifications and, hence, a higher degree of flexibility.

References

Atkinson D (2007) *Kitsch geographies and the everyday spaces of social memory.* Environment and Planning A n. 39, pp. 521–540.

Attili G, Sandercock L (2009) *Where Strangers Become Neighbours. Integrating Immigrants in Vancouver, Canada,* Springer-Verlag, Berlin, Heidelberg, New York.

Baldeschi P (2008) *Sulla lettera di Massimo Morisi e Sulla replica di Edoardo Salzano* 18 January www.eddyburg.it

Barrett SM (2004) *Implementation studies: Time for a revival? Personal reflections on 20 years of implementation studies,* Public Administration n. 82(2), pp. 249–262.

Bevir M. (2003) *A decentered theory of governance.* In: Bang H (ed) *Governance as Social and Political Communication,* Manchester University Press, Manchester, pp. 220–222.

Carlsson L (1993) *Samhällets oregerlighet: Organisering och policyproduktion i näringspolitiken,* Symposion Graduale, Stockholm/Stehag.

Castells M (1997) *The Information Age. Vol 2. The Power of Identity,* Blackwell, Malden, Massachusetts.

Ciaffi D et al. (2005) *Neighbourhood Housing Debate,* FrancoAngeli, Milano.

Dahl R (1989) *Democracy and its Critics,* Yale University Press, New Haven.

Davidson R, Maitland, R (1999) *Planning for tourism in towns and cities.* In: Greed C (ed) *Social Town Planning,* London, New York, pp. 208–221.

Donolo C (2003) *Il distretto sostenibile – Governare i beni comuni per lo sviluppo*, FrancoAngeli, Milano.

Dryzek J (1982) *Policy Analysis as a Hermeneutic Activity*. Policy Sciences, pp. 309–329.

Floridia A (2008) *Democrazia deliberativa, strategie negoziali, strategie argomentative: un'analisi del Dibattito Pubblico sul "caso Castelfalfi"*. Paper presented at the annual meeting of Società Italiana di Scienza Politica, The Italian Association of Political Science, 4–6 September 2008.

Flyvbjerg B (2001) *Making social Science Matter. Why social inquiry fails and how it can succeed again*, The Press Syndicate of the University of Cambridge, Cambridge UK.

Forester J (1993) *Critical Theory, Public Policy and Planning Practise – Towards a Critical Pragmatism*, State University of New York Press, Albany NY.

Fung A, Gastil J, Levine P (2005) *Future Directions for Public Deliberation*. In: Gastil J, Levine P (eds) *The deliberative Democracy handbook. Strategies for Effective Civic Engagement in the 21st Century*, Jossey-Bass, San Francisco, pp. 271–289.

Garofoli G (2001) *I livelli di governo delle politiche di sviluppo locale*. In: Becattini G, Bellandi M, Dei Ottati G, Sforzi F (eds) *Il caleidoscopio dello sviluppo locale*, Rosenberg & Sellier, Torino, pp. 213–234.

Gjelstrup G, Sörensen E (2007) *Public Administration in Transition. Theory, Practice, Methodology*, DJÖF Publishing, Copenhagen.

Glemdal M (2008) *Gubben på kullen. Om den smärtsamma skillnaden mellan politiska intentioner och praktiska resultat*. JIBS Dissertation Series n. 50, Jönköping International Business School, Sweden.

Gorman, RA (1976) *Phenomenology, social science and radicalism*. Politics and Society n. 4, pp. 491–513.

Gow DG, Vansant J (1983) *Beyond the rhetoric of rural development participation: how can it be done?* World Development n. 11, pp. 427–446.

Habermas J (1996) *Between Facts and Norms*, The MIT Press Cambridge MA.

Habermas, J (1987) *The Theory of Communicative Action. Vol 2. Lifeworld and System: A Critique of Functionalist Reason*, Polity Press, Cambridge.

Hajer M (1995) *The Politics of Environmental Discourse: Ecological Modernization and the Policy Process*, Oxford University Press, Oxford.

Hajer M (2003) *Policy without polity? Policy analysis and the institutional void*. Policy Sciences n. 36, pp. 175–195.

Hanberger A (1997) *Lokalpolitikens möjligheter. Historisk policyanalys av problemnärhet och effektivitet i kommunal policy och dess betydelse för politisk legitimitet*. Research Report n. 2, Statsvetenskapliga institutionen, Umeå Universitet, Sweden.

Hatton MJ (1999) *Community-Based Tourism in the Asia-Pacific*, APEC publication, Toronto.

Healey P et al. (2003) *Place, Identity and Local Politics: Analysing Partnership Initiatives*. In: Hajer M, Wagenaar H (eds) *Deliberative Policy Analysis:*

Understanding Governance in the Network Society, Cambridge University Press, Cambridge, pp. 60–88.

Hjern B, Porter DO (1983) *Implementation structures: a new unit of administrative analysis.* In: Holzner B, Knorr KD, Strasser H (eds) *Realizing social science knowledge*, Physica Verlag, Wien, pp. 265–277.

Kooiman J (2003) *Activation in Governance.* In: Bang H (ed) *Governance as Social and Political Communication*, Manchester University Press, Manchester, pp. 79–101.

Latour B (1987) *Science in Action*, Harvard University Press, Cambridge MA.

Lin AC (1998) *Bridging positivist and interpretivist approaches to qualitative methods.* Policy Studies Journal n. 26(1), pp. 162–180.

Lundquist L (2007) *Public administration theory and public administration change.* In: Gjelstrup G, Sörensen E (eds) *Public Administration in Transition, Theory, Practice, Methodology*, DJÖF Publishing, Copenhagen, pp. 163–180.

Magnaghi A (2008) *Nota a Margine del dibattito su Castelfalfi* 19 January www.eddyburg.it

Majone G (1989) *Evidence, Argument and Persuasion in the Policy Process*, Yale University Press, New Haven.

Maynard-Moody S, Stull DD (1987) *The symbolic side of policy analysis: Interpreting policy change in a health department.* In: Fischer F, Forester P (eds) *Confronting Values in Policy Analysis, The Politics of Criteria*, Sage, Newbury Park CA, pp. 248–265.

Mazzoleni G (1998) *La comunicazione politica*, Il Mulino, Bologna.

Mc Kercher B (2003) *Sustainable Tourism Development – Guiding principles for Planning and Management.* Paper presented at the National Seminar on Sustainable Tourism Development, Bishkek, Kyrgystan, November 5–9.

Meethan K (1997) *York: Managing the tourist city.* Cities n. 14(6), pp. 333–342.

Miller D (2003) *Deliberative Democracy and Social Choice.* In: Fishkin JS, Laslett P (eds) *Debating Deliberative Democracy*, Blackwell, Malden-Oxford, pp. 182–199.

Morisi M (2007) *Castelfalfi: il garante risponde alle critiche* 27 December www.eddyburg.it

Reese Schäfer W (1996) *Jürgen Habermas – en Introduktion*, Daidalos, Göteborg.

Roggio S (2007) *Garanzie di parte nella partecipazione per Castelfalfi* 27 December www.eddyburg.it

Rothstein B (1998) *Just Institutions Matter. The Moral and Political Logic of the Universal Welfare State.* Cambridge University Press, Cambridge UK.

Sabatier PA (1986) *Top-down and bottom-up approaches to implementation research: a critical analysis and suggested synthesis.* Journal of Public Policy n. 6(1) pp. 21–48.

Sabatier PA (1999) *The Need for Better Theories.* In: Sabatier PA (ed) *Theories of the Policy Process,* Westview Press, Oxford, pp. 1–17.

Salzano E (2008) *Morisi: Autodifesa o autodenuncia?* 18 January www.eddyburg.it

Scheyvens R (2002) *Tourism for Development: Empowering communities*, Pearson Education Limited, Essex UK.

Schön DA, Rein M (1994) *Frame Reflection: Toward the Resolution of Intractable Policy Controversies*, Basic Books, New York.

Simmons DG (1994) *Community participation in tourism planning.* Tourism Management n. 15(2), pp. 98–108.

Stone D (1988) *Policy Paradox and Political Reason*, Scott Foresman & Co, Glenview.

Stone D (1997) *Policy Paradox. The Art of Political Decision Making*, Norton & Company, New York.

The World Travel and Tourism Organization and International Hotel and Restaurant Association (1999) *Tourism and sustainable Development. The Global importance of Tourism. Background Paper n.1.* Commission on Sustainable Development. Seventh Session 19–30 April 1999, New York.

Timothy DJ, Tosun C (2003) *Appropriate planning for tourism in destination communities: Participation, incremental growth and collaboration.* In: Singh S, Timothy DJ and Dowling RK (eds) *Tourism in Destination Communities*, CABI Publishing, Cambridge, pp. 181–205.

Timothy DJ (2007) *Empowerment and stakeholder participation in tourism destination communities.* In: Church A, Coles T (eds) *Tourism, Power and Space Contemporary Geographies of Leisure, Tourism and Mobility*, Routledge, Abingdon, Oxon, pp. 199–216.

Wiklund H (2002) *Arenas for democratic deliberation: decision-making in an infrastructure project in Sweden.* JIBS Dissertation Series n. 13, Jönköping International Business School, Sweden.

Name Index

Subject Index

Lightning Source UK Ltd.
Milton Keynes UK
UKOW06f0842090717

304913UK00002B/179/P